e-Business

e-Business

Roadmap for Success

Ravi Kalakota and Marcia Robinson

Addison-Wesley

An imprint of Addison Wesley Longman, Inc.

Reading, Massachusetts • Harlow, England • Menlo Park,
California • Berkeley, California • Don Mills, Ontario •
Sydney • Bonn • Amsterdam • Tokyo • Mexico City

Many of the designations used by manufacturers and sellers to distinguish their products are claimed as trademarks. Where those designations appear in this book and Addison-Wesley was aware of a trademark claim, the designations have been printed in initial caps or all caps.

The authors and publisher have taken care in the preparation of this book, but make no expressed or implied warranty of any kind and assume no responsibility for errors or omissions. No liability is assumed for incidental or consequential damages in connection with or arising out of the use of the information or programs contained herein.

The publisher offers discounts on this book when ordered in quantity for special sales. For more information, please contact:

Corporate Government, and Special Sales
Addison Wesley Longman, Inc.
One Jacob Way
Reading, Massachusetts 01867

Library of Congress Cataloging-in-Publication Data

Kalakota, Ravi.
  E-Business : roadmap for success / Ravi Kalakota, Marcia Robinson.
      p.   cm.
  Includes bibliographical references and index.
  ISBN 0-201-60480-9
    1. Electronic commerce. I. Robinson, Marcia, 1964–
  II. Title.

HF5548.32.K348   1999
  658'.054678—dc21   99-26564
                                                              CIP

Acquisitions Editor: Mary T. O'Brien
Production Coordinator: Jacquelyn Young
Compositor: NK Graphics
Cover Designer: Simone R. Payment

Text printed on recycled and acid-free paper.

ISBN 0201604809

6 7 8 9 1011 MA   02 01 00 99

6th Printing November 1999

Praise for *e-Business: Roadmap for Success*

e-Business: Roadmap for Success provides unique insight into the emerging electronic business place. Economies around the world are undergoing a wholesale rejuvenation; businesses are reinventing themselves. In this new economy, the Internet and technologies like the Java platform have helped businesses streamline business processes, have helped companies compete in new ways, and have engendered all together new types of business opportunities. It's clear we're on the cusp of a new era. e-Business: Roadmap for Success serves as a guidebook to the new electronic business place where the rules of engagement are changing and where only one thing is certain: The status quo will not be maintained. It's rare to find one book that covers this much ground so effectively.

DR. ALAN BARATZ
PRESIDENT, JAVA SOFTWARE
SUN MICROSYSTEMS, INC.

e-Business is the first book I have read which captures in any depth the full spectrum of business processes that are being redefined and improved by leveraging the Internet and its associated technologies. Equally important, it relates these redefined processes to underlying business objectives and benefits. This book is going to stimulate a lot of thinking in corporate boardrooms and executive suites.

DAVID M. ALSCHULER
VICE PRESIDENT,
E-BUSINESS AND ENTERPRISE APPLICATIONS
ABERDEEN GROUP, INC.

This is the book for creating a serious e-business strategy. A must-read for managers who are creating tomorrow's e-business companies today.

DR. FRANCES FREI
ASSISTANT PROFESSOR
HARVARD BUSINESS SCHOOL

This is the best book on e-business for the decision-maker. It provides a great overview of the e-business landscape.

ANDREW B. WHINSTON
HUGH CULLEN CHAIR PROFESSOR OF
INFORMATION SYSTEMS,
ECONOMICS AND COMPUTER SCIENCE
GRADUATE SCHOOL OF BUSINESS
UNIVERSITY OF TEXAS

This book is dedicated to:

Bill and Judy Robinson
                              —MMR

Vijay and Vinod
                              —RK

Contents

CHAPTER THREE THINK E-BUSINESS DESIGN, NOT JUST TECHNOLOGY   53

CHAPTER FOUR CONSTRUCTING THE E-BUSINESS ARCHITECTURE   81

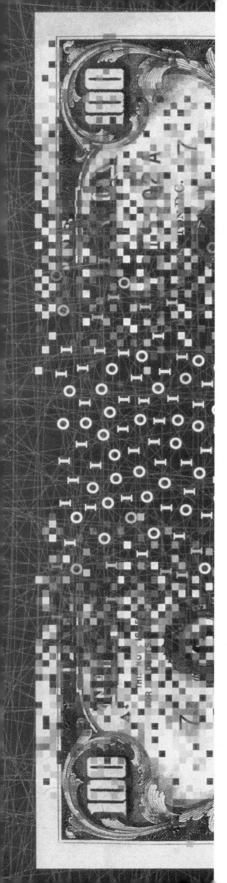

Foreword

New Business Models and the Creation of Wealth

The basis of competition and wealth creation in the digital economy is not good use of information, quality, process reengineering, speed, effective decision making, empowerment or the other countless management techniques popular today. It is business model innovation.

Throughout the twentieth century, wealth was created by the integrated industrial age corporation. A clear model of the firm was established, along with many assumptions. Organizations were structured as hierarchies with reporting relationships and an internal economy. Marketing-based print and broadcast technologies became central to revenue generation. Manufacturing plants and processes that had many similarities across industries were established. A theory of management was developed. Information technology applications were developed. Information technology applications were created embodying these assumptions.

However, as the world shifts from a broadcast to interactive paradigm, most of this is changing profoundly. In the emerging economy there is a new infrastructure, based on the Internet, that is causing us to scrutinize most of our assumptions about the firm. As a skin of networks—growing in ubiquity, robustness, bandwidth, and function—covers the skin of the planet, new models of how wealth is created are emerging.

e-Business: Roadmap for Success

If it is true that new business models based on networks are the key to competitiveness and wealth creation, then Ravi Kalakota and Marcia Robinson's book is very timely.

The term e-business began as a marketing slogan for technology companies. It is now a central theme at the heart of business strategy. However, most managers still view e-business and e-commerce as the buying and selling of goods on the Internet. Ravi and Marcia show how it is much more than this. They provide a wealth of information about the key technologies that are enabling new business models, as well as some helpful practical advice on how to get from there to here.

Once you've read this book you'll know why all business will soon be , e-business.

Don Tapscott
Chairman, Alliance for Converging Technologies
April 1999

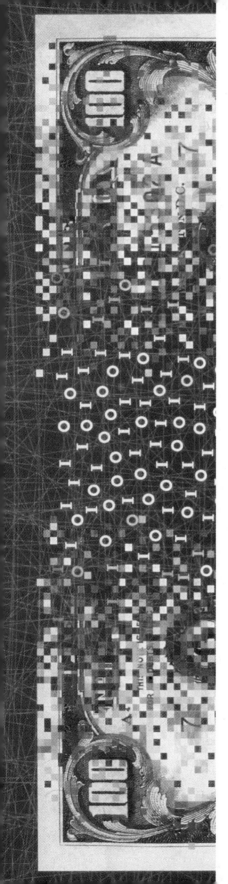

Preface

e-Commerce is changing the shape of competition, the speed of action and the nature of leadership.

Managers everywhere are feeling the heat: Their companies are at the e-commerce crossroads and there are many ways to go. But which road will lead to success? What are the roadblocks they will be forced to navigate? Which business models, management strategies, and tactics will make them successful? What will be the characteristics of the next generation of business applications, and which vendors will lead in delivering them? And to whom can they turn for help?

If these are the questions you're losing sleep over, you've picked up the right book. We'll help you find the road to take. *e-Business: Roadmap for Success* tackles the nagging questions:

- Why are some companies successful at e-commerce while others flounder?

- What are businesses that are solving customer problems doing differently?

- How are successful companies moving from traditional applications to the new breed of integrated e-business architectures?

Through detailed case studies of some of the best-known companies, this book examines the e-business blueprint, offering step-by-step guidance in choosing and implementing the right strategies to survive the e-commerce onslaught and succeed.

Moving from e-Commerce to e-Business

e-Commerce is here to stay. As we approach the new millennium, the Web and e-commerce are key industry drivers. Few companies or industries are immune to the effects of the e-commerce tidal wave. It's changed how many companies do business. It's created new channels for our customers, making leaders in many different industries sit up and take notice.

Are you e-commerce ready? Managers of established companies are struggling to comprehend this new phenomenon. And just as many have started to grasp e-commerce, the next wave—e-business—is already reaching the shore. Intensified competition and new e-commerce opportunities are pressing traditional companies to build e-business models that are flexible, fast moving, and customer focused. In other words, the core of the enterprise itself is going through a metamorphosis. The next stage of this structural evolution is e-business.

Are you e-business savvy? e-Business is the complex fusion of business processes, enterprise applications, and organizational structure necessary to create a high-performance business model. The message is simple: Without a transition to an e-business foundation, e-commerce cannot be executed effectively. Considering the inevitability of moving toward an e-business foundation, senior management is being galvanized into tactical action. Those who fail will pay a high price.

If managers seriously want to develop effective strategies for competing in the new economy, they must understand the fundamental structure of the next-generation e-corporation built on an interconnected web of enterprise applications. We wrote this book to provide a master blueprint for building an innovative e-corporation that can survive and thrive in the digital world.

What Makes This Book Different?

Many books have been written about how the old economic rules of scale, scope, efficiency, market share, and vertical integration are no longer sufficient. New rules must be applied, and that requires new organizational capabilities. Managers everywhere understand the urgency; they're itching to get going and make change happen.

Unfortunately, the first generation of e-commerce strategy books is long on vision but short on detail. Many organizations know it's easy to talk about the e-commerce future, but the real management challenge is to make it happen in a systematic way without derailing existing business. What does this mean to a CEO, CFO, and CIO? If customers are moving online, then the whole IT investment paradigm must shift toward creating an integrated e-business model.

The focus of this book is practical: How can senior management plan for and manage e-business investments? The first step is to design a comprehensive e-commerce strategy, then evaluate prospective line-of-business (LOB) application framework investments based on how well the technology or application advances the strategy. Companies often make the mistake of focusing first on e-commerce applications and then trying to bend a legacy IT strategy around this outline afterward. To succeed, managers must have a strong e-business strategy in place before considering specific e-commerce application investments. Otherwise, most e-commerce efforts are doomed to fail.

But what do these internal e-business architectures and investments look like? This is the focus of *e-Business: Roadmap for Success*. It's the first book on e-business that looks at the structural migration problem: how to transform an old company into a new agile e-corporation. It provides a unique view of the next generation, integrated enterprise and the LOB application investments necessary to compete. In this book, we highlight the critical elements—business processes, back-office and front-office applications, and strategy—that managers need to be successful in the digital economy.

In other words, corporations involved in e-commerce must rethink their visions of the future. *e-Business: Roadmap for Success* shows that understanding how to lead one's company into the e-commerce arena requires a new point of view about integration and the business design. It offers step-by-step navigation of the uncharted e-business terrain. This is a guide that executives in the Fortune 2000 companies need to succeed in the information economy.

Who Should Read This Book?

e-Business will play a significant role in determining the success of corporations. Management needs to learn that the real challenge surrounding e-business is the task of making it happen. This book focuses on the business architecture that managers must build in order to achieve e-business success.

Virtually every discipline is affected by e-commerce and e-business architectural efforts. This book's timeliness and insights into the changes in organizational practice make it appealing to a broad management market:

- Senior management and strategic planners who are charged with developing business strategies

- Corporate executives who must drive their companies' competitive future

- Information technology managers who need to lead their teams with strategic decisions

This book is a must-read for all managers, consultants, entrepreneurs, and business school students who have been discussing and reading about e-commerce and are interested in knowing how they can capitalize on e-dynamics.

How This Book Is Organized

Building the foundation for the era of e-commerce is very exciting! The first four chapters describe a new e-business design composed of building blocks called *enterprise applications.* Market leaders are developing intricate e-models resting on a set of intertwined enterprise apps—customer relationship solutions, enterprise resource planning systems, order management solutions, or supply chain solutions—and then building their strategies around it. Each enterprise app demands a distinct strategic fusion of customer-centric processes, information systems, management systems, and culture.

Most managers are apprehensive of tackling strategic fusion issues because they represent such a formidable task that transcends the organizational structure and line-of-business considerations. This book offers a way to structure this widespread strategy problem, slice it into manageable pieces, and create actionable plans that can be executed quickly.

Chapters 5 through 10 explore the various e-business design elements in the new e-corporation. The goal is to identify clear, rational, strategic design choices that are responsive to evolving customer needs. Each chapter ends with a "Memo to the CEO" that provides a set of normative questions that must be answered convincingly if the building blocks of strategic integration are to be constructed effectively and profitably.

The last two chapters are prescriptive. They focus on the challenges of moving your organization to an e-business firm. In today's business environment, the stakes are high and failure is swift and ruthless. How an organization mobilizes itself into constructive action will determine its survival and ultimate success.

Acknowledgments

Since this book contains information on many companies struggling with their e-business initiatives, we would like to thank them all for their hard work as they continue to tackle this tough issue.

We have learned much through our consulting engagements and extend thanks to the many people we have talked to. In particular, Kemal Koeksal and Peter Zencke at SAP, Shirish Netke at Sun Microsystems, Alex Lowy and David Ticoll at the Alliance for Converging Technologies, Angela Schwartz at Microsoft, and Nagesh Vempaty at Healtheon Corporation.

Thanks to the many people at Addison-Wesley who made this book possible, in particular, our editors Elizabeth Spainhour and Mary O'Brien. Many thanks to our reviewers, who took time out of their busy schedules to read through the manuscript page by page and indicate areas that needed attention. To Lorna Gentry and Jill Hall, thank you for your patience and expertise in editing and improving our book. We appreciate the long hours and honest feedback that made this book much better.

Thank you to Dean Harris, Dr. Richard Welke and colleagues at Mack Robinson College of Business, Georgia State University, for providing support of this project.

To our family and friends who have helped us throughout the writing of this book. In particular, Bill and Judy, who we miss every day; Shelley Cicero, whose regular e-mails brighten our day; and Lynn Lorenc, who always makes us smile.

Ravi Kalakota
Kalakota@mindspring.com
www.ebstrategy.com

Marcia M. Robinson
Marcia.Robinson@mindspring.com
www.ebstrategy.com

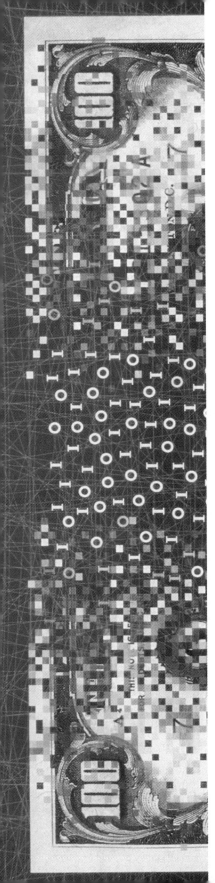

CHAPTER ONE

From e-Commerce to e-Business

What to Expect

New economy, new tools, new rules. Few concepts have revolutionized business more profoundly than e-commerce. Simply put, the streamlining of interactions, products, and payments from customers to companies and from companies to suppliers is causing an earthquake in many boardrooms. Managers are being forced to reexamine traditional definitions of value as we enter a new millennium.

To thrive in the e-commerce world, companies need to structurally transform their internal foundations to be effective. They need to integrate their creaky applications into a potent e-business infrastructure. In this chapter, we'll look at the mechanics of e-business and its impact. We describe what e-business is and how it is changing the market. Included are steps you can take to disaggregate and reaggregate value chains to create the e-business model.

- How did Amazon.com, an online bookstore that started in 1995 with two employees in a rundown warehouse in Seattle, grow revenues in only three years to more than $600 million in 1998, outmaneuvering the two 800-pound gorillas in the book retail business, Barnes & Noble and Borders Books & Music?

- Why is it that consumers can go online to buy a $1,999 built-to-order PC from Gateway Computer, but they cannot go online to buy a customized $5,000 color copier from Xerox?

- Why can you trade stocks and options online through Charles Schwab, but you can't go online to view or make changes to your Cigna or Kaiser health insurance plan?

- Why does it take only a few minutes to choose a flight, buy an airline ticket, and reserve a hotel room and a car through Microsoft Expedia, an integrated online travel transaction site, but it takes twice that long to speak with an American, United or Delta travel agent?

- How can FedEx and UPS make it easy for customers to track their packages, create airbills, and schedule pickups on the Web, but banks cannot tell their customers the status of online bill payments made to the local phone company?

- Why is it that Cisco, an internetworking company that makes routers and switches, can overhaul its product line every two years, but Kodak cannot seem to deliver rapid innovations to meet changing customer requirements?

In short, what makes some companies successful in the digital economy? Visionary companies understand that current business designs and organizational models are insufficient to meet the challenges of doing business in the e-commerce era. If you take a close look at such leading businesses as Dell, Cisco, and Amazon.com, you'll find a new business design, one that emphasizes a finely tuned integration of business, technology, and process. In many cases, these companies are tapping technology to streamline operations, boost brands, improve customer loyalty, and, ultimately, drive profit growth.

Visionary firms are setting new rules within their industries via new techno-business designs, new interenterprise processes, and integrated operations to support changing customer requirements. They realize that the next wave of customer-centric innovation requires businesswide integration of processes, applications, and systems on an unprecedented scale. We call this businesswide integration *e-business,* the organizational foundation that can support business in the Net economy, and it's forcing companies to ask three questions:

1. *How will e-commerce change our customer priorities?*

2. *How can we construct a business design to meet these new customer priorities?*

3. *What technology investments must we make to survive, let alone thrive?*

Look around your own company. Look at the problems that are preoccupying senior management, and look at current priorities: market share versus short-term profits, revenue growth versus cost. What are the high-profile projects that have been initiated or proposed recently to accomplish these priorities? Now think about the digital future and analyze your company's ability to compete with new entrants that don't have your company's baggage: legacy applications, calcified processes, and inflexible business models.

Next, ask yourself questions about strategy: *Does my senior management have a clear understanding of how our industry is being shaped by new e-business developments? Do they suffer from flawed assumptions, or blind spots, in interpreting industry-level changes? Do they recognize the threat posed by new and unconventional rivals? Are they willing to make changes to the business model before it's too late? Are they setting the right priorities to be rule makers, rather than rule takers?*

Now be brutally honest with yourself about your company's readiness to execute change. Does management understand the implementation side of strategy? Do they know that the entire business platform is being transformed by a new generation of enterprise applications? Do they understand the risks, challenges, and difficulties in integrating and implementing complex enterprise applications necessary for an e-business enterprise? Do they understand what it takes to build interenterprise applications such as supply chain management, which is the backbone of e-business?

These are not rhetorical questions. Thoughtful answers will help you shape the transformation agenda that forms the e-business backbone. Our goal is to show the logic of e-business, so that everyone on your management team can participate in creating a new infrastructure. If understanding is to be our guiding principle, then many enlightened managers are better than one. If technology is to be our driving force, then its principles must be accessible to management, not reserved, as is sometimes the case, for only an anointed few who have managed to penetrate its thick fog and hype. So let's get started in linking today's business with tomorrow's technology.

Linking Today's Business with Tomorrow's Technology

It's happening right before our eyes: a vast and quick reconfiguration of commerce on an evolving e-business foundation. What is the difference between e-commerce and e-business? We define *e-commerce* as buying and selling over digital media. e-Business, in addition to encompassing e-commerce, includes both front- and back-office applications that form the engine for modern business. e-Business is not just about e-commerce transactions; it's about redefining old business models, with the aid of technology, to maximize customer value. e-Business is the overall strategy, and e-commerce is an extremely important facet of e-business.

Why is e-business a big deal? CEOs everywhere are faced with shareholder demands for double-digit revenue growth, no matter what the business environment is. They've already reengineered, downsized, and cut costs. Consequently, CEOs are investigating new strategic initiatives to deliver results, and many are looking at using technology to transform the business model—in other words, harnessing the power of e-business.

e-Business is being driven by a profound, evolving development: Every day, more and more individuals and companies worldwide are being linked electronically. While on the surface this does not appear to be a big deal, digitally binding consumers and companies in a low-cost way is as significant as the invention of the steam engine, electricity, the telephone, and the assembly line. It's causing the stodgy old conventions of business built on information asymmetry[1] to be cast aside. So it's no surprise that the rules of the game are being rewritten (see Table 1.1).

Let's start by looking at the first rule of e-business:

Technology is no longer an afterthought in forming business strategy, but the actual cause and driver.

While the effect of technology on business strategy may not be clear initially, it is relentless and cumulative, like the effects of water over time. Technology comes in waves. As the ocean erodes the shore, so will technology erode strategies, causing an entire business model to behave in hard-to-predict ways. Consequently, e-commerce is not something that businesses can ignore.

e-Commerce poses the most significant challenge to the business model since the advent of computing itself. While the computer automates tasks, increasing business speed, it hasn't fundamentally altered the business foundation;

Table 1.1: The Rules of e-Business

Rule 1	Technology is no longer an afterthought in forming business strategy, but the actual cause and driver.
Rule 2	The ability to streamline the structure, influence, and control of the flow of information is dramatically more powerful and cost-effective than moving and manufacturing physical products.
Rule 3	Inability to overthrow the dominant, outdated business design often leads to business failure.
Rule 4	The goal of new business designs is to create flexible outsourcing alliances between companies that not only off-load costs, but also make customers ecstatic.
Rule 5	e-Commerce is enabling companies to listen to their customers and become either "the cheapest," "the most familiar," or "the best."
Rule 6	Don't use technology just to create the product. Use technology to innovate, entertain, and enhance the entire experience surrounding the product, from selection and ordering to receiving and service.
Rule 7	The business design of the future increasingly uses reconfigurable e-business community models to best meet customers' needs.
Rule 8	The tough task for management is to align business strategies, processes, and applications fast, right, and all at once. Strong leadership is imperative.

e-commerce does. **If any entity in the value chain begins to do business electronically, companies up and down that value chain must follow suit, or risk being substituted.** Therefore, rethinking and redesigning the business model is not one of many options available to management, it is the first step to profiting— even surviving— in the information era.

Are executives at large companies aware that the impact of these changes is of seismic proportions? Some are; most are not. The majority of managers are too busy dealing with a multitude of operational problems. Executives can't afford to think too much as they try to get more juice from their current business models. Time is tight; resources are tighter. If they sit around inventing elegant strategies and then try to execute them through a series of flawless decisions, the current business is doomed. If they don't think about the future, the business is doomed.

To do business differently, managers must learn to see differently. As John Seely Brown, chief scientist of Xerox, puts it, "Seeing differently means learning to question the framework through which we view and frame competition, competencies and business models."[2] Maintaining the status quo is not a viable option. Unfortunately, too many companies develop a pathology of reasoning, learning, and attempting to innovate only in their own comfort zones. The first step to seeing differently is to understand that e-business is about structural transformation.

e-Business = Structural Transformation

If e-commerce innovation is the cause of a revolution in the rules of business, what is the effect? In short, structural transformation. The results are a growing pace of application innovation, new distribution channels, and competitive dynamics that are baffling even the smartest managers.

As technology permeates everything we do, business transformation is becoming harder to manage because the issues of change play out on a much grander scale. Increasingly, value is found not in tangible assets such as products, but in intangibles: branding, customer relationship, supplier integration, and the aggregation of key information assets. This observation leads to the second rule of e-business:

The ability to streamline the structure and to influence and control the flow of information is dramatically more powerful and cost-effective than moving and manufacturing physical products.

This rule is the core driver of structural transformation. Ironically, it seems that few companies have developed the necessary information-centric business designs to deal with the issues of business change and innovation. Changing the flow of information requires companies to change not just the product mix, but perhaps more important, the business ecosystem in which they compete.

Unless an enterprise develops an explicit strategy to accommodate the accelerated flow of information, the enterprise will find itself scrambling, working harder and faster just to stay afloat. There is always hope that some magical silver bullet will appear and pierce the walls blocking the smooth flow of information, but that isn't likely.

Transformation Stakes Are Very High

Why do successful firms fail? The marketplace is cruel to companies that don't adapt to change. History shows that organizations best positioned to seize the future rarely do so. As Alvin Toffler pointed out in *Future Shock,* either we do not respond at all or we do not respond quickly enough or effectively enough to the change occurring around us. He called our paralysis in the face of demanding change "future shock." Too often, senior managers fail to anticipate change, become overconfident, lack the ability to implement change, or fail to manage change successfully. For example, in the 1980s, IBM and Digital Equipment were positioned to own the PC market, but they did nothing when upstarts such as Compaq, Dell, and Gateway took the market by storm. Why? Because their commitment and attention were directed elsewhere. Even as late as the early 1990s, Digital's official line was that PCs represented a niche market with only limited growth potential. Digital Equipment dug itself into a hole from which it was impossible to escape and consequently was acquired by Compaq, a company it could have bought many times over in the 1980s. In hindsight, Digital's management should have transformed its business design to rely less on mainframe computers and more on tapping into the PC, client/server, and Web revolution.

As this case illustrates, perhaps the greatest threat companies face today is adjusting to nonstop change in order to sustain growth. Constant change means organizations must manufacture a healthy discomfort with the status quo, develop the ability to detect emerging trends faster than the competition, make rapid decisions, and be agile enough to create new business models. In other words, to thrive, companies will need to exist in a state of perpetual transformation, continuously creating fundamental change. Throw in the resulting time-to-market pressures, and you have a serious challenge indeed. This observation leads us to the third rule of e-business:

Inability to overthrow the dominant, outdated business design often leads to business failure.

If a business design is faulty or built on old assumptions, no amount of fixing and patching will do any good for competing in the digital economy. It's become accepted wisdom that the survival of a company depends on its ability to anticipate, gauge, and respond to changing customer demands in a timely manner. Standing still and waiting for the silver bullet leads only to heartbreak, and working harder and longer leads only to companywide frustration. Neither is realistic for addressing an issue that affects the very future of the enterprise: *How should a company design itself to compete in the new, networked economy?*

e-Business Requires Flexible Business Designs

In order to deal with change, companies and autonomous business units need an effective business design that allows them to react rapidly and continuously, innovate ceaselessly, and take on new strategic imperatives faster and more comfortably. Are companies organized to deal with dynamic change? Not really. Virtually every enterprise finds itself stretched to the limit, attempting to maintain viability and profitability in the face of unparalleled uncertainty and change in every dimension of its business environment. And there is no relief in sight.

To deal with dynamic change, many organizations have sought refuge in outsourcing, the argument for which is simple: Individual companies simply cannot do everything well. True enough. In the first generation of outsourcing, the focus was on gaining efficiency and cost reduction, not on pleasing customers. For instance, because of the increasing complexity of computers and networks, more and more firms began outsourcing their technology management. Among the biggest beneficiaries of this trend have been computer service firms, such as IBM, Andersen Consulting, and EDS. BellSouth outsourced its entire information technology (IT) function to EDS and Andersen Consulting in a contract worth more than $4 billion.

But the outsourcing boom extends well beyond computers. In recent years, outsourcing in the form of contract manufacturing has caught on considerably as companies search for ways to cut costs. Examples of contract manufacturing abound in the high-tech industry: Solectron, Flextronics, and SCI Systems. Outsourcing is changing the nature of the relationship between contract manufacturers and the original equipment manufacturers (OEMs). In the past, they danced like detached partners, but now they're cheek to cheek. Why? If the objective is to please customers, the best relationship for both parties is to behave as a single company—truly cooperative and integrated. This means that firms have to share sensitive design information, link internal applications systems, and provide shared services throughout the supply chain. In a growing number of cases, outsourcers finish the product, slap on the logo, and ship it to the user or distributor. It's the wave of the future. As companies face complex business challenges, they increasingly farm out many tasks to cut down on time to market. Increasingly, new entrants in e-business use outsourcing alliances as a business model to gain market position against a leader. This strategy is often called GBF, "get big fast."

This new generation of outsourcing alliances is called a variety of names, including e-business communities, clusters, and coalitions. While successful strategies differ widely from industry to industry, a common thread runs through them. They all seek to nullify the advantages of the leader by using outsourcing to quickly create reputation, economies of scale, cumulative learning, and preferred access to suppliers or channels. Amazon.com successfully attacked Barnes & Noble using this strategy, and Yahoo! used it to overtake Microsoft Network in the portal business. This trend brings us to the fourth rule of e-business:

The goal of new business designs is to create flexible outsourcing alliances between companies that not only off-load costs, but also make customers ecstatic.

With emerging technology, outsourcing alliances are becoming less painful to implement, especially if both sides are using similar business application software. This trend makes every market leader vulnerable. Distributors are especially threatened, because new online intermediaries are able to replicate their business model at a very low cost. New entrants in the distribution business are differentiating themselves in two key ways: They're easy to do business with, and they add value through innovative services, such as inventory management. Ease of doing business is seen as critical as costs go down, even if the new entrant does not lower prices.

Complex outsourcing arrangements are not optional anymore: They are the only way companies can fill voids in their arsenals. Currently, there are very few guidelines for managers to follow as they go about the task of creating new business designs that leverage outsourcing. Still, in our work with several leading companies, we find a recurring theme that firms are implementing to fashion new business models: disaggregation and reaggregation.

Value Chain Disaggregation and Reaggregation

The value of any business is in the needs being served, not the products being offered. Disaggregation allows firms to separate the means (products) from the ends (customer needs). Disaggregation requires identifying, valuing, and nurturing the true core of the business: the underlying needs satisfied by the company's products and services. This approach allows managers to disassemble the old structure, rethink core capabilities, and identify what new forms of value can be created.

Intel, with its constant innovation in chip design and manufacturing, is a prime example of the disaggregation and reaggregation strategy. Disaggregation is crucial for leaders such as Intel because successful organizations may need to abandon old paradigms (systems, strategies, and products) while they possess equity. The foresight to cannibalize a working business design takes courage because it involves risk, but the payoff can be enormous.

Reaggregation enables businesses to create a configuration that streamlines the entire value chain. It can also help to create an unparalleled customer experience that satisfies a need while engaging, intriguing, and connecting clients. Evidence abounds that new reaggregated business designs are being built on a well-integrated set of enterprise software applications (or killer apps). These enterprise applications represent the backbone of the modern corporation.

Reaggregation enables new entrants to compete differently, even though they're competing with the same scope of activities as well-established leaders. Amazon.com reaggregated the value chain to perform individual activities differently, although it offers the same scope of activities as leader Barnes & Noble. The objective of reaggregation is to either lower cost or enhance differentiation. Using technology to reaggregate value chains is central to the digital economy.

The Road Ahead: Steps to a New Beginning

The steps in disaggregation and reaggregation follow a systematic logic, and they're the same for everybody—startups, visionary firms, and established companies:

1. Challenge traditional definitions of value.

2. Define value in terms of the whole customer experience.

3. Engineer the end-to-end value stream.

4. Integrate, integrate, and integrate some more. Create a new techno-enterprise foundation that is customer-centric.

5. Create a new generation of leaders who understand how to create the digital future by design, not by accident.

Let's focus on established companies, because they need the most help in transforming themselves. It is critical for established companies to understand that we are at a crossroads in history, a time when e-commerce is making a transition from the *fringe market,* dominated by innovators and early adopters, to the *mainstream market,* dominated by pragmatic customers seeking new forms of value. Established companies that don't pay attention to this shift are going to face hard times.

Why is it difficult for established companies to see the writing on the wall? Primarily because most want to "stick to the knitting," that is, to continue to do what made them successful. They don't want to cannibalize existing product lines, and they tend to fall back on simple formulas: lower cost, operational efficiency, increased product variety. They should look at technology as a way to make their lives easier and give them more value for their money. Established companies must challenge traditional definitions of value. They must learn to take advantage of new technologies to create and deliver new streams of value.

Challenge Traditional Definitions of Value

Customers want companies that they do business with to continuously improve the following:

- **Speed.** Service can never be too fast. In a real-time world, there is a premium on instant, accurate, and adaptive response. Visionary companies embrace constant change and consistently deconstruct and reconstruct their products and processes to provide faster service.

- **Convenience.** Customers value the convenience of one-stop shopping, but they also want better integration between the order entry, fulfillment, and delivery—in other words, better integration along the supply chain.

- **Personalization.** Customers want firms to treat them as individuals. Artificial constraints on choice are being replaced with the ability to provide the precise product customers desire.

- **Price.** Nothing can be too affordable. Companies that offer unique services for a reasonable price are flourishing, benefiting from a flood of new buyers.

In every business, managers should ask how they can use new technology to create a new value proposition for the customer. If they figure it out, they will succeed. Lots of firms are already doing it, including such companies as Domino's Pizza, Dell, Amazon.com, and Auto-By-Tel. These visionary companies are meeting new customer expectations by improving products, cutting prices, or enhancing service quality.

Domino's Pizza's mission is to be the leader in off-premise pizza convenience to consumers around the world. Founded in 1960 by Thomas S. Monaghan, Domino's owes its success to a few simple precepts. The company offers a limited menu through carryout and delivery, and every pizza is delivered with a Total Satisfaction Guarantee: Any customer not completely satisfied with the Domino's Pizza experience will be offered a replacement pizza or a refund. By raising the quality of service and the level of innovation that customers expect, market leaders like Domino's are constantly pushing the competitive frontiers into uncharted territories and driving their slower-moving competition back to the drawing board.

The ability to view the world from the customer's perspective often prevents visionary companies from starting in the wrong place and ending up at the wrong destination. Innovators look for what new things customers value, rather than focusing on differences among customers. Often companies rely too much on market segmentation and forget that segmentation techniques work well only in stable settings. Segmentation is difficult to execute in a turbulent environment in which the value proposition constantly changes.

e-Commerce Is Changing the Notion of Value

In subtle ways, e-commerce is fundamentally changing the customer value proposition. In recent years, value innovation across all service dimensions—speed, convenience, personalization, and price—has accelerated due to technological innovations such as the Web and e-commerce. These innovations have substantially changed the underlying value proposition, which in turn has changed the capabilities and competencies needed by companies.

What do we mean by value innovation? Faced with similar products, too many options, and lack of time, the customer's natural reaction is to simplify by looking for the cheapest, the most familiar, or the best-quality product. Obviously, companies want to locate themselves in one of these niches. A product or service that is 98 percent as good, isn't familiar, or costs 50 cents more is lost in a no man's land. Companies that follow middle-of-the-road strategies will underperform. This leads to the fifth rule of e-business:

e-Commerce is enabling companies to listen to their customers and become either "the cheapest," "the most familiar," or "the best."

"The cheapest" isn't synonymous with inferior. It means a value-oriented format that has taken out many of the inventory and distribution costs, such as Southwest's "No Frills Flying" and Wal-Mart's "Every Day Low Prices." The best example of the value-oriented format is Wal-Mart, which helped define a revolution in American retailing with its discount superstore format. That format, combined with friendly customer service, superb inventory management, and an entrepreneurial corporate atmosphere, helped the company steamroll competition. Recently, Wal-Mart has taken "the cheapest" model and applied it to the grocery business. The company is experimenting with 40,000-square-foot Wal-Mart Neighborhood Markets that will compete head on with grocers.

With "the most familiar," customers know what they're getting. McDonald's is a great example of a familiar brand. Often visitors to foreign countries seek local McDonald's just because they know what to expect. It took the brand giants of the past, such as McDonald's and Coca-Cola, decades to make their products household names. By contrast, it's taken so-called Internet megabrands, such as America Online and Yahoo!, only a few years to carve out strong identities.

Being "the best" involves reinventing service processes, being able to turn the company on a dime, and raising relationships with customers and suppliers to unprecedented levels of intimacy. The most obvious example of the best in exceptional service is American Express, exemplified in their Return Protection Plan. This customer benefit refunds cardmembers for items purchased with an Amex card within 90 days from the date of purchase, if the store won't accept returns. Amex will refund the cardmember's account for the purchase price, up to $300 per item, up to $1,000 per year. By continuously generating innovative improvements to customer service and benefits, Amex retains high customer loyalty.

Wherever firms are in the value continuum, customers want continuous innovation. Microsoft CEO Bill Gates calls it the "What have you done for me lately" syndrome. Faced with the burden of increasing time pressure and decreasing service levels, customers are no longer content with the status quo. They want companies to innovate and push service to a new frontier to make their lives easier in some way. Clearly, companies are caught in the midst of a tornado of spiraling business transformation. A good example is the book retailing industry.

Learning from Value Innovation in the Book Retailing Industry

The story of the Internet book retailing war between market leader Barnes & Noble (B&N) and upstart Amazon.com is one of the most written about in recent years. At stake is a significant share of the worldwide book market, estimated to be more than $75 billion (international sales constitute some 30 percent of several players' online business). Given the high stakes, Amazon.com forced the entrenched leader, B&N, and to a lesser extent Borders, to respond to its challenge.

Conventional logic dictates that B&N would dominate Amazon.com on the Internet due to its high name recognition, already advanced fulfillment process (it can leverage its catalog experience), and low prices (in contrast to smaller players, B&N purchases a large number of titles directly from publishers). One would also assume that online customers fit the same profile as those who shop in stores, that their needs are the same.

True? No! The needs and demographics of the online customer are different. In preliminary research, B&N indicated that online book shoppers buy five to ten times as many books as traditional book buyers. Online book customers have an interesting profile: They live in remote or international locations; they're interested in incremental price savings (an estimated "all-in" savings of around 15 percent); they are pressed for time; and they don't mind waiting one to three days for delivery. Clearly, value is influenced by the demographics of online shoppers.[3]

At this stage, it is too early to declare the winner in the online book wars. It's fair to say, however, that market leaders will need to provide value by finding the most interesting and simple way to use the Web, providing the best service (via speed and control) and giving customers the lowest price, because it's so easy to point and click to the competition.

What does this example mean for executives? Amazon.com has identified and innovated one component of value to a level of excellence that puts its competitors to shame. Jeff Bezos, CEO of Amazon.com, isn't unique. He's following the footsteps of other business entrepreneurs who took advantage of technology to build giant businesses from scratch: Sam Walton, Craig McCaw, Bill Gates, and Charles Schwab, to name only a few.

The role of an executive is to help the company understand the threat posed by value migration. Some industries will be profoundly affected, while others will feel little impact. It's vital that executives monitor the impact of readily available digital information on their industries. To do that, executives should answer these questions:

- Is there an Amazon.com that can squeeze margins in your business? If not, can you create one?

- Are there any new entrants in your industry that are leveraging the Web to rewrite the rules?

Watch out for a new generation of infomediaries attempting to harness the efficiencies of the Web. Bottom line: Don't take your industry's conditions as a given. You must understand that technology can create conditions in which companies that once were king of the mountain can wake up one day to find no mountain at all.

Define Value in Terms of the Whole Customer Experience

Identifying new sources of customer value is an important step, but it is not enough. Firms need to innovate the complete customer experience. The ability to streamline the end-to-end experience provides a complete solution and sets visionary companies apart. Amazon.com, for instance, makes the mundane process of comparing, buying, and receiving books an interesting experience that customers find convenient and easy to use. This discussion leads us to the sixth rule of e-business:

Don't use technology just to create the product. Use technology to innovate, entertain, and enhance the entire experience surrounding the product, from selection and ordering to receiving and service.

Amazon.com has undertaken revolutionary initiatives in customer experience through its user interface. We are aware of few other companies that have bundled experience innovation with traditional elements of brand building as successfully. Amazon.com's layout and linkages are logical, intuitive, and, just as important, entertaining. To create a satisfying shopping experience, the company created an e-retail infrastructure that meets the unspoken needs of customers. For example, hard-to-find, relatively unpopular, out-of-print titles can be traced through Amazon.com's special orders department. When a customer inquires about an out-of-print book, the special orders department contacts suppliers to check availability and, if a copy is located, notifies the customer by e-mail for approval of the price and condition prior to shipping the book. This level of service for a national and international audience is unprecedented in the book retailing business.

Amazon.com also provides third-party content, a valuable part of the book purchase process. It includes author interviews and prerelease information, which build a sense of urgency and also help to cement the relationship with heavy users (bibliophiles, in particular); instant order confirmation; customized search engines; editorial analysis; and carefully managed delivery expectations (which set up the user for a positive surprise). These elements combine to create the richness of the Amazon.com experience and have garnered the company a very high customer loyalty rate of more than 58 percent.

As business environments become electronic, firms need to think like Amazon.com in terms of resetting consumers' expectations and experiences. Established firms often discount the importance of the experience offered by a product or service as a key differentiator. Traditional customer experiences have temporal and geographic bounds: Customers must go to a specific store at a specific location between certain hours. But the online experience is quite different, and it needs to be familiar, informative, and easy to use.

Any company that can wrap experience attributes around a commodity product or service has the chance to be an industry revolutionary. However, implementing an effective experience means more than having an attractive, interactive front end. In the first phase of e-commerce, too many firms got carried away by the interactive front ends that are so easy to generate on the Web, ignoring the fact that there must be an integrated business back end that drives the enterprise to success. Providing satisfying front-end and back-end experiences is a critical skill that separates the men from the boys in e-business.

The Case of Microsoft: Creating New Holistic Experiences

Microsoft anticipates changing customer experiences by reengineering several value chains, including travel (Expedia), automotive sales (CarPoint), real estate (HomeAdvisor), and finance (Investor). The success of the new reaggregated value chains depends on an integrated infrastructure that yields easy-to-use, sophisticated customer interaction. Let's meet the new infomediaries:

- Expedia provides travelers with a large number of resources and tools, including an interactive travel agent, a fare tracker, a hotel directory with maps, travel reviews and tips, weather information, and even a currency converter.

- CarPoint provides a wealth of automotive information, such as news, reviews, dealer invoice information, complete model listings, and a dealer locator.

- Microsoft Investor is designed to help individual investors research, plan, execute, and monitor their investments. Investor supplies news, commentary, quotes, portfolio tracking, historical information, and market information, as well as direct links to online trading with Charles Schwab, E*TRADE, Fidelity Investments, and PCFN.

- HomeAdvisor facilitates the home buying process by arranging mortgage sales over the Web and offering information useful to potential home buyers, including real estate agent referrals, home sale listings, and a property valuation estimator. The company functions as a pure infomediary, the online middleman. Because HomeAdvisor posts loans from hundreds of mortgage lenders, home-loan shoppers can immediately view the many options available.

The targets of these online services are vast, according to a Microsoft strategy memo prepared as part of a three-year planning process. Microsoft plans to win a major share of not only the $66 billion advertising market, but also of sales and distribution charges in the markets for airline tickets ($100 billion), automobile sales ($334 billion), and retail goods ($1.2 trillion).[4]

Expedia illustrates how Microsoft is reshaping the economics of the markets it's entering. In less than three years, Expedia was selling more than $5 million to $10 million in tickets and travel services every week, making it one of the three largest online travel agencies. Expedia has established itself as a travel agency and negotiated deals with American Express and major airlines to sell tickets for a fraction of the standard travel agency commission rate.[5]

What is the value to the customer? Travelers can find reams of ready-made information about related travel plans that is often hard to find or time-consuming to gather. The Expedia strategy is simple: Selection, ease of use, and aggressive pricing builds customer traffic, but integrated, personalized service keeps customers coming back. Increasingly, end-to-end integration differentiates the winners from second best. Begin with customer need and work back along the fulfillment chain. This outside-in strategy requires thinking from the customer's perspective and working inward into the company's capabilities and direction.

Microsoft's e-business infrastructure enables innovation and allows the firm to deliver newer and richer customer experiences. Using this infrastructure, Microsoft is creating an entirely new set of service dynamics in various industries. Microsoft is a great example of a market leader that survived a competitive attack from Netscape and came out leaner, meaner, and stronger. *Is there a lesson to be learned from Microsoft about how to manage in a fast-moving environment?*

Microsoft appears to have mastered the art of driving in turbulent weather. It's not very difficult to drive a car fast on a crowded freeway in good weather; we do so without giving it much thought. But the worse the weather and heavier the traffic, the more frequently you have to change direction and speed. Therefore, few of us are capable of driving well at high speeds in inclement weather. Similarly, few companies are capable of thriving in demanding, changing conditions.

e-Business Communities: Engineering the End-to-End Value Stream

To create the future, a company must be capable of engineering the entire end-to-end value stream, which is not a radically new concept. Experienced managers know to redefine business designs and processes when implementing new forms of value. What's different in this new environment is the widespread use of synergistic clusters, business ecosystems, coalitions, cooperative networks, or outsourcing to create end-to-end value streams. e-Business communities (EBCs),[6] as these networks of relationships are known, link businesses, customers, and suppliers to create a unique business organism. This trend leads to the seventh rule of e-business:

The business design of the future increasingly uses reconfigurable e-business community models to best meet customers' needs.

For instance, Amazon.com, Microsoft CarPoint, E*TRADE, and other e-commerce startups are essentially complex EBCs built for the sole purpose of organizing and energizing cross-enterprise relationships to create end-to-end value for the customer. Competition is no longer between companies, but between EBCs.

EBC strategists see companies as part of an extended business family that pools the resources and benefits of each company's expertise. An EBC can play a powerful role in attacking market leaders, and new entrants are using them to gain access to resources, customers, technology, and products. However, EBCs are not just restricted to e-commerce startups. They are everywhere. Large established companies are also moving to the EBC model, but at a slower pace. Why? EBCs are difficult to integrate, and coordination among partners can prove troublesome. Large companies are therefore taking a more incremental approach to EBCs by first concentrating on creating flexible supplier communities vis-à-vis supply chain management.

Let's take a look at a strategy problem in the automobile retailing industry that illustrates the challenge that e-business community engineering poses for car manufacturers worldwide.

e-Business Car Community: Creating the Dealership Network of the Future

Buying a new vehicle is the second largest purchase the average consumer makes.[7] The new vehicle retailing business is fiercely competitive. A significant number of dealers compete not only with dealers franchised by other manufacturers, but also with dealers located in the same geographic area that are affiliated with the same manufacturer. These factors have fostered industry consolidation, considerably reducing the number of dealerships in the last 25 years.

Although it attracts significant consumer dollars, the vehicle sales process has not changed substantially in the last 25 years. However, with the advent of the Web, the process of purchasing these big-ticket items is undergoing radical change. The interactive capabilities of the Web, combined with the easy availability of automotive information, have enabled the establishment of Web-based vehicle marketing services like Auto-By-Tel, an online/telephone sales intermediary.

Using technology—principally the Web—Auto-By-Tel has revolutionized the way cars are bought and sold and, in the process, promises to redefine the auto industry itself. The business proposition is simple. For customers, Auto-By-Tel offers a painless, straightforward, money-saving alternative way to buy a car; for participating auto dealers, Auto-By-Tel provides a cost-efficient, volume-enhancing sales system. In short, the company has reinvented the business model for buying, selling, and financing cars.

What does the new process look like? Customers research the car at Kelley Blue Book or Edmunds.com, which provides such information as the factory-to-dealer price of a car free of charge. The increasing consumer use of the Web has encouraged information providers to post their automotive information online and let consumers do the research. By researching car purchases on Edmund's site, consumers can quickly determine a fair price for the model they want. Then they fill out a form on Auto-By-Tel's Web site specifying make and model, options, description of trade-in, need for loan financing, and so forth. Auto-By-Tel forwards the information to a dealer in the purchaser's area, who offers the shopper a quote on the vehicle. Armed with accurate information to bargain for the best price, trade-in value, and loan interest rate, consumers can cut favorable deals.

Consumers do not pay for the service, but dealers pay annual and monthly fees to be marketed by Auto-By-Tel and for exclusive territorial rights. Auto-By-Tel's new business model features partnerships with an information site, an insurance company, a warranty company, and a car accessories company. In essence, Auto-By-Tel makes money from Web customer referrals.

What does this new process mean for traditional car companies? In a speech at the 1997 National Automobile Dealers Association's annual meeting in New Orleans, Chrysler Corporation Chairman Robert Eaton urged dealers to acknowledge that the Internet is changing car-buying behavior forever by giving car buyers more information and choices. Eaton said, "The customer is going to grab control of the process, and we're all going to salute smartly and do exactly what the customer tells us if we want to stay in business."[8]

This change in customer buying behavior is forcing the Big Three automakers to rethink the future of car dealerships. Today, automakers are asking these fundamental questions about customer value, which shake the very foundation of their business:

- Is online car buying a fad or a new consumer trend? If customers increasingly want to purchase cars online, what kind of business model is needed to support this process?

- If the current model of car dealerships doesn't provide customer value, what will the dealerships of the future look like?

- If customers want to do business online, what kind of e-business application and technology architecture is needed to support it?

These are important corporate strategy questions because the answers will shape the future of dealer networks.

The auto industry is a great example of the rapid evolution of e-commerce from an untested novelty into a mainstream information and transaction channel. The auto manufacturers can control their destiny only by understanding how the entire industry value stream is being transformed. Insight concerning the implications will allow companies to proactively answer such questions as these: *How should we organize for opportunities that don't fit current process models? What skills and competencies must we build now to create the new value stream?* The goal is a transformation process that is revolutionary in design, but evolutionary in execution.

Integrate, Integrate, Integrate: Create the New Techno-Enterprise

Providing end-to-end process integration is not as easy as it looks. End-to-end process integration demands major application overhaul to develop an integrated back-end infrastructure that allows the processes to flow seamlessly. Most firms don't have integrated infrastructures. And the inefficiencies, inaccuracies, and inflexibilities of information technology systems within corporations need no introduction.

The lack of an integrated application architecture is not a new difficulty. It's just that with the advent of e-commerce, these problems are starting to matter more. The reason is simple: When customers had little choice and all competitors were equally bad, there was little incentive for a company to do better. But since customers now have more choices, thanks to new entrants flooding the already competitive marketplace, they are no longer willing to tolerate inefficient service.

With the threat of losing customers, integrated infrastructure problems rocket to the top of the business agenda. Clearly with e-commerce, the definition of enterprise architecture must change. It's gradually dawning on managers that they are not going to get very far in e-commerce if they apply piecemeal solutions to process problems that range from customers to suppliers.

Forward-thinking companies are beginning to understand the enormity of the task that lies ahead, and that a number of barriers must be eliminated before they are ready to use e-commerce to a competitive advantage. The typical barriers that organizations face are process inefficiencies, lack of application integration, fragmented and distributed information, and lack of accurate information. Removing these roadblocks won't be easy. The functional model of the past can't deliver for today's world. As new technological integration problems continue to create potholes in the smooth road of business, managers eventually run out of asphalt and ideas. Enter e-business.

Are You Ready for e-Business Integration?

Today, many senior managers are struggling with this question: What kind of e-business architecture—vision, strategy, cross-functional processes, integrated applications, and IT infrastructure—is needed to support new ways of doing business? Most nontechnology executives are flying blind in terms of emerging technologies at a time when it's necessary—even critical—to adopt them. Generally, they rely on their IT people. But senior executives who rely on IT managers to relate technology to overall business strategy do so at their own peril. Executives can eliminate their strategic blind spots by taking responsibility for understanding the implications of up-and-coming technologies and anticipating when they'll affect business strategy.

Some companies are quite adept at creating business value out of technology. For example, Federal Express sees itself at the crossroads of e-business. The company, now known as FDX Corporation after merging with Caliber Logistics, spends about $1 billion a year on information technology, which buys them not just a system to track packages, but something much more valuable. They can position themselves to be the warehouse, fulfillment, and shipping departments for any company.

The FDX partnership with National Semiconductor is a good example. Orders from the chipmaker's home office in Santa Clara, California, go directly over a dedicated computer line to an FDX computer in Memphis. That's the last time National Semiconductor has anything to do with the order until it receives confirmation from FDX. The order is sent to FDX's warehouse in Singapore (which keeps inventory for National Semiconductor), filled, then shipped by FDX. This system has cut the average customer-delivery cycle from four weeks to seven days and reduced distribution costs at National Semiconductor from 2.9 percent of sales to 1.2 percent.

From each customer like National Semiconductor, FDX accrues revenue by both managing inventory and shipping product. According to FDX, the global express market, which was $35 billion in 1996, is projected to grow to $250 billion in the next 20 years. The percentage of product shipped to meet the requirements of just-in-time manufacturing is expected to grow to more than 40 percent in 2000, up from about 25 percent in 1996. That places FDX at the convergence of two powerful market trends, which it leverages by investing in e-business architecture to manage the customer's supply chain.

Smart firms like FDX transform themselves proactively, using technology to gain advantage in the changing market. As the competition becomes heated, e-business strategy takes on new meaning, yet the task of creating an effective e-business strategy and infrastructure can be daunting. The fortunate firms scramble and adapt. Companies that cannot address new customer trends will either suffer losses or become history.[9]

The tough part of e-business is getting strategy implemented. *Fortune* magazine reports, "Less than 10% of strategies formulated are effectively executed." With a one-in-ten chance of success in the implementation of strategy, the landscape is littered with failed attempts. Add to the mix the fact that upstart, innovative competitors are streaming out of the woodwork, and the plot thickens.

The New Priority: e-Business Execution Framework

How do we make e-business strategy work? The top priority is to understand the elements of the e-business execution framework, which must

- Provide a structure for defining, communicating, and monitoring new realities.

- Redesign core business processes to align with new organizational vision.

- Enable IT infrastructure to support change, innovation, and business goals.

Our goal in this book is to develop an e-business framework that will help managers communicate their goals and do their jobs better.

What is the premise behind this e-business framework? Firms have reached the limits of automating existing functional processes. While many firms have improved on cost, quality, speed, and service, differentiation on the basis of these variables is harder to come by. To be profitable in the future, firms must turn their attention to new architectures that support organizational agility in terms of business applications.[10] From a business perspective, agility describes the company's ability to meet the needs of the market without excessive costs, time, organizational disruption, or loss of performance.

Is this simply old wine in a new bottle? No. The current business climate demands that companies live and breathe agility in dealing with customers. For the e-business architecture to succeed, its elements must be aligned with customers' most important priorities: variety, quality, competitive price, and fast delivery. An isolated functional model can satisfy none of these needs. Consequently, the love affair with silo-oriented IT infrastructure is being replaced by a new passion: integrated customer-centric models that are capable of supporting complex business designs.

Engineering an integrated, yet agile, infrastructure requires critical choices along a number of dimensions. CEOs, CIOs, and CFOs in established firms are acutely aware that the business systems they are mandated to implement are extremely difficult to create. It's not that the technology isn't good, it's that somewhere between the problem and the execution, the objective was lost or changed, or it wasn't there to begin with. Research shows that the vast majority of technology infrastructure investments fail to deliver expected returns because they were poorly linked to organizational plans, the strategies and tactics were flawed, the plan wasn't properly executed, or the organization failed to understand everything needed to support its objective.[11] This failure is clearly a management problem, not a technology issue.

Needed: A New Generation of e-Business Leaders

e-Business is an alluring concept for most business executives: buying and selling online, expanding the customer base; improving customer loyalty, and interacting seamlessly and efficiently with suppliers and business partners. Managers, however, need to look past the hype to realize that e-business is bringing about fundamental changes as it reshapes the structure of entire industries, creates niches for new sets of infomediaries, and enables businesses with well-executed business applications to take quantum leaps forward, while those without them suffer.

As e-business innovation gains momentum, companies, regardless of their industry, size, or location, are reformulating business strategies in the face of critical challenges. Collectively, these challenges require organizations to build new capabilities. But who is currently responsible for developing those capabilities?

Everyone and no one. That vacuum is senior management's opportunity to play a leadership role.

Continued innovation in infomediary processes is one of the best levers corporations have to add value to their web of suppliers and customers. However, changing infomediary processes is intimidating to some CEOs and senior business managers (see Table 1.2). Often they have a can't-teach-an-old-dog-new-tricks mentality. Although spending on technology has reached record levels, these executives continue to put their businesses at risk by not aligning processes with technology.

Clearly, the rapid pace of high-tech activity is forcing senior managers to understand where the set of applications on which their businesses run is heading, and it's crucial to reduce risk. The problem is that there's a lot to know and not much time to learn, given the short life span of new applications. A conceptual understanding, from top to bottom, of how business applications can support growth is critical to the future of any large organization. Keeping ahead of the pack means developing a superior understanding in order to construct the right strategy. And this fact leads us to the eighth rule of e-business:

The tough task for management is to align business strategies, processes, and applications fast, right, and all at once. Strong leadership is imperative.

As business flexibility drives the evolution of e-business, a leader's greatest challenge includes gaining an intimate understanding of the knowledge behind products and service delivery channels in order to answer the following question: *Do we stay with the status quo, seek a challenge in the relatively safe haven of improving the existing product mix, or return to the chaos, risk, and uncertainty of new products and services?*

Table 1.2: Challenges Facing Market Leaders

Manage top-line growth . . . Acquisitions

Meet or exceed customer expectations

Customer-driven . . . Become responsive

Market evolution . . . Become flexible

Implement partner/alliance strategy . . . Become competitive

Integrate multiple channels and multiple business units

Brand migration and product transition issues

Implement supply chain management . . . Shorter lead times–forecasting and
    component availability

Change internally to gain competitive advantage

A tough choice, right? Not really. Meeting new customer needs demands a new mindset. The task facing managers now is how to recover the entrepreneurial spirit from which their companies sprouted. Joseph Schumpeter, a Vienna-born professor of economics at Harvard in the early 1900s, talked about the force of "creative destruction" that exists at the heart of entrepreneurial activity. By destruction he meant breaking free from the encrusted habits of the past and the inertia of the tried and true. Nearly 100 years later, Schumpeter's words are still extraordinarily valuable because they help managers realize that much of the conventional management wisdom, which might work very well in stable environments, is not always appropriate when attempting to create new business models in the age of volatility.

Memo to the CEO

Whether they are in Berlin or Bombay, Kuala Lumpur or Kansas, San Francisco or Seoul, companies around the globe are developing new models to operate competitively in a digital economy. These models are structured, yet agile; global, yet local; and they concentrate on maximizing the risk-adjusted return from both knowledge and technology assets.

Many leading companies are aggressively pursuing e-business. Arthur Ryan, CEO of Prudential Insurance, has publicly stated that his company will spend $1 billion over the next two years updating its IT infrastructure. The spending will target e-business architecture that can deliver diverse sources of competitive advantage. Smart CEOs have gotten closer to their CIOs in the last five years as they realize that information technology may be the single most important tool they have to advance their organizations through technology.

However, the CEO must be aware of the fact that the real threat to the firm comes not just from outside, but also from inside the company. In order to navigate the treacherous waters of technology, leaders must plunge into them; they cannot manage e-business at a distance by hiring consultants or knowledgeable people and giving them adequate resources. e-Business methods and technology must not be a black box to managers, because their ability to position the company, respond to market changes, and guide internal innovation depends on this knowledge.

Today, the senior management committee must see around corners, anticipate competitors coming from left field, and execute at Internet speed. Yesterday's crystal ball sheds no light on how to strategize in this new age of e-commerce. Classic economic "theory of the firm" provides little insight into the dynamics of digital business designs. Yesterday's successful companies or Harvard Business School case studies are of limited help in a fluid marketplace in which success is measured in response agility and Internet time.

Leaders must also understand that the e-business concept encompasses the entire business model of a company. While it's not important for CEOs or senior managers to have in-depth knowledge about specific technologies, it does help for them to *have a conceptual understanding* in order to be closely involved in shaping and directing the way e-business architectures are created and used. To fight the new war, CEOs must **listen, understand, respond, and learn.** While they know what strategies they want to use to achieve their goals, CEOs need help figuring out how to support their efforts with technology. Working hard to create an integrated business/technology plan can have a significant impact on the bottom line.

All we can say is that you ain't seen nothing yet! Innovation, on many fronts, is causing business today to move faster than ever.[12] The next ten years are going to be even more suspenseful and action-packed than the 1990s have been. Not since the early electric power era or the first assembly line has there been such profound change. The focus in the next decade will be on e-commerce and e-business.

A few key points emerge to guide our journey into the twenty-first century:

1. Emphasis will shift to the broader e-business from the narrower e-commerce discipline, to derive the greatest value.

2. e-Business will provide true competitive advantage only when new concepts, practices, and performance are combined to sharply affect companies' and customers' bottom lines.

3. e-Business companies must harness the leading external drivers of change, including rising consumer demands, globalization, and information/communication.

4. The future responsibilities of the manager will change, although his or her organizational level may be similar to today's.

To really appreciate the journey that lies ahead, firms need to realize that e-commerce is no longer an appendage of business; rather, it's becoming businesses' most vital weapon. Welcome to the new era! Welcome to e-business!

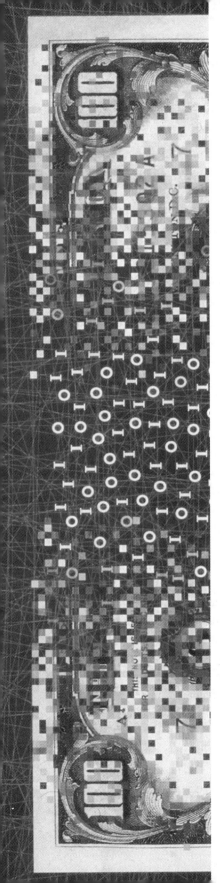

e-Business Trend Spotting

What to Expect

Never mind what worked, or did not, in the past. The rules have changed. Which strategies will be most profitable in the future? To create effective strategies, companies must be able to spot trends quickly. In this chapter we'll identify 15 trends you must be aware of before you begin your e-business journey. These trends cover consumer buying habits, service and processes, organizations, and enterprise technology. We'll show the impact of these trends on e-business.

Do you long for days gone by as you stare into the steely eyes of the future? Managers can no longer rest easy in the knowledge that today looks like yesterday and that tomorrow will be more of the same. Planning for the future requires managers to become trend spotters in an environment in which the globalization of markets and the pace and scope of change make it hard for companies to follow rapid shifts in technology, processes, and consumer taste. They must learn to identify *discontinuous change,* unsettling shifts arriving on an uncertain schedule. This provides an entirely new landscape for managers to navigate, and only the trend spotters can hope to conquer it.

The Achilles' heel of large corporations is often the inability to spot trends and act on them quickly. Michael Eisner, CEO of Disney, said that if Disney does not discern consumer trends, Tomorrowland could become Yesterdayland before they know it.[1] Warren Buffett, the legendary investor, has a knack for describing such conundrums articulately: "The rearview mirror is always clearer than the windshield." Benjamin Franklin said it even more succinctly: "Look before, or you'll find yourself behind."

These insights show that identifying trends is a neat way to synthesize consumer behavior, help eliminate uncertainty, and identify new opportunities. In the 1980s, the most significant trends were increasing competition from all corners of the globe, greater demands for quality, shorter product life cycles, process improvement, and the need to create an agile work force. Most of these trends are now considered boilerplate, and experienced managers understand them quite well.

So, what are the new trends today? What is going to be different about the next 10 years? Most obvious is the Internet. With 50 million people connected in only five years, the Internet has become the fastest accepted communications medium ever.[2] It took the telephone 70 years, radio 40 years, and television 15 years to reach that milestone. The Internet is no longer just a data network; it's a sales and distribution channel, and it's facilitated e-commerce, the ability to do business over the Web. e-Commerce is enabling the integration of information industries—content, storage, networks, business applications, and consumer devices—that have been isolated until recently. This integration is leading to industry convergence: the melding of consumer electronics, television, publishing, telecommunications, and computers for the purpose of facilitating new forms of value. Clearly, the Internet groundswell is starting to affect every facet of our lives—personal and business.

e-Commerce is slowly affecting the distribution channels through which consumers and businesses have traditionally bought and sold goods and services. The online channel provides sellers with the ability to reach a global audience and operate with minimal infrastructure, reduced overhead, and greater economies of scale, while providing consumers with a broad selection and unparalleled convenience. As a result, a growing number of consumers conduct business on the Web, such as buying products, trading securities, paying bills, and purchasing airline tickets. But remember that the Internet is an infant technology. People run into such problems as browsers that crash and Call Waiting interrupting their dial-up connections. So e-commerce has to offer overwhelming value to compensate for inconvenience.

The time to think about the following questions is now: What are the implications of e-commerce on the form and function of twenty-first-century organizations? How will existing companies make the transition into e-commerce companies? Can existing companies ward off the threat posed by new entrants? The tension between the old guard and rival upstarts is palpable. Take as an example the $21 billion U.S. toy industry, which is shaping up to become the runaway success of the Internet.

Toys are well suited to online sales: They're usually small, easy to ship, and kids don't need to try them to know they love them. The convenience factor for busy parents boosts this retail category even more. Imagine traveling mothers or fathers being able to shop for and order toys from their hotel rooms to arrive at their house precisely at 9 A.M. on Saturday. This type of convenience is invaluable for busy parents. Supporting this convenience is the new guard, represented by FAO Schwartz and eToys, which wants to become the Amazon.com of toys. Opposing them is the old guard represented by big retailers, such as Toys "R" Us, and manufacturers of brand names, such as Mattel, Hasbro, and Parker Brothers. The old guard is worried that selling to customers directly will wreak havoc on their finely tuned retail channels, pricing structures, and channel distribution. The toy industry is not unique. Increasingly, the tussle between new and old centers on new distribution channels.

Unquestionably, the opportunities for digital revolution are many and largely unexplored. How should an entrepreneurial manager begin? By looking for ways to anticipate consumer trends, foresee technology trends, and envision new organizational forms. A lot of what we find surprising and unpredictable in today's environment is actually a series of events that has been played out in pretty much the same way in industry after industry. Once we see the pattern, we can understand and predict change—and begin to master it.

Trend spotting isn't just for entrepreneurs looking to start new companies or for marketers attempting to sell old products in new packages. It is useful for identifying new business opportunities as well. Consider, for example, the growing emphasis on well being.[3] This trend encompasses several mini trends: the yearning for stress relief, a desire for greater balance in one's life, a revitalized interest in family and home, and a new focus on the environment. The business response: Grocery stores now stock natural and organic foods, medicinal herbs, and ready-to-eat meals. Insurance companies are beginning to cover alternative medicine. Travel agencies increasingly sell spiritual vacation packages. Hardware stores carry air and water purifiers and nontoxic paints.

Mastering the patterns of e-business requires understanding that the future will be built on a new set of operating assumptions. But first we must become expert in differentiating fads from trends. Fads catch on quickly, spread, and then die a fast death. Eileen Shapiro, in her iconoclastic book *Fad Surfing in the Boardroom,* defines fad surfing as "the practice of riding the crest of the latest management panacea and then paddling out again just in time to ride the next one; always absorbing for managers and lucrative for consultants; frequently disastrous for organizations."

In contrast, trends often start slowly but spread like wildfire as mass-market consumers and companies fan the flames with their pent-up demands. Trends are global, tend to last approximately five to ten years, and may evolve dramatically. The Web is a great example of a trend. It started slowly in 1989 in a remote lab in Switzerland and, with the advent of the Mosaic browser, burst onto the mass market, taking everyone by surprise. Did you identify the Web as a major trend in 1994?

The smart manager stands at the forefront of trends, such as the Web, before they become mainstream topics. Since it takes years to steer large organizations in new directions, toward new horizons, company captains must be aware of what lies ahead or their companies will sink as quickly as the *Titanic* when it hit the iceberg. Trend spotting has fast become a "plan or be planned for" issue.

In this chapter, we describe the major trends that are driving organizations to become e-business enterprises (see Table 2.1). As a manager, your ability to comprehend core trends will improve your chances of better grasping the opportunities facing your company. As you read through this chapter, ask yourself, *What is the common thread running through these trends?* We will address this question in the final section.

Increase Speed of Service: For the Customer, Time Is Money

Customers count speed of service as a key reason why they do business with certain companies. Customers hate delays and, more specifically, hate waiting for service. Just look at the success of drive-through oil changes, drive-through fast

Table 2.1: Major Trends

Consumer trends	Speed of service
	Self-service
	Integrated solutions, not piecemeal products
Service/Process trends	Convergence of sales and service: Customization and integration
	Ease of use: Make service consistent and reliable
	Flexible fulfillment and convenient service delivery: Streamline your supply chain
Organizationed trends	Contract manufacturing: Becoming brand intensive, not capital intensive
	Retain the core, outsource the rest: Business process outsourcing
	Increasing process transparency and visibility
	Continuous innovation and employee retention
Enterprise technology trends	Enterprise applications: Connect the corporation
	Infrastructure convergence: Increasing melding of voice, data, and video
	Multichannel integration: Computer telephony integration and voice recognition
	Wireless applications enter the mainstream
	Leveraging legacy investments: The rise of middleware for application integration

food, and other quick-turnaround businesses. As their time quotas shrink, customers look for companies that serve them faster. Look at new trends in online car purchasing and home refinancing. The message to the marketplace is clear: To succeed, companies must reduce the processing time between search, selection, order entry, and order fulfillment. Delays at any step of the process are unacceptable!

Why do delays occur? Often they're due to excessive hand-offs. Consider the case of a specialty stainless steel producer that wanted to improve its unacceptable 40-percent on-time delivery record. The company identified unnecessary hand-offs as delaying the production process. For example, each order was entered into the system three times. First, customer service would enter the information after writing down the buyer's specifications and use printed lists to check whether the order could be produced. They then checked printed schedules to determine a ship date. Second, operations would verify whether a particular grade of steel could be produced; information was then entered into operations' system. Third, production control would use its own files to verify the scheduling, and then reenter the information as well. This repetition caused significant delays and errors.

To solve the hand-off problem, companies are investing billions of dollars in integrated systems, which is exactly what the stainless steel producer did. After taking a close look at its problem, the company decided one possible solution was an integrated system for most of its business operations: accepting orders, triggering receivables, sending orders to production, sending requisitions to the warehouse, updating inventory, updating accounting, and replenishing stock with suppliers. This scenario is not an isolated example, but rather a common "hand-off-itis" ailment afflicting many companies.

What does this trend mean for e-business? When one considers the challenge of meeting the demands of busy, time-starved, dissatisfied consumers in an environment of hostile competition, low margins, and countless sales outlets selling similar products, it becomes clear that changing the entire business model is the only plausible strategy. e-Business applications must cut the time customers wait for service. Customers now penalize companies that infringe on their time through delays, mistakes, or inconveniences. If companies don't expedite processes, customers will go to someone who does it faster. If one company doesn't make it easy for the customer to do business, another will.

It is very important that managers understand and diagnose the cause behind service delays. They need to analyze if an integrated system can speed service. If so, they need to strategize, design, and implement such systems as soon as possible. Unfortunately for some companies, their managers may wake up too late to heed the sound of customers' fists pounding on the counters for faster service. These companies will not be in business for long.

Empower Your Customer: Self-Service

Inconvenience and poor service make customers impatient, and they're beginning to look for solutions that increase the value of their time. Today, customers with more money than time increasingly avoid difficult, slow business experiences that involve dealing with intermediaries. They are embracing 24-hours-a-day, seven-days-a-week self-service systems in which they look for information and merchandise without the aid of sales personnel.

Self-service is rapidly forcing change on a huge sector of business: the intermediary, or middlemen.[4] From real estate, insurance, travel, and car purchases to auctions, parts sourcing, and retailing, very few intermediaries are left standing when buyers and sellers realize they can meet directly online. For some, extinction is almost certain. Others are finding fresh opportunities on the Web, though virtually all will have to change how they do business.

e-Commerce is a big enabler of self-service, and market leaders are giving customers the means to serve themselves whenever possible. For instance, customers of Gateway Computer can assess their needs, then configure, order, and pay for new systems—in addition to getting limited technical support—without ever having to talk to a person.

Another example of self-service can be found in online trading. Companies such as E*TRADE and eSchwab are setting the pace. These firms make it easy for customers to trade by themselves without the help of a broker. Round-the-clock availability gives customers access to their account anywhere, anytime. In fact, the business model is predicated on the disintermediation of the broker.

The growing acceptance of self-service can be seen in the online travel industries as well. Leisure and business travelers increasingly make travel reservations over the Internet, and as a result, Internet travel agencies such as Microsoft Expedia, Preview Travel, and Internet Travel Network (ITN) have emerged as an attractive option. Using these services, customers can access a central reservation service via the Web for faster, more convenient flight booking. The electronic medium enables companies to automate the processing and confirmation of travel reservations, thus lowering the cost and reducing the need for expensive physical facilities.

For service organizations, the impact of the customer push for self-service is quite dramatic. Before self-service can become a reality, a new infrastructure must be built, and new protocols must be designed to streamline the process. Integration of processes will be essential for serving the customer well. Established companies are thus at a severe disadvantage because they have to quickly transform and integrate their existing applications, processes, and systems to enable self-service, which is no small task.

Provide Integrated Solutions, Not Piecemeal Products

In the last decade, there has been an interesting shift toward convenient integrated solutions. A good example of an integrated solution is the Microsoft Office Suite. When was the last time you shopped individually for word processing, spreadsheet, and presentation packages? The Office Suite product is one of the biggest moneymakers Microsoft has because customers love its integrated functionality. Microsoft is betting that this demand for integrated products will continue. In fact, a core design objective in many of their products is seamless integration.

It is quite extraordinary how quickly consumers in the last decade have moved away from point, or best of breed, solutions toward integrated solutions. This trend can be observed in retailing. In today's time-strapped society, shopping is a low priority on people's "to do" lists. Increasingly, customers are demanding one-stop, all-under-one-roof solutions. In response, the retail industry has created various models: one-stop life-needs providers (e.g., Wal-Mart), one-stop lifestyle providers (e.g., The Gap), and one-stop life-path providers (e.g., Toys "R" Us).

The trend of life-needs integration can be observed in the success of the Wal-Mart superstore, which is marketed as an integrated retailer for the busy, price-sensitive shopper. Wal-Mart's execution of one-stop shopping has increased customer loyalty, the number of items sold per transaction, and the average transaction size. Other retailers have picked up on this successful formula and are pursuing strategies that include selling more to the same customer out of the same store (or Web site) and making shopping more convenient.

For an example of the image lifestyle integration trend, look at the Gap in the apparel retailing business. The Gap provides a great illustration of a company that has effectively marketed an image to its customers. Gap mannequins are outfitted with three or four layers of shirts, blue jeans, a belt, a baseball cap, sunglasses, socks, shoes, gloves, and a knapsack. Customers are drawn to the hip image. Other apparel megabrands, such as Polo, Tommy Hilfiger, and Donna Karan, have improved their brand loyalty by adopting "collections," a form of lifestyle merchandising whereby one brand/concept shop can outfit a customer from head to toe. During a time when customers demand fewer shopping trips, apparel retailers must move toward becoming one-stop lifestyle providers.

Toys are a model of life-path integration. Life path basically means businesses that grow with us. Consider the strategy of Toys "R" Us, a life-path retailer for kids that sells to parents. The Toys "R" Us marketing strategy is three-pronged: baby goods at Babies "R" Us, kids' clothes at Kids "R" Us, and toys at Toys "R" Us. However, although Toys "R" Us has leveraged its core customer through each of its three concepts, it faces one key challenge: The products are sold from three separate types of stores, each of which requires its own infrastructure, buildings, management, and associates.

What does this trend mean for e-business? Consumers don't need another retailer or another electronic distribution channel. They want integrated-service-offering businesses that solve their one-stop shopping needs. There are too many choices, products, and stores. To solve the "choice" problem, customers increasingly seek integrated solutions because they make the decision process easier.

Integrate Your Sales and Service: Customization and Integration

The need to attract, acquire, leverage, and retain customers is still of primary concern to most businesses. Revenue growth through customer acquisition and retention remains a major competitive requirement. Several studies document that the average company loses half its customers every five years, and that it costs five to ten times as much to obtain a new customer as it does to keep an existing one.

To improve retention, companies are developing and managing customer relationships via better sales/service integration and new technology. The concept of maximizing customer relationship as a competitive differentiator gained attention in the late 1980s, when managers realized that customers do not exist in the aggregate and that a one-size-fits-all philosophy, therefore, doesn't work. The sales and service message needs to be tailored to each customer. Therein, of course, lies the problem. *How do you market to a diverse customer base? How can any organization effectively and efficiently address the opportunity? How can technology help bring about better customer relationships?*

Of course, technology is not just about customer acquisition or retention; it is also about generating revenue by selling more to existing customers through cross-selling and up-selling. This strategy requires firms to sell to customers while serving them. You can see it at your local bank when the teller tries to sell you a new product while you're making a deposit. In other words, the bank is attempting to become an integrated sales and service environment. However, most companies view sales and service as separate functions. A sale occurs during the sales cycle, and service is an after-sale activity. Where a prospect or customer is in this cycle determines which department in the company he or she must contact. However, cross-selling and up-selling are closing the gap between sales and service.

How does this trend affect the e-business enterprise? New organizational models need to be developed to further narrow the gap between sales and service. For instance, telephone call centers must blur the lines between sales and service. How do we design such enterprises? Look at Home Depot, which services the do-it-yourself customer. Home Depot blurs the lines between sales and service by being in perpetual service mode. This, in turn, attracts prospective customers by giving them easy access to information about products and services before they buy. After the sale, the same level of service builds the kind of loyalty that turns customers into company advocates, which leads to better up-selling and cross-selling opportunities, as well as new customer referrals.

The success of Home Depot illustrates that consumers want fast, accurate, consistent information. And they want service before *and* after the sale, not traditional service, whereby a company sells a product then hands off the customer to a service group. Today, service must start before the sale and be inherent in every interaction customers and prospective customers have with the company.

Customer relationships are the key to business growth. Firms must take absolute responsibility for a customer's satisfaction throughout the "want-it-buy-it-and-use-it" experience. This requires learning and tracking customers' needs, behaviors, and lifestyles and using this information to create a specific value proposition. This strategy is the path to consumer loyalty and is called relationship selling.

Ease of Use: Make Customer Service Consistent and Reliable

The following story is true; it happened to us. We received a letter from AT&T, our long-distance telephone carrier, informing us that we owed $ 0.00 dollars (yes! zero dollars) and that we were delinquent in paying it. If we didn't pay the $0.00 balance, the letter informed us, they were going to turn our account over to a collection agency. Naturally, we immediately called AT&T. The service representative at AT&T's call center was no help and referred us to our local service provider, BellSouth. But when we called BellSouth, we were told that it was an AT&T problem. After several minutes of negotiations, the BellSouth service representative took pity on us and called AT&T with us on the line. After repeating the problem and account information for the third time, we were elated to be making progress.

Boy, were we wrong! After getting assurances from AT&T that they would handle the situation, the BellSouth representative got off the line and, in the process, disconnected us. We were right back where we started. Believe it or not, it took us over one year to resolve this problem with AT&T. This whole incident left an indelible impression on us that AT&T cares very little for its customers. *Has something similar ever happened to you?*

Managers must understand that as customers value their time more, they are less tolerant of screw-ups in customer service. As the speed of service increases, the expectations for customer service grow higher. Making customer service easy and solution oriented is probably one of the most important trends in business today. The customer service process must be friendly and easy to use. Companies must present customers with single points of contact, rather than shuffling them from one department to another so they have to start anew each time. Ask yourself, *how often have you called a company only to suffer a hand-off to partners or outside vendors? How often have you been satisfied with the hand-off?* It's likely you were dissatisfied.

Increasingly, customer service is no longer one customer talking to one enterprise. With outsourcing of business functionality and the increasing complexity of products, many service calls require the coordination of two or more firms. To provide the kind of service that guarantees customer loyalty, companies need to better coordinate their partners and vendors. The best approach involves considering partners and vendors to be part of the company's extended enterprise, which enables the company to seamlessly share customer service issues with everyone who comes in contact with the customer. Also, the sharing of customer information beyond company boundaries is a key trend as companies increasingly depend on third parties for support.

Companies must take a close look at their customer service processes. Are they easy to use? Too often, "disconnect" occurs as a consequence of the way business processes have been built over the last few decades. Customers today need to be able to call in or log into any area of a company, immediately be recognized, and have their requests or purchases processed smoothly. If not, customers are left with an uneasy sense of company apathy and will probably think twice before calling again.

What is the impact of this trend on e-business? To achieve business objectives, companies need to adopt integrated applications that address the entire customer relationship, rather than focusing on departmental solutions that address only one part of the customer account relationship. These integrated applications will be critical not only within a company, but also with their partners. As a result, organizations should develop customer relationship solutions that go beyond the boundaries of the company to encompass the entire extended enterprise.

Provide Flexible Fulfillment and Convenient Service Delivery

The hectic schedules and multiple responsibilities of today's consumers are forcing retailers to produce innovative products and services. Home delivery and other unique fulfillment services will continue to gain importance as consumer-direct sales explode.

Today, companies bring service to the customer, rather than waiting for the customer to come to them. Consider Gevalia Kaffe, a White Plains, New York, importer that maintains the largest share in the home-delivery coffee market. Gevalia's goal is to provide its customers with reliable service and quick delivery at unbeatable prices. The company processes some 200,000 transactions a week in its customer-direct niche. But to stay ahead of the competition, the company has had to increase its sales volume and service, while at the same time lowering its shipping costs.

To lower costs while simultaneously eliminating large lead times and data rekeying errors, Gevalia developed an e-business infrastructure. In the past, receiving, sorting, and shipping orders to customers were tasks performed without automated procedures. The process involved a paper trail of communications between distant offices and the headquarters in New York, the customer service center in Des Moines, and the fulfillment and shipping complex in Phoenix. It was not only time-consuming, but also laden with inefficiencies and opportunities for errors.

Today, after the Gevalia customer makes a purchase, the network takes over tasks that were previously done manually. First, it looks for the least-cost routing, determining where the customer is in proximity to the warehouse. Second, it determines if the product is available at that location. If not, it then goes to where the inventory is available. Finally, the system automatically splits the order for the shippers. By streamlining its distribution system and improving communications with its outsourcing partners, Gevalia improved access to data and enabled flexible reporting.

Technology has enabled the coffee importer to focus on marketing to the consumer. Even during peak and promotional seasons, Gevalia can handle the demand efficiently and cost-effectively. According to one operations executive, the company has cut outbound shipping costs to consumers by about 20 percent through enabling practices at the distribution center, such as pick and pack. Also, much of the lead time has been reduced and errors eliminated, even though one outsourcing agent handles customer service while another physically fills orders.

To deliver the right product to the customer, companies must streamline their supply chain as Gevalia has. The simple view of the integrated supply chain is as follows: Take an order, give an accurate promise date, manufacture the right goods, allocate properly, ship efficiently, and do all of this in a cost-efficient manner while maintaining a minimal finished goods inventory. Whatever bells and whistles you add to the basic foundation are wonderful, but if you can't do the simple stuff, there's no way you can support the newer applications or leading-edge technology.

e-Commerce-enabled supply chain management has been growing in popularity for the past couple of years. All the software companies are gearing up to support it, the consulting firms are preaching it, and the trade press is eating it up.

So what is it? And does it affect you? Yes, it does. Supply chain management is really a combination of inevitable and constant trends in manufacturing and distribution: moving closer to the consumer; reducing waste (time, inventory, etc.) in the supply chain; ensuring technology-enabled, real-time information access between customers and suppliers; and building closer partnerships with virtual coordination. The development of integrated supply chains is by far one of the most important business trends.

Contract Manufacturing: Become Brand Intensive, Not Capital Intensive

Are you an asset-intensive company? If the answer is yes, it's likely that you are heading toward using e-commerce to become a virtual manufacturer. Many old-line manufacturers are attempting to copy the success of companies in the computer industry and others that contract out much of their manufacturing.

Contract manufacturing has its roots in the high-tech industry. Take Sun Microsystems, for example. The company's founders decided to focus on designing hardware and software and subcontracting or purchasing virtually all the workstations' components. Its own manufacturing efforts are limited to prototypes, final assembly, and testing. By relying on outside suppliers, Sun was able to introduce four major new product generations in its first five years of operation, doubling the price-performance ratio with each successive year.[5] The objective: Achieve better quality, dependability, speed, flexibility, and cost advantage.

The trend toward contract manufacturing is spreading beyond the high-tech industry. Take, for instance, Sara Lee, the Chicago-based consumer goods company. Sara Lee disclosed "a fundamental reshaping" of the company that would move it away from manufacturing the brand-name goods it sells. Sara Lee is selling factories in order to concentrate on managing its stable of famous brand names: L'eggs hosiery, frozen desserts, Wonderbras, Coach briefcases, and Kiwi shoe polish, to name a few.

The trend toward specialization (marketing versus manufacturing) means that companies have to focus on what they do best. The goal: Move from a capital/asset (or manufacturing) intensive company to a knowledge (and marketing) intensive firm. John Bryan, Sara Lee's CEO, said, "It's imperative for companies to focus on new products, managing brands and building market share."[6] Sara Lee aims to outsource its manufacturing, much like Nike did in the shoe industry.

In a relentless drive to obtain more profits from fewer assets, companies are using contract manufacturing more and more. This trend is largely due to pressure from Wall Street, where investors constantly demand higher returns. To achieve better asset utilization, technology is being used to enable organizations to segregate marketing from manufacturing by quickly developing contract partnerships and distributing manufacturing globally. The new trend is to be innovative through technology, change product offerings constantly, and keep overhead as low as possible.

Learn to Outsource: You Cannot Be Good at Everything

As the going gets rougher, the business climate demands that companies live and breathe cost reduction. To survive, firms are turning toward business process outsourcing (BPO), which is defined as the delegation of one or more business processes to an external provider to improve overall business performance in a particular area. For example, gas and electric companies are outsourcing their cost centers—human resources and purchasing functions—so they can concentrate on their core competence, making and selling energy.

BPO offers businesses innovative ways to save money and enter or create new markets rapidly, without a significant up-front investment. It provides a modular environment in which it is possible to scale up and ramp down depending on seasonal forces and production needs. The market trends that are driving the adoption of BPO include pressure to increase earnings and reduce costs, and an increased need to create and maintain a competitive edge. Processes that are not core competencies are increasingly being outsourced. This flattening of organizations is parsing operations from vertical strategic business units into horizontal business processes. Process owners are outsourcing entire processes for business performance rather than IT efficiency.

Traditionally, outsourcing has been used as a cost-control technique to move cost centers such as data processing, payroll processing, and systems development to outside specialists. However, as globalization spreads and networking technology becomes more widespread, companies are realizing that outsourcing is really a way to create a true virtual enterprise. It is a way to change corporate culture, gain access to premium thinkers, and implement world-class capabilities and technologies.

What does outsourcing mean for e-business? Outsourcing lays the foundation for creating the virtual enterprise, the core of the e-business concept. It's clear that a single organization working alone is no longer a justifiable business model. The complexity of operations, the regulation and deregulation of markets, the steady, rapid advance of technology, and the need for constant growth are conditions that require core competency in too many functional areas. Outsourcing strategies herald the beginning of a new era.

Increase Process Visibility: Destroy the Black Box

Process visibility implies that business customers need to have access to order status, product information, pricing, and availability. Providing visibility to products and services helps create additional demand. A great example of process visibility is the United Parcel Service (UPS) tracking system. Customers can use the Internet to track air and ground parcels anytime, anywhere, anyplace. UPS and FedEx have changed customers' expectations so that flawless delivery is now considered the norm, not the exception. Part of the change in attitude comes from the view that customers now have into the overnight package delivery business. Sophisticated information systems allow shippers to call any time of the day or night and find out exactly where their packages are. Within minutes of delivery, couriers can tell customers not only when packages were delivered, but also to whom they were delivered.

Process visibility is an essential business feature as package delivery companies compete with one another. What began with a promise to deliver "absolutely, positively overnight" escalated to promises of delivery the next morning, then before the morning coffee, and now "same day, next city." Customers now expect deliveries between specific hours, not just on certain days. Clearly, changes in business operations based on accurate delivery times serve to increase delivery expectations and simultaneously increase the consequences of service failures.

Process visibility is especially important in business-to-business commerce. Consider Solectron Corporation. With 7,000 employees worldwide, Solectron is a major supplier of circuit boards and electronic assemblies for companies such as IBM, Hewlett-Packard, and Intel Corporation. It has manufacturing facilities in California, Washington, Malaysia, France, and Scotland, and it has an office in Japan. Initially, each facility acted independently in automation projects because it was so hard to provide data access to them all. There was no way to pull results into a common database or to track circuit board assemblies across divisions. As a result, managers weren't getting the high level of information needed to monitor the shop floor, and customers weren't getting the information they needed in a timely manner.

To provide more insight into the manufacturing process for their business customers, Solectron developed a Shop-Floor Tracking and Recording System (STARS), which enables workers to record the movement of circuit boards through the assembly and testing processes. Bar code readers capture and enter subassembly information, test results, quality information, and a variety of other data directly into the STARS application. Customers can access information remotely to learn the status of their jobs. The ability to publish real-time information and interact with the system gives users, especially in the critical, event-oriented world of process control, new methods for monitoring, controlling, and regulating manufacturing processes.

What does process visibility mean for e-business? Companies must strive to build internal applications and processes that open the black box and make internal operations more transparent. For instance, why can't customers know exactly what is happening with the mortgage or car loan applications they filed with the bank? It would let them know exactly what's going on and enable them to plan their lives accordingly. It also allows for more accountability. Increasing visibility can have a significant impact on creating demand, as well as on retaining customers. Through close customer contact and high-quality service, a company's competitive edge and long-term relationships with its customers are maintained and strengthened.

Learn the Trends in Employee Retention

To continually grow, deliver better service, or reduce prices, an enterprise must become a learning organization that can prosper in a fast-paced, demanding business environment. Meeting these demands requires answering this question: *How does management develop an organization that is capable of innovating constantly and learning continuously?* The upscale retailer Nordstrom is an excellent example. Long considered to set the standards in retail service, Nordstrom has a legendary policy of bending over backward to please the customer. Nordstrom's gold-plated service and no-questions-asked return policy make for strong repeat business. In fact, the company figures about 90 percent of its sales come from 10 percent of its loyal shoppers.

A key element of Nordstrom's success is its employees. Nordstrom uses exceptional incentives to motivate employees, including paying very high commissions and using undercover shoppers to evaluate service, with cash rewards given to employees who score a perfect 100. They also give workers a great deal of autonomy in decision making, telling them to use their best judgment. This practice gives an entrepreneurial zeal to the store's service.

The Nordstrom example illustrates that sustainable innovation depends on employees. The lesson to be learned is that, with changing technology and business trends, management needs to worry about employee retention, because it's critical to long-term success. The trends in employee retention are:

- **Better incentives and compensation.** Pay and bonuses should be tied into continuous improvement, both for individuals and the organization.

- **Earned advancement.** Promotions must be based on the proven ability to lead and manage a strong group of people. If employees are given the hope that they can move up in the company, they will stay longer and work harder.

- **Better motivation.** A real commitment must be made to employees. If people believe they're working so that senior management can get a bigger bonus, change will not happen. The workforce has to be self-motivated to continuously improve processes and themselves.

What does all this mean for e-business? Supporting and sustaining a culture that can succeed and innovate is not only a requirement, but also a prerequisite for doing e-business. The old ways of command and control over knowledge workers will not work well in the future. Technology is a key weapon in employee motivation. New opportunities await companies that can become employee-friendly.

Integrated Enterprise Applications: Connect the Corporation

Integration of the enterprise has emerged as a critical issue for organizations in all business sectors striving to maintain competitive advantage. Integration is the key to success. It is the key to unlocking information and making it available to any user, anywhere, anytime.

Why is integration hard? Most companies separate their business applications, creating functional specialists: accounting, finance, manufacturing, and customer service. This is the concept of divide and conquer: If the job could be defined specifically enough, a specialized application could optimize functions in a particular area. The assumption was that if all functional links in a company were optimized, the company itself would function at an optimal level. In recent years, business theorists have challenged that view, recognizing that if a chain of processes is to run at a high-performance level, the individual functional applications must be tightly linked with other processes around them.

This thinking gives birth to the notion of a connected corporation built on a foundation of well-integrated enterprise application software. Enterprise applications help companies connect disparate systems, provide greater access to information, and more closely link employees, partners, and customers. There is little doubt that the future techno-enterprise will be built on a well-integrated set of enterprise software applications. These enterprise applications, offered by packaged-software vendors such as SAP, PeopleSoft, and Baan, represent the backbone of the modern corporation.

There is growing debate within organizations about build versus buy. Why buy some outside vendor's packaged software rather than build it internally? The combination of more data, users, systems, and applications, compounded by a lack of time and resources, has contributed to a crisis of complexity for IT organizations. These organizations are under increasing pressure to quickly deliver bottom-line benefits to their customers. And building complex applications under severe time-to-market pressure is not easy to do. If you fail, you risk alienating customers, as well as losing money and your competitive advantage. Buying packaged software helps IT organizations relieve some of the time-to-market pressure. There is no black-and-white answer to the question of build vs. buy, only shades of gray that make the decision complicated.

One thing companies must be watchful of if they buy packaged software is the failure to differentiate between packaged application support and takeover. In Stanley Kubrick's 1968 film *2001: A Space Odyssey,* the spaceship computer, HAL, takes over the ship, killing several crewmembers in the process. HAL's original role was to support the ship, not control it. In the same vein, an enterprise application must support company operations, not completely take over.

If managers let enterprise applications run the company rather than support the creation and delivery of value to the customer, jobs can be lost. This happened to FoxMeyer Drugs, a very large distributor. FoxMeyer miscalculated the difficulty in implementing an enterprise resource planning (ERP) solution. They also did not understand the consequences of what they were doing. This resulted in the company filing for bankruptcy—sobering food for thought about the perils of poorly implemented technology.

Meld Voice, Data, and Video

A major trend in the infrastructure for e-business is the convergence of various data and voice transport networks. Throughout the world, telephone networks, cable TV networks, wireless networks, and computer data networks are ceasing to be separate, isolated systems. Instead, they're converging into a powerful, unified network based on the Internet Protocol (IP), the packet-switching network layer that has proven to be a versatile workhorse that can transmit any kind of information quickly and cheaply.

Infrastructure convergence encompasses many mini trends happening simultaneously:

- **The race to improve last-mile bandwidth.** Increasing the amount of bandwidth in the "last mile," that is, from the telephone switching office to the home, is by far one of the biggest barriers to Internet usage. The resulting trend: Faster connections are becoming available through innovations in optical technology.

- **The race to provide quality of service.** Dependability and predictability of service in the network are increasing. Imagine trying to talk to someone when all you can hear is static, a few words, and more static. Chances are you will be very frustrated. The resulting trend: Companies are competing to provide solutions that provide a guaranteed quality of service.

- **The race to provide integrated services.** Major long-distance carriers such as AT&T, Sprint, and MCI/WorldCom have announced plans to set up unified networks that will carry voice and data over the same line, thus saving the huge expense of maintaining separate networks. These companies join newer service providers such as Qwest Communications and Level 3, which were both founded on the premise of providing integrated voice and data services. The resulting trend: The dial tone of today is evolving into the Web tone of tomorrow.

- **The race to dominate the customer home contact point.** Currently, the customer contact point is the browser and modem. As technology improves, the consumer is beginning to use the cable set-top box (e.g., WebTV) to access content and services. The resulting trend: There will be multiple customer contact points at home, resulting in the proliferation of network appliances.

The business driver behind infrastructure convergence is service convenience. For example, the recent formation of EnergyOne, a venture that jointly markets phone, security, gas, and electric services to homeowners, highlights this growing market for convenience and one-stop shopping. Telecommunications companies want to offer customers a bundled package of services that includes local and long-distance phone service, online services, high-speed Internet connections, wireless phone, paging, pay TV, and tailored billing.

Another business driver behind infrastructure convergence is user convenience. An example of user convenience can be found in the ability to have telephone conversations over the Internet. New systems are allowing data networks to handle voice calls as well, by translating the analog sound into digital data. Venture capitalists, phone, cable, and Internet service provider companies are spending billions of dollars to realize infrastructure convergence. Beneath the hype lies a very real long-term trend.

What is the impact of this trend on corporations? Like railroads in the 1830s, electricity in the 1870s, and the interstate road system in the 1950s, the infrastructure for e-commerce is in its infancy and evolving quite rapidly. Understanding how infrastructure convergence is playing out is quite important for managers whose responsibility it is to make long-term strategic plans. If you base investments on outdated telecommunications and networking technology, you can have a serious negative impact on the competitiveness of your company.

Multichannel Integration: Look at the Big Picture

The brick-and-mortar office was for a long time the only service channel available to customers for conducting business. Then came the telephone. Today, there's an explosion of access alternatives and capabilities—the Web, direct dial-up, interactive voice response (IVR), and kiosks. With all these service channels proliferating, customers are demanding multichannel service integration.

Multichannel integration is critical because customers expect consistent service—no matter which channel they use—when they interact with a company. For instance, suppose Judy walks into a bank branch and deposits $50,000 into her account. She goes home and logs onto the Internet branch of the same bank to pay her utility bills. Unless she is overdrawn, she should not get a message that her account has insufficient funds. If she gets this message in error, it's because the channels (the physical branch and the Internet site) are not integrated. This is not acceptable.

Multichannel service integration is not a technical issue; It's a management issue. You have to get managers to look at the whole picture. The success of the individual parts must be defined in sync with the overall system. Otherwise, each delivery channel may be considered a success, but the delivery system as a whole is not. There are all kinds of managers scrutinizing each channel, but few look at the overall picture.

The level of technical investment needed to create integrated services is huge. There are a lot of emerging technologies, such as middleware, that could make it less expensive, but many of them are untested and not ready for 24×7 mission-critical applications. Thus, multichannel integration is a long-term trend that is going to take more work than most people realize.

Wireless Applications Enter the Mainstream

With the widespread rollout of a wireless infrastructure, a new wave of both consumer and business applications will begin using airwaves for much more than phone calls. The power and convenience of these wireless applications, when combined with the decreasing cost of wireless usage, will increase the efficiency with which consumers perform everyday tasks like making phone calls, organizing business and personal affairs, sending e-mail—even finding the best restaurant within walking distance.

The first-generation devices that deliver these services will vary from cell phones to handheld devices like 3Com's PalmPilot and the Nokia 9000 Communicator, which consists of a phone, a Web browser, and a personal-messaging and data-organizing system bundled into a single (though rather cumbersome) unit. New consumer applications will help these devices gain market share, unshackling technology users from their desktops in the process. Take, for instance, 3Com's PalmPilot, which provides instant two-way personal communication in a text format and offers flight schedules, news headlines, and online transactions such as movie ticket purchases or stock trades.

However, the true potential of wireless applications lies in the enterprise applications marketplace. As data proliferates throughout corporations, managers are under increasing pressure to make analytical decisions. This means pushing data outward to managers via the wireless network. We are on the cusp of a new generation of decision support applications that are coupled with the wireless infrastructure.

The demand for being mobile and yet productive, combined with the build-out of the wireless infrastructure as an alternative to wire-line technologies for basic telephone service, will create tremendous demand for e-commerce applications.

Middleware: Supporting the Integration Mandate

There is a buzz in boardrooms and at company water coolers around the world: *"We have to become more customer-centric."* Customer information must be available across the board, spanning several departmental domains and stovepipe legacy applications. This is easier said than done. Departmental isolation, no matter how efficient in its own microcosm, no longer provides the speed that companies need for staying competitive. To become truly customer-centric, firms must integrate legacy applications developed in the 1970s with more modern applications, thereby providing seamless business process integration.

Compelling business reasons to endure the cost, complexity, and risk of integrating stovepipe applications have been missing until recently. The heat of competition is forcing organizations to rethink and broaden their views on application integration, just as many *customer-care* initiatives are forcing companies to present a single view of the customer relationship. In addition to business trends such as globalization, several technology mini trends—Internet/intranet architectures, quick and inexpensive data access, multimedia capabilities, open standards, and the increasing demand for distributed applications—are driving the need for robust, distributed applications that are scalable and reliable enough to run mission-critical business applications.

To meet business and technology integration needs, a new class of technology, called *middleware,* is emerging. Integration based on middleware makes financial sense. Customers are reluctant to throw away their existing legacy investments. The old systems cannot be replaced easily and are not going away. Most major mission-critical operations still run on mainframe-based systems due to concerns about security, reliability, and speed. For this reason, companies are looking for robust connectivity and seamless interoperability between their mainframe and Internet applications. As corporations and vendors respond to these demands, they are discovering that middleware provides the essential glue that enables large, complex business software (like electronic commerce, decision support, and database applications) to run effectively and reliably. However, this is difficult to do, since the available technology is not yet mature.

The middleware problem is bound to get more management attention as spending on technology spirals out of control. According to *InformationWeek,* the 500 largest corporate users of IT in the United States will spend a total of nearly $97 billion worldwide on IT products and services this year. The nine top spenders account for nearly $18 billion, or one-fifth of that total.[7] To combat chaos resulting from a hodgepodge of unrelated systems, middleware products provide the essential plumbing that enables the linking (interoperability) of mainframe, client/server, and Internet environments. By leveraging existing legacy systems and skills within organizations, middleware prolongs their useful life, which in turn generates potential cost savings. The middleware trend is significant and must be watched carefully, because it plays an integral role in creating customer-centric, distributed, and virtual organizations.

What Is Common to All These Trends?

In the e-business world, innovation is derived from spotting the trend before anyone else and from the sophisticated exploitation of information and technologies to create value. It is the senior managers in particular who will be called on to lead the innovation charge. Today, every manager is wondering how the Internet can remake his or her business. In a concerted search for growth, corporations are intent on mastering the art of trend spotting in order to discover new products and services, design new business processes and structures—even to create completely new businesses.

The 15 trends that we have illustrated contain three common threads—*effectiveness, efficiency,* and *integration.* Effectiveness trends are those that directly affect the relationship between the enterprise's customers and its environment. Efficiency trends, on the other hand, affect the internal structure and operating activities of the enterprise. Integration trends are those that push for one-stop-shopping consolidation.

Most of these trends will ultimately result in the formation of many new companies. *Why?* The answer is quite simple. The long-term goal of any business is to be more effective in meeting the needs of customers. Unfortunately, most of management's time and attention is spent on internal efforts designed to make day-to-day operations as efficient as possible. Therein lies the paradox. The companies best qualified in terms of resources to take advantage of new trends are often the least structurally capable of taking advantage of them. That situation often leaves the door open for new startups to come in and fill the void.

Memo to the CEO

In the good old days, there was time to notice fads and watch them unfold into trends, which then became full-blown requirements. Today, through the continuous march of technology, we speak in terms of nanoseconds and talk of instant industries. How many people knew much about the Internet a few years ago, much less that it was going to change business?

What are these new, blisteringly fast-paced trends? Technological innovation, new product introductions, changes in customer requirements, declining prices, and evolving industry standards, among others. New products and new technology often render existing services or value propositions obsolete, excessively costly, or otherwise unprofitable. As a result, success depends on the ability to innovate and integrate new technologies into service offerings. In order to know what is on the horizon, executives must become proficient in trend spotting.

New trends will cause many existing companies to fail. Today's businesses have spent the past decade scaling the change mountain, which was created by the collision of technology, consumer, and quality trends. But despite how high each company manages to climb on the change mountain, they all reach the same chasm: the digital revolution, which affects them equally, regardless of industry, size, or business principles. The big question is whether they have the energy to ascend the peak before a young, energetic upstart overtakes them and reaches the summit first.

The new generation of leaders in e-business will have to be imaginative to radically change the value proposition within and across industries. Freud once wrote, "What a distressing contrast there is between the radiant curiosity of the child and the feeble mentality of the average adult." Perhaps the critical management issue today is unleashing the imagination, which will be vitally important for the transformation of large industrial-age companies into nimble digital enterprises.

Deregulation, the ubiquity of information, and new customer demands provide additional opportunities to transcend industry's current boundaries. Industry's bounds are meaningless as customers increasingly look for end-to-end process integration. As customers self-serve and input orders digitally, their service expectations are bound to increase. To meet these expectations, firms must invent new processes that help compress the order-to-delivery service time.

As customer demand patterns change, be prepared for consolidation to accelerate at a fearsome pace in order to exploit new national and global economies of scale. For instance, with e-commerce technology, any industry that was local, such as retail banking, becomes national. Any industry that was national, such as the book retail business, becomes international. Of course, an industry can be scaled down as well as up. In the face of such unprecedented chaos, firms need agility in three dimensions: business models and strategy, product mix and customer experience, and easy-to-use business processes. In the past, firms dealt with these three dimensions of agility differently. All this has changed with the advent of e-commerce. e-Commerce forces firms to think about agility in a holistic way.

In summary, successful companies understand that pleasing new customers means capitalizing on new trends. They understand that customer and technol-

ogy trends have a natural tendency to evolve unpredictably, often creating opportunities as established firms are caught off guard. In the face of innovation, established firms behave like ostriches, hiding their heads in the sand. They resist
change because they have reached their zone of comfort, and therefore, their operating models tend to be fairly rigid. This creates a tension and opens the door
for innovative upstarts who can satisfy customers' most important priorities.
Thus begins a new era.

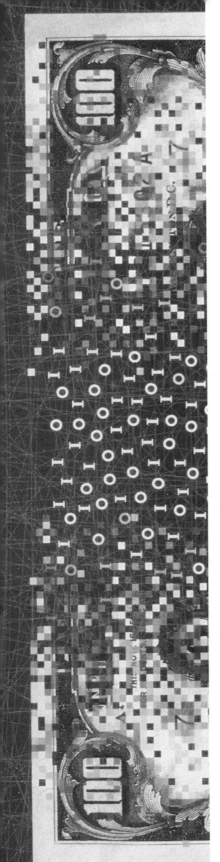

CHAPTER THREE

Think e-Business Design, Not Just Technology

What to Expect

It is becoming crystal clear that with e-commerce, we have entered a new phase: the age of e-business design. Competition is not so much product versus product, but traditional business design versus e-business design. The challenge confronting managers is in the creation and execution of the e-business design. How do you construct an e-business design? How do you transform a traditional business design to an e-business design? In this chapter, you'll learn e-business design secrets from three superstar market leaders. You'll learn what questions to ask and what the answers should be.

Demands on managers in charge of strategy have never been greater. CEOs are asking them to come up with the next generation of breakthrough products, innovative ways to cut costs, new ways of managing channels, a strategy to get products to market faster, and ways to achieve quality. More than ever before, strategists need to get it right the first time in cost, time to market, and quality. Aside from the obvious competitive pressures, there are huge dollar amounts at stake. Choosing the right strategy accelerates market penetration and minimizes cost, whereas choosing the wrong strategy causes years of repercussions in cost, quality, customer satisfaction, and supply chain issues—serious problems that no amount of tinkering will fix.

Why is it that some companies always seem to be in the right place at the right time with the right strategy? How does American Express constantly improve service in the competitive charge card and business travel markets? How was Dell Computer able to operationally outmaneuver Compaq, IBM, Hewlett-Packard, and others in the cutthroat computer industry? Why are Cisco Systems' competitors losing market share to this innovative supplier of networking products?

What sets truly great organizations apart is their ability to use state-of-the-art technology to transform themselves. They do three things well:

1. Redefine value for their customers.

2. Build powerful e-business designs that outperform the competition.

3. Understand customer priorities and consistently raise customer expectations to new heights.

Companies that succeed in doing these three things are practicing technology management in its highest form: creating new e-business designs. In other words, they are using business designs that leverage emerging trends before the rest of the world catches on. Take for instance, the burgeoning car warehouses CarMax and AutoNation. These firms recognized that customers are looking for a more friendly experience in buying a car: no-hassle treatment, low prices, and a wide selection of new and used vehicles. By understanding that they are selling experience as much as product, these firms have reshaped the car dealer network.

The focus is no longer limited to process design; it's shifted to business design. Innovation in business design is gathering momentum with e-commerce. Consider the case of retail drug stores. Retailers CVS, Walgreen, and Rite Aid are suddenly facing competition from Internet startups such as Drugstore.com and Soma.com which sell over-the-counter medicines, medical supplies, and prescription drugs (an $87.8 billion market).[1] The race to become the Amazon.com of health care is on. Established companies are responding by revamping their business models. Now, members of Merck-Medco Managed Care, which handles prescriptions for more than 51 million consumers, can refill their orders electronically. Walgreen customers can also order refills on the Web, and Rite Aid not only offers online refills, but also uses the Web to remind its customers when their prescriptions are due to be refilled. The repertoire of innovators knows no bounds. Nothing is sacred anymore. No company is untouchable. No longer do huge corporations have sole access to the capital markets. Today, it's possible for relatively unknown but talented people to raise huge sums of money.

Success depends on how quickly companies can formulate novel business designs and adapt them to their markets. Incremental improvements won't work. If you're pressed for time, would you take a horse-drawn carriage if you had the option of taking a car or, better still, an airplane? Today's business environment is driving the switch to e-business design.

In many ways, the pressure to rethink business is similar to what happened in the 1980s, when many American industries were threatened by competition from Japan and other Pacific Rim countries. The auto, steel, and textile industries lost gobs of market share to a wave of imports, while American TV, camera, and consumer electronic companies were all but wiped out. American companies had grown fat and slow, leaving themselves vulnerable to nimble competition from abroad. To survive, many corporations went through a painful period of restructuring, reorganizing, and reengineering. Old-line companies were ill suited to compete with companies flashing better technology. However, out of the upheaval emerged leaner, more nimble, and more competitive companies. Sound familiar? This is what's going on today with e-commerce.

Business designs are strategic weapons in the digital economy. In an environment in which multiple variables—technology, customer requirements, supply chains—are changing simultaneously, the old weapons of differentiation—low cost, quality, and incremental process improvement—are of little hope for sustaining growth. **The business design dimension is no longer an optional part of corporate strategy; rather, it's the very core.**

Constructing an e-Business Design

The idea that companies succeed by creating value is not novel. What is new, however, is how innovative business designs are delivering value. To create innovative e-business designs, you must first answer some questions. *What business design do you need to make your customers' experiences unique and memorable?* Although it's not easy, a good way to outdo competition is to render it passé by pleasing customers in new ways. Essentially, that's what e-business is all about. e-Business uses technology and e-commerce processes to build better customer relationships and create new value propositions. Over and over we see examples of e-business innovators leapfrogging over competition by delivering end-to-end service. Such service delivery is important because it's what a customer experiences and, moreover, truly cherishes. *When assessing a business design's value, ask yourself if it meets customers' priorities, not only today, but tomorrow as well.*

Next, define capabilities needed to match customers' most important priorities. *What capabilities and competencies do you need to create rich experiences?* These decisions determine what the customer sees when interacting with an e-business design. For instance, value according to Dell Computer translates into convenience of purchasing a high-quality product at a low cost. Making the purchase process convenient has resulted in an explosive growth of Web-based sales for Dell. The company says it's generating sales of more than $10 million per day using a Web-based direct-sales model, and that Internet-based sales could soon account for 50 percent of its business. Dell was not only innovative in how it sells, but also in how customers purchase computers. The company uses a build-to-order (BTO) business model. Dell won't start building a machine until an order is received. This perhaps helps hold down inventories of components and finished computers, which in turn controls costs. Competitors Compaq and IBM are working overtime to replicate Dell's BTO e-business design.

Now, answer these questions: *How much does your company manufacture internally and how much does it outsource? How do you structure your organization for efficiency? Are you function or process oriented? How do you sell to the customer—through a sales force, reseller channels, or a call center (direct)? How do you distribute your product?* These elements must align in order for your company to excel at providing exactly what customers wish to experience in doing business with you.

Once you make the tough decisions required to coordinate these processes, you must then figure out how to change your company. *How can you move from where you are today to where you want to go? How do you integrate and tailor legacy infrastructure to meet new requirements?* Like a battlefield surgeon, who assumes great loss in order to ensure future success, executives must cut their losses and abandon important projects in order to reallocate resources vital to the survival of the company. Although it's risky, time to formulate plans is running out. To preserve the entire business, executives must be vigilant and learn to prioritize in a constantly changing environment. *Are you ready?*

The First Step of e-Business Design: Self-Diagnosis

Before embarking on your journey to create an e-business design, you must first diagnose your company. Ask yourself these questions about the impact of customer, business, and technology trends on your company:

- Has the recent wave of technology innovation created new ways of doing business and reorganizing priorities?

- Is your company responding to changing customer expectations? Is it aware of the dimensions of value that your customers care about?

- Is your company willing to question and change countless industry assumptions to take advantage of new opportunities, while preserving existing investments in people, applications, and data?

- Is your company successful at lowering operating costs while making complex business applications adaptive and flexible to change under the relentless pressure of time to market?

If all your answers are yes, then you are in the *innovator* or *market leader* category. You are lucky and rare. Savor the moment.

If most of your answers are yes, then you are in the *early adopter* or *visionary* category. You too are rare. You are among the first to exploit new technological innovations to achieve a competitive advantage over your rivals. Let's take a look at an example of an early adopter, Charles Schwab. In an industry in which the pace of innovation is not for the faint of heart, Schwab has built a discount brokerage colossus of more than 4 million customers placing more than $253 billion worth of total assets into Schwab accounts. Schwab is building its entire business model around an e-business infrastructure. This includes eSchwab, the largest online brokerage service, with more than 1.5 million customers. In 1998, eSchwab customers moved more than $100 billion worth of assets through online connections. What can we learn from Charles Schwab? *Even large, established firms can be early adopters and compete successfully with small, fast-moving innovators.*

If most of your answers to the questions are no, then your firm belongs in the *silent majority* category. Interestingly, as Geoffery Moore points out in *Crossing the Chasm,* the silent majority is often made up of three types: pragmatists, old-guard conservatives, and die-hard skeptics. These three types vary in the degree of risk they are willing to take. The management of these three types chooses to believe that e-commerce is a fad and will never become a key facet of mainstream business. In the process, they are missing one of the biggest stories in modern times: the transformation of society. As we dissect each one of these types, no doubt you'll recognize them.

Management of pragmatic firms sees the world changing around them, but they want proof that the changes are long-term before they commit to action. Pragmatists often stay very close to their current customer base in order to keep focused on delivering superior customer value. Pragmatists, who often find it hard to be creative in the day-to-day grind of business, should read the opening lines of A. A. Milne's classic, *Winnie-the-Pooh:* "Here is Edward Bear, coming downstairs now, bump, bump, bump, on the back of his head, behind Christopher Robin. It is, as far as he knows, the only way of coming downstairs, but sometimes he feels that there really is another way, if only he could stop bumping for a moment and think of it." Too many demands keep managers bumping along, unable to concentrate on changing business designs.

Old-guard conservative companies are in a state of denial. Conservatives avoid growth prospects that do not align with their distinctive core competencies. Management remains pessimistic about the ability to gain any value from technology investments and undertakes them only under duress. Only the threat of impending bankruptcy can convince this type that their business model is changing despite them.

Robert Galvin of Motorola is reported to have said that in the 1940s his father viewed 14 firms as key competitors, but today most of them don't exist.[2] Why? Each stuck to its knitting too long. Since the 1920s, Motorola has routinely abandoned markets, even though it meant relinquishing considerable equity. The company jumped from car radios to two-way radios, to televisions, to microprocessors, to cellular pagers and wireless systems. Each transition was full of risk, but had Motorola not taken those risks, it wouldn't be here today. What can we learn from Motorola? In the face of continuous product innovation wrought by technological changes, sticking to your knitting leads to business failure.

Die-hard skeptic companies are destined to fade away. These companies are like Luddites, the nineteenth-century British reactionaries who feared competition from machinery. They smashed machines with sledgehammers in a futile attempt to arrest the march of progress fueled by science and technology. Die-hard skeptics' stubbornly obsolescent management is convinced that technological change will never affect them. They see almost everything as media hype. One example of shortsighted skepticism is the railroad industry, which in its heyday refused to believe that consumers would prefer air transportation to railcars. Another more up-to-date example is the mainframe computer industry, which refused to believe that personal computers would ever amount to much. What can we learn from the railroad and mainframe industries? Not taking technological change seriously can lead to failure, or worse, extinction.

These three categories of companies—market leaders, early adopters/visionaries, and the silent majority (pragmatists, old-guard conservatives, and die-hard skeptics)—comprise the current business landscape. If you see where you are in the picture and don't like it, then you must make a path to get to where you'd rather be. This requires understanding how customer needs are changing, making customer priorities your priorities, and adopting an e-business design. You'll find this is a complete reversal of the value-chain strategy model taught in MBA programs and preached by consultants everywhere! So, where does that leave you? Read on . . .

The Second Step of e-Business Design: Reversing the Value Chain

The greatest challenge in e-business is linking emerging technology to new business designs. If it were just a matter of linking emerging technologies to existing markets or vice versa, the management challenges would be relatively easy. But when both are emerging, it's a delicate process. As technologies emerge, they affect customer needs; customer needs influence business designs. As business designs emerge, they affect processes; processes influence the next generation of technology.

Technology alone cannot make a business design dynamic, but it can make a dynamic design a real dynamo. As new technologies and customer needs emerge, managers find creating new business designs difficult for two reasons. First, most have been trained to concentrate on improving products, increasing market share, and growing revenues. Second, in the e-business world, the distinction between products and services often blurs. Therefore, success depends on creating new "product offerings" in which customers see value.

Successful companies no longer just add value, they invent it. To invent value, managers must reverse the traditional value-chain thinking (inside-out models) by which businesses define themselves in terms of the products they produce (see Figure 3.1). In the traditional model, managers concentrate on being effective and competitive by putting well-understood products on the market. In the new world, however, the business design is outside in.

In an outside-in approach, the strategy revolves around the customer. Why is this crucial? From time to time, conditions suddenly change direction, causing industries to completely rethink the way they do business. Often, a business-

Traditional Business Design

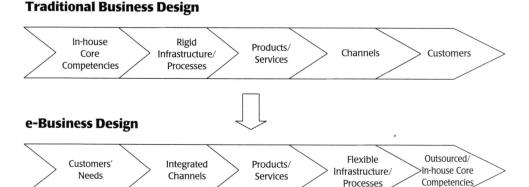

Figure 3.1: The Reversing of the Value Chain

condition change is due to a new entrant that does not play the game by the understood rules. The challenger reconfigures the offering and suddenly starts running away with the business.

Traditional coffee companies such as Folgers and Maxwell House experienced this change firsthand when they failed to see the shifting consumer trend toward gourmet coffee. Starbucks saw it and created a business around the gourmet coffee drinker. If the management at the established coffee companies had stayed focused on changing customer tastes, they would have migrated toward gourmet coffee, changed delivery systems, and restructured prices. In the process, they would have made it much harder for Starbucks and others to break into the market and steal their customers.

The need for an outside-in approach becomes essential in times of great structural transition, when old categories suddenly become obsolete. Businesses must redefine themselves in times of flux, a danger for companies married to a business definition that's fixed to specific products. How do you navigate these dangerous waters? By defining new offerings born of customer needs (see Figure 3.1). Dell, American Express, Charles Schwab, Microsoft, and Wal-Mart are shining examples of firms that seem to understand what the customer wants.

How can one create the most effective experience for one's customers? Business designs are an outcome of the reconfiguration and integration of one's competencies, channels, application infrastructure, and employee talent to answer this question. New companies such as Amazon.com, E*TRADE, and Microsoft Expedia have been quite effective at this reinvention process. How can established companies follow suit?

The creation of an e-business design is inextricably linked to the manage-

ment of change. Change begins in the organizational mind with new ways of thinking that are later translated into and shaped by new ways of behaving. However, change is not an uncontrolled activity. The boundaries of change are set by choosing a narrow focus. In the next section, we describe three types of focus used by companies to narrow their creative thinking.

The Third Step of e-Business: Choosing a Narrow Focus

While technology can be enabling, it can also be disabling if firms don't concentrate. Market leaders use three types of e-business designs to narrow their focus and retain leadership, because they know that few organizations can do many things well. Look at visionary companies. None shine in every dimension of business: cost, quality, price, convenience, and ease of use. Amazon.com, for instance, doesn't ship books any faster or more conveniently than anyone else does. Dell is not the cheapest computer online. Charles Schwab doesn't offer better online trading than their competitors. These companies thrive because they provide intrinsic, narrowly focused value that their customers care about.

In order to narrow their circle of competence, successful firms choose among the following:

- **Service excellence.** Delivering what customers want with hassle-free service and superior value.

- **Operational excellence.** Delivering high-quality products quickly, error free, and for a reasonable price.

- **Continuous innovation excellence.** Delivering products and services that push performance boundaries and delight customers.

The objective is simple: To succeed, focus on one e-business design, then put a lot of resources behind it. The rest of this chapter describes the philosophy and operation of these three e-business designs and provides a detailed case study exemplifying each.

Service Excellence

Imagine you frequently fly between Atlanta and London. Now imagine what your trip might be like if every airline employee with whom you come in contact—at the ticket counter, the gate, as you take your seat—knew you by name and knew all your travel preferences. For example, they would know that you prefer evening flights, an aisle seat, that you're on a low-fat diet, and that you don't watch movies. As a customer, you would feel both important and valued. It would certainly strengthen your bond with that airline. You'd probably tell your friends about it.

Service excellence involves selecting a few high-value customer niches, then making a concerted effort to serve them well. If you're focused on service excellence, your company will be extremely responsive to and in tune with your customers' desires (see Figure 3.2). This strategy requires customer relationship management: anticipating the target customer's needs and frequently sharing information to provide the expediency of self-service, if that's what the customer wishes.

The operating principles of service excellence are as follows:

- **Prepare your company for the unforeseen.** For example, imagine your top competitor just dropped its price by 10 percent. A customer calls your call center to see how you'll respond to the drop in price. Are you prepared to quickly rearrange priorities, people, and processes to head off such threats and take advantage of sudden opportunities?

- **Gather and maintain all the up-to-date, accurate information you need, where you need it, and when you need it.** Your company must be able to blend intelligence and information in order to make wise decisions.

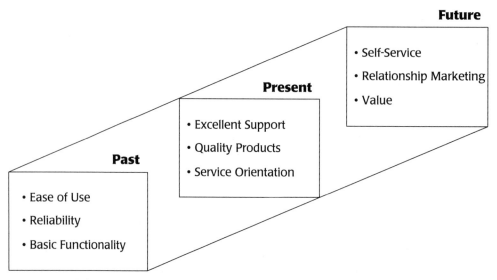

Figure 3.2: Shifting Customer Service Expectations

- **Employ customer contact management.** You must know when a customer's last encounter with your company was, which channel he or she used to contact you, the nature of the encounter, and the outcome. Few companies have this level of sophistication in tracking their key assets, customers.

- **Develop a forward-thinking corporate philosophy about customer service.** Business practices that result from this companywide attitude will encourage insights into customer service and breakthrough thinking about how to improve the customer's value proposition.

Operational Excellence

Imagine if you could break down barriers between organizations so you could work better with your vendors and suppliers. Imagine how much simpler it would be if you could let your vendors access the information they need to service your company. If they could see such things as inventory levels, production plans, and product designs, your suppliers could be much more responsive in meeting your needs. You'd spend a lot less time on the phone or at the fax machine coordinating routine purchasing. Likewise, imagine how much easier life would be if you had access to your vendor's shipping schedules, materials availability, and production plans. You could work together as a single virtual organization rather than as separate entities. Think of the edge that such operational excellence would give you in producing and delivering products.

Operational excellence involves providing the lowest-cost goods and services while simultaneously minimizing problems for the customer. A business with a focus on operational excellence finds that working with customers and partners can be a lot like working with departments within its own company. Knowing customers intimately and working closely with partners gives companies a clear advantage (see Figure 3.3).

The success of operational excellence depends on several key principles:

- **Efficient leveraging of assets.** Resources are allocated in the most efficient manner and at the lowest cost possible.

- **Management of efficient transactions.** For greater efficiency and speed, processes between suppliers and the organization are often integrated.

- **Management of sales intelligence.** Imagine that you're a personal computer manufacturer. You need to know what's selling, where it's selling, and when

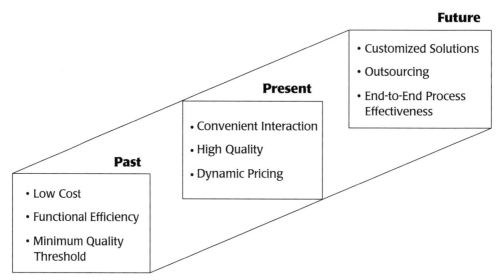

Figure 3.3: Shifting Operational Expectations

it's selling. You need to know what trends are catching on. And you need to convert all these facts, details, and insights into information you can use.

- **Dedication to measurement systems.** Businesses dedicated to operational excellence monitor and measure all processes, continually searching for ways to reduce cost and improve both service and quality.

- **Management of customer expectations.** Under the principle that "variety kills efficiency," operationally excellent companies provide a manageable set of product or service options, and manage customer expectations accordingly.

Continuous Innovation Excellence

Change, change, change—create it or die from it. Continuous innovation demands dedication not only to providing the best possible products, but also to offering the customer more exciting features and benefits than your competitors (see Figure 3.4). Why is continuous innovation critical? The marketplace is a dynamic playground. Clearly, continuous innovation results in product leadership. For instance, Microsoft is expert in continuous innovation in several markets, including operating systems, productivity packages, and online services. SAP excels in the business application market, and Nike eclipses competition in the sports shoe market. Failure to adapt to the speed and turbulence of technological change causes even the best to lose ground. For example, lack of innovation has

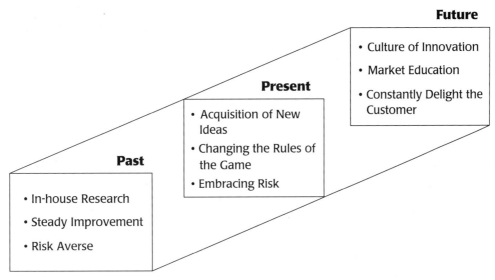

Figure 3.4: Shifting Innovation Expectations

pulled down such mighty giants as AT&T, Eastman Kodak, Sears, and General Motors.

Continuous innovation is based on the following principles:

- **Risk-oriented management style.** Product leadership companies are innovators, and innovation requires recognition that there are risks (as well as rewards) inherent in new ventures.

- **Growth by mergers and acquisitions.** A company's current success and future prospects lie in its acquisition of new products and those who design them.

- **A market-education style.** Recognize that your company must lead the market in educating your customers about how to use and benefit from new products.

- **Encouraging innovation.** If you develop an "experimentation is good" mindset and create compensation systems that reward success, then constant product innovation will be encouraged.

Case Study: Service Excellence at American Express

For a century and a half, American Express (Amex) has been successful by regularly betting the company on innovative new products and services. It began as a cargo agent that forwarded freight on the railroads. While this business was still growing, Amex made a transition to money orders, primarily for the immigrant community. Later, the company branched out into retail travel services, credit cards, and traveler's checks.

In the 1980s, the company expanded into integrated financial services, including banking and financial planning. In essence, the business shifted from money transfer to money storage. Amex bought investment banks and brokerage companies to ensure product diversification, which it hoped would counter the inherent cyclical nature of financial services businesses. However, this strategy backfired and Amex had to shed several noncore businesses in the early 1990s.[3] Why did the diversification strategy fail? Because there was no customer focus. Everything was management by numbers. Since senior management knew little about its diverse businesses, it had no idea what was going on in the divisions, which led to chaos and poor results.

In the 1990s Amex's charismatic CEO, Harvey Golub, transformed the firm from its global financial services one-stop-shopping model to a more narrowly focused service model. This latest transition has resulted in a new e-business design that concentrates on the profitable management of customer relationships.[4]

Amex Business Overview

Amex provides services in travel, financial advisement, and international banking in more than 160 countries. The business is organized around three segments: Travel Related Services, Financial Advisors, and the American Express Bank.

Travel Related Services (TRS) issues the Amex charge card, the Optima card, Traveler's Cheques, and other stored-value products, targeted mostly at the high-end customer. Their strategy: The more customers spend, the more perks they get. Depending on the type of card, Amex encourages members to remain loyal through "membership rewards," benefits such as savings on airline tickets and other purchases. TRS is also the leading provider of travel services to large and small businesses as well. Corporate cards are integrated with business travel services as a means to help businesses manage their travel and entertainment budgets. Services include trip planning, reservations, and ticketing.

Amex Financial Advisors (AEFA) provides financial services and products to both individuals and businesses. Products include financial planning, sales of insurance and annuities, mutual funds, limited partnerships, retail brokerage services, trust services, and tax preparation. Advisors provide financial planning that addresses financial protection, investment, income taxes, retirement, estate planning, and asset allocation for a fee.

Amex Bank is a subsidiary focused on providing financial services for corporations and affluent individuals primarily outside the United States. Commercial banking is provided to corporations with trade finance and risk management services in emerging markets. Wealthy entrepreneurs are targeted by the bank for investment and trust management services.

Amex faces new challenges, as depicted in Figure 3.5. The business environment is changing, and many products are mutating and transforming due to new customer priorities. Also, profits and margins are under pressure. Like all credit card companies, Amex needs to acquire and retain more customers to compensate for shrinking margins. Superior service provides a much-needed competitive edge.

Service Strategy Shall Lead the Way

As Table 3.1 illustrates, Amex's business design is changing from a traditional model to an e-business model based on customer relationship management (CRM). CRM means segmenting customers and tailoring offerings to create value.

The word *value* is mentioned quite frequently in business. Just what is value, anyway? It consists of price, quality, intrinsic product features, brand, service, and a very pleasurable experience. Often it means different things to different people. Many times, service is of utmost importance to customers, in part because prod-

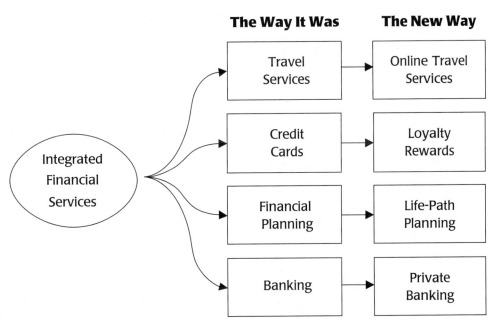

Figure 3.5: The Transformation of American Express

Table 3.1: Business Design Evolution at American Express

	Traditional Amex Business Design	e-Business Design
Key trends	• Product focused	• Customer focused
	• Rigid, functionality-oriented systems	• Flexible, integrated service applications
Key assumptions	• Cost reduction is key to success	• Customer relationship is key to success
	• Task oriented	• Solution oriented

uct quality and pricing in many industries are close to parity. **Put another way, in an era of limited time, customers appear to be more concerned about service, in particular, simplicity, flexibility, and consistency in service.**

Amex understands this and plans to excel at CRM by combining detailed customer knowledge with service flexibility. For instance, Amex's CustomExtras, built on strategic use of technology to cull information from its extensive databases, enables the company to offer custom discounts and deals directly on card members' bills. This gives customers more service without charging extra, a smart way to add value. Amex hopes the program will engender tremendous customer loyalty.

Creating "Customer Relationship Statements" (CRSs), also known as monthly bills, is a technology-intensive task. Convincing people to spend more means hitting the right customers with exactly the right offer at the right time. By extracting spending patterns from the company's mainframe databases, which are jam-packed with customer transactions, the system comes up with a custom set of promotions for each customer. The result is printed right on the cardholder's monthly statement. Thus, customers who frequently purchase jewelry are likely to find an offer for a $100 discount on their next purchase of jewelry at their favorite store. The program is a powerful incentive for customers to use their Amex cards and for merchants to accept them.

The CRS is a great place to entice customers with discounts because bills are required reading, unlike most promotional mail, which goes straight from the mailbox to the trashcan. The message inserted with a bill has close to a 100-percent readership rate and costs zero in extra postage. The goal is to transform the monthly billing statement into a communications channel and a vehicle for delivering added value to customers. Amex intends to encourage merchants to grant discounts displayed on favorite customers' CRSs.

The focus on value has forced Amex to rethink service, such as offering service before a sale to help customers make better choices. To build the base for service excellence, Amex is investing roughly $1 billion annually in the construction of a sophisticated service infrastructure. The scale and scope of service is quite incredible: Amex handles 215 million customer service inquiries a year. Across the financial services industry, these expenditures can provide a means to develop a competitive advantage and also raise competitive barriers to entry.

Lessons for e-Business Design

In financial services, technology is not a luxury, it's absolutely mandatory. The case of Amex illustrates that service excellence is closely tied to technology for brand enhancement. Continuous enrichment of the Amex brand is a critical element of future growth. Amex is currently trying to bring customer targeting capabilities to the Internet. Already card members can check their balances, view their statements, and look up offers from merchants on Amex's Web site. The goal is to integrate all Amex products into a cohesive service framework that further enhances the brand.

Case Study: Operational Excellence at Dell Computer

At age 13, Michael Dell was a successful businessman. From his parents' home in Houston, Dell ran a mail-order stamp-trading business. At 16, he sold subscriptions to the *Houston Post*. Dell started college as a premed student, but found time to establish a business selling memory chips and disk drives for IBM PCs from his University of Texas at Austin dorm room. Dell bought his products at cost from IBM dealers, who, at the time, were required by IBM to order large monthly quotas of PCs, which frequently exceeded demand. Dell resold his inventory through newspapers (and later through national computer magazines) at 10 to 15 percent below retail.

Dell's dorm-room computer business was grossing about $80,000 a month in early 1984, enough to persuade him to drop out of college. At that time, he started making and selling his own IBM clones under the brand name PC's Limited. Dell sold his machines directly to end users, rather than through retail computer outlets as most manufacturers did. By eliminating the retail markup, Dell could sell his PCs at about 40 percent of the price of an IBM.

Company Overview

In 1988, Dell went to the NASDAQ stock market and raised $34.2 million in an initial public offering. Dell tripped in 1990, reporting a 64-percent drop in profits. Sales were growing, but so were costs, mostly due to efforts to design a PC using proprietary components. Also, the company's warehouses were oversupplied. Within a year, Dell turned itself around by cutting inventories and coming out with new products. It added international sales offices and started to focus on selling to government agencies and Fortune 1000 customers.

Dell entered the retail arena in 1990 by allowing Soft Warehouse Superstores (now CompUSA) to sell its PCs at mail-order prices. In 1991 the company made the same agreement with office-supply chain-store Staples. In 1992, Xerox agreed to sell Dell machines in 19 Latin American countries. That year, Dell sold a new line of PCs through Price Club (now Price/Costco). In 1994, Dell abandoned retail stores to go back to its mail-order and telephone-order origins.

Today, Dell is growing rapidly in the European and Asian markets. How does Dell sell overseas? Just as it does in the United States. Hundreds of sales reps court large international accounts such as Deutsche Bank, Michelin, and Sony. And while it's true that 800 lines are in their infancy overseas, Dell has things arranged so that customers all over the world can dial toll-free to one of six call centers in Europe and Asia. A customer in Lisbon, for instance, places a local call that is automatically forwarded to Dell's center in Montpellier, France. There, the customer is connected to a Portuguese-speaking rep. Dell ramped up its efforts in Asia with new mail-order service in Hong Kong, Japan, and Singapore; a new Asia/Pacific customer center in Malaysia; and direct-sales operations in South Korea and Taiwan.

Build-to-Order e-Business Design

So, what is central to Dell's success? Superb low-cost manufacturing and fast-cycle product development. In other words, end-to-end operational excellence. Dell's focus on operational excellence came at a time when the PC business was changing and old-line companies such as IBM and Compaq seemed ill suited to meet the needs of rapid change. The integration of demand from the direct-sales channel with the back-end supply chain is reshaping the industry by enabling the cost-effective selling of build-to-order computers directly to customers, thus bypassing the resellers and their markups.[5]

Dell is leading this revolution with supply chain innovation that no competitor has matched. It is more focused than any competitor on quickly manufacturing and delivering inexpensive top-quality machines. How does build-to-order work? Dell assembles its U.S. PCs in Austin, Texas; its European PCs in Limerick, Ireland; and its Asian PCs in Penang, Malaysia. All the plants are close to suppliers such as Intel; Maxtor, which makes hard drives; and Selectron, a motherboard manufacturer that ships parts just in time. An order form follows each PC across the factory floor, starting when the machine is nothing more than a metal chassis. Drives, chips, and boards are added according to the customer's request. At one spot, partly assembled PCs roll up to an operator standing before a tall steel rack with drawers full of components. Little red and green lights flash next to the drawers containing parts the worker must install. When the operator is done, the machine glides on down the line.

To compete in the cutthroat personal computer and desktop server market, Dell needs a supply chain that is very flexible and agile for the following reasons:

- When products become noncompetitive, Dell must be agile enough to move to a line of new products that are compatible with existing capital and human resources.

- As customers' incomes rise, they demand better selection and higher-quality products. Therefore, customized, build-to-order products and services become commonplace.

- As competitors introduce new models, Dell must make design changes quickly by switching supply sources. Also, when competitors start offering multiple quality and price levels, Dell needs more flexible product mixes.

- When customers want fast delivery and are willing to pay premium prices, or when competitors start offering expedient deliveries, Dell's supply chain needs to be more flexible in transportation and deliveries.

- Since new microprocessors and other innovations prompt changes in customer demand, Dell needs to respond quickly and supply new products, offer a variety of items on a trial basis, and identify hot items in a short time.

Build-to-order definitely gives Dell several advantages:

- Dell has no finished-goods inventory. The company manufactures the central processing unit, but purchases monitors and keyboards from others. Upon receipt of an order, UPS Worldwide merges the shipments of the processor, monitor, and keyboard from different origin points at one of their facilities in Reno, Nevada; Louisville, Kentucky; or Austin, Texas. The entire system is delivered intact.

- Dell's tailor-made computer systems contain the latest high-margin components. This is important because inventoried components depreciate quite rapidly.

- Unlike manufacturers that use resellers, Dell has direct contact with its customers. If a trend pops up and customers request 18GB drives, Dell knows immediately.

- Selling directly means that Dell isn't getting paid by resellers; it's getting paid by the likes of NationsBank and Boeing. Dell receivables have a great credit rating, higher, in fact, than Dell itself!

- Consumers and small businesses pay for their orders by credit card, which means Dell has its money in the bank before the motherboard meets the chassis. Dell has a cash-conversion cycle—the difference between the time it pays its creditors and the time it takes to get paid—of eight days.

Another key element of Dell's operational excellence is the interface to the supply chain. In the build-to-order model, the link with the customer is extremely critical. In Dell's case, this link is its Web site. Originally (phase 1), the site presented customers with simple product and price descriptions, rather like an online catalog. In phase 2, visitors are able to take advantage of more sophisticated services, such as the ability to enter specifications of the hardware or software they require. They then receive information on machines and prices that match these criteria.

In phase 3, currently under way, customers will be able to take advantage of a more sophisticated online customer support system, including an order-tracking system complete with courier-tracking technology. Customers will be able to find out exactly where their orders are, from the time they enter their purchase to the moment the goods arrive. In phase 4, a Dell customer will enter a tag code located on the back of the machine and will be able to view pages of technical support that correspond to that particular computer's hardware and software. Increasingly, the service side will be the differentiator in operational excellence.

The company's supply-chain excellence strategy is definitely paying off. Dell has grown to $12.3 billion in revenue, and profits are more than $1 billion. Dell is growing more than twice as fast as any of its competitors, and its worldwide PC market share has doubled. Then there's the stock. Ah, the stock! Between 1995 and 1998, Dell stock has risen more than 26 times. In fact, Dell is the top-performing big-company stock of the 1990s. Since 1990, Dell's stock has risen 29,600 percent!

Lessons for e-Business Design

What can we learn from Dell? The goal is to make the internals of the company agile enough to respond to the ever-increasing and ever-changing needs of cus-

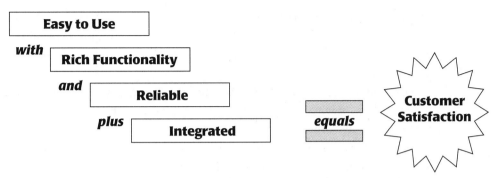

Figure 3.6: Operational Excellence Model Leading to Customer Satisfaction

tomers. Operational excellence implies that successful companies succeed by developing flexible business designs built on a solid technical foundation.

As Figure 3.6 illustrates, the operational excellence model that delivers the highest customer satisfaction is built on an e-business infrastructure that has four characteristics: it is easy to use, has rich functionality, is reliable, and delivers integrated performance. These characteristics imply a need for supply chain excellence in anticipating and responding to change.

Case Study: Continuous Innovation at Cisco Systems

Cisco is the leader in the rapidly growing market for internetworking equipment, enabling its customers to build large-scale integrated computer networks. Driving the exponential growth for internetworking equipment is a surge in data traffic, which results from the strong demand on the part of companies worldwide to move an increasing amount of digital information within and between their sites.

Cisco's story provides one of the best depictions of the new model of continuous innovation management. Cisco believes that continuous innovation demands that organizations build on change (not stability), organized around networks (not a rigid hierarchy), based on interdependencies of partners (not self-sufficiency), and constructed on technological advantage (not old-fashioned bricks and mortar). Technology aids and abets this business design.

Company Overview

Cisco was founded in 1984 by Stanford University husband-and-wife team Leonard Bosack and Sandra Lerner and three colleagues. Bosack developed technology to link his computer lab's network with his wife's network in the business school. Deciding there could be a market for internetworking devices, Bosack and Lerner mortgaged their house, bought a used mainframe, installed it in their garage, and got friends and relatives to work for deferred pay. They sold their first router in 1986.

In the beginning Cisco targeted universities, the aerospace industry, and government facilities, relying on word-of-mouth advertising and contacts made via the Internet. In 1988, the company decided to expand its marketing to include large corporations. Short on cash, Cisco turned to venture capitalist Donald Valentine of Sequoia Capital. Valentine bought a controlling stake in the company and became chairman.

As the market for network routers opened up in the late 1980s, Cisco, whose products already had a proven track record, had a head start on competitors. In addition, the company was the first to offer reasonably priced, high-performance routers. Cisco sales exploded, jumping from $1.5 million in 1987 to $28 million in 1989. Cisco went public in 1990.

With the explosion of the Internet and the coming of age of the networked economy, Cisco's products became the foundation for the networked business model. Today, the company's products are at the heart of nearly every big network, and Cisco intends to keep it that way. They are using acquisitions to broaden their product line so they can offer customers one-stop shopping for networking gear. Cisco Systems is emerging as the strategic internetworking vendor of choice and a powerhouse equal in stature to such household names as Microsoft and Intel.

Exponential Growth: Playing the Acquisitions Game

Most companies struggle to absorb one or two acquisitions. Cisco is considered a master at the acquisitions game, having accomplished more than 30 in the last five years. Increasingly surrounded by bigger competitors, Cisco eventually made acquisitions the cornerstone of its strategy. For instance, by 1991 Cisco's sales had reached $183 million, but they faced increased competition from startups as well as computer giants IBM and Digital Equipment Corporation (DEC).

To survive, Cisco began a program of rapid expansion via acquisition in 1993, swapping about $95 million in stock for Crescendo Communications, another California-based networking company. It also debuted products for the lower end of the router market. The following year it bought Kalpana, the leading maker of Ethernet switches. In 1995, Cisco pumped up its position in the fast-growing ATM (asynchronous transfer mode) switching market when it bought LightStream.

In 1996, Cisco acquired Statacom to enter into the frame-relay marketplace. That year the company increased its presence in the Internet connectivity market with the purchases of MultiNet software maker TGV Software, and Internet Junction, which makes software that connects Novell NetWare users with the World Wide Web. In 1997, Cisco acquired Granite Systems. This company manufactures Gigabit Ethernet switching, which can move data as fast as one billion bits per second.

Earnings growth via acquisitions has made Cisco the darling of Wall Street and among the best performers on the NASDAQ stock market. A $10,000 investment in 1990 was worth well over $1.5 million in 1998. Cisco's market capitalization also passed the $200 billion milestone, a landmark feat for a company just in its teen years. A rising stock price is a critical element in modern business strategy because it provides currency for companies like Cisco to use stock to buy other companies. As voice and data networks increasingly become one, Cisco faces competition from 800-pound gorillas Lucent Technologies and Northern Telecom. It will be interesting to see this battle unfold in the next decade.

Continuous Innovation via Acquisitions

Cisco's acquisitions are managed and carried out by an acquisitions group that fulfills two functions: strategic and tactical execution. On a *strategic* level, the acquisitions group must identify companies that help Cisco enhance its product line and keep up with the changing marketplace. Based on what customers are saying and what competitors are doing, Cisco might see a hole in one of their areas because they haven't moved fast enough or moved in the right direction. Acquiring a company that has the necessary technology already in place provides a quick fix.

On a *tactical* level, the acquisitions teams must make sure Cisco absorbs each acquisition without skipping a beat. From the day the transaction closes (a window of between one to three months after the acquisition is announced), Cisco integrates the target company into its operations. This ensures that the new product line quickly adds to Cisco's revenues.

Cisco's tactical integration strategy is not unique. Other market leaders follow similar strategies. Consider the case of Newell, which merged with RubberMaid. This gigantic maker of housewares, hardware, and office products—everything from Levolor blinds to Mirro cookware and Rolodexes—has devoured more than 40 companies in the past decade. Its dynamism comes from the company's ability to meld merged entities. How? Through integrated application infrastructure, of course. All 47 of its disparate manufacturing plants use the same program from American Software for processing and purchasing. All payroll is handled by Cyborg; all financials are handled by Global AP & GL. Oracle's IRI Express runs the company's data warehouse, tracking point-of-sale information on each and every Newell product. Newell says that because of standard applications, it realizes significant cost savings in integrating acquisitions.[6]

Lessons for e-Business Design

Cisco's e-business architecture must be flexible enough to support the organizational structure imposed by an acquisition strategy. The acquisition strategy creates an innovative structure: a strong center surrounded by freewheeling satellites (business units). The challenge is to manage such a loosely coupled structure while continuing to provide seamless product integration to the customer. This harmony is very difficult to achieve, and, if Cisco isn't careful, this strategy could be its undoing.

Business Design Lessons Learned

The successful businesses of the next decade will not be found among those companies fighting today's battles with yesterday's tactics and tools. The objective is not to catch up with competition, but to outperform it by quantum leaps. What market leaders are really doing is finding new ways to delight their customers.

Effective business design and execution depends on how managers use technology to deliver services faster, cheaper, and with better quality than their competitors. Technology is the only theme common to the three case studies discussed in this chapter. However, their *management of technology* to reconfigure underlying business infrastructures and deliver outstanding value provides important lessons to be learned. A quick review follows.

Be customer focused. Of the many imperatives to which organizations must respond, none is more difficult, more perilous, or more vital than being customer focused across multiple business units. To accomplish this, innovative companies are using the Web and the Internet to build interactive relationships between prospects, customers, resellers, employees, and suppliers.

Value creation is a continuous process. Even the best business designs have short life spans. Today's rising stars can become complacent, move too slowly, incorrectly anticipate competitors' moves, or miss strategic opportunities. Then they may face the unpleasant question of whether value is beginning to migrate toward startups with better business designs.

Transform business processes into digital form. A fundamental premise of an e-business enterprise is that all information must be available in digital form. In other words, there's nothing available on paper that isn't also available electronically. This may sound obvious, but it's an essential concept. Digital information is more efficient to create and maintain. Rather than entering the same information multiple times, each item is entered only once. That's significant. Even more important is that words and numbers on paper are dead—you can't work with them. In digital form, information comes alive. It can be analyzed creatively, searched quickly, updated easily, and shared broadly.

Decentralize management but centralize coordination. Taking an enterprise perspective brings with it some challenges and some opportunities. Integration efforts to coordinate complementary but independent departments or enterprises must find ways to deal with the inability to control everything from one point. This approach calls for breaking up large applications into smaller pieces that each have defined responsibilities and can communicate with one another using a common language. It calls for designing the business and the technology around the information flow.

Create an e-business application architecture. The American Express, Dell, and Cisco case studies repeatedly emphasize the power of having a forward-thinking application architecture. The architecture addresses three critical requirements:[7]

- **Interface.** Innovators do not just want new technology. They want their new systems to support key business practices within their industry, so that they can continue to interface with their suppliers and customers without losing rhythm.

- **Integration.** Innovators want to streamline and integrate their business processes using their new information systems.

- **Innovation.** Innovators demand new and more advanced applications that help them grow quickly.

The foremost objectives of the application architecture are to improve customer satisfaction and reduce operating cost. Process integration allows innovators to gain operating efficiencies, improve information flow between various departments, and build predictability and repeatability within their processes.

Integrate, but plan for continuous growth and change. Integration efforts over a very large functional scope must work with the prospect of continuous change. Nothing is permanent. However, managers may find that in conquering the vexing problems, they will have acquired an ability to exploit change and maximize the value they derive from their technology investment. The solution to the e-business architecture problem calls for an approach that fits business reality by organizing application software the same way companies organize business units.

Memo to the CEO

If you are reading this book, it's probably safe to assume that you are a forward-thinking manager responsible for steering your company or business unit through the stormy waters of continuous growth, cost reduction, and customer retention. At this very moment, you are seeing the emergence of the electronic enterprise and noticing more opportunities than ever before to add value to your company and make money. But it is tough to figure out how deep the business impact of technology is, where to invest, and what changes to make. So here you are at the beginning of the twenty-first century searching for a place to start, a path to follow, a destination to reach.

Creating an e-business design is only the first step. The most difficult part comes next: execution. In recent years, many best-selling management books have exhorted managers to be innovative and develop a vision for the future. Also, the "strategic" consulting industry is making a killing by guiding executives to render strategy intelligible, develop strategic vision, make choices about product and service offerings, develop better competitive timing, segment and target customers, and outsource noncore competencies. Analyzing core competencies, planning strategy at the 50,000-foot level, and developing mission statements make great reports that, unfortunately, few read. Almost all firms these days have great visions and strategies, but relatively few execute them, and even fewer execute them well.

Execution of the e-business design is the name of the game. **e-Commerce technology must be embedded in an effective business design or it isn't a viable approach to generate differentiated or sustainable value.** While this seems obvious, it's amazing how many firms fall prey to the lure of the technology silver bullet. The source of differentiation lies not only in how well you plan, but how well you execute your plan using technology.

It is becoming crystal clear that with e-commerce, we have entered a new phase: the age of e-business design. The challenge is in the creation and execution of the e-business design. For instance, American Express aims to improve the quality of customer interaction while cutting costs and increasing market share. But these opportunities can be realized only if organizations take advantage of emerging electronic business designs and overcome some of the obstacles standing in the way.

To execute designs well, however, focus of management time and resources is required. Realistically, a firm can choose only one of three disciplines—service excellence, operational excellence or continuous innovation excellence—in which to specialize. Unfortunately, most companies do not specialize in any of these, and therefore, realize only mediocre or average levels of achievement in each area. In no sense are these companies market leaders. In today's business environment of increased competition, the need for competitive differentiation is greater than ever, and complacency will not lead to increased market share, sales, or profits. In fact, it could lead to bankruptcy or extinction.

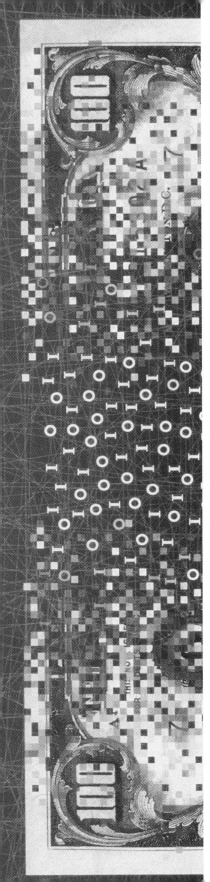

CHAPTER FOUR

Constructing the
e-Business Architecture

What to Expect

The e-business design built on an application architecture is no longer merely a concept; it's become a widespread reality as more companies than ever integrate applications to streamline operations and compete in the e-commerce arena. But disparate applications are like building blocks—they have to be put together systematically to create an e-business enterprise.

In this chapter, we'll show you what application integration is, why it's important, and what business and technology megatrends are driving application integration. We present real-life case studies of companies that have embraced integrated applications and explain how they did it. We then show how you can integrate various applications to create an e-business architecture.

Chief information officers (CIOs) face an overarching challenge from the CEO: "Give us enterprise applications that make us more competitive and deliver benefits quickly, so we can improve our business performance today, not years from now." There is growing recognition among CIOs that the fastest and most effective way to deliver dramatic business benefits is to bridge the information chasm between customers, back-office operations, and the supply chain. The cost of this information gap? Tens to hundreds of millions of dollars in higher product costs and longer order fulfillment cycles.

According to Bill Gates, "Virtually everything in business today is an undifferentiated commodity, except how a company manages its information. How you manage information determines whether you win or lose. How you use information may be the one factor that determines its failure or success—or runaway success."[1] That brings us to the question, How does a company manage its information? The simple answer is through its business applications (apps), order and inventory management, financials, and customer service.

Modern business designs are constructed from well-integrated building blocks called *enterprise applications.* Enterprise application examples include enterprise resource planning, customer relationship management, human resources management, and supply chain management apps. These apps form the backbone of the modern enterprise. The migration of companies toward enterprise apps is a big deal. While the Web and Internet may have grabbed most of the media attention recently, the business world's steady embrace of enterprise apps may, in fact, be the most important development in the corporate use of information technology in the 1990s. Emphasis on enterprise apps increased significantly in the mid-1990s as companies scrambled to find ways to root out old legacy apps incapable of meeting the stresses of the global economy. Today, as companies race toward the information economy, their structures are increasingly made up of interlocking business apps. Isolated, stand-alone applications are history.

So, in reality, e-business design is about how to integrate an intricate set of apps so they work together like a well-oiled machine to manage, organize, route, and transform information. This vision is not easy to achieve. For instance, TCI attempted to create a massive computerized customer billing service called Summitrak. It was supposed to handle customer service and billing functions, but three years and $132 million later, the system barely ran. TCI extricated itself from the mess and sold the system to CSG Systems International, a cable billing services company.

As this example illustrates, creating large-scale applications is not easy. The reason is quite simple. As the rate of change increases, the complexity of the problems increases. The more complex these application problems are, the more time it takes to solve them. The more the rate of change increases, the more the problems change, and the shorter the life of the solutions becomes. Therefore, by the time one finds solutions to many of the problems being faced (usually the most important ones), the problems have changed so much that the solutions are no longer relevant or effective; they are stillborn. In other words, many of the solutions are to problems that no longer exist in the form they did when first analyzed. As a result, companies that attempt massive application projects are digging themselves into a deeper hole. Many companies in the future will either suffer huge losses or go bankrupt due to bad application development.

Little wonder, then, that making application investment decisions is rising to the top of the management agenda. As businesses apply technology to address new opportunities, the relationship between the business model and its application architecture inevitably grows closer, and the question of how to steer this relationship becomes more and more urgent. How well you manage and use information depends on the e-business architecture that your company's "C"-level executives—CEO, COO, CIO, and CFO—are building. Senior management must play the role of corporate architects in order to shape the information technology (IT) infrastructure and business processes so that they can meet the demands of customers and build lasting value by connecting business strategy with operational reality. They cannot afford to leave this important task to developers or lower-level management who don't see the big picture.

The challenge facing management is evident: Create and deliver customer value through integrated business apps. That brings us to the questions managers must ask:

- What are the key trends and events that will drive new e-business application investments over the next five years?

- What is the role of packaged application software in creating the next-generation e-business architecture?

- How will technology advancements and business changes affect e-business application deployment decisions?

- What is the ideal e-business application architecture needed to compete in the twenty-first century?

- What integrated architecture will radically improve the way companies manage information and will run organizations like clockwork?

- How can we create a management structure that will help my organization harness and exploit business apps despite ever-increasing complexity and volatility?

Clearly, integrated business apps are becoming catalysts for the corporate change that e-business requires. However, with firms increasingly banking on grand visions of an e-commerce-enabled, "wired" enterprise, separating market hype from technology reality demands new levels of insight and shrewd decision making. Taking a multiyear planning perspective, this chapter will focus on the most important business and technology megatrends driving application deployment, as well as key areas of investment necessary to harness and exploit business apps effectively.

Why Is Application Integration Important?

How should you integrate your back-end systems to provide accurate, real-time information to your customers? With all the changes happening in the marketplace, an organization is not safe with an outdated, ineffective application infrastructure. To deploy a workable e-business design, management must be on top of which application infrastructure will best meet the company's needs. This takes work and a lot of vision.

Whether you like it or not, your company may be forced to take the integration route for a variety of reasons, including better customer care, new competitive conditions, or the need to offer more integrated services. Let's take a look at each of these in detail.

New Customer-Care Objectives

Needless to say, an integrated application architecture is key to serving the customer seamlessly, especially in e-commerce. This strategy is exemplified by Amazon.com, the integrated seller of books, CDs, videotapes, audiotapes, and other products. The goal of Amazon.com is to create a seamless buying experience for the mainstream Internet customer. Seamless buying and fulfillment is important because as the novelty of Internet retailing fades and customer expectations increase, rapid, error-free fulfillment will increasingly play a major role in retaining customer loyalty. Realizing this, Amazon.com's business goal is to significantly improve order fulfillment and shipment speeds. Most people don't realize that

Amazon.com maintains a significant inventory of only the most popular titles in two big warehouses, a 70,000-square-foot facility near downtown Seattle and a 200,000-square-foot facility in Delaware. The main purpose of these facilities on the East and West coasts is to reach a same-day, first-time fulfillment rate for 90 percent of popular titles.[2]

How does their integrated business process work? Once an order is placed on the Web site, Amazon.com uses an integrated packing and shipping system via an online connection to the order management system. This system monitors the in-stock status of each item ordered, processes the order, and generates warehouse selection tickets and packing slips. Once picking and packing is done, the package is sent via Airborne or UPS to the customer. The high level of integration in order fulfillment means that Amazon.com can turn its own inventory much more frequently than traditional competitors, who average three to four times longer. This helps keep inventory and warehousing costs down, making them more competitive.

The Amazon.com example shows that to achieve the business goal of creating a richer customer experience, firms need to integrate their Web sites with their back-office systems, the heart of their operations: inventory management, order processing, financials, and customer service. Again, easier said than done. Do you know that companies spend billions of dollars on application software every year and still do not have the information they need to run their businesses well? Why? Because they lack integration across apps. This happens because, unfortunately, most application software automates some tasks, but not entire processes. Clearly, the problem facing companies is how to integrate enterprise apps for seamless flow of information that e-business designs demand.

Managers everywhere must understand that the Web is a powerful tool for slicing margins and increasing interactivity with customers and prospects, but if companies don't practice the fundamentals of fast, error-free integrated service, they will fail miserably. In the same vein, as customers become more Internet savvy and realize the efficiencies to be gained through online interactions, their tolerance for wasted time and lack of integrated processes diminishes. To survive, companies must refine their business processes if they hope to win the hearts of fickle consumers and reap the benefits of integrated front-office and back-office apps.

New Competitive Conditions Require Integrated Apps for Survival

The changing competitive environment is driving the need for integrated apps. Consider the case of NB Power, located in Fredericton, New Brunswick. NB

Power has provided electricity to customers throughout the Canadian province of New Brunswick since 1920. With 2,500 employees and assets of $4.3 billion, NB Power has developed one of the most diverse power-generating systems in the world, with a mix of hydro-, nuclear-, coal-, oil-, and diesel-generating units.

Deregulation and the growing demand for better customer service began to strain the limits of its existing apps. Pending regulatory changes leading to a far more deregulated and competitive environment forced the company to reevaluate its business processes, especially its customer service functions. NB Power anticipated that the existing software and system infrastructure would soon lack the functionality and flexibility needed to meet changing business requirements.

As the power industry deregulates, NB Power and other utilities are quickly realizing that integrating internal apps is merely a down payment on a competitive advantage. In order to remain a player in the next century, firms better start thinking about ways to tie their various apps together tightly and smoothly. Another important goal for NB Power is to improve the quality of services it provides. This requires improving the quality, timeliness, and types of information available to the corporation, and increasing control over resources through improved process integration.

Unfortunately, business objectives are often in conflict with existing apps. NB Power's previous application infrastructure included purchased apps as well as in-house apps running on IBM mainframes. Within that mainframe environment, access to information was cumbersome; software and hardware had become obsolete; and maintenance, support, operation, and integration of the systems were becoming increasingly difficult and expensive.

To achieve better alignment between competitive needs and application capabilities, NB Power decided to migrate to a more flexible environment. After exhaustive research and a thorough comparison of various application solutions, NB Power decided that its demands would be met best by implementing a standard application infrastructure provided by packaged software provider SAP. But the game is far from over after choosing a packaged application architecture.

The challenge for managers is to make sense and good use of what packaged apps offer. Not all purchased apps add value. In the coming years, managers will need to figure out how to make an integrated application architecture a viable, productive part of the work setting. They will need to stay ahead of the information curve and learn to leverage information for business results. Otherwise, they risk being swallowed by a tidal wave of data, which is not a business advantage.

Fast-Moving Competitors Force the Need for Better Application Integration

Established companies are forced to scrutinize their existing application architecture and determine if they are capable of competing with new entrants who enter their turf with new products and services. This is the question facing Norwest Mortgage, a leading residential mortgage lender. Norwest faces challenges from new online services such as homeshark, eLoan, and Microsoft's HomeAdvisor. These upstarts provide consumers with mortgage marketplaces on the Web, where they can shop easily for home loans from a number of companies.

Norwest presents a good case study because it's in a traditional, nonautomated industry caught in the midst of an e-business transition. To understand the application challenges facing Norwest, we must first understand their business. Norwest provides funding for 1 of every 15 homes in the United States and serves more than 2 million customers. Norwest has grown rapidly, with more than 11,000 employees and more than 750 branches in all 50 states. Growth has come from internal expansion as well as aggressive acquisition, most recently the 1996 purchase of Prudential Home Mortgage. Along with Prudential's $45 billion portfolio, Norwest acquired an added complement of legacy computing systems.

Postacquisition Norwest faced many challenges, including how to take advantage of new economies of scale, leverage existing technology assets, and use new Web and Internet technologies in the best way to provide real-time quotes to agents, telemarketers, and other online users. The issue is not how much information exists, nor how to store it, but the speed and agility with which the "right" information can be transmitted to solve a particular customer problem. The idea is simple: Put information at the customers' and employees' fingertips so they can act faster and make better decisions.

Norwest's strategy is to enable customer convenience. In the old days, customer convenience in the mortgage business was defined by three simple words: location, location, location. Web access, however, makes geographical proximity an obsolete virtue. Today, consumers define convenience as access to any information, in any form, anytime, anywhere. To meet their customers' needs, Norwest must offer a range of delivery and access options to customers, insurance agents, and employees and provide customer convenience.

Norwest's first task is to simplify the application infrastructure by evaluating and selecting the best systems in each of the newly merged firms. Next, it has to find a way to integrate all business systems into a single, unified platform that will support an expanded user base and a growing revenue stream. The most difficult task is integrating various apps, since most rely on proprietary solutions.

Norwest realizes that in the rapidly changing and fiercely competitive financial services industry, the firms that flourish are those that offer the best service and deliver it ahead of the competition (see Figure 4.1). With this understanding, Norwest quickly recognized the necessity for a completely flexible and scalable e-business architecture that allows them to:

- Enhance customer service and quality of operations through enterprisewide apps.

- More closely link technology to business objectives.

- Develop apps faster, reliably and cost-effectively, with minimum training or cultural change.

- Meet the standards for performance, reliability, and security of mission-critical systems.

The case of Norwest may sound familiar because many large companies are going through similar experiences. Today's e-business architecture must enable companies to analyze their businesses like chessboards, on which they seek to be two, three, or four moves ahead of the competition.

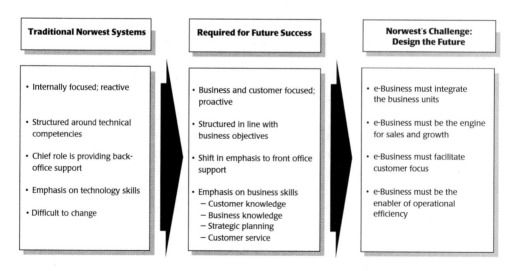

Figure 4.1: e-Business Architecture Challenges

Bad for Your Health: Problems Caused by Lack of Integration

The lack of integrated application architecture can bring companies down rather quickly. Consider the case of Oxford Health Plans Inc., a $4 billion health maintenance organization (HMO). Oxford Health, whose motto is "The health and healing company," operates in New York, New Jersey, Pennsylvania, Connecticut, and New Hampshire. The company offers traditional HMO service, point-of-service plans, Medicare/Medicaid plans, employer-funded plans, and dental plans. Oxford has been a juggernaut in the managed-care arena, buoyed by strong membership growth and keen marketing. Beyond this, they have been praised for use of the Web, which gives members access to lists of providers and allows physicians to check the status of claims.

At the end of 1997, Oxford Health announced that a computer problem in the accounting and billing system caused the company to underestimate medical costs and overestimate revenue. The announcement that it was poised to post its first-ever loss stunned investors, and the stock fell more than 80 percent. Who is to blame? Initially, Oxford Health blamed computer conversion for rendering it unable to bill customers and make payments to doctors and hospitals. However, Oxford later discovered that the problems stemmed from the fact that the company's internal financial controls were virtually nonexistent. A chastened (and now former) Chairman Stephen Wiggins didn't duck culpability, conceding, "At the end of the day a computer problem is probably a business problem, and somewhere along the line I obviously made a mistake."[3] No kidding.

Oxford Health's example illustrates that careful design of application architecture is essential for business survival. Getting the integration right is even more important. However, there are many minefields. Some of them are system related (see Figure 4.2), whereas others are related to the organization. The typical organizational barriers to be dealt with are as follows:

- Focusing too much on efficiency and cost-cutting. This often leads to myopia and the inability to take advantage of opportunities for revenue growth in new lines of business.

- Not listening to the customer's perspective and using it as the best arbiter of success.

- Rehashing competitors' ideas (often positioned as "industry best practices"), resulting in diminished returns. Businesses need fresh ideas.

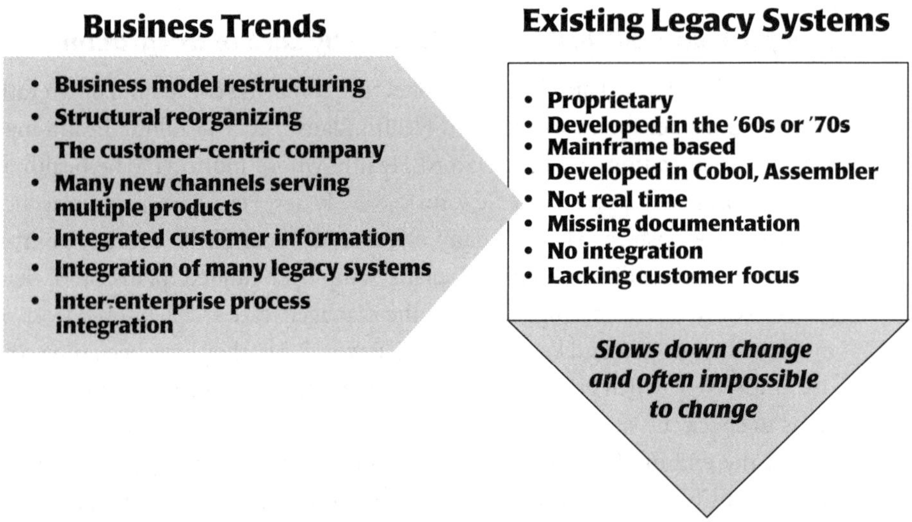

Business Trends

- Business model restructuring
- Structural reorganizing
- The customer-centric company
- Many new channels serving multiple products
- Integrated customer information
- Integration of many legacy systems
- Inter-enterprise process integration

Existing Legacy Systems

- Proprietary
- Developed in the '60s or '70s
- Mainframe based
- Developed in Cobol, Assembler
- Not real time
- Missing documentation
- No integration
- Lacking customer focus

Slows down change and often impossible to change

Figure 4.2: System Challenges Facing Large Organizations

- Pursuing drawn-out, enterprisewide projects in search of a "perfect" answer, thus failing to address today's need for faster response.

- Frequently reorganizing, which often leads to weak executive involvement and support. Consistently, this is one of the top five causes for the failure of e-business initiatives. An effective transition strategy must be in place before executives are shuffled around.

- Placing too much emphasis on outside consultants for execution. Often, consulting firms focus their change efforts exclusively on bleeding-edge technology, which may achieve nothing more than incremental benefits.

Businesses today need to automate a much broader process, cover a bigger chunk of the organization, and pull together more information from more places than in the past. By "bigger chunk of the organization," we mean the cross-functional business processes, such as customer management, that often cut across many departments and are bigger in scope than any one existing application.

The New Era of Cross-Functional Integrated Apps

We are entering an era of complex, cross-functional integrated apps, called *application clusters,* which represent the foundation of e-business. To understand how we got here, however, it's important to understand the evolution of business apps.

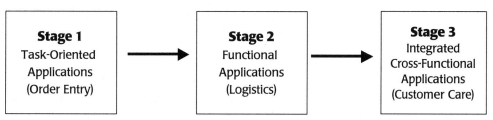

Figure 4.3: Evolution of Business Apps

It has been a process of stages, as illustrated in Figure 4.3. Let's look at each stage in more detail.

 Stage 1: Simplification and Segmentation. Historically, business apps were narrow in focus and more task oriented, simplifying processes such as order entry. While task specialization improved productivity dramatically, it also fragmented processes beyond recognition. In a task-centric world, processes tend to fall between the cracks. They become slow, inflexible, error prone, and replete with the costs of the managerial overhead needed to hold them together.

 Stage 2: Reintegration and Transformation. In the 1980s, the task-oriented nature of apps evolved to become more functionally integrated. Fortunately, information technology is allowing us to reintegrate tasks into connected processes. For instance, order entry was transformed into sales apps. But in the reality of today's global economy, functional specialization can be crippling. What is needed is the ability to provide solutions, which requires that everyone comprehends the big picture and remains flexible in the face of new or complex situations. This requirement has created the need for cross-functional application integration.

With the early 1990s came the advent of "business process reengineering," and organizations began focusing on managing and optimizing cross-functional business processes. A process perspective transforms a group of ad hoc and fragmented functional activities into a system that is organized, repeatable, and reliable. The shift from task-oriented to process-oriented organization may not sound very dramatic. In fact, it is the kind of discontinuous change that occurs only rarely.

Clearly, the trend in business is toward software-enabled process support. This is accomplished by deploying business apps that fuse multiple functions into a collection of well-orchestrated clusters. For instance, increasingly sales apps are being integrated with customer service and marketing apps to form customer relationship management solutions. Why is this fusion of disparate apps necessary? Price wars, market share wars, and quality wars are forcing companies to streamline and integrate processes at unprecedented levels to become solution oriented and more effectively serve the needs of customers.

 Stage 3: Cross-Functional Integration and Fluid Adaptability. Application clusters are of different types, each of which represents a related cluster of functionality. The implementation of application clusters represents a total overhaul of enterprise systems. These application clusters are designed to integrate an array of internal functions, including

- Customer relationship management (e.g., Siebel Systems)
- Enterprise resource planning (e.g., SAP)
- Supply chain management (e.g., I2 Technologies)
- Selling-chain management (e.g., Trilogy)
- Operating resource management (e.g., Ariiba)
- Enterprise Application Integration apps (e.g., CrossWorlds)
- Business analytics, knowledge management, and decision support apps (e.g., SAP)

Companies are pursuing the application cluster route by buying and deploying packaged apps developed by business application vendors such as Siebel, SAP, Baan, PeopleSoft, J.D. Edwards, Vantive, and Clarify, among others. The logic behind buying packaged apps is simplified by using an analogy of a car. Companies should buy cars instead of building them from scratch if the objective is to serve the customer by getting him from point A to point B. It's better to focus on driving than building the car.

The same logic applies to application cluster development. Companies should focus on buying the applications rather than spending precious dollars on developing complex applications. These packaged apps have helped some organizations adapt significantly to shifting conditions, improved the competitive standing of others, and even have positioned a few for a far better future. The following sections describe each of these application clusters with a detailed example.

Charles Schwab: Customer Relationship Management Apps

Consider application integration at Charles Schwab. Millions of do-it-yourself investors rely on Schwab, which has some $200 billion in assets, for its wide range of brokerage services and mutual fund products. As executing stock market trades becomes a commodity, Charles Schwab has successfully made customer service the core of its strategy. Still, there was a slight problem. Most of Schwab's business is done over the phone or in person. This means that sales reps and service people need to have easy access to the most current information on the company's clients and products. A few years ago, Schwab realized that its salespeople weren't getting enough information to best serve their customers. The existing systems were fragmented, and it would be too expensive to integrate them.

Thus began an exhaustive evaluation process to buy an integrated sales and service application. Schwab selected Siebel's Sales Enterprise system, which has a wide array of customer relationship management (CRM) functionality. Sales Enterprise allows Schwab's sales reps, who handle more than 10 million telephone calls every month, to gain real-time access to customer profiles and histories and to improve responsiveness to the needs of its nearly 3.5 million active customer accounts and prospects. The integrated apps also enable service reps to market new products while talking to the customer. Now service reps are able to develop a big-picture view of their customers and the company's relationship with them, which shapes how they communicate with and sell to them.

What does Charles Schwab's example tell us? Schwab no longer manages customer service as an isolated function. In order to address the needs of its customers, the company has linked all its sales and customer service organizations with one another and with all the customer-interfacing parts of the company. Key to the implementation of this initiative has been a new information infrastructure to capture information about customers and their behavior.

Integrated CRM apps (see Figure 4.4) provide immediate value to the Fortune 500. Even large and resource-rich companies are resorting to purchasing and implementing packaged apps over custom-built solutions. For most organizations, selecting a packaged CRM application is more economical than building

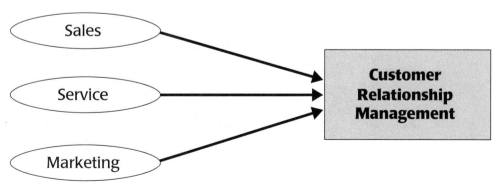

Figure 4.4: The Trend toward Integrated Customer-Centric Apps

one with a set of low-level tools. No longer do they have to wait through long development cycles to realize the benefits of a CRM application.

Does the Charles Schwab example sound familiar? Is your organization going through similar sales and service integration issues? Is your company facing a build vs. buy decision for integrated customer relationship management solutions?

Nestlé: Enterprise Resource Planning Apps

Nestlé, an international company operating in 69 countries, sells products that range from drinks, sweets, and foods to pharmaceuticals, and has 210,000 employees and 498 factories. The business challenge facing Nestlé is how to integrate systems and business activities while gaining high-quality, consistent, and efficient management of information.

Sustained optimization of business processes throughout the entire logistical chain, plus closer linking of international locations, were among the goals Nestlé set for itself before selecting an integrated application suite. Ineffective integration of information is an issue of great concern to Nestlé's managers, who are charged with increasing market share, reducing costs, and improving service. Management also wanted software that was able to speed up information flow and standardize reporting to improve international comparability of results.

Nestlé selected an enterprise resource planning (ERP) application suite from SAP to run its order entry, purchasing, invoicing, and inventory control. Figure 4.5 captures the various functions that form the ERP integrated suite. The key benefits that materialized after implementing the ERP suite were optimized ser-

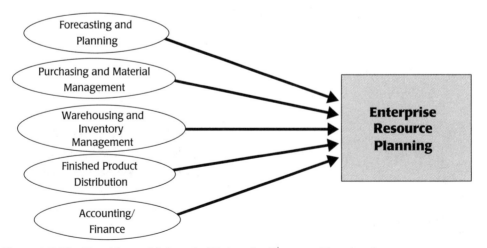

Figure 4.5: The Trend toward Integrated Enterprise Resource Planning Apps

vice, integration of worldwide logistics, an improved ability to meet deadlines, shorter turnaround times from customer inquiries to delivery, and a shift away from stock-oriented to demand-driven production.

Is your organization going through similar application integration issues? Is your organization attempting to integrate diverse functional areas in order to align your business and application strategies?

Ford Motor Company: Supply Chain Apps

The Visteon Division of the Ford Motor Company manufactures chassis components: axle and drive shaft assemblies designed for such cars as the Mustang and Crown Victoria, as well as for limousines, pickup trucks, and sport utility vehicles. Balancing production capacity with market demand is one of the division's biggest challenges. In the automotive industry, missing scheduled delivery due dates is not an option, since delay of a key assembly can cost millions of dollars in lost productivity. To help balance demand, planners are responsible for scheduling various sections of the plant. They used unconnected Excel spreadsheets for production scheduling, a process that was difficult and time-consuming. Efficiency and throughput were not optimal, and inventory was higher than it needed to be.

To solve the problem, Ford chose an integrated supply chain management (SCM) application. The scheduling application was integrated with the company's market demand database and legacy systems that stored resource and capacity constraints. The integrated functionality enables planners to perform scheduling independently over ten sequential production departments, standardize and link reports, and integrate scheduling with supplier functions. Ford calculated that, with an advanced scheduling solution, its total inventory was reduced by 15 percent—significant savings.

As businesses like Ford increasingly move toward real-time reaction to demand fluctuations, multicompany supply chain management apps are becoming a way of life. SCM apps are designed to help streamline production schedules, slash inventories, find bottlenecks, and respond quickly to orders (see Figure 4.6). Used properly, the software removes logistical barriers by creating a seamless flow of supplies and finished products.

Supply chain management is getting a lot of attention in e-business. Why? Existing supply chains are mostly outdated for the e-business era, in which inventories and costs must be eliminated wherever they are found. Traditional supply chains were designed in a time of modest competition and slow response time. To succeed in today's customer-driven environment, firms must streamline

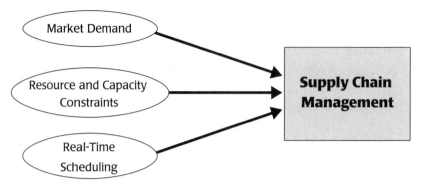

Figure 4.6: The Trend toward Integrated Supply Chain Apps

intercompany processes just as they do with processes that reside within a company's boundaries. By reengineering the intercompany supply chain, corporate boundaries are becoming meaningless. The result: enormous payoffs for all partners in the chain.

Whirlpool: Selling-Chain Management

Whirlpool is the world's second largest producer of major home appliances. The company makes washers, dryers, dishwashers, dehumidifiers, microwave ovens, ranges, refrigerators, freezers, and air conditioners. Whirlpool suffered from a labyrinthine pricing process that stifled its profitability and frustrated customers.

To reduce operating costs, Whirlpool is taking a hard look at streamlining their sales processes. Whirlpool's selling organization consists of hundreds of account managers and field marketing representatives who promote and sell products. In addition to its convoluted pricing, Whirlpool's promotions ran amuck. The company implements thousands of promotional programs per year, but because they lack analysis tools, many of these programs have been launched without understanding how they affect the overall business.

Whirlpool's paper-based pricing system consisted of multiple price sheets that were updated several times a year. The actual pricing calculations were modeled in an 180,000-cell Excel spreadsheet that took about 110 days to update.[4] Manual reentry, constant repetition, and 15-day pricing blackouts for price book printing were standard procedures.

To manage its pricing and promotions, as well as to provide its channel partners with the tools to facilitate the sales process, Whirlpool decided to overhaul its sales processes. What did it require? An integrated set of apps that makes it easy for customers to do business with Whirlpool. Whirlpool bought an enterprise software suite to integrate each function in its sales and marketing operation, including pricing management, product management, sales, commissions, promotions, contract management, and channel management. The goal was to allow Whirlpool to sell products more quickly and profitably at reduced overall costs.

What pressures is your company facing from the mass-customization trend? As firms move increasingly toward a mass-customization world, the contemporary business environment puts extraordinary demands on sales and marketing organizations. Facing sophisticated customers and intense competition, salespeople must configure custom solutions from an enormous range of complex and changing products, then price them appropriately. Traditional sales and pricing processes are unprepared for this challenge. This situation gives rise to a new cross-functional application cluster (see Figure 4.7) that is called selling-chain management apps.

CIBC: Operating Resource Management Systems

A new class of procurement-oriented apps, known as operating resource management (ORM) systems, is emerging. ORM can be defined as the procurement of the goods and services it takes to operate a business—anything from industrial supplies, office supplies, and capital equipment to services, travel, and entertainment. Figure 4.8 shows the various categories of procurement that come under this class of integrated apps.

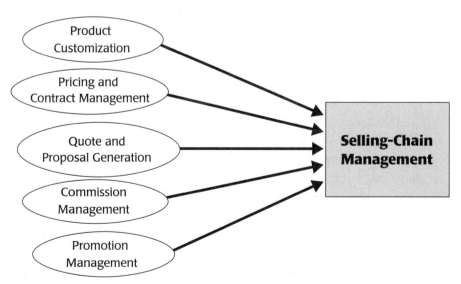

Figure 4.7: The Trend toward Integrated Selling-Chain Apps

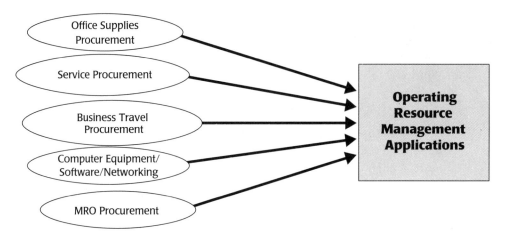

Figure 4.8: The Trend toward Integrated Procurement Apps

Consider the case of Canadian Imperial Bank of Commerce (CIBC). CIBC is looking to slash more than $100 million a year by implementing ORM apps. Though plans are to start slowly, the purchasing system aims to support more than 1,400 branch offices and 40,000 employees. CIBC projects a savings of up to $130 million annually, or 10 percent of the bank's annual $1.3 billion in purchases. The ORM solution will include software to manage employee travel and expense reports, as well as high-volume transactions conducted with the top several hundred of CIBC's 14,000 suppliers.

The goal of CIBC is to create an ORM application cluster that enables employees to buy online from designated suppliers, while maintaining approval routing and purchasing consistency. By hooking up employees to preferred suppliers, ORM apps route employee purchase requests internally before turning them into orders. The potential cost savings from ORM is quite high because it's estimated that close to 95 percent of the procurement process is paper based.

ORM is one of the last nonautomated processes in large companies. The goal of ORM apps is to empower blue-collar and white-collar employees by automating the procurement process, thereby cutting purchasing costs. You may not know this, but the overhead of processing a purchase order runs from $70 to $300. By automating the purchase process, organizations are looking to cut the overhead by at least 50 percent. For low-cost, frequently used items, allowing employees to act as purchasing agents makes a lot of sense. Another advantage is control. ORM apps enable companies to consolidate information and negotiate better with suppliers. They also permit companies to track expenses by category:

employee, department, month, and so forth. ORM represents a new wave of employee self-service apps.

Does the CIBC example sound familiar? What challenges is your company facing? Is your organization going through procurement automation decisions?

Bay Networks: Enterprise Application Integration Apps

Bay Networks provides a complete line of products that meet the connectivity requirements of corporate enterprises, service providers, and telecommunications carriers. Bay Networks sells its products through multiple channels: resellers, field sales, and support personnel. Bay Networks resellers include network and systems integrators, value-added resellers (VARs), distributors, and original equipment manufacturers (OEMs). Bay Networks leverages sales channels to provide appropriate coverage, integration services, and specialized vertical market support.

In support of their global customer service operations, Bay Networks built a custom interface between their customer relationship management application (Clarify) and enterprise resource planning application (SAP). This interface ensured that product deliveries to customers recorded in SAP were recorded in the installed product base information that resides in Clarify for contract and warranty validation. This custom interface processes over 10,000 new delivery records per day. This example highlights a new breed of apps called *connectors,* Enterprise Application Integration (EAI) apps that unite front-office customer relationship management apps with back-office, core-operation ERP apps (see Figure 4.9).

Why are EAI apps essential? These apps become important in companies that have different vendors for their front-office and back-office apps. For instance, a purchase order or purchase requisition can be generated in the ERP application,

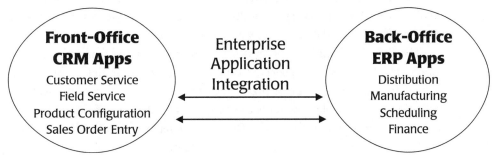

Figure 4.9: The Trend toward Order/Service Integration Apps

and a repair order or restock request can be created in the customer relationship management call-center application. If the two application clusters are not integrated, customers will not be able to get prompt replenishment of their spare parts inventory. How do you get disparate front-office and back-office apps to work as well together as they do independently? In other words, how can you coax your independent enterprise apps to collaborate as a seamless, integrated suite? This issue is central to the emergence of EAI app frameworks.

Without EAI apps in a multivendor environment, your sales force cannot immediately respond to customers' order status requests, your customer service reps cannot initiate stop orders or process returns online, and you can't bill your customers as you provide service. EAI apps

- Empower call-center operations

- Streamline sales order processing, allowing organizations to deliver products and services faster

- Improve the customer experience by helping companies become more responsive to customer demands

CrossWorlds Software is an example of a vendor providing this functionality. Another marketing term for this class of enterprise application software is "processware." *What is your company doing to resolve EAI issues?*

Business Analytics, Knowledge Management, and Decision Support Apps

Business analytics (BA), decision support systems (DSS), and knowledge management (KM) apps enable both active and passive delivery of information from large-scale databases, providing enterprises and managers with timely answers to mission-critical questions. The objective of these apps is to turn the enormous amounts of available data into knowledge companies can use.

The growth of this class of apps has been driven by the demand for more competitive business intelligence and increases in electronic data capture and storage. In addition, the emergence of the Internet and other communications technologies has enabled cost-effective access to and delivery of information to remote users throughout the world. Due to these factors, the overall market for BA, KM, and DSS is projected to grow substantially.

The following scenarios illustrate the importance of this class of apps.

- Someone is trying to use your MCI Phone Card to make a call to Pakistan. Since this usage is unprecedented and potentially fraudulent, MCI forwards a notification to your two-way pager, along with a request for permission to place the call. A detailed breakdown of every call made in the previous two weeks will be on your fax machine by the end of the day.

- It's Monday morning and your PC at work is creating a report detailing all significant week-to-date customer transactions in your territory. It automatically computes comparisons with previous months and years. When budgeting time arrives, a spreadsheet model is automatically populated with last quarter's performance statistics. You tweak some growth and cost parameters and e-mail it to the CFO.

- A customer sends inventory replenishment requests and purchase order codes directly to your mobile phone, taking advantage of the digital messaging capabilities of the new PCS digital phones. In the event of a stock-out situation, you will know within minutes. When things are running smoothly, your phone remains silent.

What's new with these apps? For the first time we are seeing the integration of data capture, analysis, and delivery into comprehensive solutions (see Figure 4.10). This class of apps enables users to query and analyze the most detailed, transaction-level databases, turning data into business intelligence any time and distributing it anywhere through a broad range of pull-and-push technologies such as e-mail, telephones, pagers, and other wireless communications devices.

Integrating Application Clusters into an e-Business Architecture

Effectively managing the transformation to a process-centered organization will be critical to the success of the twenty-first-century organization. Every aspect of the modern organization is being transformed by integration of disparate processes. First applied to manufacturing and order fulfillment, the cutting edge of process integration is now found in sales, employee self-service, and customer service. An integrated process view infuses support areas, such as finance and human resources, with a strong customer orientation.

Fundamentally, enterprise business apps are process systems. The popularity of apps that automate, integrate, or transform a major portion of a firm's

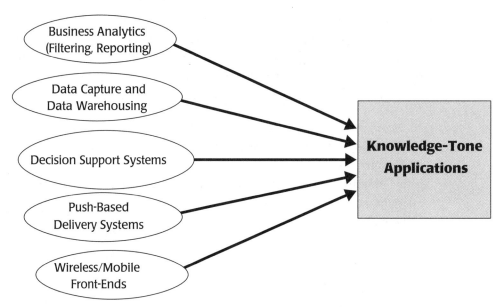

Figure 4.10: The Trend toward Integrated Knowledge Management

processes is a new phenomenon in the world of information management. In the past few years, application vendors introduced cross-functional apps such as enterprise resource planning, customer relationship management, and supply chain management that feature integrated process functionality. Tight integration, the smooth information exchange between functions, is a factor for which firms adopt integrated application clusters. Cross-functional apps provide new ways to compete, and their broad functionality makes it easy for firms to focus on the automation of areas in which they can achieve a distinct advantage.

No one vendor, however, can respond to every organization's needs; hence, customers purchase multiple apps from multiple vendors. As a result, large companies usually have multiple applications that are not designed to work together, and find themselves having to integrate business solutions. This situation sets the stage for understanding how disparate functional clusters can be integrated into an e-business architecture.

e-Business designs must be based on an organization's process capabilities, which in turn are embedded in the apps. Only by focusing on end-to-end processes and business apps can organizations achieve the levels of performance that the global economy demands. A clear roadmap of the various cross-functional apps and how they integrate to form the backbone of the enterprise

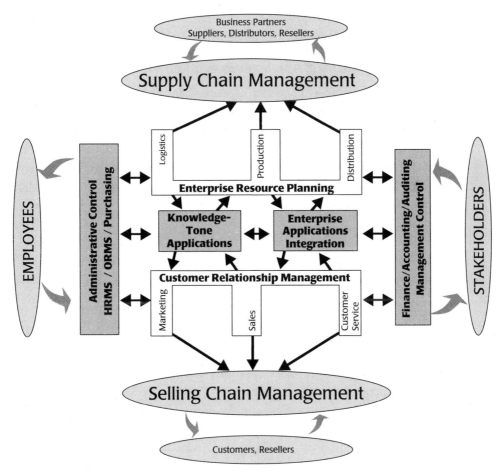

Figure 4.11: e-Business Application Architecture

becomes essential. Without such a roadmap, managers cannot have a clear idea of what steps to take and decisions to make.

Figure 4.11 shows how all the various application clusters are integrated to form the future model of the twenty-first-century organization. This blueprint is useful because it assists managers in identifying near-term and long-term integration opportunities, based on predefined strategies. Most of all, it helps managers grasp the big picture, so they can set priorities.

Figure 4.11 also illustrates the underlying premise of e-business design: Companies run on interdependent application clusters. If one application cluster of the company does not function well, the entire customer value delivery system is affected. The world-class enterprise of tomorrow is built on the foundation of world-class application clusters implemented today.

Integrating e-Business Applications Is a Journey, Not a Destination

The complete enterprise, including customers and suppliers, cannot be integrated in one fell swoop. A staged approach is often useful in aligning software with business requirements. Consider the case of Wal-Mart, the $93 billion consumer goods retailer. Legendary founder Sam Walton maintained a view of business that has long been one of end-to-end integration, from store systems to merchandising systems to distribution systems. Like many companies, Wal-Mart started down the road to total integration by first linking its internal systems. Then the focus shifted toward an emphasis on integrating Wal-Mart's systems with those of its suppliers. More recently, Wal-Mart has initiated efforts to bring processes and systems from the customer side of its business into the loop.[5] What's left is a customer-to-supplier architecture that allows Wal-Mart to follow its customers' shopping habits so closely as to know their likes and dislikes and to parlay that information into pinpoint promotions.

The Wal-Mart example illustrates that creating the e-business application architecture is a continuous process of integration, encompassing the enterprise's entire operating base—apps, information, communications, and infrastructure—to support the business. To achieve this goal, Wal-Mart managers took a very high-level view of the overall apps landscape: stepping back, looking at the entire system as a whole, then considering how integration should be initiated to support their strategic goals.

Unfortunately, cases like Wal-Mart are rare. Integration in established companies is often easier said than done due to infighting, turf issues, and lack of strong leadership. A high level of mergers and acquisitions within large organizations further exacerbates the problem. Also, large-scale integration of customer-facing apps, supplier-facing apps, and internal apps requires business transformation and reengineering of legacy apps.

Clearly, creating an integrated application architecture like the one in Figure 4.11 is a top-management issue. Unfortunately, senior management in many companies is not paying attention to the critical issue that seems to be just over the horizon. While management is currently overwhelmed with such issues as mergers and acquisitions, or is busy implementing solutions for isolated apps, the challenge of creating an integrated infrastructure or initiating major mission-critical application development efforts around the e-business paradigm falls through the cracks.

Aligning the e-Business Design with Application Integration

Companies are expecting e-business to increase profitability, create competitive differentiation, and support innovative business practices. To achieve these goals, companies must evolve through distinct stages, from integrated processes to truly synchronized interenterprise communities, managing with each step the changes required to sustain a competitive advantage through each phase of development.

The first question to ask is, Who is responsible for creating an e-business architecture? The e-business architect is the central figure in this new kind of organization, charged with end-to-end responsibility and authority for cross-functional processes. Yet, those appointed to this vital position often lack both a real understanding of what it entails and the skills needed to discharge it. Creating an enterprisewide e-business architecture is not trivial. It takes patience and the ability to guide evolution through multiple stages of development.

Figure 4.12 charts five general stages in developing e-business architecture, ranging from cross-functional process integration to multicompany integration. *Where is your organization in terms of these stages? What kinds of management systems does each stage require?*

At each one of these stages, it is very important to align the scope of e-business design with the nature of application integration. If the scope of the

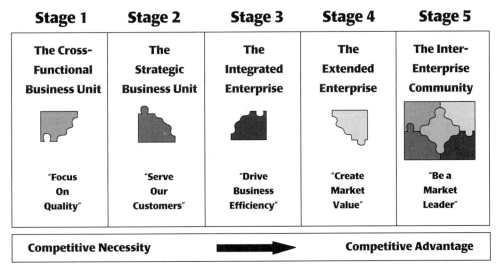

Figure 4.12: Roadmap to an e-Business Architecture

e-business design is restricted to a single strategic business unit, it makes no sense to create a grandiose integration plan that goes across 20 other business units. Often, companies create visionary designs that don't get implemented because there's misalignment between the scope of the design and the magnitude of the application integration problem. In other words, application integration must be closely aligned with the e-business design strategy.

Why is alignment of the organization with integrated apps important? Companies must be smart enough to understand that success doesn't come simply from choosing the right apps, Web-enabling the right process, or forging the right links to legacy systems. **It requires fundamental changes in organizations, corporate behavior, and business thinking—inside and outside corporate boundaries. Technology is often the easy part. Changing organizations to align with the technology is more difficult.**

Let's examine the five stages of e-business design.

 Stage 1: The Cross-Functional Business Unit. The driving goal of the organization in this stage is to produce dependable, consistent, quality products and services at the lowest possible cost. In order to accomplish this goal, companies in stage 1 typically focus on automating existing functions and tasks. Most companies are striving to reach this level. The majority of the cross-functional examples found in this chapter (e.g., Whirlpool, CIBC) depict stage 1 companies.

 Stage 2: The Strategic Business Unit. Companies moving toward stage 2 concentrate on serving the customer end to end, for example, in order acquisition and fulfillment. Companies in this stage are beginning to consolidate their supply chains in some areas, such as combining distribution and transportation into logistics, and manufacturing and purchasing into operations, with the ultimate goal of better meeting customer demand. In the past decade, strategic business units (SBUs) have increasingly taken the role of application strategy formulation away from corporate headquarters. The shift makes sense: SBUs are closer to customers, competitors, and costs. American Express is an example of a stage 2 company. However, in a high-velocity environment rife with mergers and acquisitions, SBUs can fail to create organizational agility by losing their focus on the organization's priorities and capabilities.

 Stage 3: The Integrated Enterprise. Companies in stage 3 focus mostly on cost reduction and internal efficiency. The driving goal is to be highly customer responsive, leveraging the ability to quickly deliver high-quality products and services at the lowest total delivered cost. Stage 3 companies become highly responsive by in-

vesting in operational flexibility as well as integrating their internal supply chains, from the acquisition of raw materials to the delivery of product to the customer. Companies implement a strategy of decreasing costs by achieving "preferred partner" status with key suppliers. Chapter 3's example of Dell Computer depicts an integrated enterprise.

 Stage 4: The Extended Enterprise. As companies move into stage 4, creating market value becomes important. *Extended enterprise* describes a multienterprise supply chain with a shared information infrastructure. The extended enterprise enables supply chain integration, more effective outsourcing, and self-service solutions for both internal and external users. The extended enterprise allows for sophisticated online business processes that interweave line-of-business apps with other internal and external information or sources. The goal is profitable growth, which such companies accomplish by providing customer-tailored products, services, and value-added information. This differentiates them from competitors. McKesson, a health-care distributor, is an example of a stage 4 company.

 Stage 5: The Inter-Enterprise Community. This stage focuses on market leadership. Companies consolidate into true interenterprise communities whose members share common goals and objectives across and among enterprises, using forward-looking technologies such as the Internet.[6] Stage 5 companies are able to streamline their business transactions with their partners to maximize growth and profit. Microsoft Expedia and E*TRADE are examples of stage 5 companies.

Memo to the CEO

Let's be realistic and not fool ourselves about the difficulty of the task that lies ahead. To succeed in the digital economy means we must design our business soundly for the long term to take on competitive challenges, bring in new customers, and keep old customers happy, while maintaining a smooth operation. This is a feat similar to changing tires on a car while it's going 60 mph.

Success depends on a flexible and forward-thinking business architecture. Organizations, however, have to eliminate a number of barriers before they are ready to use e-business for competitive advantage. One barrier is that old ways of doing business powered by legacy applications seem to live on forever within companies, leaving not so much an efficient business architecture as a graveyard of computing. The problems posed by legacy infrastructure are clearly illustrated by the year 2000 problem.

The accelerating rate of change in business cycles and the difficulty in maintaining an equivalent rate of innovation within an enterprise's application architecture are causing many organizations to lose their edge and suffer dire consequences, such as missed opportunities, inflexible processes, and poor customer satisfaction. Unfortunately, engineering change in enterprise apps is very difficult. It is estimated that a high percentage of change efforts fail. A proportion of this failure occurs because, although the business environment has changed radically in the last ten years, the approach of big firms has changed little.

To create value via e-business design, managers need to address serious architectural questions:

- How do you structure your company on an e-business apps architecture to assimilate ever-increasing rates of business change?

- How do you structure a robust application architecture that can not only survive but thrive in a business environment characterized by rapid technological change, frequent introduction of new products, changes in customer demands, and evolving industry standards and practices?

The e-business architecture must be very well thought out in order to survive an introduction of products embodying new technologies and functionality that can and will render existing business apps obsolete. As a result, any organization's future success will depend, in part, on its ability to continually enhance its existing apps and develop and introduce new apps that keep pace with technological developments, satisfy customer requirements, and achieve operational objectives.

e-Business integration is a far cry from the data-processing days. Forty years ago, data processing was wrestling with relatively simple challenges; for example, how best to relieve the tedium of daily tasks such as typing checks. Today, the cutting edge for line-of-business apps lies in integrating and leveraging an enterprise's relationships across the entire business chain.

Only with relentlessly integrated systems does a firm stand a chance of keeping up. The acceptance of packaged software, however, leads many managers to wonder how they can differentiate their businesses if everybody is running the same systems. How can they achieve differentiation from their huge financial investments in software? We will address that question in the next section of the book.

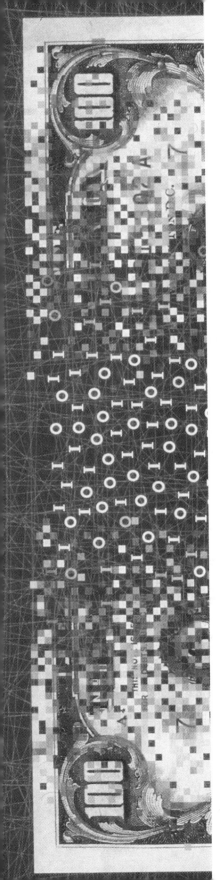

CHAPTER FIVE

Customer Relationship Management: Integrating Processes to Build Relationships

What to Expect

Most companies consider themselves customer focused, but in reality, they're product-centric. Meanwhile, e-commerce has increased customer expectations, and customer expectations have raised the bar on service levels. If companies fail to leap over it, they're out of the game.

In this chapter, we'll take the often-vague notion of customer focus and put it in a concrete application framework. We'll dissect customer relationship management and show you how to add it to your arsenal. We present the tools you'll need to build an excellent customer relationship infrastructure.

Some facts[1] to chew on before we get started:

- It costs six times more to sell to a new customer than to sell to an existing one.

- A typical dissatisfied customer will tell eight to ten people about his or her experience.

- A company can boost its profits 85 percent by increasing its annual customer retention by only 5 percent.

- The odds of selling a product to a new customer are 15 percent, whereas the odds of selling a product to an existing customer are 50 percent.

- Seventy percent of complaining customers will do business with the company again if it quickly takes care of a service snafu.

- More than 90 percent of existing companies don't have the necessary sales and service integration to support e-commerce.

Why Customer Relationship Management?

Customers don't care how a company stores information, or that data from different sources must be combined to give them what they want. They don't even care if they've called the wrong location. All customers know is that they want excellent service and they want it now. Out of this comes customer relationship management (CRM).

Is CRM critical to the survival of companies? Industry leaders think so. Increased competition, globalization, the growing cost of customer acquisition, and high customer turnover are major issues in such disparate industries as financial services, telecommunications, and retail. CRM is a combination of business process and technology that seeks to understand a company's customers from a multifaceted perspective: Who are they, what do they do, and what do they like?

Research shows that effective management of customer relationships is a source of competitive differentiation. Key findings, such as those listed at the start of the chapter, are driving an enormous investment in CRM. In fact, we believe that CRM will remain one of the highest growth software markets well into the next century, growing into a multibillion-dollar opportunity. This trend is driven by corporations' focus on improving customer satisfaction and loyalty, as well as increasing revenue from existing customers.

It's been repeated so often it's nearly a cliché, but in the contemporary world of sophisticated customers and intensifying competition, the only way for an organization to succeed is to focus diligently on the needs of the customer. To keep the best customers, management must concentrate its energies on quickly and efficiently creating new delivery channels, capturing massive amounts of customer data, and tying it all together to create an unique experience. Customer incentives such as frequent flyer loyalty programs and buy-*x*-amount-and-get-one-free punch cards don't go far enough any more. Only by creating an infrastructure that integrates sales and service with all aspects of operations can management expect to see a change in customer relationships. Yet few companies have succeeded in making customer focus a reality because prior business models didn't require it, technology wasn't accessible, and organizational resistance remains quite high.

The goal of this chapter is to take the nebulous concept of customer focus and put it in a sound application framework. In the process, we show how marketing practices and systems have to be reworked to support the e-commerce environment.

Defining Customer Relationship Management

Anyone can keep one ball in the air; some can even juggle two or three. But what customer relationship management requires is that the whole company work together to keep the flaming sticks, bowling pins, and razor-sharp knives of customer demands in the air. CRM is defined as an integrated sales, marketing, and service strategy that precludes lone showmanship and depends on coordinated actions. The goals of this business framework are as follows:

- **Use existing relationships to grow revenue.** Composite a comprehensive view of the customer to maximize his or her relationship with the company through up-selling and cross-selling. Enhance profitability by identifying, attracting, and retaining the best customers.

- **Use integrated information for excellent service.** Use customer information to better serve his or her needs. It's about saving time and easing frustration for customers. For instance, they shouldn't have to repeat information to various departments over and over again. Customers should be surprised by how well you know them.

- **Introduce more repeatable sales processes and procedures.** With the proliferation of customer contact channels, many more employees are involved in sales. In order to enjoy continued success, companies must improve consistency in account management and selling.

- **Create new value and instill loyalty.** It can be your point of difference, your competitive advantage, to become a company known to prospects and customers for the ability to respond to needs and accommodate requests, a company well deserving of their patronage, a company to which they will become loyal.

- **Implement a more proactive solution strategy.** Use a customer-focused business solution that works across the entire enterprise. Instead of just gathering data and eventually using it, eliminate issues before they reach the crisis stage. Move from reactive data collection to proactive consumer relations that resolve problems on the first call.

Becoming customer focused doesn't necessarily mean improving customer service. It means having consistent, dependable, and convenient interaction with customers in every encounter. As you can see, CRM is an integration framework or a business strategy, not a product. Putting the CRM business strategy into practice requires developing a set of integrated applications that address all aspects of front-office needs, such as the need to automate customer service, field service, sales, and marketing. To succeed, companies are looking to application software vendors to support integration across the range of business functions.

By investing in CRM applications, companies are hoping to build better customer retention programs that will maximize the lifetime revenue. In many industries, customer retention is a driver of profitability. **Even a five percent increase in customer retention can increase profits by as much as 85 percent!** It's no wonder that business strategies that can help companies achieve a close relationship with their customers—while containing costs—have taken center stage in most industries.

In addition, new technologies are increasing demands on customer service. As customers assimilate technology, their expectations are changing about service, support, and how they make purchases. Enterprises that don't use application software to tie their customers on the outside with their line-of-business systems on the inside will be at a competitive disadvantage.

CRM applications are also gaining a foothold in small and mid-sized companies. Technology enables these organizations to enjoy the customer relationship capabilities that until a couple of years ago only the largest enterprises with deep pockets could afford. Integrated applications that provide complete views of customer information to such areas as sales, marketing, customer service, and accounting are now within reach of organizations with fewer than 100 employees.

As a result, CRM will drive the next major wave of investment in information technology. Estimated to have been $153 billion in 1998, CRM spending will continue to grow by 25 to 30 percent over the next five years. Now that we have established the importance of CRM, let's turn our attention to the different phases of a CRM solution.

Managing the Customer Life Cycle: The Three Phases of CRM

In personal relationships, the level of understanding and intimacy grows over time, as long as both parties are committed to making the relationship work. The same is true in the world of business. Learn this quickly, because competition is increasing so fast that consumers are rapidly finding out that they have a wide selection of dance partners from which to choose.

There are three phases of CRM: acquisition, enhancement, and retention. Each has a different impact on the customer relationship (see Figure 5.1) and each can more closely tie your company to your customer's life and dance card.

1. **Acquiring new customers.** You acquire new customers by promoting product/service leadership that pushes performance boundaries with respect to convenience and innovation. The value proposition to the customer is the offer of a superior product backed by excellent service.

2. **Enhancing the profitability of existing customers.** You enhance the relationship by encouraging excellence in cross-selling and up-selling. This deepens the relationship. The value proposition to the customer is an offer of greater convenience at low cost (one-stop shopping).

3. **Retaining profitable customers for life.** Retention focuses on service adaptability—delivering not what the market wants, but what customers want. The value proposition to the customer is an offer of a proactive relationship that works in his or her best interest. Today, leading companies focus on retention much more than on attracting new customers. The reasoning behind this strategy is simple: If you want to make money, hold onto your good customers. But don't be fooled; it's not as easy as it seems.

All the phases of CRM are interrelated. However, doing all three phases well is a difficult proposition, even for the best of companies. Companies often have to choose which one of these dimensions will be their primary focus. Keep in mind that choosing one dimension to master does not mean abandoning the

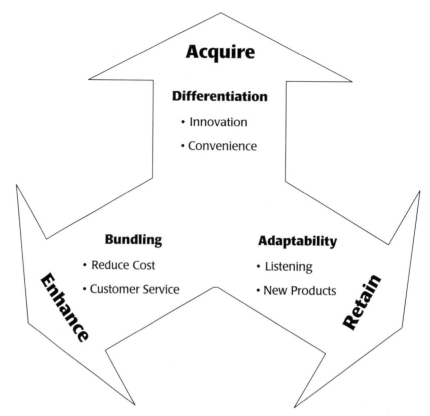

Figure 5.1: The Three Phases of CRM

other two. It simply means the company is selecting a dimension of value on which to stake its market reputation. Ask yourself which dimension your company has chosen to master.

This choice is important because it dictates the technology infrastructure strategy. Not choosing means trouble. It means hybrid processes with diverse technological requirements that are neither here nor there and consequently cause confusion, tension, and loss of focus. It means steering a ship in several conflicting directions. Let's look at each phase and examine the implications closely.

Acquiring New Relationships

Beginning a new business relationship is much like going on a first date. There is insecurity, hesitation, some fear, and anticipation. It takes a determined suitor to overcome these obstacles. Similarly, acquiring new customers demands a great deal of planning, and in the new e-business world, this translates into an integrated experience. Imagine that you're surfing the Web looking for a new laptop computer. You land on the IBM site. Interesting stuff, you say! The IBM ThinkPad looks like just what you need. So you go to the product information page, fill out the online request form, press the Enter key, and submit it. Then you hang around the Web site to read some more. All of a sudden, your phone rings. "Hello, this is Patti from IBM. I just received your request for information about our products." She asks you about your requirements, walks you through an online demo of the product, and before you know it, you're on your way to acquiring the system you need.

Such instantaneous response is not magic, though it feels like it. It's the result of an intricate and finely tuned sales-and-service integration strategy. Potential customers or prospects are very impressed when companies call them while they're still browsing their Web site. Preliminary research shows that the probability of sales goes up when prospects receive a response to their request within one to three minutes. The goal is to ease those first-date jitters and create a smooth transition from prospect to customer.

Enhancing Existing Relationships

In an established personal relationship, what happens when something goes awry? Most people do not run away, at least not until they have discussed the issue. A healthy couple takes time to listen and work through the problem. The result is a richer relationship. Companies prove their commitment on a daily basis by taking time to hear customers' concerns and by developing a service focus.

Consider the case of Best Buy, a specialty electronics retailer with more than 300 stores in 32 states. On average, the Best Buy Consumer Relations Call Center receives about 3,000 calls a day, the average length of which is 15 minutes. More than 50 percent of the calls are computer-related inquiries. These calls cover a wide variety of topics, as well as specific questions about products. Customers request assistance for many reasons, including whether a computer repair issue is a hardware or software problem, challenging the return policy, taking advantage of manufacturer rebates, and checking on coupons, gift certificates, or delivery schedules.

The call center's primary concern is customer satisfaction through effective resolution of issues and concerns. As competition increases, companies such as Best Buy realize that CRM-capable call-center applications are a necessity for attaining and maintaining relationships. For instance, when a customer calls about a product, the agent can automatically suggest a complementary item (cross-selling). For example, a buyer who has selected a camera can be offered a tripod. Or an agent can suggest a similar product of better quality (up-selling). By accessing and using customer information more effectively, Best Buy can offer superior service, which provides competitive differentiation.

Retaining Customer Relationships

Of course, no one said relationships were easy. On the contrary, they take tons of work, but the rewards are usually worth the effort. So, just as personal commitments need patience and understanding, so do business relationships. Retaining customers requires a complete understanding of the needs of the customer and a determination to stay in the relationship.

State Farm has chosen to make retaining customers its primary objective. State Farm is very selective in choosing its new customers. If you have had an accident in the last five years, you cannot be a State Farm customer, because the company has decided that's not the kind of customer they want. The company tries to identify and recruit the "best" customers, with whom they seek lifetime relationships through a complete life-cycle product line.

Several of State Farm's practices are indicative of the importance they place on customer retention. The company's pricing policy rewards continuing customers. For example, those policyholders who have been with the company for two or more years receive breaks on their rates. In addition, rather than monetarily rewarding agents for attracting new customers, as most insurance companies do, State Farm gives higher commissions to those agents who retain existing customers. The company measures retention and defection rates and distributes the results throughout the company. Through this creation of a competitive, financial incentive, agents are encouraged to work harder to keep customers happy. State Farm also involves agents in decisions affecting them and their customers. These practices create a base for State Farm's "close to the customer" business objective.

As this example shows, the business of growing a company can be framed as a matter of getting customers and keeping them. While customer retention is increasingly the focus of companies that operate in a competitive environments, it will likely become an obsession for all companies as customer choice increases and switching costs become lower.

Organizing around the Customer: The New CRM Architecture

Take a moment to answer the following questions about your company:

- Are most of the company's applications designed simply to automate existing departmental processes?

- Are these applications capable of identifying and targeting the best customers, those who are the most profitable for the organization?

- Are these applications capable of real-time customization/personalization of products and services based on detailed knowledge of customers' wants, needs, and buying habits?

- Do these applications keep track of when the customer contacts the company, regardless of the contact point?

- Are these applications capable of a consistent user experience across all the contact points the customer chooses?

If the answers to these questions are no, then you should seriously consider a new CRM architecture in the near future. The timing couldn't be better. Corporate demand is on the rise for integrated applications that are built around customer life cycles and customer interactions. Rising to meet this demand is a smart new generation of CRM architecture that seamlessly integrates emerging customer-serving processes (see Figure 5.2).

What's New about CRM Architecture?

What's new is the customer-centered nature of applications, which means organizing CRM processes around the customer, rather than marketing, sales, or any other internal function. Measurements and feedback from the customer drive improvements in the CRM process. The customer's viewpoint becomes an integral part of the process, allowing it to change with the customer's needs. In other

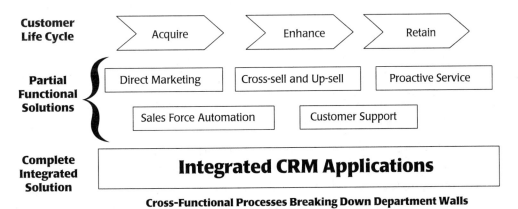

Figure 5.2: Integrated CRM

words, companies base their actions not on the priorities of functional fiefdoms, but on the overall corporate objective of providing customer satisfaction.

However, before aggressively deploying CRM applications, managers might have to restructure customer-interaction processes. Functional and organizational structures tend to compartmentalize the various activities that go into serving the customer. Such fragmentation prevents customer information from being dispersed far enough within the organization to be useful; in fact, it often stands in the way of efforts to build a relationship. As a result, customized service is difficult and, consequently, organizations tend to treat all customers the same—a damning impediment to building closer relationships.

To counter fragmentation, leading-edge companies strive to take a more customer-centered approach to CRM. There's a growing trend toward managing all the activities that identify, attract, and retain customers in an integrated fashion, that is, managing them as a process that cuts across functional departments. By addressing these activities as a set of CRM processes, organizations can create end-to-end communications and performance accountability for entire sets of activities. In short, a CRM infrastructure is really a portfolio of process competencies.

Portfolio of CRM Process Competencies

The core CRM process competencies are cross-selling and up-selling, direct marketing and fulfillment, customer service and support, store front and field service, and retention management (see Figure 5.3).

Identifying these process competencies is important because you must understand that a company cannot manage and develop its CRM infrastructure if its managers don't share the same view of what the core CRM competencies are, realize that these competencies form the soul of CRM and are distinctly different from the underlying technical infrastructure, and be able to identify what core competencies are missing in order for your company to develop goals. As you read through these core competencies, ask yourself which ones apply to your company.

Cross-selling and Up-selling

Consider the following scenario. Gail Brown is on the phone with her claims agent discussing an auto insurance claim she has made. While they are talking, the agent accesses a synopsis of Gail's insurance information. The agent notices that Gail has no life insurance policy. The agent takes the opportunity to ask Gail

Figure 5.3. Core CRM Process Competencies

if she has ever considered buying life insurance. What started as a service situation has now become a sales opportunity.

Cross-sell and up-sell software typically include the capability to qualify prospects, track contacts, and refer them to salespersons when appropriate. Event-driven marketing is one aspect of cross-selling that companies are beginning to recognize as a strategic advantage for their marketing departments. By implementing a cross-sell strategy, complete with the applications necessary to track customer contacts, triggers can be established to identify prospects for additional sales. For example, in a bank an event would be a large deposit, which would then trigger a salesperson to call the customer and ask if he or she would be interested in investment options.

Cross-sell and up-sell software may be used to schedule sales calls, keep detailed records about sales activities, and check on the status of customer orders. This software may also be integrated with inventory software (to see what products are in stock) or field service/external customer support (to learn how the product is working for the customer).

Cross-selling and up-selling depend on identifying life-path needs. For instance, in the finance industry, banks are attempting to build lasting relationships with customers by matching their life-path needs to complementary products and services. As customers approach retirement, banks could recommend assets such as money markets, bonds, and annuities. If customers with young children could be identified, then banks could cross-sell education savings plans or even loan consolidation plans. The bottom line is, to prosper in this day and age, companies must sell complementary products and services to deepen their relationships with their customers.

Direct Marketing and Fulfillment

Direct marketing and fulfillment is like a one-two punch—sell well and deliver fast. This includes presale interaction such as direct marketing and other advertising techniques that either influence or provide potential customers with the necessary information to make a purchase decision.

Marketing automation is critical as organizations grow larger. Why? It becomes more difficult to manage multiple, simultaneous programs and track costs across multiple channels. Campaign management, a direct marketing process, allows companies to manage, integrate, and leverage marketing programs by automating such tasks as managing responses, qualifying leads, and arranging logistical aspects of events.

Another critical core competency is fulfillment. Marketing departments today are being deluged with requests for information via the Web and other channels. The goal of effective fulfillment is to provide a myriad of information to customers and prospects quickly, easily, and efficiently. Whether it's product or service inquiries, direct mail responses, pricing or billing issues, or requests for literature, responding to requests in a timely manner is critical. This creates a need for fulfillment capabilities that can get product information, literature, collateral packages, or other correspondence into the hands of customers and prospects at a time when they are most receptive. Effective fulfillment is not trivial; it requires a sophisticated interface with campaign management, sales force automation, and posting systems.

Customer Service and Support

Customer support provides customer care and other services. The applications include support for service request management, account management, contact and activity management, customer surveys, return material authorizations, and detailed service agreements. These discrete applications work together to ensure that customer service representatives can quickly assign, create, and manage service requests, as well as look up detailed information about customer service contracts, contacts, and activities.

Customer support capabilities are used to manage customers who are having problems with a product or service and to resolve those problems. Help-desk software automates the management and resolution of support calls and improves efficiency and effectiveness. These applications typically include capabilities to verify customer status (e.g., what level of support they are entitled to), open trouble tickets, track specific tasks needed to resolve problems across multiple workgroups, monitor service-level agreements, maintain permanent incident histories, and capture support costs for charge backs. Armed with this complete customer and product information, service professionals can resolve customer issues efficiently and effectively.

Field Service Operations

There is nothing like the hands-on approach to instill faith in your customers about your company. Field service is the hands-on extension of external customer support, activated when a problem cannot be solved over the phone and requires sending a repair person to the customer site to perform maintenance or repair equipment. Field service and dispatch applications have become mission-critical tools that affect a company's ability to deliver effective customer service and contain costs.

Field service software provides service organizations with features for scheduling and dispatching repair personnel, managing inventory and logistics, and handling contracts and accounting. More and more, the field service function plays a role in increasing revenues.

Retention Management

Your resources are valuable: Spend them wisely on the customers who count. Effective CRM must be based on differentiating customers based on account and transaction histories. Today, very few organizations are able to make these distinctions. The ability to effectively segment customers depends on *decision support technology,* which most executives see as a powerful enabler of CRM.

Effective decision support depends on the ability to gather customer information at great levels of detail. Detailed knowledge about customers allows companies to treat all customers individually and, in many cases, disengage from or "fire" customers who are high-maintenance, low-margin prospects.

Now that we have identified the core CRM competencies, let's explore the integration requirements in the next generation of CRM infrastructure.

Supporting Requirements of the Next-Generation CRM Infrastructure

The hot topic, the buzzword, the sweeping universal trend that we'll ride into the next century is integration, integration, integration. Next-generation CRM infrastructure is no exception. It requires five types of integration to be effective:

- Customer content

- Customer contact information

- End-to-end business processes

- The extended enterprise or partners

- Front-office and back-office systems

Integration of Customer Content

The ability to access, manage, and process all relevant customer content, including the seamless integration of structured and unstructured customer data, has emerged as a key requirement for CRM applications today. For example, customer service agents and loan officers need access to a variety of structured data, such as customer and product information, and unstructured data, including faxes, digitized voice messages, images of applications, and credit reports.

Without a holistic view of the customer and the ability to understand his or her desires, service will continue to be mediocre at best. In the past, companies realized how important customer data was and vigorously started collecting information. The problem was that once they had mounds of data, they didn't know what to do with it. With the push for CRM, companies are beginning to recognize how to integrate this critical data. To create a clear picture of your customers and your relationships with them, all content about them must be easily accessible. This integrated picture of the customer allows for numerous service and sales opportunities, as well as level-of-service distinctions for your best customers.

Integration of Customer Contact Information

Don't force your customers to play "hot potato" every time they call. Contact management (CM) is defined as the electronic capture of customer information with the capability to access and share information throughout the organization for sales and service purposes. Managers must pay close attention to the firm's contact management capabilities because in recent years the number of opportunities for customer interaction has become enormous. Today, customer inquiries and transactions can come from the call center, the Internet, or many other channels. Capturing and sharing these interactions within an organization should be top priority.

Effective CM is the linchpin of a company's goal of zero leakage of customer information. Providing consistency in CM across all channels is all but impossible unless data from previous interactions is stored and is accessible by all customer contact personnel. Effective CM requires current information about the customer relationship, regardless of when, where, or why that customer contacted the organization. Consistent business rules must be applied to every customer contact, no matter what channel the customer uses to make contact —the Web, a call center, or a store front. This is called the *channel-independent solution*.

A well-designed CM infrastructure allows a company to create a virtual contact center that centralizes information and makes it available 24 hours a day, seven days a week across all service delivery channels. It should be noted that CM information has a dual temporal aspect. CM information can be accessed in the "here and now" to provide service during interaction with a customer, and it can also be accessed offline, extracted to a decision support system for further analysis, and used for sales opportunities.

Integration of End-to-End Business Processes

Restructure to be solution-oriented, not problem-oriented. As the business environment becomes focused on anticipating and addressing customer needs—companies must have cross-functional process integration. For example, sales and service are often viewed as separate functions. Sales occur during the sales cycle, and service is an after-sale activity. Customers often get different answers depending on whether they talk to sales or service representatives. This is no longer tenable.

The keys are consistency and simplicity. Today, prospects and customers want to access companies from a variety of places in order to obtain fast, accurate, consistent information. They want service, both before and after the sale—not traditional service, in which they're sold a product and then handed off to a service group. Today, service must start before the sale and be inherent in every interaction a customer has with the company. Imagine the following scenario. Bill Robinson, a long-time customer of Eastwest Mortgage, realizes that the 30-year fixed mortgage rates have fallen so low that it would be to his advantage to refinance immediately. Bill remembers having received a letter about submitting a refinancing application via the Internet or phone. For Bill, a self-service access channel like the Internet is the easiest choice.

Bill logs on to his mortgage company's home page. He is prompted to enter his name and policy number. The details of the policy, monthly payments, and balance due are displayed on his computer screen, seamlessly collected from several customer information databases. He fills out a form with specifics of the loan he wants. The only information the mortgage company needs is his name, e-mail address, summary of asset and liability information, current housing expenses, the money he has for closing, the price range of the property being refinanced, and how large a down payment he expects to pay.

Since Bill is on a tight schedule, he chooses a feature that says "Please call me" and selects 7:00 P.M. At 7:00 sharp, Bill receives a call from a mortgage broker, who tells him that his loan request has been processed and he qualifies for the full amount requested. The broker offers to take the paperwork to Bill's house so the transaction can be completed. Bill is delighted with this service.

As this scenario illustrates, the Web offers an unprecedented opportunity for organizations to achieve an end-to-end, integrated sales-and-service environment. Increasingly, we see the Web being transformed from a marketing channel to an interactive customer-care-and-fulfillment center that can handle multiple channels of communication, including faxes, e-mail, video, Internet calls, and, of course, traditional telephone contact. This shift places a premium on highly integrated customer self-service interactions.

Integration of the Extended Enterprise: Interenterprise Customer Care

Deploying a tightly integrated front-office solution throughout a company isn't enough. Sharing customer information with partners or third-party service organizations is absolutely critical as companies come to depend on outside alliances. Consider partners and vendors part of your company's extended enterprise. This will enable your company to share leads or customer support issues with everyone who comes in contact with the customer, regardless of whether they work for the company or not. Businesses are thus beginning to look for next-generation CRM applications that have interenterprise integration capabilities.

To provide the kind of service that guarantees customer loyalty, companies must extend to their partners and vendors a CRM infrastructure via the Internet and intranets. Through this infrastructure, partners can share information, communicate, and collaborate with the enterprise using Web-based applications, regardless of their internal network platform and without the complexity and cost issues typically associated with current applications.

Integration of Systems

The demand for complete relationship management is driving the need to integrate telephony, Web, and database technologies to provide a 360-degree view of customer attributes and account history. This integration means a company can combine information on all products and services used by a customer and share that information across all delivery channels and points of contact.

Execution of this strategy requires four enabling technologies that must work together to provide some punch to the CRM infrastructure. These technologies are as follows:

- **Legacy systems.** Many organizations still have 20-year-old systems that cannot be thrown away and must be integrated into the CRM infrastructure. The tools needed for the job are middleware and messaging tools, which increase the efficiency of extracting data from these systems.

- **Computer telephony integration (CTI).** CTI allows companies to apply consistent business logic in managing incoming calls. Real-time information about a caller is captured and linked with customer information from a company's disparate data repositories. This information is used to determine the resources needed to address the caller's requirements.

- **Data warehousing.** Data warehouses extract data from transaction systems and aggregate information so it can be effectively analyzed. When executing a CRM strategy, tremendous volumes of data need to be massaged, but this massaging isn't the repetitive and mechanical processing that traditional transaction systems use. In a real-time setting, knowledge of customer is a powerful weapon.

- **Decision support technology.** These technologies incorporate sophisticated analytical and modeling tools to determine appropriate customer decisions based on accumulated relationship data. These systems will enable companies to retain their best customers.

The explosion of alternate delivery channels primarily drives the need for integration. As companies accelerate their investment in alternative delivery channels, the integration problem is becoming more difficult. Clearly, the next generation of front-office applications needs to be quite powerful. Don't underestimate the difficulty of implementing CRM infrastructure and channel applications. The gauntlet has been thrown down.

Organizational Challenges in Implementing CRM

Nothing is ever simple. This is an unfortunate truth, especially when change is in the air. And change is churning the air with hurricane force these days, threatening to blow away those comfortable with the status quo. For the storm chasers of the e-business world, however, CRM offers another exciting, progressive challenge.

Implementing CRM requires a high degree of political, cultural, and organizational change. Political resistance arises because CRM generally cuts across autonomous business or functional units that are not typically required to cooperate with each other. However, under a CRM program, data that originates in one unit is used in another. Corporations may temporize by allowing individual business units to set their own strategies, which may result in the handling of customers differently across lines of business. CRM can handle these situations, but it can't overcome cultural resistance, which arises when individual business units lose the power to make decisions.

Organizational resistance to CRM is unfortunate, but almost inevitable. The organizational issues that companies must tackle to implement CRM include the following:

- CRM may reduce an individual business unit's contribution, even though the whole company benefits. Current incentive systems work against CRM because they reward only part of the customer's relationship with the company. Therefore, a sales manager who is evaluated on individual product sales has no vested interest in ensuring that the service organization is meeting the needs of the customer. Most companies today lack financial incentive programs that promote CRM.

- CRM requires making a careful transition from an existing "silo-centric" infrastructure to an integrated customer-centric infrastructure. Over the years, however, large enterprises have built, bought, or inherited a wide variety of customer management applications. Some of this software is proprietary and will be difficult to share across departments.

- Organizations with global operations must manage customer interactions in different languages, time zones, currencies, and regulatory environments. In this environment, providing consistent, customized service is difficult to accomplish using traditional technology.

CRM has a definite impact on the shape of the organization and the roles of employees. This impact is especially evident on the corporation's front line, the critical point where the process and the customer make contact. All companies should recognize that the effectiveness of CRM processes depends on the close link between front-line activities and internal operations such as product development, strategic planning, and financial processes. The goal is to make it easy for the front line to relay customer requirements and issues to upstream portions of the process; in other words, to carry the voice of the customer deep into the organization and use it to guide processes.

Next-Generation CRM Trends

It's important to note that a CRM infrastructure alone isn't sufficient. The growth of the CRM market is also happening at customer contact points, such as call centers, and the Web. Management must pay close attention to the dynamics that occur in these places (see Figure 5.4). As CRM infrastructure becomes more widely accepted, we anticipate that customer needs and expectations are going to change subtly across various channels.

Clearly, management needs to reevaluate customer contact points. Begin by asking two questions: How will the emergence of Internet-delivered customer service affect traditional communication channels of support? Will online customer

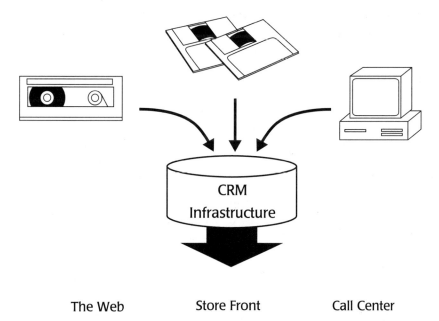

Figure 5.4: The Channel Interface to the CRM Infrastructure

service really be cheaper than traditional support channels? In this section, we will address some future customer trends we see emerging at customer contact points.

The Rise of the Call Center as a Powerful Customer Contact Point

The call center is one of the main growth areas of customer contact. Although there's a lot of hype surrounding Web channels, 70 percent of all customer contact occurs at the call center. The scale and complexity of call centers are growing at an unprecedented rate. For example, British Telecom operates 35 call centers across England, Scotland, Ireland, and Wales that serve 24 million customers, with 18,000 products and services.

A call center is a group of agents and voice response units (VRUs) that assist customers with support, inquiry and transaction functions. As the call center evolves into a sales-and-service channel, understanding the dynamics of this channel will help us prepare for the future. Why? Because the Web is also evolving into a self-service sales and service channel. While it's currently a tiny market, we expect the Web to be one of the fastest-growing portions of the CRM software market, leveraging the rapid growth of the Internet. However, the trick is identifying where the changes will take place and where growth will happen in the near future.

Service industries, including communications, banking/financial, insurance, and utility companies, recognize the importance of customer interaction via the call center in retaining and expanding their businesses. Service industries lack a connection with their customers because there is no tangible product to hold and use. That's why the connection via the phone—and soon the Internet—is so important.

For service companies, the call center's focus has evolved from a customer service interaction center to a selling channel. All questions must be answered correctly, eliminating lengthy hold times and annoying call transfers. An agent answers a call from a customer armed with sophisticated software that gives a detailed record of the products the customer uses and his or her spending habits. The agent also has a script to follow in selling additional products or services, which ensures companywide consistency. Managers need to think about how to transfer the high-touch capabilities of the call-center to the low-touch medium of the Web.

Listening to the Customer

The call center and Web channels must be transformed into listening outposts that keep track of what customers are talking about. However, be careful to listen to the right set of customers. Most organizations fail to maximize their sales potential because they make the mistake of asking the wrong customers for feedback on how to improve their performance. One company that made this mistake and paid heavily for it is the now-defunct Manhattan bookstore Shakespeare and Co. The bookstore was unperturbed when a larger bookstore chain opened shop across the street. Although it took some precautions by asking customers for feedback on how to improve their service, this feedback didn't help them prepare for competition. Those surveyed were loyal Shakespeare customers who were quite pleased with the bookstore; therefore, they failed to offer any suggestions for improvement. Because the firm limited its survey to existing customers, it didn't learn about the additional services offered by the competition. The experience of Shakespeare and Co. underscores the fact that feedback from competitors' customers also counts.[2] Ask yourself, *how does my company listen to its customers? What systems are in place for doing this effectively?*

Customer Loyalty: Luke-warm or Fanatical

In this changing and challenging environment, customers have more choices. Once-apathetic customers are becoming increasingly engaged, well-informed, and demanding. Customers are beginning to ask companies, "What have you done for me lately?" This may be the biggest challenge corporations face as they move forward in the call center and Web channels. Like it or not, the juggernaut of change driven by the Internet has made people smarter, more aware of the business landscape, and better able to find information about you and your competitors—what you sell, what you don't sell, and what people have to say about you. Take a moment to think about this. *How can your call center help you build customer loyalty? When your customers call you, do they get courteous service? Are they delighted when the call is over?* If you did not respond with a quick yes, you need to think about how loyal that customer will be to your company.

That's why more firms are starting to look at their relationships with valued customers over time and figuring out how to acquire and retain them. The clear leader in customer loyalty is Harley-Davidson (HD), the motorcycle manufacturer. The fact that Harley-Davidson is the only corporate logo found tattooed on its customers demonstrates its model relationship with them. HD keeps tight quality control on a small line of well-known products, supports its dealers, listens to customers, and uses licensed products as advertising.[3] Ask yourself how to build HD-like customer loyalty through your call center.

New Integrated Service Experience

You are still undecided which car in the $15,000 to $20,000 range you want to buy. You visit the Web home page of a car manufacturer and browse the features and options of their latest model. You click a button and an agent from the manufacturer calls you within a minute. She answers your questions and schedules a test drive at your home on Saturday morning.

The very same technologies that are raising customer expectations can also be used to meet and exceed them through integrated solutions that offer superior customer service at every contact point—the Internet, call centers, storefronts, ATMs, kiosks, and person-to-person selling. No matter how or why customers reach you, or you reach them, you can offer a uniformly effective (and therefore positive) customer experience. Ask yourself, *is my company creating an integrated service experience?*

Higher Service Expectations

Customer dissatisfaction with service is widespread, and expectations of customers interfacing with call centers are higher than ever. Consider what's possible in customer service. For example, you call your insurance company with a question about your homeowner's policy. The agency's telephone system identifies you and greets you by name. The agent knows your policy, answers your question, and asks if you would like information on a new line of auto insurance that could save you money. You say yes and begin to rattle off your address, but the agent already has it and says the information will be in the mail to you that day.

Customers are beginning to take what used to be exceptional service as a starting point. As competition intensifies, they're expecting more from the organizations with which they have ongoing relationships. They're raising the bar for customer service to a higher level. As organizations with long-standing customer bases attempt to meet customer expectations, they often find they lack the information and data that would enable them to make good business decisions. Therefore, decisions are being made that are less than optimal; as a result, companies are not able to either satisfy customers or maximize profit.

For ongoing relationships with customers to be strong, companies must view the world through their customers' eyes. Firms must take a customer-focused view and move away from the more traditional account- or product-centric perspective. Old paradigms for interacting with customers are becoming less successful, and failure to move toward a CRM environment will result in suboptimal business practices. Ask yourself, *has my company taken an outside-in view in creating a service experience?*

New Competition Creates New Headaches

Are new startups creating new value propositions for your customers? Globalization and deregulation are opening up new markets, increasing the reach of competition. New and nontraditional competitors are entering established markets as industry lines become blurred. Enabled by e-business technologies, these companies often have lower cost structures and broader geographic reach. At the same time, they are very creative in addressing customer needs.

When competition is fierce, go back to basics: create value for thy customer. Executives at many companies now find themselves contemplating new value creation issues. In the 1980s, years of cost cutting and downsizing led to record corporate earnings and stock price performance. But by the early 1990s, executives began to realize that this success was a house built on sand. As their gaze shifted from cutbacks to growth, many senior managers saw that in their zeal to run lean, they had lost touch with their customers, who were slipping away. To complicate matters, those customers who were left had grown—and continue to grow—more sophisticated and discerning. Today, any advantage based on product or service innovation is short-lived; instead, creating new value propositions for customers is key to survival in an increasingly dynamic market. Ask yourself, *does my infrastructure allow the creation of new value propositions?*

Building a CRM Infrastructure: A Manager's Roadmap

Recent significant changes in the competitive business environment have made CRM a necessity. As companies have fostered account and feature proliferation, there has been a corresponding increase in transactions, resulting in a further explosion of customer data. Customers are beginning to understand that companies are compiling enormous stores of data about them, and they are becoming intolerant when it's not used to better serve them. General customer dissatisfaction does not appear to be abating—and likely will not abate—until companies embrace CRM and the proactive use of customer information.

For some companies, CRM represents a radically new approach that will require them to do many things in different ways and for very different reasons. **For the customer-centric perspective to take root in the organization, the entire management team must understand and participate in creating the CRM infrastructure.** So, where do you start?

1. Define a vision of integrated CRM. Understand what services and products you want to offer your customers and how you want to track customer interactions. It's critical to look at the whole relationship with the customer and not limit yourself to a stovepipe view.

2. Understand the customer. How does he or she use the existing products and services you offer? What is good or bad about the current process from the customer's perspective?

3. Develop a business case. Analyze where you currently stand and where you need to go. Do not use subpar technology as an excuse for inaction. There will always be technical weaknesses.

4. Evaluate current readiness. Determine your company's position relative to the competition. Assess the ability of existing sales and service infrastructures to gain and retain existing customers.

5. Establish the CRM strategy and specific objectives. Adopt a strategy consistent with the overall company strategy. Involve marketing, sales, and service organizations, and understand how each deals with customers. Ask about current and future product and sales offerings.

6. Evaluate appropriate applications with an uncompromising focus on ease of doing business. Ensure that the applications meet today's needs *and* the strategic direction of the firm. Look at the applications from an *integrated* viewpoint.

7. Take the customer's view, not the product or account view. After selecting an application, ensure that the process redesign will benefit and retain the customer.

8. Identify and target quick wins. Set aggressive and realistic milestones. Accomplish attainable objectives early in the process to build support and ensure completion. This allows you to implement incrementally and successfully. Celebrate your successes along the way.

9. Put the ownership of the end-to-end project in the hands of a single manager. Partner your team members with experienced business leaders and developers who understand how to deliver and deploy integrated applications.

10. Implement in stages. Due to the cost and complexity of CRM, a staged approach will offer a greater chance of success and allow for continuous evaluation of strategy. Also, challenge the solution. The usefulness and benefits of

a CRM strategy constantly change in the real world. Be ready for it. Be proactive about change.

11. Be sure to create a closed-loop CRM environment. The goal of the CRM strategy is zero leakage of information. As customers contact the company, regardless of the channel, purpose, or outcome of the interaction, make sure it is captured.

12. Finally, create concrete measurement goals. Through ongoing measurement and continuous improvement, you will be able to monitor the project and ensure its success.

So, how is your company doing with regard to CRM? When implementing any new strategy, it is critical to measure progress and continuously assess performance. Measurement is often overlooked in the rush to make things work. Often the hardest part of this process is deciding what the critical success factors are and when we are successful.

When implementing a CRM strategy, use the scorecard in Figure 5.5 to help determine if you are on the right path to relationship management. Although the

	Legacy Apps	Evolving Legacy Apps	Data-Centric	Relationship-Centric
Applications	No cross channel systems	Customer information	Limited functional integration	Functional integration
Service and Support	No access to customer information	Access to customer information	Access to relationship information	Integrated sales and service information
Marketing	No marketing tools	Batch processes for marketing	Customer information file	Closed loop integrated marketing
Decision Support	No customer analysis	Limited customer analysis	Data warehouse applications	Data model analysis

Figure 5.5: CRM Scorecard

CRM scorecard is at a very high level, it shows the importance of measurement at both the organizational level and at the project level. Other goals to consider when setting up critical success factors are scheduling, relationship agreements, costs, and customer satisfaction. Measuring results is a critical component in determining current and future success.

Memo to the CEO

Is managing the relationship between your business and your customers fundamental to your company's success? Is customer service a critical component for achieving and sustaining competitive advantage? Should the process of fulfilling your customers' requirements differentiate you from the competition?

If you answered yes to any of these questions, then your company is a candidate for CRM. If you answered no to these questions, then you, above all, should take this chapter to heart: CRM should be your company's lifeblood. CRM means offering the right product or service to the right customer at the right time and price via the right contact point. CRM paints a compelling picture: sales-and-service integration is changing what is feasible, and more important, resetting the bar on what customers have come to expect.

Why should CEOs care? Because the ability to capitalize on this new trend and to deliver new information-based services effectively rests on corporate leadership. Companies that change to a customer-centric service garner a competitive differentiation in the e-business world.

The goals of the new CRM infrastructure are as follows:

- Create a single, long-running customer dialogue across all business functions and customer access points.

- Create an integrated approach across functional units that enables company-wide management of customer relationships rather than departmental management of customer transactions.

- Ensure that every channel your customers use is easy and consistent.

- Understand customer behavior. All interactions with the customer should be recorded. Segmented marketing and trigger events are important uses of data.

- Understand when to take action. Learn how and when to create appropriate marketing offers and opportunities.

To remain competitive and maximize profits, companies must align people, processes, strategy, and technology and search for innovative, cost-effective ways to build, retain, and deepen the lifetime value of customer relationships. You must understand your customer like never before and use this knowledge to serve your customers. Clearly, a well-planned CRM infrastructure that allows for the capture, storage, and analysis of customer interactions is essential.

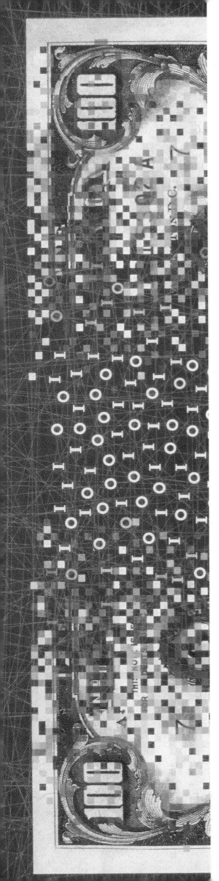

CHAPTER SIX

Selling-Chain Management: Transforming Sales into Interactive Order Acquisition

What to Expect

Technology has steadily spread across virtually every business function of the enterprise and has finally arrived at one of the last bastions of manual processes: sales. We are beginning to see integrated selling-chain applications that streamline the order cycle by moving information faster among respective buyers and sellers so buyers can make quicker, more confident decisions.

In this chapter, we'll examine the future implications of the integrated selling-chain trend. We'll look at the business trends driving the corporate adoption of selling-chain solutions. Success in the next generation of sales means a significant shift in strategy. We'll show you a blueprint for building an integrated order acquisition application framework that gives on-demand product availability, pricing, and interactive configuration capability.

The business of business is selling. Companies implementing a strategy that aims to please the customer are facing a wide range of problems with existing sales processes.

- It's difficult to find the right information because marketing information is not consistent, printed marketing collateral material is old, and pricing information is out of date. This is a problem in self-service selling environments.

- Sales people are inundated with non-value-added tasks, spending 30 to 50 percent of their time on administrative tasks.

- Fragmented order support is a problem after the order is placed. This forces customers to deal with multiple company contacts who have difficulty accessing order status information.

- Current sales applications are not responsive or flexible because the IS staff is backed up with requests for new functionality.

- Current systems are not integrated, which means orders are rekeyed multiple times.

These problems wreak havoc on a company and its customers. Not only do they increase costs and reduce quality, but they also decrease customer satisfaction.

The selling process is evolving (see Table 6.1), which raises the question: What new business practices will have to be in place to support real-time, one-to-one selling? What new applications are needed to support the changing orientation of selling? A new generation of business practices for one-to-one relationship selling is emerging under the moniker *selling-chain management*. The purpose of selling-chain management is to create new real-time links between previously disconnected sales functions and to build a complete sales cycle, from initial customer contact and product introduction to billing transactions and sale completion.

Defining Selling-Chain Management

Selling-chain management is defined as an integrated order acquisition strategy. As we move forward, a broader definition for the selling-chain strategy should be "the application of technology to the activities in the whole life cycle of an order—from inquiry to order."

The underlying premise for implementing selling-chain applications is simple: Success in the next generation of sales will mean a significant shift in strategy.

Table 6.1: Evolution of the Selling Process

Salesperson Titles	Selling Orientation
• Drummer or peddler (1750–1900) [Demand exceeds supply]	Negotiate price and/or barter with customer
• Salesman (1900–1960) [Demand equals supply; limited competition]	High-pressure selling; manipulative and canned; transaction oriented
• Account Executive; Sales Consultant; Marketing Rep.; Sales Engineer (1960–1990)	Building long-term relationships; solving problems; adaptive selling
• Partnering Value-Added Relationship Manager (1990–Present)	Synergistic relations with suppliers; real-time visibility into the process; customer needs are paramount

Companies will move away from automating discrete tasks, such as lead management, configuration, and pricing, and move toward an integrated infostructure that views order acquisition holistically, as an end-to-end process involving every department, from marketing to logistics (see Figure 6.1).

By approaching sales or "order acquisition" as a process rather than as a function, companies will begin to see things from their customers' point of view, arguably the best vantage point from which to win their loyalty, respect, and purchasing dollars. In other words, look at selling-chain applications as tools to streamline the integrated set of activities businesses perform to acquire and ful-

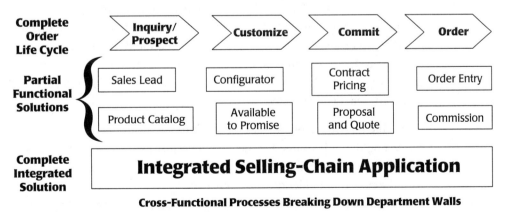

Figure 6.1: Complete Order Life Cycle

fill orders. To support this view, you need a new application framework to enable the integration of information that's fragmented across the organization.

Selling-Chain Application Framework Goals

Companies such as Dell, Cisco and Amazon.com redefined order acquisition processes that involve direct interaction with the customer, such as providing product information, configuration, pricing, and order entry. By helping companies redefine the selling process, the aim of the next generation of selling-chain solutions is to help companies focus their direct sales force on the most appropriate and profitable business opportunities; shorten sales cycles by keeping all members of a sales team up to speed on what actions to perform and when; increase repeat sales by knowing more about customers and their interests; improve visibility in order pipelines, leading to better sales forecasting accuracy; and deliver more timely market intelligence to decision makers.

The basic change in business lies in the movement from functionally oriented sales automation to process-oriented selling-chain management. To be successful, sales must be managed as a cross-functional process. This change is much more than a question of semantics. Sales processes must smash functional boundaries, center on customers, and possess end-to-end measurement. Focusing on interactive selling means turning your organization on its side and rethinking everything you do.

The goals of this business strategy are as follows:

- **Make it easier for the customer.** This means making the entire order process seamless. For example, consider Haworth, a manufacturer of office furniture. Traditionally, if you needed an office system, you'd go to an architect to have it designed for you, but it could take a couple of months just for them to figure out what you want. So Haworth put in a computer system that allows the customer to do more of the work. The customer and dealer sit in front of a screen and design the office system in real time. Instead of taking weeks, it takes only an hour. Then, when it's delivered, you don't send it back, because it's exactly what you expected.

- **Add value for the customer.** This means thinking about the order process as something that adds value for the customer. Just being an order taker isn't going to cut it. Companies really have to be involved in a collaborative effort with the customer to identify the requirements, configure a solution to meet their needs, and then deliver it. The personal computer manufacturers have mastered this.

- **Make it easy to order custom products.** This means match what customers want and what companies sell. This reduces unsold inventory and increases sales. Companies are beginning to explore the possibility of integrating the front-end sales configuration system with the back-end planning engine that bases delivery-date promises on material availability in the supply chain. The goal is to increase overall sales revenue by meeting customers' orders quickly, accurately, and, of course, profitably.

- **Increase sales force effectiveness.** Despite the tactical productivity advances represented by technology, little has been done to improve the strategic effectiveness of salespeople, or to increase sales volume, trim sales cycle times, or lower costs per sale. The focus on sales effectiveness is increasing as companies look for ways to increase revenues while reducing the cost of operations.

- **Coordinate team selling.** As more companies become multinational organizations and service customers in many different countries, there is a much greater need to store customer information in a central location and to coordinate sales activities. The need to coordinate activities and share information is an especially critical process in complex, team-selling environments in which various members of the team work concurrently to close a deal.

Clearly, the order acquisition environment today is very different from the way it was five to ten years ago, and the pace of change is only getting faster. Many of these changes—regulatory changes, shifts in reseller channels, and product line expansion—are increasing the pressure on sales organizations.

Why an Integrated Selling Infrastructure?

The selling environment is getting tougher and tougher. Shorter product life cycles, intensified competition, and, above all, more sophisticated and demanding customers are making the salesperson's life ever more difficult. Increasingly, customers are demanding solutions designed and configured to meet their needs. These challenges are exacerbated by difficulties in the management of pricing, promotions, and commissions, in addition to other sales parameters. Sales organizations must add more value for the customer, operate with greater speed and accuracy, and cut their own costs—all at the same time.

Consider the following scenario: A sales representative meets with a customer. Despite being armed with volumes of product information, the salesperson cannot answer the customer's questions: "Can you deliver the product with these modifications by this date? How much will it cost with these modifications?

When can I have it?" The salesperson cannot answer these questions because the company's product and service offerings have intricate structures and seemingly endless variations, with associated pricing combinations and discount structures.

So, the salesperson tells the customer, "I'll get back to you in a couple of days." She has to go back to the office and begin the time-consuming process of configuring the order, developing and submitting a price quote, and negotiating with manufacturing and shipping for an acceptable delivery date. Several days or weeks later, the customer finally receives the answers to his questions. In the meantime, a competitor with the ability to answer the customer's questions with the most timely, accurate, and actionable information has walked away with the business.

On hearing that the order is lost, the salesperson complains to the manager, "Give me the ability to configure orders in real time and deliver a price quote and related product availability on the spot. Also, give me software that will seamlessly integrate with the back-office processes [manufacturing and distribution] so that we can track orders and provide customers with accurate commitment dates." Now, ask yourself, *does this scenario sound familiar? How are your salespeople spending their time? How effective are their tools? What obstacles do they face before closing a sale? Does your organization have the necessary selling tools that can facilitate order acquisition?*

Salespeople have a difficult enough time getting the prospect's attention, co-ordinating schedules, and keeping the prospective client on the telephone. But maintaining the prospect's attention is even harder, especially if he or she has questions or objections that the salesperson can't respond to quickly. That is why the sales force must have integrated applications close at hand that provide real-time access to all current product, price, and availability information so that they can answer customer questions completely, handle objections skillfully, and, ideally, close the sale on the spot.

Traditionally this process has not been easy. During a typical conversation with a customer, a salesperson may need to confer with manufacturing to ensure that a product can be configured with certain features, contact engineering to verify that a solution meets the customer's needs, or check with distribution to confirm that a product is in stock or is ready to ship. Obtaining all this information can be an arduous, time-consuming task that slows down the sales cycle. But without this information, the risk of order errors (which can cause delays, annoy customers, and, ultimately, result in lost revenues) is huge.

The bottom line is that the order acquisition process, in most enterprises, has undergone little or no automation to date. However, recent technological advances now make selling-chain automation solutions feasible. Clearly, in the networked economy, the sales organization has a profound impact on downstream decisions made across the enterprise, as well as decisions that relate to outside suppliers. Unfortunately, there's widespread confusion in management ranks as to what should be included in the selling-chain life cycle and how to support it using software applications. Exacerbating the confusion are the fluid scope of software capabilities, the dynamic nature of the market and vendors, and ever-changing tools and technology. In this chapter, we aim to shed some light on this complex and dynamic topic. But before going any further, let's look at the business trends driving the corporate adoption of selling-chain solutions.

Business Forces Driving the Need for Selling-Chain Management

Several fundamental market issues are driving the interest in selling-chain applications: the rise of self-service, the excessive cost of presales support, the increasing cost of order errors, changing sales channels, increasing product complexity, and the rise of mergers and acquisitions. Companies can cope with these issues by implementing selling-chain management systems. To achieve successful implementation, companies must integrate their sales systems with other enterprise systems in order to bring enterprise information to bear at the point of sale (e.g., kiosks, salespeople's laptops, Web sites, and on call-center representatives' PCs).

To reduce selling costs, companies need to integrate isolated sales and order acquisition applications with their other core front- and back-office enterprise systems. They then will be better positioned to increase sales throughput, lower costs, reduce order errors, and increase customer satisfaction.

The Rise of the Self-Service Order

The sales process is getting increasingly complex as customers demand higher levels of service, faster turnaround times, and more customization. The early 1990s brought the concept of mass customization to the marketplace, which has evolved to serve a "market of one." Consumers want what they want, when they want it, and they want it packaged uniquely to meet their individual needs. In this new market, companies need to reexamine their sales procedures for ease of use. For years, Citibank captured a significant share of the college student market for credit cards simply by making it easy for students to obtain credit, while competitors made it difficult.

One aspect of selling that has been significantly influenced by self-service is the selection process. Today, after a consumer has narrowed the possibilities, he or she looks for a final selection process that is more comfortable and convenient and less irritating. An example of this dynamic can be found in the online used-car business. For many potential customers, the experience of choosing a used car is an ordeal. But new methods for selecting used cars are transforming the industry. Companies such as Auto-By-Tel, Microsoft CarPoint, CarMax Auto Super-store, and AutoNation USA have targeted the selection experience as their competitive focus. At a CarMax showroom, customers sit in front of a computer and specify what features they want in an automobile. They can scroll through detailed descriptions of cars that might meet their needs. The final, no-haggle price for each vehicle is listed. A sales assistant then lets the customer inspect the autos that interest them, and handles all the paperwork if they decide to buy. The "selling" is done not by the salespeople, but by the customers themselves.

The Excessive Cost of Presales Technical Support

Companies that fail to systematically address the quality and turnaround time associated with preparing sales quotes and proposals are likely to lose sales and market share to more responsive competitors.

The effective translation of prospect needs into product specifications results in the increased use of technical sales specialists during the presale phase of a sales process. Generally, technical sales specialists have a superior grasp of the capabilities of the entire product line and a better understanding of how these capabilities may meet a prospective customer's needs.

While effective, using technical support drives up the cost of selling and shifts the burden of expertise from the salesperson to the technical sales specialist. The result: excessive time consumed preparing complex sales quotes and proposals. As the pace of business accelerates and consumers expect shorter response times, it's imperative that companies deliver accurate and thorough sales proposals in record time.

The increasing trend toward the "market of one" makes it more difficult to create standardized proposals because each document is as unique as the product it proposes to sell. The cost of preparing high-quality, accurate quotes and proposals rises relative to the level of complexity and customization per product.

The Increasing Cost of Order Errors

The increased sophistication of custom products, services, and systems has resulted in an overall increase in the cost and frequency of order errors, which occur throughout the sales-and-delivery cycle. At the point of sale, an error can be made by simply proposing a product configuration that does not actually meet a customer's technical requirements or by offering a product that can't be manufactured.

Errors occur in order entry because incompatible options are not rejected or ancillary equipment has not been included in the order. In manufacturing, an invalid configuration can shut down the production line. If a miscalculated, multivendor product configuration is actually shipped to a customer, the cost of correcting the mistake in the field can be excessive, if not irrecoverable.

Human errors often account for order mistakes: insufficient access; noncurrent, inaccurate back-office information; misinterpretation of what's valid; misunderstanding the product line or how a product will perform; and simple typographic errors when processing an order. Companies that do not automate these processes and integrate their selling functions with their back-office systems will continue to be plagued with order errors. No matter what the cause or where the errors occur in the sales cycle, increased costs will result.

The Increasing Channel Proliferation Problem

Selling is not as simple as it used to be, due to the rapid proliferation of channels. The channel applications that serve the order acquisition side are manifold:

- Field sales and in-store/branch sales: assisted in-person selling

- Telesales: assisted call-center selling

- Self-service: unassisted selling via the Web

- Third-party resellers or channel selling

The relative success of direct-to-the-end-user and build-to-order models are beginning to put pressure on companies to improve the information flow through various sales channels in order to improve time to market, reduce costs, and compete more effectively.

In addition, to achieve global expansion and/or market penetration more quickly, many organizations are attempting to implement integrated multichannel sales strategies. These require the efficient passing of leads and the even tougher challenge of keeping all parties informed on the status of the sales process.

The Increasing Complexity of Products

The increasing complexity of products and the rise in customers' demands for time-efficient ordering processes have put pressure on companies to increase the productivity and responsiveness of their sales force. Furthermore, the pace of introducing new products has accelerated dramatically, causing shorter product life cycles, which makes the salesperson's job of staying current even more difficult.

Sales efficiency and productivity remain major issues in many industries that are experiencing tight labor markets for seasoned sales professionals. The sales force must become adept at dealing with an ever-growing, ever-changing set of products (and/or services) as companies seek to broaden their product portfolios to sustain or accelerate growth rates.

All this makes it difficult for sales representatives and end users to keep up with changing product and compatibility information. These difficulties underscore the need for tools and a central repository of up-to-date product information in order to increase the productivity and accuracy of sales representatives and to enable end users to independently select, configure, and order products.

The Rise of Deregulation, Mergers, and Acquisitions

While some organizations may face new sales and marketing challenges due to new channels and product line expansions, others face dramatic changes within their industries, such as the impact of deregulation on both the telecommunications and utility industries. Until now, companies in these industries haven't had to worry about having efficient and effective sales and marketing departments because they've enjoyed a monopoly. Now that they must compete, many of these companies are rapidly adopting selling-chain applications, not only to improve service, but to survive.

In addition to deregulation, mergers and acquisitions have created corporations with diverse product lines, often sold by a consolidated sales force with little experience in selling the entire range of products. In fact, mergers can create interesting problems for salespeople. For instance, one software company has a habit of merging with suitors and changing the name, function, and physical attributes of its product lines without strong justification. Worse, it changed the company name at regular intervals and confused existing and prospective customers about the product. As a result, customers have had great difficulty in locating the product and the firm. The company was forced to spend a substantial amount of money on retooling and repackaging sales applications.[1] Not paying attention to customer needs during mergers is often the primary cause of company failure.

Technology Forces Driving the Need for Selling-Chain Management

Business drivers highlight the importance of watching customer preferences and trends in selling-chain management. Just as important are the technology issues and trends that steer a company in a direction that will either position it for the future or for failure.

Managers should not make application investment decisions without a clear understanding of technology limitations. Many of the sales automation applications have mixed reputations in corporations due to vendors who made promises that didn't come to fruition. The reasons for these failures are varied:

- Integration was not a factor considered in the selection and implementation of applications.

- Many of the then-current software solutions were unwieldy or difficult to implement.

- The breadth of product functionality did not meet business requirements.

- Sales and marketing staff refused to use the products because they didn't increase sales effectiveness.

Let's further examine application issues and look at recent technology advances in the mid-1990s that have helped overcome some of the problems.

The Selling-Chain Application Continuum

The driving business forces and limitations of existing applications, coupled with the emergence of necessary enabling technologies, have companies scrambling to invest in sales automation solutions so they aren't left behind by more technically advanced competitors. In order to understand where we're going, however, we need to understand the application continuum (see Figure 6.2).

The current business environment requires offering the right product or service to the right customer for the right price via the right channel at the right time. This requires more customer-centric sales functionality. Yet effective *sales* require a broad range of capabilities for integrating, automating, and managing sales interactions throughout an enterprise. This requires relationship-oriented

	Traditional Sales Force Automation	Evolving Sales Force Automation	Customer-Centric Sales	Relationship Oriented Order Acquisition
Integration	Task oriented	Functionally isolated	Lines of business and select integration	Enterprisewide and highly integrated
Sales/Service Approach	Account-centric	Account-centric	Customer-centric	Relationship-centric
Application Emphasis	Productivity	Productivity	Effectiveness = closing the order	Effectiveness = revenue growth

Figure 6.2: The Selling-Chain Application Continuum

order acquisition (see Figure 6.2), which leading companies are implementing. Where is your organization in the selling-chain continuum?

The selling-chain continuum allows us to see where most companies are focusing their energies today and in which direction we need to move. Integration has become a hot topic at many corporations, but few understand why it's so critical. People are concentrating current integration efforts via functionally isolated efforts or line-of-business organizational structures. Both are insufficient for moving toward an enterprisewide order acquisition environment.

Problems with Existing Sales Force Automation

The first generation of selling-chain solutions burst onto the marketplace in the form of sales force automation (SFA) software, which is used to manage the entire sales process by capturing data at every step, from lead generation to contract closing.

The first generation of SFA software included stand-alone, task-oriented tools, such as personal organizers (appointment calendars and address/telephone directories). The focus of these products was to coordinate and manage the diverse activities of a direct sales force throughout the entire sales cycle.

Second-generation SFA software focuses on improving the administrative productivity of salespeople by automating functions such as contact management, opportunity management, sales forecasting, and commission tracking. Another aspect of second-generation SFA is telesales. Telesales automation increases the productivity and efficiency of call centers, with the goal of increasing sales closure rates. Many companies spend bushels of money implementing second-generation SFA, yet success has been limited.

The reason for the lack of success is that SFA tools suffer from the following problems:

- **Limited, task-oriented functionality.** These systems have archaic interfaces that are inflexible, have limited capabilities, and often require different sessions to access various core programs.

- **Functional isolation.** These products have limited back-office integration to perform such activities as inventory availability checks, fulfillment functions, real-time pricing, and account management, all of which emanate from sales-initiated customer contact.

- **Organizational resistance.** No enterprise wants to buy an off-the-shelf sales automation solution. Almost every company views its sales processes as a unique, key part of its competitive differentiation. Although most companies realize the inefficiency of building and maintaining a custom application, they won't accept a cookie-cutter approach either.

- **Limited view of the customer.** Salespeople don't sit at desks, so it's difficult to tie them directly to the enterprise applications and provide a 360-degree view of the customer. Also, sales activities are organized by product or account for operational efficiency. Thus, incomplete understanding of the total customer situation propagates throughout the entire customer interaction and destroys sales opportunities.

Sales professionals often find the current crop of applications to be more administrative burdens than productive tools and eventually stop using them. Clearly, new sales applications need to be developed that closely mimic the sales and order acquisition process.

Limited Process Functionality

Many sales applications are built for some limited subset of product and functionality, which results in narrow process capabilities. For example, a banking sales application may serve only credit card, mutual fund, or insurance products.

The ability to take a customer view—an integral part of CRM—is thus severely restricted. This results in lower productivity from the sales force, more customer call-backs when needs can't be met in one phone call, and an increased possibility of error when data has to be entered more than once.

Sales professionals are typically mobile users operating in "frequently disconnected mode." Users require applications that allow them to operate offline generally and to connect occasionally to a network to synchronize their local data store with a central database. **Selling-chain applications, by definition, must automate processes across multiple user types and functional areas. These issues add a significant degree of complexity to the selling-chain application.**

Selling-chain vendors today are just now bringing to market first-generation solutions that address the issues of variations in customer requirements, mobile computing, and cross-functional process integration. The selling-chain market is poised for take-off, mainly because of the quality and sophistication of the products now available, the increasing integration of the technology into enterprise systems, and the increasing number of success stories. Businesses also are influenced by the current marketing hype surrounding this hot topic, fearing that if they don't take advantage of the technology, they may be left in their competitors' dust.

Limited Sales Effectiveness:
The Need for More Integrated Applications

Salespeople can be only as effective as the systems in which they work. Companies are demanding more integrated applications to help improve sales efficiency. Why is sales effectiveness critical? The challenge for companies today lies in gaining market leadership by helping their global sales force effectively sell a variety of products, from the simplest items, such as office supplies, to the more complex, such as build-to-order systems like a Boeing 777 aircraft. Businesses that develop, manufacture, and market customizable products, services, and systems must meet their customers' unique needs, respond quickly, and offer high quality, competitive cost, excellent service, innovation, and flexibility, while ensuring that orders are accurate.

How does integration facilitate effective selling? Salespeople are demanding the integration of sales applications into their enterprises' back-office systems. The implications for any company are far-reaching because all departments will be affected. For example, with full integration, a completed sales transaction will book the sale automatically, update the demand forecasting model, affect the production and delivery schedules, update the customer relationship file, and provide input to the calculation of sales performance metrics.

To facilitate effective selling, focus is placed on ease of use, which is also closely related to staff retention and training. Why? Because it's difficult for companies to quickly train and deploy new salespeople who can effectively sell rapidly changing product lines.

Managing the Order Acquisition Process

Clearly, great salespeople and great products are no longer enough. Increasingly, customized products and services, new distribution channels, and multiple pricing options are making the order acquisition process dramatically more complex and difficult to manage. As shown in Figure 6.3, the process of order acquisition entails performing needs assessment; facilitating option selection; performing configuration; and generating a quote and proposal, complete with drawings, schematics, and performance metrics.

In nonautomated situations, account managers often perform ad hoc need assessments that vary according to selling skills, product knowledge, and experience. This process requires subsequent sales calls that involve technical sales specialists who, in order to configure the most advantageous solution, create alternative scenarios by extracting detailed needs from customers and mapping them against the company's abilities. This scenario is particularly found in markets that require complex products such as high-tech systems.

The technical sales specialist then transfers his or her understanding of the solution into production terms, such as price and delivery schedules, or passes the technical information to someone else who figures out the pricing and manufacturing schedule. The information is then either given back to the salesperson or to a proposal specialist, who creates a complex document recapping the customer's needs and proposing the manufacturer's best product configuration, price, delivery date, and other relevant terms. This manual process leaves a great deal of information (e.g., engineering, pricing, and manufacturing issues) up to individual interpretation. The likelihood of human error in the process is high and the cycle time is long.

Ask yourself, *What does my sales process look like?* The first step toward creating applications that provide strategic differentiation is to map the customer's entire experience with the sales order process. We recommend that companies perform this exercise for each important customer segment. To begin, assemble groups from all areas of your company, in particular those who use marketing data and those who have face-to-face or phone contact with customers. Charge the groups with identifying, for each major market segment, all the steps through

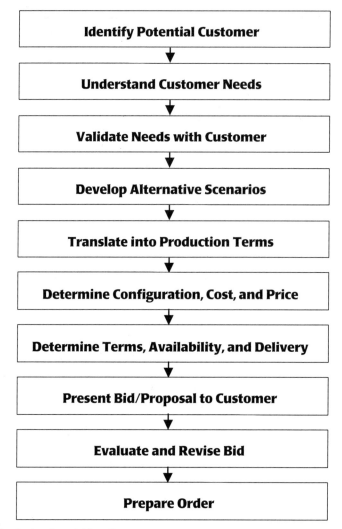

Figure 6.3: The Order Acquisition Process

which customers pass from the time they become aware of your product to the time the order is entered into the system.

Specific industries may increasingly need selling-chain automation for different reasons, but corporations worldwide are turning to these solutions as they look to gain and use more intimate knowledge about their customers in the order acquisition process. It's simply easier for any company to sell when the sales team is equipped with comprehensive information about customers and can demonstrate their ability to respond quickly to customers' possible needs or concerns.

Sometimes reengineering the entire order acquisition process may be very difficult. In such cases, it makes sense to optimize the elements that are causing the most grief.

Cisco and Selling-Chain Management

In early 1996, Cisco Systems embarked on a project that would completely change the way it sells routers. Cisco's customers are resellers that sell all kinds of networking products to retail outlets, businesses, and end customers. Cisco used to process orders in a way typical of most businesses today. Either salespeople would go on site to help fill out order sheets, or customers would fill them out themselves. Order sheets were then faxed to Cisco's headquarters, where someone would type them into an order processing system.

Cisco realized that much of the process could be automated to reduce errors and the number of people involved in the ordering process, which would save time. It would also free the salespeople from order taking, allowing them to devote more time to selling and end-marketing. Moreover, Cisco envisioned a system that went beyond automated order taking and was integrated into the company's operational planning process. It would allow them to give the company better forecasts of demand, streamline planning production, and reduce the lead time between when a customer ordered a router and when it showed up at the customer's door.

Cisco put together a phased plan on how to establish leadership in e-business (see Figure 6.4). Phase 0 was the old way, in which people faxed purchase orders, called for pricing, and, typically, reconfigured selling and delivery of complex products multiple times. In phase 1, Cisco built an Information Center, which pretty much offered one-way information. For example, customers could look up pricing and product information and get the status of their order.

In phase 2, Cisco built the Marketplace and Internetworking Product Center, which provides the capability to configure and order all the products that Cisco offers. Cisco is thus harnessing the power of Web technology to mass customize its products and services to serve each customer efficiently and uniquely. Cisco is currently working on phase 3, which involves customer fulfillment. The company is planning phase 4, which is relationship management of their e-business strategy. Phase 4 will use the Web as a way to build customer relationships with special customers that have unique requirements. Plans include building a customer profile agent and custom order scheduling.

Business architecture changes often cause a ripple effect. As Cisco implements the different phases of their e-commerce architecture, every organization

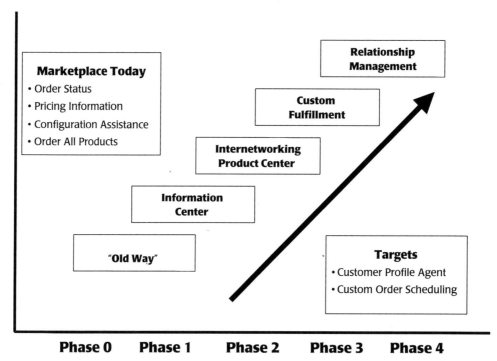

Phase 0   Phase 1   Phase 2   Phase 3   Phase 4

Figure 6.4: Evolution of Cisco's Architecture

that does business directly with Cisco's customers, partners, or resellers worldwide needs to determine how it can work with those constituents in an electronic orientation rather than by paper, fax, mail, and telephone.

Interenterprise Order Acquisition: Cisco Connection Online

Cisco is unique because it's one of the few companies that has effectively created an interenterprise process architecture using the Internet to link companies. To serve its reseller customers, Cisco established a business-to-business commerce area (Cisco Connection Online) on its Web site in June 1996, and it estimated that Web-related sales reached a $6 billion run rate in 1998. Cisco estimates that more than 60 percent of orders are coming over the Web. Note that the company's products sell at prices ranging from hundreds of dollars to hundreds of thousands of dollars. The efficiencies and gross margins that Cisco is able to achieve through selling on the Web are amazing. The company keeps its customers happy by providing fast response time and around-the-clock service and support.

Cisco's online commerce side provides customers with a complete product catalog, a configuration agent, a pricing agent, and an order-tracking agent. Increasingly, Cisco is attempting to act as the integrator and to let the resellers self-serve. To illustrate how the process works, consider the status, pricing, configuration, and order-tracking agents.

- The status agent takes the purchase order or sales order number to look up the status of an order or get a full backlog report. It can also hotlink to FedEx, UPS, or DHL for immediate status on the exact location of the shipment.

- The pricing agent has the ability to generate an ad hoc price list by product line, product family, individual product, or by solution in any price list currency to which the user has authorized access.

- The configuration agent has the ability to allow customers to custom configure the order exactly to their needs.

- The order-tracking agent is designed to provide real-time tracking of all orders across all internal systems 7 days a week, 24 hours a day, 365 days a year on a worldwide basis.

Cisco Connection provides competitive advantage by streamlining customer interactions and increasing clean orders. Consider this former process: Resellers make a proposal to an end customer, who generates a purchase order that goes to the reseller's customer service department, which then sends the purchase order to Cisco. If Cisco finds there is a configuration or pricing problem, the company informs the reseller, who tells the end customer, who must completely redo the order, causing significant delay. **With electronic order entry, Cisco is able to achieve a lead time reduction of more than three days. The company is also able to provide better personalized service and support.**

Cisco is increasingly taking over back-office functions from resellers, which allows them more time to concentrate on selling the products. For example, Cisco can give its customers a private label delivery service. The customer provides Cisco copies of its corporate logo, tag lines, and watermarks, and Cisco reproduces them on packing slips and shipping labels before shipping to the end customer. This helps resellers effect a more efficient model for their operations. The objective is to maintain contact with their customers and avoid undermining the reseller and, in the process, avoid channel conflict.

Elements of Selling-Chain Infrastructure

How did the selling-chain infrastructure evolve? First, isolated applications were developed to automate key aspects of the order acquisition process. These applica-

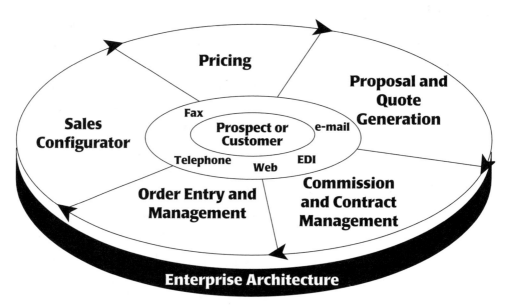

Figure 6.5: Elements of Selling-Chain Infrastructure

tions included product catalog and marketing encyclopedias, sales configuration systems, pricing engines, proposal/quote generation systems, sales compensation systems, and order management systems (see Figure 6.5). Then these various sales applications were interconnected, followed by an integration of the applications.

Why is application integration a big deal? **Today, most sales opportunities occur in complex team-selling environments, in which various members of a sales team (e.g., telemarketing, presales rep, field sales rep, regional sales manager, VP of sales) need to coordinate activities and share information to develop and execute the optimal sales strategy.** Coordination of activities is absolutely essential when organizations sell products with long, complex sales cycles, when there are multiple organizations jointly selling, and when there are many decision makers to keep informed.

With integration, sales team members can share information such as pricing updates, history of the customer relationship, and other orders in the pipeline. They also can coordinate prospect management, which includes the timing of the next meeting, identifying who the key decision makers are and what their current attitudes are, identifying those responsible for "working" key decision makers before and after the meeting, and outlining appropriate follow-up actions for each team member in order to close the deal. Integration also provides sales managers with complete visibility into all the elements of the sales process.

Let's look at individual aspects to see what's important in each and why each is a critical component of the order acquisition process.

Product Catalogs and Marketing Encyclopedia

Easy access to product information is an essential requirement in modern selling systems. The rapid growth of catalog sales in channels formerly dominated by retail chains can be attributed to the ease of finding product information. Consumers are able to obtain detailed, up-to-the-minute information about a wide range of products over the telephone or through the Internet, without having to endure the inconvenience of visiting a showroom and the frustration of interacting with an often-unknowledgeable floor sales staff.

For assisted selling, a valuable tool is a marketing encyclopedia, an intelligent electronic catalog that connects sales representatives and customers to a company's most current product and service information. It provides a single point of entry for harnessing and distributing all product information. Product managers can update information in the database and immediately broadcast the changes throughout the enterprise. Some critical requirements of any marketing encyclopedia are the ability to easily create and maintain a repository of product information; the ability to create multiple search mechanisms to assist in locating information; and the ability to alert sales representatives and customers to bundled products and services, promotions, and complementary products.

This enterprise application uses cutting-edge technology to display product information, perform searches, and share data with other applications across the organization. The marketing encyclopedia provides immediate access to product information, brochures, pictures, and pricing and availability data, dramatically increasing an organization's ability to be flexible and responsive to customers.

Sales Configuration Systems

In many companies, the process of selling configurable or customized products is cumbersome at best. From the time a sales quotation is prepared, through product manufacturing and shipment, requirements must be captured and configuration questions must be accurately answered. Salespeople (either direct or channel partners) are forced to "check with the home office" because they lack the tools and information they need to provide accurate and complete configuration quotes in the field.

As far back as the early 1970s, companies began implementing configuration-checking tools for sales, order entry, manufacturing, and support. These early tools were either options of manufacturing resource planning (MRP) and enterprise resource planning (ERP) systems or customized solutions, the latter being written from scratch by each company. The ERP/MRP configuration solutions guaranteed accurate configurations; however, they checked configurations for accuracy only after they were sent to manufacturing. They thus prevented incorrect orders from hitting the manufacturing floor, but they didn't catch problems until after the order had been placed. Identifying misconfigured orders early is critical to reducing rework costs and customer returns.

Another problem: Custom solutions tend to be very difficult to maintain as business and product lines change. One of the best examples of a custom configuration system is one built by Digital Equipment Corporation for configuring minicomputers. It was abandoned because it could not be maintained at a reasonable cost. Unlike off-the-shelf software, customized solutions don't benefit from the large investments in development tools, graphical user interfaces, and core technology that commercial suppliers must make to stay competitive.

Modern configurators are designed to go beyond checking configuration to embracing the needs of the customer, enabling a sales force to generate requirements-based, accurate configurations and quotes at the point of sale, whether it's in front of the customer or over the Web.

An example of a modern configurator is Concinity from Calico Systems, a sales configuration system used by Cisco Systems in their Connection Online channel management system. Concinity allows users to select a large set of features and options that must work together. Concinity enables creating custom orders from a diverse product line, especially where the number of options for each product is large. For complex processes, such as build-to-order, configuration is a prerequisite for doing business.

Pricing Maintenance, Distribution, and Configuration

Does your company have complex pricing and discounting structures? Does your company need flexible pricing to deal with market conditions by market areas or trading/channel partners? Does your company suffer from high customer adjustment claim rates due to promotional pricing and customer deductions? Does your pricing vary by customer contract or rebates? Do expensive pricing maintenance costs or untimely pricing distributions plague your company? If the answer is yes to any of these questions, you suffer from "pricing complexitis." Many enterprises with extended selling channels, such as resellers and partners, have difficulty responding to changing market conditions due to elongated pricing update cycles, ineffective pricing strategies, and poor price distribution to their channel partners. These problems can result in lost market share, poor margins, or increased inventory.

Selling complex products requires effective pricing strategy support. Pricing varies by the sales strategy, such as tiered customer hierarchies, multiple distribution channels, varying product lines, "effectivity" dates, and authorization ranges. Because of these and many more issues, a new sales configuration type has emerged: pricing configuration. Pricing configuration and update management assists companies as they develop, manage, and deploy complex pricing and discounting structures to selling channels.

Proposal and Quote Generation

The goal of proposal and quote generation systems is to enable companies to provide an intuitive, professional layout to customers who require complex quotes. Such applications include the following features:

- **Opportunity creation/tracking.** This enables salespeople to organize, locate, and restore versions of existing quotes and configurations by customer, session, or date.

- **Interactive needs assessment.** This enables salespeople and customers to articulate their buying criteria and solution requirements.

- **Automatic quote generation.** This generates quotes directly from the sales configuration, with the ability to add spare parts, apply custom discounting, select currency type, apply special charges or discounts based on geography, and affix special shipping and packaging charges.

- **Proposal wizard.** This automatically generates tailored proposals from configurations, needs assessments, and quotes, reducing the time and effort required to generate custom proposals.

A further goal is to allow sales representatives to include information relevant to the individual customer on each quote, such as product promotions or company legal statements. Product details also can be expanded or contracted to illustrate different levels of product information.

Sales Incentives and Commission Processing

Systems for processing sales incentives and commissions can be potent levers for increasing sales effectiveness. These systems are used for designing, processing, and analyzing sophisticated incentive programs for large sales organizations.

Commission systems have three core modules: incentive design, incentive processing, and incentive analysis. From an incentive design standpoint, systems need to enable a company to:

- Create sophisticated commission and bonus rules that reward salespersons based on different sales credit points, including booking, shipping, and payment.

- Create individualized and account compensation programs using an unlimited number of commissions, bonuses, and quotas.

- Create and use customized performance measures, including profit margin, net discount, and customer satisfaction.

From a processing standpoint, systems need to be able to use nonrevenue performance metrics such as customer satisfaction and service quality to calculate commissions and bonuses.

Incentive analysis capabilities allow managers to get an accurate view of the entire sales process. These capabilities also enable detailed account-, product-, and customer-level analysis, and examination of profit margins and discount trends.

The realm of compensation design, planning, and processing, however, is one of the most complex, error-prone, and time-consuming areas facing today's sales executive. Another challenging management problem: What should incentive and commission systems look like in an online or in a self-service setting?

The Custom Foot: Transforming Shoe Sales with Technology

In previous sections of this chapter, we discussed business and technology drivers that force us to closely examine selling-chain management in our companies. We also looked at the elements of the selling-chain management infrastructure, which clearly illustrates the complexity of this issue. After this discussion, it would seem that mastering these issues would lead to ultimate success. To further drive home the message of the complicated nature of selling-chain management, let's consider the case of Custom Foot, which attempted to completely reengineer the sales process using technology.

How would you like to shop for made-to-order shoes without leaving your house? The shoe industry's biggest business challenges are providing value to the customer (e.g., quality, selection, and convenience at the right price) and, at the same time, minimizing inventory-holding costs. Custom Foot, based in Westport, Connecticut, aimed to solve customer value and inventory problems through a selling-chain solution in which customers could have shoes made to their specifications in about three weeks—starting at less than $100.

How did it work? First, the customer placed his or her feet on an infrared scanner that measured foot size. The scanner operated in 3-D and translated the data of each foot's contour into one of 670 shoe sizes. Next, the customer sat at a kiosk to select options (e.g., leather grade, style, color, and type of sole). Custom Foot used a sales configurator from Trilogy Software that allowed salespeople to interactively configure orders. The shoes were dynamically depicted as the customer selected configuration options. Customers could also see in real time how their choices changed the price of the shoe.

Once the customer was satisfied with the style, features, and price, the order was routed to the back-office system. The shoe specifications were sent electronically to a manufacturing plant in either Italy or Maine. Three weeks later, the shoes were either shipped to the store for pick up or delivered directly to the customer. Custom Foot hoped this system would enable them to carry no inventory or associated stocking costs, because each pair of shoes was manufactured only after it had been specified and ordered by a customer. The goal was to eliminate 30 to 50 percent of the warehousing and distribution costs typically associated with retailing.

The case of Custom Foot illustrates the opportunities created by using new selling techniques coupled with new configurators. Many analysts and experts thought Custom Foot would be an overnight success. Unfortunately, this was not the case. Custom Foot ceased operations and filed a bankruptcy petition on June 1, 1998. What went wrong? What can we learn from the battle scars of this selling-chain pioneer?

Custom Foot grappled with a complex process and a new business model and faced glitches. The first problem was a conflict between size and fit. Initially the company relied solely on its scanners for precise sizing. But when Custom Foot began selling shoes, many customers complained that, although the shoe might have been the "right" size, they didn't like the fit.[2] Some people like shoes to fit snugly, whereas others prefer a looser fit. Also, many people's right and left feet are different sizes. According to James Metscher, the company's CEO, the single biggest mistake that Custom Foot made was misjudging the importance of subjectivity in shoe fitting.

The outcome of this glitch: Custom Foot lost money as customers returned shoes, forcing the company to remake many shoes. To solve the problem, the company replaced the scanner with a new one that advised three possible sizes for each foot measurement. Before an order was finalized at one of Custom Foot's five stores, a customer tried on left and right shoes in various sizes and expressed a preference. This tactic resulted in a sharp decline in returned shoes.

The second problem: Forecasting demand for different kinds of leather proved to be tough. Early Forecasting snafus caused the company to often miss its three-week guarantee. To better predict demand, Custom Foot modified its process to capture orders in a centralized database that it tallied daily.[3]

The experience of Custom Foot illustrates a basic tenet: **The flow of precise order information from customers to companies dealing in customized products or services is crucial to success.** When information is lacking or misleading, it can undermine the whole system.

Memo to the CEO

Selling-chain management is one of the fastest-growing market opportunities in enterprise software. The demand side of the equation has always been there: the need to make sales organizations more productive, increase revenue per customer, and more accurately forecast future sales. If anything, these needs have only intensified in recent years, due to the increased level of global competition, shorter product life cycles, and the use of more complex multichannel and/or team-selling strategies.

What has changed the most in recent years, however, is the emergence of several technologies that have, for the first time, enabled the development and successful deployment of large-scale field sales automation solutions. In particular, these new technologies address the fact that, unlike most other users of enterprise applications, salespeople are not desk-bound; ergo, they are not tethered to the corporate infrastructure. Rather, they are located in small, remote offices and spend most of their time on the road meeting with customers and prospects. As such, the emergence of the Web, powerful laptops, intuitive graphical user interfaces, and mobile computing capabilities have been critical to the very rapid emergence of the selling-chain market.

Selling-chain management is part of a shift in enterprise computing. The spotlight, once almost exclusively on back-office (e.g., accounting) applications, has moved to increased spending on front-office applications. Selling-chain software is a new breed of application that concentrates on automating many of the order acquisition functions, such as configuration, pricing, quoting, and service. Meanwhile, companies operating in highly competitive markets can't afford to sit back and wait until the dust settles. They must support selling-chain management applications. In addition to increasing sales and return on investment, selling-chain management gives many companies a strategic competitive advantage.

The biggest challenges for managers who want to implement these applications are

- How to keep up with all the changes in vendors, applications, technologies, pricing, and tools.

- How to sort through vendors and software to select the best fit.

- How to ensure a successful implementation and deployment.

A complete selling infrastructure is necessary for companies to seamlessly manage all facets of an order. In this infrastructure, prospects turn into customers only when they are offered the best presales service. Companies attract prospects by allowing easy access to information about products and services before buying. After the sale, the same level of service builds the kind of loyalty that turns customers into company advocates, which leads to better up-selling and cross-selling opportunities, as well as new customer referrals.

The success of early adopters of selling-chain software (such as a payback on investment in six months or less) and the strategic value of enabling businesses to increase revenue opportunities and expand market share have caused market research firms to expect the selling-chain market to grow into a multibillion-dollar market.

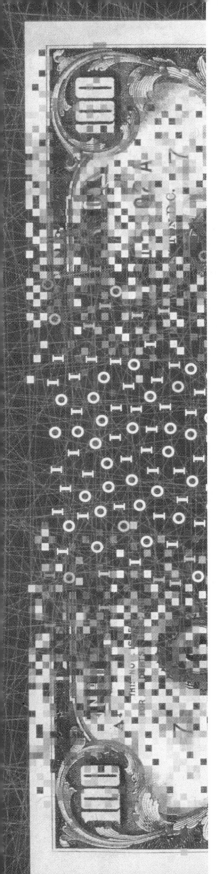

CHAPTER SEVEN

Enterprise Resource Planning: The e-Business Backbone

What to Expect

While the Web stampede and Internet gold rush have seized most of the media spotlight, the business world's steady embrace of enterprise resource planning (ERP) apps may be one of the most significant events of the 1990s. ERP apps are reshaping the business structure because they appear to solve the challenges posed by portfolios of disconnected, uncoordinated applications that have outlived their usefulness.

In this chapter, we'll place the spotlight on ERP and give you real-world examples of how market leaders have embraced ERP in order to gain operational efficiencies. But the process is not pain-free. Adopting ERP significantly affects a company's architecture, processes, people, and procedures. We'll discuss how senior management can make the right choices.

What do Microsoft, Coca-Cola, Cisco, Hershey Foods, Colgate, Eli Lilly, Alcoa, and Compaq have in common? Unlike the majority of businesses, which operate on 25-year-old back-office systems, these market leaders turbocharged their businesses to run at breakneck speed on a transactional backbone called enterprise resource planning (ERP). These companies swear that ERP systems have helped them reduce inventories, shorten cycle times, lower costs, and improve overall operations.

ERP works like an information lubricant, facilitating the exchange of data among corporate divisions through the unification of key processes. More than 70 percent of Fortune 1000 companies have either begun implementing an ERP system or plan to do so over the next few years.[1] The ERP phenomenon is not restricted to large firms. Smaller firms are slowly adopting ERP solutions as prices drop and larger manufacturers are beginning to demand that suppliers be ERP compliant. As a result, leading ERP vendors, such as SAP, Oracle, PeopleSoft, J.D. Edwards, and Baan, have become familiar names.

What set off this ERP adoption frenzy? For large companies, the ERP revolution represents the Holy Grail of corporate computing. Traditional corporate computing typically is a 20-year-old general ledger system on a mainframe that is too old and slow for modern business. The old system worked well in its day, when customers expected orders to be fulfilled in several weeks, but today, in the age of overnight delivery and split-second Internet speeds, that just doesn't work. Top management realizes that outmoded systems must be fixed—fast.

Overhauling the antiquated systems is the first step in back-office transformation. Enter the magic bullet—ERP integrated application suites. ERP is not a single system, but a framework that includes administrative apps (finance, accounting), human resource apps (payroll, benefits), and manufacturing resource planning (MRP) apps (procurement, production planning). ERP unites major business processes—order processing, general ledger, payroll, production— within a single family of software modules.

ERP is the backbone of e-business. In other words, ERP is the business operating system, the equivalent of the Windows operating system for back-office operations. Nevertheless, the maturation of this vision has taken time. In the early 1990s, only large manufacturers felt the pull of ERP, but medium-size firms must now recognize the necessity of an integrated back office if they wish to succeed in the e-commerce world.

Who Really Uses ERP Suites?

Does your company rely on ERP as the foundation for e-commerce? If the answer is no, then you are setting yourself up for potential integration problems. As the information economy metamorphoses to e-business, ERP suites are here to stay as the backbone of the enterprise. Developing, deploying, maintaining, and continuously improving ERP systems are at or near the top of many large corporations' agendas.

Consider 3Com Corporation, the data networking company. 3Com operates in an industry in which the ability to respond quickly to changing customer needs is the cornerstone of competitive advantage. The company made its business case for an integrated back-office infrastructure around gaining a strategic and operational edge. Its requirement was a platform that could handle hypergrowth, support expanding worldwide operations, and adapt to changes in business and customer needs. Another key desire was support for the extended enterprise model. Unlike the classic vertically integrated leviathans of the past, 3Com and other high-tech organizations are, in reality, often a widely dispersed collection of subcontracting producers of specific products, glued by technology into an extended enterprise.[2]

Consider Chevron Products Company, the refining and marketing arm of Chevron Corporation. Chevron Products represents about $16 billion of Chevron's $39 billion total revenue, employing some 8,500 people who are responsible for more than 10,000 facilities—storage terminals and service stations—across the United States. Chevron Products takes crude oil and refines it for sale as gasoline, jet fuel, and lubricants. The information systems supporting their business had been based on approximately 120 disparate, mainframe-based apps. Chevron made its business case for an integrated back-office infrastructure that could support the massive cost cutting and business process changes in procurement, accounting, and plant management.

Consider General Motors (GM), which developed a business case for back-office integration to standardize financial information and processes throughout its global enterprise. Financial information is critical to linking GM with all its factories, engineering and marketing operations, as well as its growing international base. The move is part of the company's continuing effort to cut costs by updating GM's legacy infrastructure. In the past, operations varied so much from one division to another that systems had difficulty communicating. It was reported that the impetus for the ERP deal was to reduce the cost of computer systems as GM builds an array of new auto and component plants throughout the world.[3]

What do 3Com, Chevron, and GM have in common? These companies have chosen to buy preintegrated ERP software frameworks to run their businesses. **Their back-office foundations are evolving from business operations bureaucracies to service-delivery networks.**

Effective Service Delivery Requires Integrated Back-Office Applications

Service delivery excellence requires placing the entire corporation into a unified transaction environment. This strategy implies having one common platform instead of many software pieces that don't talk to each other. Take, for instance, Ericsson, the wireless giant. To support the migration from a purely functional to a truly integrated operation, Ericsson's manufacturing and distribution division made ERP a critical element of its business reengineering effort. Following the implementation of an ERP system from Glovia, the company reportedly enjoyed significant operational improvement:[4]

- Sales order processing lead time was reduced from 1 hour to 10 minutes.

- Purchase order lead time was reduced from 1 to 4 hours to less than 5 minutes.

- Production scheduling run time was reduced from 18 hours to 30 minutes.

- Ninety-eight percent of orders are now delivered on time.

Clearly the benefits are quite impressive. Ericsson's ERP applications track such information as orders, materials, money, labor, and asset utilization. Ericsson's goal involves acquiring a single integrated view of all information resources: general ledger, accounts payable/receivable, order entry, billing systems, sales, marketing, materials, purchasing, product data management, shop floor control, and manufacturing operations, to name only the most common variables.

Figure 7.1 illustrates the core asset-tracking applications that form the backbone of a standard ERP suite. The multiple applications comprising ERP are themselves built from smaller software modules that operate specific business processes within functional areas. For example, a manufacturing application normally includes modules that permit sales and inventory tracking, project raw material requirements, and plan plant maintenance.

The underlying integration across various modules provides operational transparency, which allows managers to follow what's happening in even the

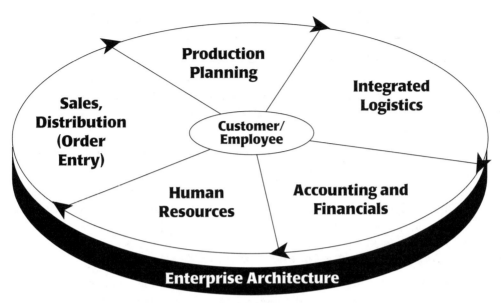

Figure 7.1: Elements of Enterprise Resource Management

farthest-reaching parts of their business. Is operational transparency worth investing millions of dollars? Management seems to think so. Let's look at some business reasons why.

Why Is Management Willingly Paying Millions for ERP Suites?

Companies are rushing to buy packaged ERP applications to address their business needs. Why such high demand? The forces driving ERP are:

- The need to create a framework that will improve customer order processing. Most companies have ignored their back-office systems for years, and they are looking for solutions that will save them from their myopic neglect.

- The need to consolidate and unify business functions such as manufacturing, finance, distribution/logistics, and human resources.

- The need to integrate a broad range of disparate technologies, along with the processes they support, into a common denominator of overall functionality.

- The need to create a new foundation on which next-generation applications can be developed.

ERP suites that are designed for a multisite, multinational company like Coca-Cola are quite sophisticated. To function effectively, Coca-Cola needs to integrate business information across the organization; accommodate diverse business practices and processes that are integrated into a synergistic whole; manage resources across the enterprise; and support multiple languages, currencies, and jurisdictions. Automating even a small portion of Coca-Cola's operations is a complex undertaking.

Preparation for the year 2000 is often cited as a big reason for ERP adoption. Hundreds of companies will "go live" in 1999 as they switch off their legacy computer systems and fire up newly installed ERP software. However, these companies realize that going live is just the end of the beginning because ERP has a second wave—e-commerce.

The Second Wave: e-Commerce Drives ERP Demand

e-Commerce and other business drivers are compelling companies to replace homegrown, industry-specific applications with ERP apps. The key business drivers forcing structural migration include replacing legacy systems, gaining greater control, managing globalization, handling regulatory change, and improving integration of functions across the enterprise. In a nutshell, core business reasons are motivating executives to undertake major ERP projects. These drivers vary in intensity across different industries, but their combined impact is inciting managers to reevaluate application capabilities.

• **Replacing creaky legacy systems.** Too many systems and too little integration is not good for business. The entire business core, which consists of financials/accounting, logistics, and human resources (HR) management, has applications that are in the midst of a huge replacement cycle. The HR market alone represents a $30 billion installed base of software migrating from legacy systems to e-business solutions. The goal is to deploy application frameworks that reflect current business practices and are capable of change.

• **Gaining greater control.** Too many expenses and too many administrative headaches. Managers want to know how much they've sold, what they've shipped, their complete inventory status, and why inventory looks the way it does. Most legacy apps cannot provide managers that information. As one manager of a large company told us, "You can't manage what you don't know. Before our ERP implementation, it was four to six weeks after the close of the month before we had information reconciled, and we still weren't sure of the accuracy. Previously, information was integrated manually and, therefore, was not reliable or timely. That was at the heart of my needs."

• **Managing global operations.** Too many operations, not enough control. To manage local activities and coordinate worldwide operations, applications must change. This change must happen for three reasons: stringent business conditions accentuated by channel and brand proliferation, the pressures of managing globally, and intense service demands by customers. With globalization has come price pressure as customers insist that manufacturers produce higher-quality goods with shorter delivery times and lower prices. To meet these demands, companies must have a more accurate, timely information flow. At the same time, the span and scope of these global implementations expand daily. For instance, Dow-Corning's ERP installation includes about 1,400 concurrent users and 8,000 regular users in 84 sites across 17 countries.[5] Dow must be able to handle the currency, language, tax, and statutory requirements of many countries, and its goal is to support regional needs with a minimum amount of customization.

• **Handling industry deregulation and regulatory change.** Too much change, no way to manage it. In many industries, new government demands such as deregulation drive application requirements. For example, under the Telecom Act of 1996, U.S. telecommunications companies must resell local phone service to competitors, forcing them to manage inventories, prices, and customer arrangements in formats not even tracked today. Other recent regulatory changes include Year 2000 compliance and euro conversion.

• **Improving integration of decisions across the enterprise.** ERP links information islands. Many companies have grown up with disparate, decentralized systems that prohibit different functional units from communicating easily. Often, finance doesn't talk to manufacturing, which doesn't talk to marketing. This fragmentation has been a hard problem to solve. As a result, most large enterprises find themselves contending with a hodgepodge of disparate apps. The disjointed infrastructure can create an environment of confusion, misunderstanding, errors, and limited use of corporate information assets. The ERP model attempts to minimize coordination problems by creating an integrated core of administrative and financial apps that serve as a focal point for all enterprise apps.

The first step in accomplishing these objectives is for firms to gain an integrated view of their business operations. The idea behind integration is quite simple: Use technology to develop process standardization across multiple business units in order to generate continued margin expansion and greater return on capital. **The attempt to gain control over aggregations of disparate mission-critical apps has spawned the multibillion-dollar ERP industry.**

The ERP decision, however, is very complex and can make or break a company. Let's look at why making the ERP decision is increasingly being equated to planning enterprise architecture.

ERP Decision = Enterprise Architecture Planning

Increasingly, large and medium-size companies are being called on to make strategic decisions about enterprise architectural issues as they choose among prepackaged ERP application product families. To find a good fit between the ERP apps and an organization's business requirements, managers must ask, *"What kind of company do we want to be?"* rather than *"What features are in each application?"*

Getting the fit wrong can destroy an organization's competitive capabilities. FoxMeyer Drugs, a $5 billion pharmaceutical wholesaler, filed for bankruptcy protection due to a bad case of ERP "implementitis." FoxMeyer filed a lawsuit against SAP's U.S. subsidiary and its implementation partner, Andersen Consulting, for $500 million each for allegedly making false assurances about the software. FoxMeyer argues that the implementation, which began in 1993, did nothing but drive it to the wall. After filing for bankruptcy protection in August 1996, FoxMeyer was bought by competitor McKesson Drugs. ERP implementations are rarely this bad, but corporate frustration with the inability to find the right fit between the ERP apps and the business is rising.

With horror stories like FoxMeyer and others, why do companies continue to invest in ERP software? The answer is simple. When implemented properly, this stuff works. It streamlines processes, facilitates better coordination within an enterprise, improves customer service, and, in general, enhances a company's bottom line. Often the problem lies not with the ERP concept, but in the demand for quick fixes and rapid cures to underlying structural problems. ERP suites can't fix these problems, and companies that don't recognize this will fail. More savvy companies, however, have gained significant business benefits from ERP.

Remember that ERP provides a business foundation. Selecting and installing a new ERP solution is one of the most important—and most expensive—endeavors an organization will ever undertake. It's also the single business initiative most likely to go wrong. A lack of alignment between the ERP applications business processes and e-commerce objectives can derail even the best-run companies. So, what should managers do? In particular, managers must be able to assess the technological and architectural issues surrounding a product, in addition to its core function. Unfortunately, most managers, unwilling to face such matters, turn the situation over to the company's information technology (IT) department with a mandate to "find an ERP system that will solve all our problems." This often results in less-than-optimal solutions.

Don't make light of the difficulty of making a transition from old systems to ERP suites. Managers often underestimate the speed of change. Change is a gradual process because it involves moving decades of process baggage—knowledge and information—to a new platform. The case of FoxMeyer illustrates a key lesson that every manager must keep in mind: **Technology itself isn't the only challenge in managing transformation.** In an effort to stay ahead of the technology curve, managers tend to lose sight of their customers. FoxMeyer did. As companies adopt new technology, they must ask themselves, *"Is this something our customers will recognize as valuable?"* For example, *"Will it shorten the time between order and delivery? Will it improve our product?"*

The impact of ERP is not limited to software. ERP adoption significantly affects the organizational architecture, processes, people, and procedures. To make sound decisions, senior management needs to understand the technical basis for business and e-commerce functionality, as well as the relationship between technology and return on investment. The broadening of the ERP app market has meant that managers now have a variety of choices concerning the type of foundation on which they seek to build. To make the right choice, they must ask the right questions: *What is our business? What are our issues today? What will be important tomorrow?* The ability to make these assessments is critical to the ERP decision.

ERP Decision: Build or Buy Software

No doubt, ERP applications are defining the overall corporate architecture. An ERP application affects the whole corporation; therefore, the decision to build versus buy is very strategic. A misguided ERP selection will hinder a company's ability to achieve strategic e-business objectives. The ERP selection dilemma is, Do we build it ourselves or do we buy it from others?

Traditionally, organizations had two alternatives when choosing an ERP architecture: a highly complex, custom-designed application to meet the organization's specific requirements, typically developed in a legacy environment; or an off-the-shelf application designed to be amenable to a changing environment and to be implemented more rapidly at a lower cost. While custom-designed apps provide the desired degree of functionality, their size and complexity require lengthy design, development, and implementation efforts. Maintaining, updating, and upgrading these apps require substantial internal resources, and often the assistance of outside consultants as well. In addition, these apps have limited flexibility to support diverse and changing operations or to respond effectively to evolving business demands and technologies.

To address the limitations of custom programming apps, a new breed of software solutions—off-the-shelf apps—has emerged. These off-the-shelf apps aim to provide broad functionality, better integration with existing systems, greater flexibility to change and upgrade, and a lower total cost of ownership. Never run into these packages? Odds are you will soon, because most businesses are adopting them en masse. SAP, Baan, PeopleSoft, J.D. Edwards, Oracle, Lawson, QAD, and SSA offer by far the most popular ERP packages available today.

The build vs. buy decision is being tilted toward purchasing commercial off-the-shelf (COTS) software from third-party vendors for several reasons:

- Only organizations with deep pockets can viably maintain the high total cost of ownership and complexity associated with developing and maintaining custom-designed apps.

- Installed applications are becoming technically outdated and the ongoing re-design of business processes makes existing software functionally obsolete—even a business impediment.

- Off-the-shelf solutions integrate the best business practices from a variety of industries. The ability to import and adopt these best business practices translates into bottom-line improvements.

- Companies realize that software development may not be a core competency. It's estimated that more than 70 percent of internal software projects fail. To minimize risk, companies increasingly outsource development activities.

Together, these trends provide the rocket fuel for COTS application vendors to sustain strong growth.

COTS solutions, however, come at a price. These apps require organizations to reengineer established business practices to accommodate application constraints, or to customize the apps with labor-intensive reprogramming to fit their needs. The limitations of COTS apps result in an initial higher total cost to the organization. The largest components of such cost are the necessary consulting and programming resources associated with implementation and maintenance. These requirements significantly challenge resource-constrained organizations.

COTS solutions also do not provide a competitive edge for long—any technology your company can buy today your competitors can buy tomorrow. Every company must view a COTS solution within the context of its overall business. Senior executives must consider a new set of questions: *What business processes bring us our identity and competitive advantage? How can we ensure that we enhance these with COTS solutions? How can we support our e-commerce initiatives with COTS solutions?*

The Capabilities of COTS ERP Solutions

COTS ERP solutions have become very sophisticated over the years, providing the following functionality critical for effective e-commerce:

- **Consolidation of the back office.** Consolidating back-office functions allows companies to better leverage their capabilities and present a single face to suppliers. The goal is to centralize operations, yet this is rather risky. Many companies have previously tried—and failed—to consolidate systems. So what has changed? The focus and attention management place on consolidation.

- **Creation of a single back office that supports multiple channels.** Consolidated back-office functions become an even bigger deal when firms must communicate with multiple customer-interaction channels. Companies are looking for one seamless back office capable of supporting all paths to the customer. But this issue is complex. How can firms add new delivery paths when it's difficult to support even existing ones? As it is, their many information systems already have problems communicating with one another.

- **Facilitation of changes in business practices.** Trying to change encrusted business practices is like pulling teeth—very painful. To get around this, companies take the best practices canned in various ERP solutions to bring about change.

- **Facilitation of changes in technology.** The ERP architecture is designed to mask the complexities of underlying platform technologies, thus enhancing flexibility and simplifying software modification. Using flexible software tool sets, customers modify the application suites to accommodate their business practices, without regard for the underlying hardware, software, and network technologies.

The broad benefits from these changes should encompass lower total delivered costs, excellent service to trade partners, and increased revenue growth. To understand the COTS ERP functionality better, let's look at the leader: SAP R/3.

The COTS ERP That Keeps on Ticking: The SAP Juggernaut

After Microsoft, SAP is the second-largest software developer in terms of market capitalization. The history of this German company makes an interesting story. In Mannheim, Germany, in 1972, five ex-IBMers had an idea.[6] They wanted to produce and market standard software for integrated business solutions. So, they started a company called Systemanalyse and Programmentwicklung (SAP). In 1993, the company released its first product, a financial accounting package called R/1, and in 1979, replaced it with R/2. Both R/1 and R/2 were designed to operate on a mainframe. Although R/2 was successful, the company's growth was driven by the 1992 introduction of the R/3 product suite.

The founders envisioned developing application software from a business viewpoint. They created software that could assist companies of all sizes to link their business processes, tie together disparate business functions, and run their whole enterprises more smoothly. From the beginning, the software was designed to work on a multilingual/multinational level, gaining it quick acceptance in countries all over the world. Soon, SAP was the top software vendor in Germany.

The fortunes of SAP took off in the early 1990s with the advent of business process reengineering.[7] In the mid-1990s, Fortune 2000 companies, like lemmings in the "Pied Piper" folk story, were led by management gurus to adopt ERP apps en masse. Also, a coincident flurry of mergers and acquisitions left many large companies encumbered with an assortment of incompatible legacy systems. Instead of waiting for their IT staffs to implement new integrated systems, large companies simply took the alternative path of buying the SAP R/3 solution.

Aided by several large contracts, the first being the oil company Chevron, and benefiting from a long gap between the launch of R/3 and the emergence of rival offerings, SAP quickly built a strong lead in the ERP market. One of the keys to SAP's success has been the $50 billion to $60 billion consulting ecosystem that grew around the product. SAP's sales and support infrastructure is complemented by a network of implementation partners such as Andersen Consulting, Deloitte & Touche, and Price Waterhouse Coopers, which have been instrumental in managing the deployment of the R/3 product. This network caused SAP to grow exponentially and gain visibility.

SAP R/3 has become the catalyst for a major information systems overhaul. Its success is based on its ability to provide complete and integrated business administration solutions for an ever-widening range of industries and clients more cheaply than their in-house developers can. The R/3 package is a technical tour de force that incorporates many desired features and automates the basic processes

Table 7.1: Some Functions and Processes Supported by SAP R/3

Accounting and Finance	Production Planning and Materials Management	Human Resources	Sales and Distribution
Assets accounting	Purchasing	Travel expenses	Sales planning
Cash management	Vendor evaluation	Personnel planning	Order management
Cost center accounting	Inventory management	Payroll	Distribution planning
Product cost accounting	Warehouse management	Billing	Project management
Profitability analysis	Material requirements planning	Financial consolidation	Quality management
Profit center accounting	Plant maintenance		
General ledger	Production planning		
Accounts receivable and payable			

of business: taking orders, checking credit, verifying payments, and balancing the books. A partial list of the functions and processes supported by SAP R/3 appears in Table 7.1.

The SAP R/3 enterprise solution consists of an integrated collection of pre-configured apps that enable companies to plan and manage resources on a real-time basis. When changes are entered into one module of the system, other related data elements and modules are automatically updated. The R/3 modules are delineated by core business functions such as finance, manufacturing, sales, and human resources. The business processes are addressed via smaller modules, which operate specific business processes, including sales and inventory tracking, raw material procurement, and plant maintenance. For instance, a financial package can offer a complete suite of integrated apps: general ledger, fixed assets, accounts payable/receivable, and cost accounting. In short, integration is SAP's value proposition.

We are often asked if SAP will continue to dominate. We think so. SAP continuously improves its basic product, and ERP solutions are devilishly hard to build. As long as SAP continues along the innovation path shown in Figure 7.2, it will play a major role in shaping the business milieu. However, the critical question facing managers is: *How do I leverage my SAP R/3 investment to compete in the e-commerce world?*

ERP Usage in the Real World

No doubt the success of the SAP R/3 ERP solution has been quite phenomenal. However, there is widespread misunderstanding that ERP equals production

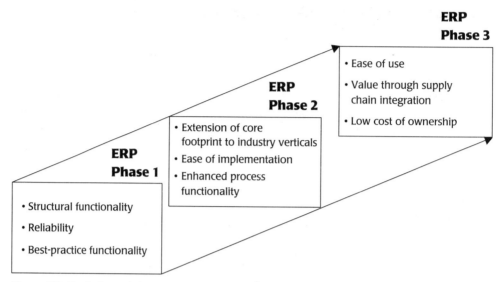

Figure 7.2: Evolution of the SAP R/3 Product

scheduling. This is not the case. The fundamental ideas behind ERP apps have a broad range of applicability.

As consumers, most of us are oblivious to the processes that go into the products we buy and use every day. We are also oblivious to the raw materials used to make them. But the acquisition of raw materials, the accounts payable and receivable processes, and the manufacturing and distribution processes provide the basic building blocks for virtually every commercial product.

Let us consider three companies that have built their business around ERP: Microsoft in the software industry, Owens-Corning in the building supplies industry, and Colgate-Palmolive in the consumer products industry.

Microsoft

In general, ERP software is used for divisionwide or enterprisewide business-critical purposes and involves significant capital commitments by customers. Microsoft spent ten months and $25 million installing SAP R/3 to replace a tangle of 33 financial-tracking systems in 26 subsidiaries. As a result, Microsoft puts its annual savings at $18 million, and Bill Gates calls SAP "an incredible success story."[8]

As the world's largest software company, Microsoft employs more than 25,000 people, operates more than 50 subsidiaries around the world, and expands every day. In fact, the company's expansion has skyrocketed to the point that, at times, it has struggled to keep up with itself. Microsoft's tremendous growth rate was straining the systems supporting its business. More than 30 separate systems supported the company's financial, operations, and human resources groups alone. These systems had been implemented in a piecemeal fashion over time, with significant customization in many Microsoft subsidiaries. Based on diverse platforms such as IBM AS/400 and Digital VAX technologies, the applications communicated through a complex series of costly custom interfaces.

Microsoft's application environment was by no means integrated. Batch processes moved information among the systems, but as the company grew, the window required to run the batch grew to more than 12 hours. Indeed, Microsoft analysts estimated that over 90 percent of the more than 20,000 batch jobs that ran each month retrieved the same information. The complexity of the systems inhibited efficiency and didn't provide company managers with easy access to the information they needed.

Microsoft executives realized that they needed a new solution to support the core business—one that was both global and integrated. According to John Connors, Microsoft's CIO, "What we needed was to develop a unified general ledger solution that streamlined and standardized the business processes around the world—one that would enable us to gain control over capital assets, establish worldwide business performance standards, and get rid of the multiplicity of legacy systems."[9]

The requirements were divided into three areas: financials, procurement, and human resources. The primary goals for financials were to simplify and consolidate. The objective was to bring together multiple systems into a single, worldwide chart of accounts. In the area of procurement, the goals were to increase transaction velocity, the number of procurement transactions handled at any given time, and transaction processing speed. The human resources requirements were to provide more accurate, timely, and consistent head-count information.

The SAP R/3 solution enabled Microsoft to keep pace with and support its growth. The company was able to capitalize on new business opportunities, while making the links between Microsoft and its customers and vendors more efficient and effective. However, moving from the legacy systems to a single global architecture required close coordination and extensive preparation. The requirements for the new system had to be thoroughly defined and the solution had to be championed at a corporate executive level. Indeed, Microsoft's executives and IT group understood these challenges all too well because of previously failed attempts to implement ERP solutions in 1992 and 1993.

The ERP application has proved to be a good investment for Microsoft. SAP R/3 has provided managers with better tools for making decisions with a single chart of accounts. Consolidating the financial, human resources, and order management functions provided managers real-time access to accurate and timely financial information. Timely, accurate and global information access also made it possible for Microsoft to close its books faster each quarter.

Owens-Corning

Building supplies manufacturer Owens-Corning is one of the world's top makers of glass fiber and composite materials. Owens-Corning manufactures fiberglass insulation, piping and roofing materials, asphalt, specialty foams, windows, patio doors, vinyl siding, and yarns. The company operates manufacturing facilities in the United States and about a dozen other countries. Owens-Corning continues to grow internally and geographically through acquisitions.

In 1992, CEO Glen Hiner said his goal was to grow the $2.9 billion-a-year company to a $5 billion-a-year organization through a combination of acquisitions, overseas expansion, and more aggressive marketing of the company's traditional building products. Mr. Hiner's vision is that Owens-Corning should offer one-call shopping for all the exterior siding, insulation, pipes, and roofing material that builders need. Currently, this is a work in progress, and the process is fragmented. Customers call an Owens-Corning shingle plant to get a load of shingles, but then must place a separate call to order siding and yet another call to order the company's well-known pink insulation.

One-stop shopping will give Owens-Corning the ability to integrate sales by allowing salespeople to see the inventories at any plant or warehouse and quickly assemble orders for customers. Typical goals of sales order management include:

- Accepting customer orders from any location worldwide into one system

- Assigning ship dates to available products

- Scheduling future ship dates for products not in stock

- Checking order status 24 hours a day, seven days a week

Sounds simple, but like other large companies, Owens-Corning had operated as a collection of autonomous fiefs with an estimated 211 legacy systems.[10] Each plant had its own product lines, and each had its own pricing schedules, built up over years of cutting deals with various customers. Trucking had been parceled out to about 325 different carriers, which were selected by individual factories. Clearly, Owen-Corning's business needs had outgrown its practices, and the company required a platform that could handle present demands while serving as a long-term foundation for future growth.

The case of Owens-Corning illustrates how companies operate across a series of information islands. The tendency is for various departments to function as if they were independent empires, which maintains unhealthy rivalries. ERP can be used as a battering ram to break down differences and pave the way to effectively integrating islands of information, ensuring total transparency.

For Owens-Corning to grow, it was critical to integrate order management, financial reporting, and distribution. The company chose to implement SAP R/3. The use of SAP R/3 effectively demanded that Owens-Corning staff come up with a single product list and a single price list. The use of R/3 also allowed the finished goods inventory to be tracked easily, both in company warehouses and in the distribution channel. The estimated savings were more than $65 million by the end of 1998.

The example of Owens-Corning shows that one of the major aims of implementing ERP is to develop aligned strategies throughout the organization. ERP often leads to the breakup of an organization into a focused line of cross-functional business apps, which is seen as the only mechanism to ensure competitiveness within an organization. The reason for this is that the accountability associated with focused businesses will lead to continuous improvement. Furthermore, the risk of ineffectiveness is reduced when the breadth of activities to be managed in a business unit is decreased.

Colgate-Palmolive: The ERP Benefits Are Tangible

ERP implementation has become the foundation of Colgate-Palmolive's business (see Figure 7.3). The corporation is the world leader in oral-care products (mouthwashes, toothpaste, and toothbrushes) and a major supplier of personal-care products (baby care, deodorants, shampoos, and soaps). Palmolive is a leading dishwashing soap brand worldwide, and Colgate is a top producer of bleach and liquid surface cleaners (Ajax) outside the United States. The company's Hill's Health Science Diet is a leading premium pet food brand worldwide. Foreign sales account for about 70 percent of Colgate's total revenues.

To stay competitive, Colgate's management continuously seeks to streamline its business. At the same time, one of the challenges Colgate faces is that of new product acceleration, which has been a factor in driving faster sales growth and improved market share. Also, Colgate is devising ways to offer consumers a greater choice of better products at a lower cost to the company, which creates

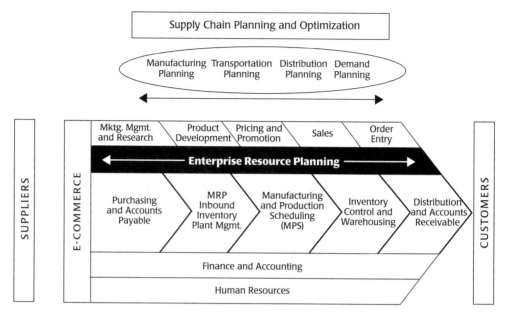

Figure 7.3: Colgate-Palmolive's ERP Implementation

complexities in the manufacturing and logistics process. To better coordinate its business, Colgate embarked on an implementation of SAP R/3 to allow the company to access more timely and accurate data, get the most out of working capital, and reduce manufacturing costs.

An important factor for Colgate was whether it could use the software across the entire spectrum of the business. Colgate needed the ability to coordinate globally and act locally. Colgate's U.S. division installed SAP by the end of 1996, a year or so ahead of most of its competitors. According to Colgate's annual report, "The implementation of SAP integrated software across the Colgate supply chain contributed to increased profitability. Now installed in operations that produce over 35 percent of Colgate's worldwide sales, SAP will be expanded to all Colgate divisions worldwide by 2001. Global efficiencies in purchasing—combined with product and packaging standardization—also produced large savings."[11]

The Colgate example proves that for organizations willing to navigate the difficult terrain of implementation, the benefits are quite measurable. The benefits from Colgate's ERP implementation include the following:

- Before SAP R/3, Colgate had 75 data centers for its global business; now, the company has two data centers, employing only 40 people.

- Before SAP R/3, it took Colgate U.S. anywhere from one to five days to acquire an order, and another one to two days to process the order. Now, order acquisition and processing combined takes 4 hours, not up to seven days. Distribution planning and picking used to take up to four days; today, it takes 14 hours. In total, the order-to-delivery time has been cut in half.

- Before SAP R/3, on-time deliveries used to occur only 91.5 percent of the time, and cases ordered were delivered correctly 97.5 percent of the time. After R/3 the figures are 97.5 percent and 99.0 percent, respectively.

- After SAP R/3, domestic inventories have dropped by one-third and receivables outstanding have dropped to 22.4 days from 31.4. Working capital as a percentage of sales has plummeted to 6.3 percent from 11.3 percent. Total delivered cost per case has been reduced by nearly 10 percent.

- After SAP R/3, accounts payable was consolidated into one location from eight, and three human resources administrative offices were consolidated into one.

Colgate's process streamlining has realized significant cost savings. But the biggest savings are expected to come downstream as Colgate changes processes and organizational structure while implementing best practices in each region. Colgate and other leading companies in the consumer products marketplace are in the early stages of making important changes to the way management runs companies and views its businesses. These changes will lead to improvement in profit margins, increased reinvestment in growing sales, further consolidation of the industry, and enhanced growth of economic profit. Clearly, Colgate-Palmolive is leveraging its ERP investment and aiming at the next generation of ERP— supply chain management (which is discussed in detail in Chapter 8).

ERP Implementation: Catching the Bull by the Horns

A combination of better products, time-to-market urgency, and thin in-house technical skills ensures that mainstream firms will embrace packaged ERP software. It's important to note that each ERP application suite has its own architecture, customization features, installation procedures, and level of complexity. Therefore, you can never approach the installation of all ERP packages in the same manner.

Take, for instance, SAP. Companies implementing SAP use a variety of implementation strategies:

- A step-by-step approach, in which one SAP module at a time is installed, tested, and integrated with other systems.

- A "big bang" technique, sweeping away all old systems at once and replacing them with SAP.

- A "modified big bang" approach, in which various modules are implemented at one time, piloting them in one area of the company and then extending the program throughout the firm. Most companies use this method.

Even if the implementation strategy is right, actually setting up the ERP solution is not easy. There are numerous obstacles (many of which are not technology related) that hinder the organization's ability to move quickly. Consider the case of Brother Industries.

Brother Industries illustrates the complexity involved in translating strategy into execution. In early 1996, Brother Industries (USA), the American typewriter and word processor manufacturing arm of Brother Industries Ltd. of Japan, figured that installing SAP's enterprise software in eight months would be a snap. Brother would simply transfer data from its existing legacy applications into the new database. And while they were at it, why not migrate from a big mainframe computer to a client/server, desktop-centric model that nobody in the company had yet been trained to use? Oh yes, and the information technology people could run most of the project.

Everything that could go wrong did. The project team was composed of technologists who didn't really understand the business side of what the application was supposed to accomplish. For example, the team added up how many people worked on each assembly line and the volume of parts and materials ordered by each plant, figuring that simple arithmetic was enough to calculate costs. But the numbers proved far too vague for operations executives, who needed an accurate gauge of the cost of making each product. They needed to know labor and unit costs and waste rates at each plant.

As a result, implementation was far over budget and months behind schedule. After bringing in a new CIO to clean up the mess, Brother slowly fixed all the problems. Finally, the application began doing what it was meant to do: keep materials flowing, log orders in, send bills out, highlight the most efficient operations, and red-flag the least. After taming manufacturing functions, Brother is expanding the footprint of the application to include a sales-and-distribution module that will convert sales orders to production orders. Next on the agenda is supply chain management. Brother is slowly and methodically building out the e-business blueprint.

Roadmap to Rapid Implementations: The Accelerated ERP Approach

As an old Chinese proverb warns, "Between here and the Promised Land can be a parched desert." Today's intense competitive pressures require fast response. Unfortunately, most ERP application suites can't keep up—systems take too long to install and, once installed, take too long to adapt to the ever-changing business processes vital to competitive success.

An analysis of many companies in a variety of industries reveals that success follows a simple implementation philosophy. Successful companies strive to understand their business processes, simplify them, and introduce automation. Unsuccessful companies start their ERP implementation effort with automation, bypassing the critical steps of understanding and simplifying their processes. These companies believe that automation alone will improve performance and lead to productivity gains. Automating complex or nonvalue-added processes, however, will not increase productivity or provide measurable improvements in performance. Automation without simplification only immortalizes ineffective processes. In other words, a badly implemented ERP is like a broken rudder on a cruise ship: Everything is beautiful and expensive, but navigation is impossible.

To reduce the pain of implementation and address time-to-deploy issues, SAP offers a methodology called ASAP, Accelerated SAP. ASAP uses a methodical question-and-answer format to guide customers through a maze of features. Other packaged applications have their own installation and integration methodologies and approaches as well. Let's look at the implementation methodology phases.

- In the project preparation phase, the project kickoff is organized and all the arrangements for the project team are made. This phase also includes the estimation of project resources, costs, and duration of each activity.

- During the blueprint phase, the consultants document the requirements of the enterprise and its business process design, including interviewing potential users.

- In the pilot phase, the software is configured to match the structure of the company with the desired business processes. The technical team members plan the interfaces and data integration infrastructure of the new system.

Table 7.2: Pros and Cons of Rapid ERP Deployments

Advantages	Disadvantages
Up and running on ERP quickly	Inability to customize software to suit business operations
Less staff time spent on project	Small core group making key decisions without involving everyone
Less business disruption	Must understand business context and processes to implement effectively
Can be lower cost over time	May require more up-front preparation costs
	Short time frame may limit IT staff's ability to support new software effectively

- In the final phase, all the work from the previous phases is consolidated, with the goal of preparing the system for final acceptance. This phase covers the final system test, user training, and final migration of the data to the new system. Moreover, all the conversion and interface programs are verified, as is the scalability of the system. Finally, the user acceptance tests are run.

- The assessment phase reviews the system to ensure that all business requirements were met. This includes checking the business processes and technical architecture as well as checking with the end users, assuring that their expectations were met. Finally, the business benefits of the new system are measured, allowing the company to determine the ultimate return on investment.

Utilizing canned methodologies reduces risk and brings consistency to the overall project. However, there are disadvantages in implementing too quickly. Table 7.2 lists some potential problems.

Implementing ERP is just the beginning. By far the most important challenges facing any company are developing a new set of leadership skills and changing management techniques.

Roadmap to New Leadership Skills

As companies find new ways to implement change, the management style that comes with issuing orders is giving way to one of coordination, or lateral leadership. Effective coordination management encompasses a combination of the following four capabilities.

Strategic Thinking. *How well does your ERP selection, implementation, and evolution strategy align with your business strategy?* To answer this question, you must first answer the following: *What are we trying to accomplish?* Companies selecting an ERP solution face a conundrum: *Should the priority be cost, functionality, or speed of implementation?* There is no easy or generic answer. The biggest mistake users make is getting caught up in the bandwagon effect surrounding some new technology without looking at what they really are trying to improve in their business. In fact, most failed implementations are doomed from the start by managers choosing the wrong system for their business.

Process Reengineering. Never underestimate the reluctance to change processes. One lesson that many managers have learned again and again is that you cannot implement large-scale systems without first changing processes. Process reengineering is essential to obtain the most benefit out of the software. This requires taking rules and procedures and mapping them in a logical manner into the software. An ERP system is really a collection of business rules and procedures (called *best practices*). Therefore, when implementing an ERP system, one set of rules and procedures is replaced by another. For this transition to work properly, a thorough alignment of both sets is a prerequisite. The decisions regarding which rules and procedures should be kept and which ones should be modified can quickly become a political nightmare.

Managing Implementation Complexity. The complexity of implementing large-scale ERP systems is giving rise to a love/hate, "can't live with 'em, can't live without 'em" partnership scenario. Instances of ERP projects behind schedule and over budget occur with alarming frequency, as do cases of companies spending millions of dollars on a system and using only a small percentage of its capabilities. Most of these problems arise due to lack of partnership governing. Most firms outsource their implementation, so effective overseeing of the outsourcing relationship is crucial. Increasingly, firms such as Bay Networks, which selected Andersen Consulting to do the implementation, put in place a "gain-share" contract, which ties compensation to on-time completion. If Andersen delivers what they promise, achieving 80-percent accuracy, they get paid an agreed-upon amount. If they do more, they're paid more. If they do less, they're paid much less. Compensation is tied to deliverables.

Transition Management. Coordinating a smooth transition and overcoming employee resistance can be critical factors for the successful completion of a project. Even after effectively completing process reengineering, an implementation can fail. Who's at fault? Most of the blame for ERP installations has been leveled at the consultants retained to assist in the implementations, with software vendors running a close second. The vendors are often criticized for overselling the benefits of the new features packed into their systems, while underselling the amount of work involved in getting all the fancy tools to work. The consultants are accused of dragging out the installation process to rack up billable hours. Often, however, it isn't the consultant or vendor at fault, but the user. There is a logical explanation for this: the underestimated resistance to change. Top management often underestimates the amount of pain involved with large-scale ERP implementations. Like shooting the messenger bringing bad news, the consultant is unjustly made the scapegoat for the mess that implementation uncovers.

There are a few ways of making the pain of change disappear: Find ways of helping users understand the vision behind the change. Get them to participate in the implementation, and get pieces of the new system in front of them as soon as possible so they can overcome their fear.

The Future of ERP Applications

Compared with even a decade ago, the ERP solutions that have become routine in corporate life today are pretty amazing. But have no doubt, they're nothing compared with tomorrow's. As a wise person once said, "The road to excellence is always under construction." Likewise, the ERP solution is also "under construction." The long-term goal is achieving more flexibility in operations.

Four crucial elements are required to achieve flexibility.

1. **Components, not modules.** Historically, ERP systems have been built from interdependent modules. In the future, freestanding components will work independently, capable of integrating seamlessly with each other, with legacy systems, and third-party solutions. Why? Companies are outsourcing business functions such as logistics, human resources, and accounting in order to concentrate on areas that improve competitive advantage. They need apps that can be pulled apart, recombined, and distributed to match new outsourcing-based business models.

2. **Incremental migration, rather than massive reengineering.** ERP systems have traditionally taken too long to implement. This must give way to a ready-to-go product that allows companies to migrate in easy steps, moving steadily from one deliverable to another, rather than waiting long periods for completion of a total project.

3. **Dynamic, rather than static, configuration of ERP systems.** Big ERP systems that are configured once and for all are no longer acceptable. ERP components must be dynamically reconfigured to suit changing business needs. No one vendor can presume to predict accurately and precisely how its customers will work and how their processes will flow. Technically, users will be able to influence the system functionality and configuration simply by changing an underlying business logic template. Critical to such reconfigurability is the ability to create dynamic suites of applications out of best-of-breed components.

4. **Management of multiple strategic sourcing and partnership relationships.** Rather than merely viewing the flow of processes, future ERP systems will model and monitor processes affecting the activity of the business, wherever those processes are occurring, up and down the supply chain. This is especially important in a business-to-business e-commerce environment.

The vision is turning into reality. Let's consider two examples of how ERP is evolving.

Next Generation: ERP Is Evolving into Supply Chain Planning

To understand where we are going next, we need to know where we came from. The root of most ERP is in the traditional inventory control that dictated the style of software packages in the 1960s. The 1970s saw the emergence of MRP (material requirement planning), which moved about the fulcrum of a master schedule. The next decade witnessed the evolution of MRP II (manufacturing resource planning), which embraced other functions such as processing, manufacturing, and distribution. The integration it embodied naturally made it attractive to other functions, and so it gradually spread its tentacles to finance, human resources, and project management. MRP II was felt to be a misnomer since it in fact covered extensive domains; therefore, it was renamed ERP.

Today's ERP systems offer little in terms of interenterprise planning. What ERP has traditionally excelled at is transaction management, that is, the ability to manage administrative activities such as payroll, financials inventory, and order processing. An ERP system has the functionality to process an order, but it provides little or no information about the profitability of the order or the best way to deliver it to the customer. All it does is process the transaction. The difference in how ERP and supply chain planning (SCP) address the planning problem is in one word: "*Should* I take your order?" instead of "*Can* I take your order?"

Today, the planning systems within ERP are rudimentary. Data from ERP systems provide a snapshot of time, but they don't support the continuous planning exercise that is central to an SCP system, one that continues to refine and enhance the plan as changes and events occur up to the very last minute before executing the plan. Attempting to come up with an optimal plan using ERP-based systems has been compared to driving down a busy freeway while looking in the rear-view mirror.

Thus, SCP systems have emerged as a complement to ERP systems to provide intelligent decision-support capabilities. An SCP system is designed to overlay existing systems and pull data from every step of the supply chain, providing a clear, global picture of where the enterprise is heading. Creating a plan from an SCP system allows companies to quickly assess the impact of their actions across the entire supply chain, including customer demand.

A good plan is useful, but if you cannot execute it, it's useless. Supply chain execution and selling-chain management must back up SCP. The integration of these functions represents the external face of the enterprise. As we move toward real-time supply chains, this integration of external and internal activities will become critical (see Figure 7.4). Tight coupling of execution and decision making is

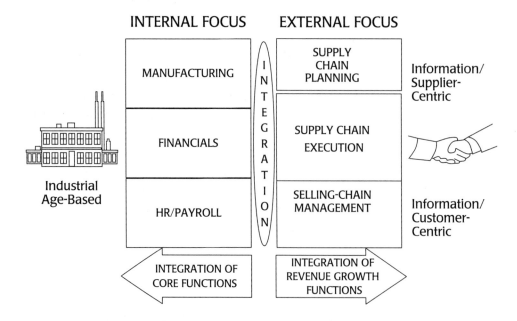

Figure 7.4: The Next Wave of Integration

an essential ingredient to effective SCP. In the next chapter we will look at SCP in detail.

ERP Application Management and Maintenance Is Big Business

In addition to the core applications, integrated ERP solutions include software ("tools") and methodologies that aid the implementation and configuration of applications to meet performance specifications required. As the complexity of ERP implementations increases, administrators want end-to-end management tools. They realize that the management of the applications is even more critical than rapid ERP deployment. In most cases, tools specific to ERP management simply have been neglected, weren't available, or were rudimentary.

Increasingly, companies realize that the best formula for managing complex ERP applications is to employ a variety of management tools. Here's a look at the primary categories:[12]

- **Service management.** Monitors the performance and availability of ERP applications, performing such functions as service reporting, availability, and performance management. For instance, how are you going to manage response time? This will require the ability to analyze the thousands of transactions that can occur simultaneously in an ERP system. Products in this category include Luminate and Envive.

- **Use management.** Manages the application during use. Functions among this class of tools include event monitoring, job scheduling, output, backup and recovery, and user access. Among the products in this class is IBM's Maestro.

- **System administration.** Manages network and systems for ERP as well as other network applications. Tools in this class perform inventory and asset management, software configuration, change management, and software distribution. IBM's Tivoli Enterprise, Computer Associates' Unicenter, and Hewlett-Packard's OpenView are among the offerings in this category.

As ERP software and implementations mature, managers are finding that application management—and the tools to make it happen—are essential to improving the return on what is typically a costly investment. Effective application management means making sure response time, uptime, and transaction volume are as fine-tuned as possible. There's little doubt that management tools are becoming a key requirement and will be an interesting area to watch in the future.

Memo to the CEO

It's ubiquitous. It's bigger and more complex every year. Its development and management are essential components of competitive performance. It's the dramatic rise of very big, integrated apps called ERP packages that form the backbone of e-business.

In the late 1980s, the ERP phenomenon first began to surface. Overnight, most Fortune 500 companies began racing to implement ERP systems in a push toward reengineering archaic systems that were strangling businesses, making them noncompetitive against low-cost producers such as the Japanese and other Asian tigers. ERP systems were seen as the magic wand that would make process reengineering a breeze. That was the first wave of the ERP revolution.

Fast-forward to the mid-1990s. To remain competitive in the e-commerce world, enterprises are continually faced with challenges to reduce product development time, improve product quality, and reduce production costs and lead times. Increasingly, these challenges cannot be met by isolated changes to specific functional units, but instead depend on the relationships and interdependencies among different entities such as sales, manufacturing, and logistics.

Faced with e-commerce, companies can no longer afford to look at their operations in a vacuum. To achieve sustained profitability, companies must be able to plan, execute, and control their processes at every point. Advantages gained by companies implementing ERP solutions include cutting costs, improving customer service, reducing inventory, and shortening time to market. It is important to note that ERP systems are enablers, but they aren't the answer in and of themselves. Essentially, they allow companies to streamline operations. The next step becomes what companies do after they are streamlined.

However, continually improving the ERP foundation is a challenge. Managing the ERP evolution is complicated because, with few exceptions, no one person or department in the corporation has total ownership or responsibility for all these elements. What CEOs need is a single point of contact, an ERP czar, who oversees the entire organization. By overseeing the entire firm, the ERP czar can better understand the cause and effect that changing ERP conditions have on his or her business. Making informed business decisions in this manner would help organizations align their business goals.

As business needs change, so must the ERP solution. Smart managers need to understand the process of enhancing and leveraging the ERP investment. **Clearly, in visionary organizations, the most critical element to business success and** competitive advantage in the twenty-first century will be the strength and integration of ERP investments and e-commerce initiatives.

e-Commerce is causing ERP apps to evolve. New innovations have given rise to terms such as "EERP" (extended ERP) and operations such as supplier-and-customer integration. The spread of the Internet has made its own contribution: the three *w*'s—Web, workflow, and warehouse—are becoming embedded in ERP. It's hard to predict the possibilities, but one could say that they're immense.

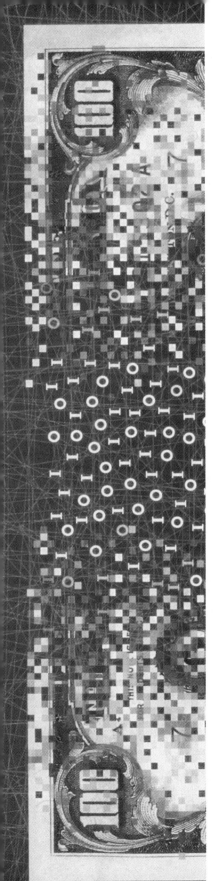

CHAPTER EIGHT

Supply Chain Management: Interenterprise Fusion

What to Expect

Supply chain management (SCM) has become increasingly important in recent years. What was a theoretical process ten years ago is now a hot competitive weapon. SCM isn't a technology issue; it's a business strategy issue that creates new, interesting opportunities.

In this chapter, we'll define SCM and also ask some important questions: What will the supply chain look like in the year 200X? Do you know how to diagnose your company's supply chain problems—and cure the root problem? Are you ready for the emergent supply chains? Don't panic. The answers are here in the form of a supply chain roadmap. And to make your job even easier, we also present eight steps to setting up your company's e-supply chain architecture.

Leading companies are the most innovative in their supply chains—and they're pulling ahead of the competition at breakneck speed. Recent developments at the following corporations show the impact Internet-enabled supply chain management (SCM) is having on modern business.

Bergen Brunswig is a major pharmaceutical and medical/surgical supply distributor. According to CEO Donald Roden, SCM has become his company's business. "We do $13 billion a year and handle billions of packages," says Roden. "We're no longer in the distribution business, but actually in the business of managing the supply channel. This means not just moving products, but managing information, and the ultimate cost-effectiveness of that supply channel."[1]

Dell Computer is built on a vision of customer-responsive order fulfillment. This vision requires a flexible supply chain that gets it made and gets it there. "We already have a quick-ship plan for large customers, where we can deliver a machine within 48 hours of an order," Michael Dell explains.[2] The frictionless flow of information through the supply chain is a central part of Dell's vision.

Procter & Gamble (*P&G*) plays its supply chain like a maestro. P&G estimates it saved retail customers millions through supply chain efficiency gains. According to P&G, the essence of its approach "lies in manufacturers and suppliers working closely together . . . jointly creating business plans to eliminate the source of wasteful practices across the entire supply chain."[3]

Boeing Aircraft was forced to announce write-offs of $2.6 billion in October 1997. The reason? "Raw-material shortages, internal and supplier parts shortages, and productivity inefficiencies."[4] Basically, poor SCM created havoc with production at Boeing, resulting in very unhappy customers.

Nabisco, the food king, disappointed Wall Street with slow innovation and a nearly 2-percent slip in sales in 1997. The problem was that the company's supply chains were not integrated. Supply chains for Nabisco Biscuit, the baked-goods segment, were handled by one system, whereas the Foods Group division (LifeSavers and Grey Poupon) ran on another.[5] The result: Unhappy retailers left with barren shelves.

The question is no longer about manufacturing costs and making the highest-quality product. It's about delivering the new value proposition: what the customer wants, when and where it's wanted, at the lowest possible cost. To support the new value proposition, companies need rapid demand fulfillment that is cost-effective and flawlessly executed (see Figure 8.1).

With e-commerce, the process focus is shifting inexorably outside the organization's four walls. Process reengineering, quality improvement, and other trends have all addressed the inner workings of the corporation. **The next oppor-**

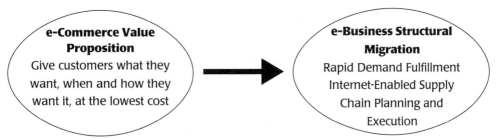

Figure 8.1: What Is Causing the Supply Chain Management Boom?

tunity lies in the fusing of each company's internal systems to those of its suppliers, partners, and customers. This fusion forces companies to better integrate the interenterprise processes to improve manufacturing efficiency and distribution effectiveness. The managerial challenge? Integration must be achieved while simultaneously achieving flexibility and responsiveness to changing market conditions and customer demands.

Without a doubt, supply chain issues are finally on the radar screen of senior management and even corporate boardrooms. So, what is an executive to do? Initiate supply chain education, planning, execution, and measurement—in that order. Let's begin with education. The supply chain market suffers from a lack of definition and structure. There is no clearly defined set of requirements or application standards. Even the buzzwords are poorly defined and confusing. Sound overwhelming? Relax. The next section equips the manager with the understanding needed to appreciate the changes taking place due to supply chain innovation.

Defining Supply Chain Management

In the simplest sense, the supply chain is a "process umbrella" under which products are created and delivered to customers. From a structural standpoint, a supply chain refers to the complex network of relationships that organizations maintain with trading partners to source, manufacture, and deliver products.

As you can see from Figure 8.2, a company's supply chain encompasses the facilities where raw materials, intermediate products, and finished goods are acquired, transformed, stored, and sold. These facilities are connected by transportation links, along which materials and products flow. Ideally, the supply chain consists of multiple companies that function as efficiently and effectively as a single company, with full information visibility and accountability.

In a nutshell, SCM is the coordination of material, information, and financial flows between and among all the participating enterprises.

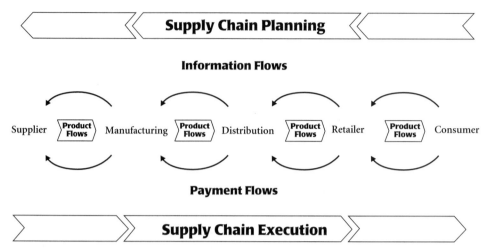

Figure 8.2: A Process View of the Supply Chain

- Material flows involve physical product flows from suppliers to customers through the chain, as well as the reverse flows via product returns, servicing, recycling, and disposal.

- Information flows involve demand forecasts, order transmissions, and delivery status reports.

- Financial flows involve credit card information, credit terms, payment schedules, and consignment and title ownership arrangements.

Interenterprise integration is a necessary goal of SCM. Since the late 1980s, businesses have focused on reengineering the processes within their organizations to improve efficiencies. Having succeeded within their own four walls, many organizations are now looking for other ways to gain competitive advantage. This includes speeding time to market, reducing distribution costs, and getting the right products to the right place at the right time, cost, and price.

To achieve these goals, enterprises are rethinking their relationships with suppliers, manufacturers, distributors, retailers, and customers. Market leaders realize that the more efficient their relationships with their partners, the greater the edge they have over their competitors. As these partner relationships become more efficient, they also become more dependent on information flow, leading to mutually beneficial interdependence and intertwined relationships. This interdependency is creating sweeping changes in the competitive landscape. Manufacturer vs. manufacturer competition becomes supply chain vs. supply chain competition. This, in turn, forces enterprises that want to remain competitive to solidify relationships with their own partners.

A supply chain perspective transforms a group of ad hoc and fragmented processes into a cohesive system capable of delivering value to the customer. This integration requires process optimization, or, in other words, minimizing the total cost of the order-to-delivery process by trading off the costs of inventory, transportation, and handling. Traditional optimization solutions may minimize a single cost, but they cannot handle the complex interdependencies that real-life situations often create. Also, the business apps of manufacturers, distributors, transporters, and retailers concentrate on controlling costs under an organization's direct control, rather than controlling the combined costs of end-to-end operations.

Consequently, until recent developments in large-scale optimization applications, no one player has had the information visibility needed to synchronize the entire channel. The result is that for most products, the supply chain contains more than double the inventory required to provide acceptable service, products are typically handled five or six times, and transportation carriers struggle to maintain profitable equipment and driver utilization.

The advent of better techniques has enabled the optimization of multiple variables simultaneously. Supply chain planning and optimization are enjoying a revival of sorts. The new generation of supply optimization tools, such as I2 Technologies' Rhythm and SAP's Advanced Planning and Optimization, provides an integrated approach through which demand prediction, inventory stocking, and transportation decisions are made together. In managing supply chains, the new generation of apps optimizes not only cost, but also service, quality, and time factors that can strongly influence customer satisfaction.

An e-Supply Chain in Action

To get a sense of how completely technology can be woven into the product delivery process, let's look at the dynamics of the entire consumer product supply chain between Warner-Lambert (WL) and CVS.[6] As you reach for a bottle of Cool Mint Listerine at your local CVS pharmacy, your action is the culmination of a complex set of events and processes that ensure that that bottle is waiting for you. The journey begins in Australia, where a farmer sells his eucalyptus crop to a processing company that extracts the oil and sells it to a distributor in New Jersey. The distributor transports the oil to WL's manufacturing and distribution facility in Pennsylvania.

Concurrently, in a Saudi Arabian desert, natural gas is being drilled for the synthetic alcohol that gives Listerine its 43-proof punch. Union Carbide ships the synthetic alcohol to Texas City, Texas, where it's refined into ethanol. The ethanol is shipped to WL's plant in Pennsylvania. In the Midwest, farmers grow corn that is converted to Sorbitol, which sweetens and adds bulk, and shipped to WL's plant. Once all these ingredients are mixed, Listerine flows through pipes to be packaged. The packages are shipped to CVS's warehouse and then distributed to retail stores.

Now, imagine trying to coordinate all the above suppliers so that every time a customer wants a bottle of Listerine, it's on the shelf. The ordering, processing, shipping, and delivering make up the supply chain. It's a complicated process that consumers don't think about, but one that companies understand to be critical to their success. Many systems are used throughout the supply chain cycle. For CVS, the Merchandise Transaction system calculates the exact quantities of Listerine needed, generates a purchase order, and sends it via electronic data interchange (EDI) to WL. CVS's warehouse management system is also sent the information so that they know to expect the order.

At WL, the supply chain planning system analyzes manufacturing, distribution, and sales data against expected demand to decide how much product to make and consequently how much of each raw ingredient is needed. The capacity planning system schedules production and generates electronic purchase orders for suppliers. WL's SAP R/3 ERP package prices the order and determines how much must be manufactured. The same day, the ERP system transfers the order to WL's Transportation Planner to determine how best to consolidate order delivery and which shipping companies to use to minimize cost. Meanwhile, the action plan downloads the information to the warehouse system for people on the warehouse floor to use for picking and packing purposes.

As soon as the truck is unloaded, the CVS warehouse system team generates an electronic receiving notice telling the CVS accounts payable department that it has received the goods from WL. The team also uploads the document to the company's data warehouse for future forecasting purposes, and to the warehouse management system, which routes the pallets to the appropriate storage site. There, the pallets will sit for up to three weeks, until they're shipped to fill orders placed by CVS stores. And so, as a customer picks up a bottle of Listerine, the demand cycle starts again.

Clearly, the ultimate objective of the CVS-WL supply chain is "scan one, make one." Market share and revenue growth are increasingly dependent on getting the right product to the right place at the right time. The goal is to provide exemplary end-to-end service that will satisfy even the most finicky customer. Why? Because customer satisfaction creates more demand. This requires increasing the production rate of in-demand goods. The term *in demand* is important because, believe it or not, there are businesses out there that build products no one buys.

Companies such as WL that react quickly to customer demand tend to produce goods customers want when they want them. Although a variety of businesses have made great strides in this area, the supply chain can be further streamlined beginning with receipt of an order and following through to delivery to the customer.

Let's now look at the market trends that are driving supply chain investments.

Supply Chain Investment Trends

Today, several forces are driving companies to expand Internet-enabled supply chain collaboration with trading partners.

- **The trend toward worldwide dispersion of manufacturing and distribution facilities.** Demand for products that are customized for local markets has increased.

- **Channel unpredictability is the norm.** New technologies are enabling firms to manage local and regional demand better. This requires sophisticated coordination of multiple distribution channels.

- **Responsiveness over efficiency.** The need for faster and more customized deliveries has disrupted traditional inventory management policies and transportation choices.

- **Companies are willing to accept lower margins to maintain and increase market share.** This is causing many companies to redesign supply chains to drive out unproductive work and complexity and, consequently, eliminate delay, error, excessive cost, and inflexibility.

The advent of e-commerce has forced manufacturers and distributors to become more responsive to retailers and consumers, which has created a need for improved planning capabilities. At the same time, competitive pressures are forcing manufacturers to reduce costs, decrease order cycle times, and improve operating efficiencies. As a result, manufacturers are under pressure to better manage the supply chain and improve manufacturing efficiency and logistics operations while remaining responsive to changing market conditions and customer de-

SCM Strategic Objectives

Figure 8.3: SCM Investment Areas

mands (see Figure 8.3). The increasing complexity and globalization of the inter-actions among suppliers, manufacturers, distributors, retailers, and consumers compound these pressures.

The implementation of new technologies can help offset these pressures. So-phisticated SCM applications are changing the rules of the game. Advances in supply chain apps built on new technology platforms have enhanced the ability of organizations to integrate their processes through collaborative information sharing and planning. These technology developments include the proliferation of the Internet environment, the introduction of data acquisition technology such as point-of-sale devices, the growth of data manipulation tools such as large-scale optimization, and the growth of data dissemination capabilities.

So, what's the big deal? **Information is replacing inventory**. The capabilities of supply chain apps are rapidly growing to manage inventory that companies can't see and don't own. Companies that are adept at managing information are less likely to carry costly inventory. Companies that don't understand this trend will be left in the dust as competition moves from a company vs. company model to a supply chain vs. supply chain model. Companies that learn how to exploit the chain fusion trend will achieve considerable advantage over less-adept competi-tors. The opportunities will be even greater in the years to come.

Basics of Internet-Enabled SCM: e-Supply Chain 101

SCM is where the action will be in the next decade. But as the SCM industry grows, so does confusion over which software apps do what functions best. With a host of products for every task from forecasting and purchasing to warehousing and shipping, and with countless variations in the terms used for various supply chain functions, managers struggling to improve their SCM infrastructure find themselves wandering in the dark. In order to turn on the lights, we must first understand the basics of SCM. Thankfully, the basics are the same whether companies make PCs or conduct financial transactions.

SCM Requires Interenterprise Integration

Interenterprise integration is the core of SCM. As Figure 8.4 illustrates, SCM is evolving from the current enterprise-centric models (e.g., Nabisco) to more collaborative, partnership-oriented models (e.g., the Proctor & Gamble and Wal-Mart continuous replenishment model in the consumer packaged goods industry). And leading-edge companies such as Intel and Dell in the high-tech industry have gone even further to create an increasingly streamlined supply chain model with mass-customization and customer-direct capabilities.

No company wants excess inventory. The rallying cry behind interenterprise integration is "drive down inventory, production, and distribution costs." The basic economic reality, however, is that retail stores and distributors maximize profits by inventory turns—frequent delivery of goods to replace sales (order cycles of less than 18 hours), whereas manufacturers maximize profits by longer production lead times (production cycles of many days or weeks). To manage the mismatch between the two, companies create stores of inventory in the supply chain. This is exactly what manufacturers like Nabisco face.

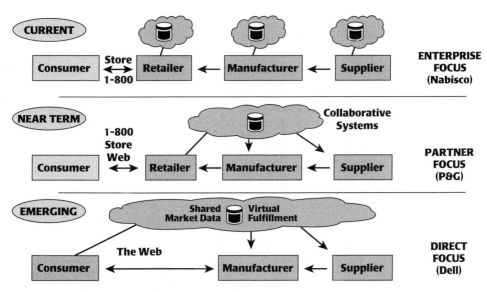

Figure 8.4: Different Supply Chain Strategies

Historically, trading partners have engaged in various promotional pricing, purchasing, and diverting strategies to coerce one party or the other to maintain the supply chain inventory or its costs. The supply chain retailers and distributors are closest to the point of product consumption and therefore have access to the most accurate consumption data. Used in conjunction with the right replenishment optimization software, this data can provide the projected replenishment needs for the supply chain *and* the production planning information so desperately needed by the manufacturers. This is exactly what's happening in the P&G collaborative systems scenario.

Today customers are very aware of their buying options, so the demands they place on suppliers often change from order to order. In response to the unpredictable customer order cycle, companies are looking to go even further in reducing superfluous inventory—actually cutting it out entirely in order to have a zero-inventory model. Dell, for one, has found great success with this strategy in their build-to-order scenario. The traditional method of forecasting demand followed by developing a production plan no longer held water for Dell once agility became the name of the service game.

Types of Interenterprise Integration

Integrated supply chains—collaborative and build-to-order direct—aren't magic, but they seem to have magical effects. Rather than magicians, however, it will take skilled managers to successfully engineer high-performance supply chains, in the shortest time possible, that will be responsive, enterprising, or intelligent.

Responsive supply chains accurately and quickly respond to customers' needs. One important feature of responsiveness is the available-to-promise (ATP) factor. Customer-oriented businesses need to know what material and resources are available before they can promise a delivery date to the customer. ATP systems provide real-time integrated checks across the entire supply chain. ATP can help set delivery expectations when orders arrive, and help companies perform against those expectations.

Enterprising supply chains can be rapidly reconfigured to adapt to changing consumer demand. To compete, companies must accelerate the rate at which they identify and respond to mutating business conditions and consumer requirements. This requires integration up and down the chain.

Intelligent supply chains are not static and must be continuously fine-tuned. They are changing more and more rapidly as companies look for that slight edge over other chains. Adaptation implies that chains are formed and reformed in an attempt to strengthen the weak links within the chain.

Which one of these types is your company trying to create to beat the competition? Service via SCM integration has become the Holy Grail for competitive advantage. Companies hard-pressed to knock out competitors on quality or price now try to gain an edge by delivering the right stuff in the right amount at the right time.

Evidence is mounting that inferior integration affects corporate performance. The lack of integration between planning and execution manifests itself in the following ways:

- Erratic levels of customer service. The cause: Inventory is either too high or too low.

- No vision of future demand and its impact on production. The cause: Production lacks confidence in marketing's forecast.

- Too many changeovers in production. The cause: lack of agreement between customer service, distribution, and manufacturing on what products are required, when they're needed, and where.

- Too many stockouts. The cause: Inventory is in the wrong place at the wrong time.

When it comes to the supply chain, diverse systems are the enemy of integration, flexibility, and cost control. A company's ultimate success depends on its ability to rapidly and cost-effectively collect, organize, and analyze data and disseminate information throughout the supply chain. Increasingly, executives, consultants, and technicians look upon controlling and fortifying the internal logic of a supply chain architecture as the best means to make the hodgepodge of application software and hardware found in most corporations consistent.

To manage and facilitate integration among various participants in the supply chain, organizations have to deploy large-scale enterprise apps to address collaborative planning and execution requirements. The collaborative planning apps use information to facilitate the delivery of the right products on time to the correct location and at the lowest cost.

Basics of Internet-Enabled SCM: e-Supply Chain 201

Now that we understand why SCM is important, let's turn our attention to a more advanced course: the apps side of SCM. SCM is a business framework comprised of multiple applications and divided into two application camps: planning and execution.

The *planning process* focuses on demand forecasting, inventory simulation, distribution, transportation, and manufacturing planning and scheduling. Planning software is designed to improve forecast accuracy, optimize production scheduling, reduce inventory costs, decrease order cycle times, reduce transportation costs, and improve customer service.

The *execution process* addresses procuring, manufacturing, and distributing products throughout the value chain. Supply chain execution apps are designed to manage the flow of products through distribution centers and warehouses and help ensure that products are delivered to the right location using the best transportation alternatives available.

Let's examine each of these processes in detail, beginning with supply chain planning (SCP).

Elements of Supply Chain Planning

In general terms, SCP modules can be placed into several categories (see Figure 8.5). *Order commitment,* or an *available-to-promise system,* allows vendors to accurately quote delivery dates to customers by providing real-time, detailed visibility into the entire fulfillment cycle, from the availability of raw materials and inventory to production status and prioritization rules. Rather than relying on rule-of-thumb estimates, order commitment links into the iterative planning module to provide much higher accuracy in the order-promising stage.

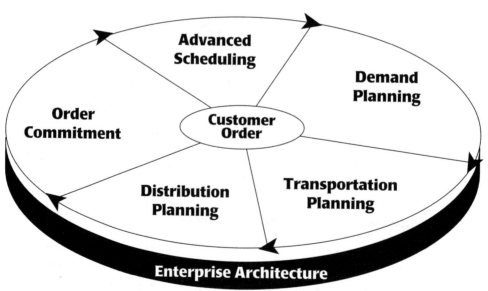

Figure 8.5: Elements of Supply Chain Planning

Advanced scheduling and manufacturing planning modules provide detailed coordination of all manufacturing and supply efforts based on individual customer orders. Scheduling is based on real-time analysis of changing constraints throughout the process, from equipment outages to supply interruptions. Scheduling is much more execution oriented and creates job schedules for managing the manufacturing process as well as supplier logistics.

Demand planning modules generate and consolidate demand forecasts from all business units in large corporations. The demand planning module supports a range of statistical tools and business forecasting techniques.

Distribution planning functions create operating plans by the logistics managers. Distribution planning is integrated with the demand and manufacturing planning modules to provide a complete model of the supply chain and the operating plan for fulfilling orders; it's also the area where customer-specified requirements are integrated.

Transportation planning facilitates resource allocation and execution to ensure that materials and finished goods are delivered at the right time and to the right place, according to the planning schedule, at minimal cost. This includes inbound and outbound, intra- and intercompany moves of materials and products. It considers such variables as loading dock space, trailer availability, load consolidation, and the best mix of available transportation modes and common carriers.

Supply chain planning modules help make better operating decisions. For example, they help determine how much of a given product to manufacture in a certain time period, at what levels raw material and finished goods inventories should be maintained, at which locations to store finished goods, and what transportation mode to use for product delivery. For most of their data, SCP apps rely on the enterprise resource planning (ERP) backbone. Too often ERP and supply chain projects are not integrated, resulting in less-than-optimal performance.

Today, as organizations cope with new customer demands, they require a certain flexibility across the supply chain that only a tightly integrated combination of planning modules can provide. Flexible SCP apps involve evaluation of multiple planning strategies, such as the following:

- Profitable to promise: "Should I take the customer order at this time?"

- Available to promise: "Is inventory available to fulfill the order?"

- Capable to promise: "Does manufacturing capacity allow order commitment?"

For example, when a priority customer places (or changes) an order on short notice, issues such as desired colors, sizes, styles, and quantities can have a widespread impact. Pricing may be affected by a change in product availability. Manufacturing may receive new production requirements and have to change job sequencing. Procurement may need to order new stocks of raw materials, which, in turn, affects suppliers. A transportation partner may need to have trucks available on a specified day.

SCP meets these needs by making the necessary adjustments to production and distribution plans. In addition, the apps allow information to be shared so that everyone who will be affected across the supply chain is given the same information regarding changes. This sharing can be important because many organizations lack one common information source. Often manufacturing has a production schedule that is not coordinated with marketing's promotions schedule or with the transportation department's shipping schedule. Without a common plan and information source, none of these departments is aware of each other's plans, making it impossible to efficiently coordinate activities.

Elements of Supply Chain Execution

Focusing strictly on planning and managing inventory levels is not enough. **Supply chain execution**—the process of fulfilling customer-specific needs for goods and value-added services in a timely, efficient, and cost-effective manner—is a **key differentiator in increasingly competitive markets.**

Why execution? Planning can cut costs by streamlining the procurement and manufacturing processes, but that may not help satisfy customers. To keep customers happy, companies must deliver as promised. Current trends show that companies need more and more detailed execution information to coordinate the supply chain. To manage sophisticated outsourcing arrangements, companies are turning to supply chain execution apps to provide fulfillment pipeline visibility and to control orders, inventory, and assets. The market for supply chain execution apps is growing due to two major factors:

- Businesses that have maximized efficiencies within their organizations are now working to achieve greater operational efficiencies in their relationships with supply chain partners.

- As they look beyond their own four walls, companies realize that planning apps are aiming for the ideal. These apps have to be constantly fed data that adjusts plans to the real world.

Within the execution applications, the focus rests on the effective management of warehouse and transportation operations and on the need for their integration with planning systems and other enterprise software applications. Supply chain execution is composed of order planning, production, replenishment, and distribution (see Figure 8.6).

Order Planning. With rising customer expectations and short fulfillment deadlines, effective execution planning that breaks artificial boundaries and bridges the chasm between planning and execution is critical. The objective is to select the plan that best meets the desired customer service levels with respect to transportation and manufacturing constraints. Increasingly, firms have to plan backward from customer priorities and fulfillment deadlines. This implies that in order to generate a feasible plan, fulfillment planning must consider all supply chain constraints simultaneously, including transportation limitations such as truck capacity and weight, alternate modes, and availability of downstream resources such as loading docks.[7]

Production. With the advent of modular designs, production is increasingly performed at dedicated warehouses and includes light subassembly and sequencing, kitting, merging, packaging, and labeling. Timing of the final assembly often drives the production plan for subassemblies. Starting with the master production

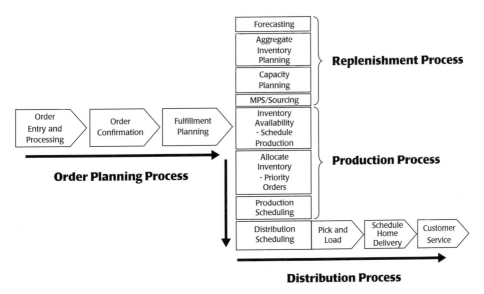

Figure 8.6: Supply Chain Execution

schedule for the finished product, a manufacturing resource planning (MRP) system expands this schedule to derive when, where, and in what quantities various subassemblies and components are required to make each product.

Replenishment. Production also includes component replenishment strategies that minimize the amount of inventory in the pipeline and coordinate product hand-offs between the various parties involved. Timely replenishment of warehouses is critical because customers no longer tolerate out-of-stock situations.

Distribution Management. Once a product is manufactured or picked, it is then distributed. Distribution management encompasses the entire process of transporting goods from manufacturers to distribution centers to final consumption. Distribution management has been innovated by integrating it with transportation planning and scheduling. Transportation management spans the life cycle of the shipment and provides customers with the ability to track their shipments across a network of multimodal transportation. Distribution gives users easy access to shipping, tracking, and delivery data and also supports the complex, ever-changing requirements of international trade, including document generation and regulatory compliance.

Reverse Distribution or Reverse Logistics. Rapid obsolescence and more generous warranties have sparked a growing trend of customers returning products. Damark International, a mail-order catalog firm offering products in six broad categories—computers, home office, consumer electronics, home decor, home improvements, and sports/fitness—stated that in 1997 its merchandise returns from customers were approximately 14.1 percent of gross product sales.[8] This figure is a reflection of the industry return rate. Reverse logistics means that due to customer dissatisfaction, items must be shipped, accounted for, and returned to the manufacturer or disposed of. Reverse logistics encompasses not only damaged or returned goods, but also products designed for remanufacture, hazardous material, and reusable packaging.

e-Supply Chain Fusion: e-Supply Chain 301

Now that you understand the basics of SCM, it's time to move to the next level. How do you create integrated supply chain structures? How do you migrate from existing nonintegrated supply chain models to more effective integrated models? Before we address the process of fusion, note that many firms struggle to implement the integrated supply chain vision because existing supply chains are artifacts of the past. These legacy supply chains are clogged with unnecessary steps and redundant stockpiles.[9] For instance, a typical box of breakfast cereal spends an incredible 104 days getting from factory to supermarket, struggling its way through an unbelievable maze of wholesalers, distributors, brokers, and consolidators, each of which has a warehouse.[10] Unclogging these inefficient supply chains means changing the way links interact, and it could greatly affect leadership positions of some or all of the companies involved.

Diagnosing Root Causes of Supply Chain Problems

Before creating an e-supply chain architecture, such as that shown in Figure 8.7, you have to diagnose what the problems are that prevent collaborative work. An old axiom says, "If you don't understand the problem, it's hard to fix it!" Fixing a business problem requires untangling underlying, symptomatic, structural trouble, such as:

- A lack of knowledge about the end-to-end demand planning function. This often results in an unstable demand figure that changes frequently in the production schedule and can lead to expedited transfers and shipments.

- Inconsistent or out-of-date data, due to a lack of integration with ERP. This can result in reactive fire-fighting decisions based on inadequate information or poor decision-support tools.

- A lack of process integration across partners. Retailers are demanding more sophisticated interenterprise purchasing, inventory management, and merchandising tools that enable them to distribute and manage goods efficiently.

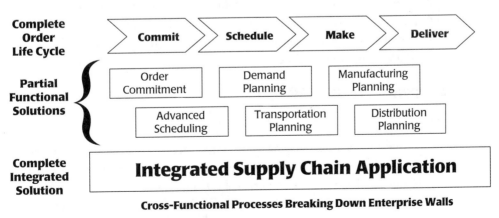

Figure 8.7: An Application View of the Supply Chain

Inventory management has become more complicated as retailers, distributors, and customers seek to reduce costs and improve margins while replenishing inventory on a just-in-time basis. But until efficient SCM is in place, inventory management plans are hard to execute well.

- Effective deployment of SCM requires structural change, because existing supply chains are sadly outdated in an era in which inventories and costs must be ruthlessly eliminated.

Historically, apps in the supply chain have consisted largely of separate legacy apps at the corporate, store, and distribution levels (see Figure 8.7). These legacy apps have primarily been host-centric systems that operate on mainframe or mid-range computers. These systems, developed and modified internally over many years or licensed from third parties, represent considerable investments and have been beneficial over the years. But in general, they don't have the flexibility to support diverse and changing operations within a company's business, nor can they respond effectively to changing technologies. Additionally, these apps have targeted only distinct levels of the supply chain and generally have not provided the full benefits of integration, which allows information to be distributed effectively. Despite these limitations, many host-centric systems are still widely deployed due to their strengths in particular segments, as well as to preserve significant hardware and software investments.

However, this situation is changing with the advent of better e-business tools. Companies such as SAP, I2 Technologies, and others are creating solutions that provide integrated functionality. These solutions are adept at handling large volumes of transactions, possess a high degree of reliability, and can rapidly capture and analyze data and distribute information throughout the geographically dispersed parts of the enterprise. Moreover, these solutions support the specialized requirements of global business, such as transportation planning and the increased prevalence of e-commerce.

e-Supply Chain Heal Thyself: Fixing the Root Cause

Supply chain fusion goes through four stages.

1. **Enable information sharing.** This stage requires a solid communication process. For instance, more and more retailers are restructuring existing operations so that consumers interact effectively with the entire enterprise from a single store or Web site. Decision makers throughout the enterprise need to have a common base of readily available sales and inventory information,

and in-store personnel need the ability to more rapidly respond to consumers' needs.

2. **Create joint performance measurement systems and collaborative planning processes.** Key challenges are creating performance measurements and developing a clear understanding of the costs and benefits involved in supply chain integration. We've seen partnerships and initiatives fail because they lacked these elements. There must be a clear way of settling risk and achieving shared information.

3. **Exchange responsibilities and realign work.** That is, what you used to do, I now do; what you used to decide, I now decide for you.

4. **Redesign products and processes so that work becomes easier or more efficient.** A challenge is to consider the entire supply chain when doing inter-enterprise process reengineering.

The majority of companies are in the information-sharing stage, the current state of the art in e-business. But forward-thinking companies are already using the new technologies to connect themselves. Once they understand all the components of the supply chain, they'll use these technologies to create tightly coupled relationships and, at the same time, learn to create, use, and discard loosely coupled relationships.

The coordination and integration of these flows within and across companies form the catalyst for modern business. Managing the flow is complex because it cuts across multiple organizations within one company or many companies, and sometimes industries. In the last few years, coordinating and integrating these flows have attracted interest among managers, practitioners, consultants, and researchers in academia and industry.

e-Supply Chain Fusion Management Issues

The business world's understanding of SCM management challenges is still quite primitive. Certainly there are exceptions by companies (Dell, P&G, Wal-Mart) and industries (semiconductors, PCs, and peripherals), but the concepts of managing and integrating the flow of products are only now beginning to invade corporate boardrooms. *Do your board and top management understand the issues behind SCM?*

SCM decisions are really business design decisions. With customer satisfaction at stake, SCM is quickly becoming an executive and boardroom issue, not a technical, functional, or storeroom issue. Senior management is being asked to make complex strategic decisions in order to create integrated SCM solutions.

Increasingly, CEOs, CFOs, and line-of-business managers are being asked to make technical decisions that can help revolutionize their businesses. Where do they start? To make an effective supply chain design, ask yourself the four fundamental questions posed in the following sections.

1. What Is the Right e-Supply Chain Structure for My Company?

To meet customers' demands, an expensive option is to keep a large finished goods inventory. But what happens when the market demands something else? The now-obsolete product becomes wasted money. Companies have to use supply chain planning to anticipate conditions and act, not react. In other words, **SCM is a prerequisite to doing business.**

Consider the computer supply chain. The consumer has a specific need for one of a thousand possible configurations of processors, hard drives, peripherals, and so forth. One manufacturer, such as Compaq, reacts by tieing up millions of dollars building an inventory of premade models (which the customer may not want), whereas another manufacturer, such as Dell with its responsive supply chain, can quickly assemble every customer's order. Which manufacturer pleases customers *and* saves money?

Clearly, SCM is not a technology issue; it's a business strategy issue. In a classic article titled "What Is the Right Supply Chain for Your Product," Marshall Fisher wrote: "Before devising a supply chain, consider the nature of the demand for your products," because "functional products require an efficient process; innovative products, a responsive process."[11]

Different strategic goals motivate companies to adopt different supply chain structures. Configuring the supply chain with a strategic view restrains the tendency to focus only on cost. A low-cost distribution network can be quite different from one designed for lead-time responsiveness. While analyzing strategies, make sure that the entire team understands and agrees on how to handle the basic elements of the supply chain, including demand and capacity planning, strategic scheduling, and performance measurement.

The objective of any supply chain design is to please the customer and to make money. It's often easy to lose sight of the fact that the supply chain exists only to support a revenue stream. Business ought to be focused on growing that revenue stream, which requires a shift in focus from reengineering costs out of processes to driving revenue growth.

2. Does the Chain Enable Effective Differentiation Capabilities?

Most profitable strategies are built on differentiation: offering customers something unique that the competition doesn't have. But most companies, in an effort to differentiate themselves, focus their energy on only their products or services. We believe that companies have the opportunity to differentiate themselves through their supply chains.

Consider, for instance, build-to-order (BTO) business models, which are used to support delivery of the mass-customization value proposition. The basic goal of build-to-order is to trigger the entire buy-make-ship cycle only when a clear demand signal is sent by a specific customer. BTO provides vendors and suppliers multiple avenues of differentiation by adjusting variables: the velocity of moving goods throughout the supply chain, exposure to inventory carrying and depreciation costs, higher volatility in demand, and transitions through product cycles.

Differentiation using the supply chain makes even more sense when you consider the fact that most companies don't have just one supply chain. They have multiple supply chains running concurrently. It's estimated that large companies such as 3M have more than 30 different supply chain configurations. In such settings, differentiated policies offer one of the most effective means for improving performance. By differentiated policies, we mean the matching of performance standards to the cost and cycle-time realities of different products.

3. Does My Supply Chain Facilitate Effective Order Fulfillment Capabilities?

Order fulfillment is the highest single cost of doing business and therefore offers a great opportunity to reduce cost and improve service. For instance, better consensus planning reduces errors that are often caused by multiple groups developing forecasts independently. The different functional groups involved in the supply chain have different priorities, and sometimes conflicting objectives. The classic example is the sales department that pads its forecast to ensure availability of a product, to the detriment of those trying to control inventory. Unless these conflicts are resolved, the supply chain can be whipsawed between extremes, resulting in increased cost and poor customer service.

Or consider order promising. Order promising gives companies the ability to accurately quote delivery dates to customers. The goal is to provide real-time, detailed visibility into the entire fulfillment cycle, from the availability of raw materials and inventory to production status and prioritization rules. Rather than relying on rule-of-thumb estimates, companies want to link into planning modules that provide much higher accuracy during the order-promising stage. By reducing opportunities for errors, companies can save valuable time and money.

A tightly integrated yet reactive chain is critical for the success of order fulfillment. Well-run supply chains are built on a premise that order forecasts are merely plans—plans that will inevitably be wrong. But instead of constantly planning, effective supply chains are configured to respond to orders. Planning establishes the level of resources—production capacity, labor, raw materials—required for a given time period. But deploying resources most effectively occurs when the chain responds to the pull of real orders, not the push of the plan. Keeping forecasts separate from orders ensures that the best, most current information drives the flow of materials needed for order fulfillment.

4. Does My Company Have the Right Infrastructure Capabilities?

Typical SCM solutions span multiple packaged applications, legacy systems, and geographies. They also include sophisticated integration of the planning and execution capabilities. Decisions about how to deploy network applications, ERP software, and other SCM systems are increasingly participatory, with line-of-business managers, marketing executives, and corporate leaders joining IT professionals in the technology review and decision-making process.

Creating a real-time SCM infrastructure is a daunting and ongoing issue, and quite often a point of failure for several reasons, chief among them being that the planning, selection, and implementation of SCM solutions are becoming more complex as the pace of technological change accelerates and the number of partners increases. SCM investments must be made surgically, while bearing in mind the existing ERP and legacy infrastructure. Large companies have already made the necessary investments in ERP systems to integrate functions such as purchasing, inventory management, production scheduling, and finance within the enterprise. The next step is to leverage ERP investments to integrate the functions and information of multiple enterprises in real time.

SCM apps are constantly in a state of flux because new technologies are fundamentally redefining the realm of what is possible. Today the Web and retail barcode readers allow a wide variety of companies to track consumer demand. With point-of-sale scanners, information is captured accurately and cheaply and can be provided throughout the supply chain on a real-time basis at a reasonable cost. Similarly, on the distribution side, logistics providers have leveraged information technology to enhance their management capability. Predicting what new capabilities technology will provide is key to making solid investment decisions.

The SCM solutions market is in its infancy. In the early 1990s, software dedicated to SCM barely existed. Today, with SCM recognized as a very important key to competitive advantage, the industry has boomed and now hundreds of software and technology suppliers are competing. As more and more companies initiate internal and external supply chain improvement efforts, the industry is expected to explode in the coming decade. However, in this boom period separating hype from capability can be difficult. *Managers, be vigilant!*

The Future: e-Supply Chains in 200X

As we move into the new millennium, a key issue on most managers' minds is what the supply chain will look like in the year 200X. In this section, we will present several examples that offer insight into the various ways modern supply chains are evolving.

Integrated Make-to-Stock. Traditional supply chains, also called make-to-stock models, are particularly useful in mass-production environments. How does this work? Production quantities and dates are provided by the forecast, with no concern for individual customer requirements. Instead, customers receive shipments from the finished goods inventory. This means that the irregular demand flow that would result from various customer orders can be smoothed, produced, and warehoused downstream.

Examples of make-to-stock users include Coca-Cola, Proctor & Gamble, and General Mills' cereal production. Typically, the resource utilization with make-to-stock models was modest due to inefficient parts purchasing, product overdesign, poor plant utilization, lengthy inventory pipelines, and a lack of streamlined logistics. Companies are now attempting to mitigate the problems associated with make-to-stock by using information to better coordinate the end-to-end chain.

A more recent innovation of make-to-stock is configuring the actual finished product to the distribution channel, which is called *postponement*. Hewlett-Packard, for instance, configures its printers for each customer's order by adding the specific type of power supply, power cord, appropriate language instruction manual, and other materials to the box before shipment. Clearly, some products have destination-driven features (particularly those for international customers) that are best handled in the distribution channel.

Continuous Replenishment. To mitigate the logistics problem and create a customer-demand pull system that stretches across several companies, new methods such as efficient consumer response (ECR), quick response (QR), or continuous replenishment have been introduced, primarily in the consumer packaged goods industry. These methods vary in the level of system integration, but all perform interorganizational boundary spanning aimed at coordinating activities in an integrated manner.

Build-to-Order. As the world moves from mass production to mass customization, the supply chain requirements also change. In other words, we're seeing the emergence of build-to-order supply chains that are more suitable for the mass-customization world. Another factor driving BTO supply chain innovation is the realization that **inventory can be substituted with information.** This is especially true in the high-tech industry, in which components change constantly, making warehousing of products foolish. Firms want to be as flexible as possible so they can move components in and out of the warehouse quickly.

Three real-world examples of these next-wave supply chains are discussed in the following sections.

Integrated Make-to-Stock: Starbucks

A high-performance supply chain best achieves corporate objectives by balancing supply against demand. Seattle-based Starbucks Coffee is one company that has succeeded at integrating the demand and supply sides to provide true end-to-end integration.

Starbucks is North America's top specialty coffee roaster and retailer. This king of café lattes has experienced more than 60-percent sales growth for eight consecutive years, including retail store growth from 11 stores in 1987 to more than 1,200 today. Starbucks serves more than 4 million customers in its retail stores every week. In fact, it's so popular the company has gone international, with locations in Tokyo and Singapore. With plans for more than 2,000 stores by the year 2000, Starbucks has elevated drinking coffee from a mundane morning exercise to a social experience.

Starbucks' strategy is to be the most recognized and respected coffee brand in the world. Growth is part of that strategy, and technology is key to supporting growth. For instance, to determine the best locations for new stores, Starbucks uses customized real estate software. And to calculate how many green-aproned staffers are needed to serve coffee addicts, the company uses point-of-sale data for efficient labor scheduling. But the best use of technology occurs in Starbucks' supply chain.

Starbucks' supply chain supports three channels: specialty, direct response, and retail or joint ventures. The specialty channel supports airlines, such as United Airlines, and retail stores, including Nordstrom's. These specialty accounts don't fall under retail business unit operations. The direct-response channel serves customers through direct mail. Joint ventures provide opportunities to leverage the company's brand into innovative products. Recent joint ventures include Dreyer's Grand Ice Cream and Pepsi-Cola. These joint ventures create different supply chain opportunities. Starbucks created a centralized supply chain operations organization that supports each of these channels, instead of running three separate business units.[12] The company recognized significant leverage in operating the supply chain operation in this way.

Starbucks is vertically integrated via the control of coffee sourcing, roasting, packaging, and distribution through company-owned retail stores (see Figure 8.8). The company uses automated manufacturing systems (Oracle GEMMS) to accomplish distribution planning and materials requirements planning (MRP). This helps determine its long-term coffee-buying requirements and positioning of the coffee beans for roasting and packaging. Starbucks manufactures an estimated 85 million pounds of coffee a year at its facilities on both the East and West coasts.

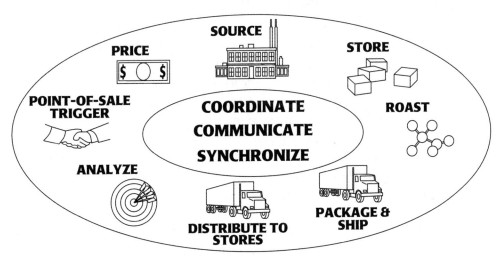

Figure 8.8: Starbucks' Vertically Integrated Supply Chain

Dealing with multiple channels of distribution for similar products requires timely and accurate reporting of inventory, allocation capabilities, and maintenance of dynamic safety stock. To manage resource allocation, the company uploads nightly sales and inventory information from the stores to the Seattle headquarters. Instead of independent demand for finished goods—whole-bean coffee and coffee beverages—Starbucks is faced with an exploding sales forecast through a dependent component demand for its proprietary coffee extract and other coffee products. The sourcing network for these products can include as many as nine levels from grower to consumer.

The benefits of SCM to Starbucks include better allocation of critical resources; reduced overhead and material costs; improved quality, faster throughput, and control of the complete material flow in the production process; and high-performance planning and integrated procurement, enabling faster time to market.

Clearly, the objective of SCM at Starbucks is asset profitability, or putting the least money in to get the most profit out. Achieving this objective requires a commitment to invest in systems, people, and talent ahead of the growth curve. Starbucks' supply chain partners are challenged at every step. Starbucks envisions its role as providing the best tools to support the success of its partners while continuing to enhance the Starbucks experience.

Continuous Replenishment:
The CVS Pharmacy–McKesson Demand Chain

CVS is the leading drug retail chain in most of the regional markets it currently serves and is growing so fast that it may soon surpass Walgreens for the number one slot nationally. In recent years, CVS has made some significant drug chain acquisitions, such as Revco, to provide itself with excellent locations in new markets. The company converted them to its own name and stocks them with CVS products. Figure 8.9 shows the entire supply chain.

The wholesale drug distributor McKesson occupies the critical position in this supply chain. Founded in 1833, McKesson is the largest U.S. distributor of pharmaceuticals, health care products, and medical/surgical supplies, with sales in excess of $20 billion per year. Customers are located in all 50 states and include hospitals, independent pharmacies, chain drug stores, food stores, clinics, nursing homes, government facilities, physician groups, HMOs, and surgical centers. McKesson supplies pharmaceuticals and health care products to roughly 35,000 customers and processes about 60,000 orders containing 1.6 million order lines daily. Customers send virtually all orders in some electronic form, using every-

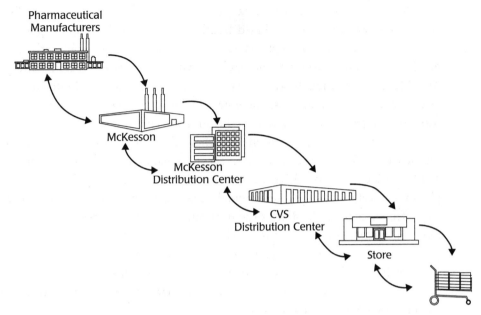

Figure 8.9: The Tightly Integrated Pharmaceutical Supply Chain

thing from handheld scanners to large mainframe computers. In addition, all major movements of funds, including customer remittances and payroll, are handled through electronic fund transfers. On the inventory management side, McKesson depends on e-commerce. Roughly 80 percent of all goods purchased by McKesson are ordered through electronic data interchange. Payments to larger suppliers are also handled in this manner.

To understand McKesson's position, you need to understand the industry structure. The drug distribution channel has experienced dramatic consolidation, with larger participants purchasing smaller companies to complement their geographic and product positioning. In ten years the number of drug wholesalers has declined from 180 to less than 50. As a result, the top five competitors account for 57 percent of the market. The chain drug stores at one time were the largest customer segment of wholesalers, accounting for roughly 28 percent of the total market, but this sector has also witnessed a number of consolidations, including the combination of CVS with Revco and of Thrift with Eckert Drugs. These chain stores continue to gain market share from independents.

McKesson is a distribution superpower. The company's objective is to become the world leader in health care supply and comprehensive pharmaceutical management across the entire supply chain, from manufacturer to customer. To accomplish this goal, the company has both pared down and focused its portfolio of businesses into a broad-based health care product distribution powerhouse. The company has replaced slower-growth, disparate, nonhealth-care distribution-related businesses with faster-growth, health-care-centered entities. Also, McKesson is using its scale, expanded product selection, and influence to help drive up its gross margins. These steps highlight the big profit leverage distribution companies can achieve with slight margin changes.

McKesson is in a great position. The wholesale drug distribution network is the most cost-effective means for pharmaceutical manufacturers to go to market. The two principal factors driving growth are a general increase in the size of the pharmaceutical market and a realization by manufacturers that wholesalers are a cost-effective channel. In short, drug distributors are able to service customers more efficiently than manufacturers, which frees manufacturers to allocate their resources to research and development, manufacturing, and marketing. Indeed, it's clear that the drug wholesaler's role is changing from that of providing only cost-effective logistics to also providing information services and marketing assistance to suppliers and customers.

Moreover, customers, including CVS, benefit from this paradigm shift by having the convenience of a single source of supply for a full line of pharmaceutical products, lower inventory costs, more timely and efficient delivery, and improved purchasing and inventory information. Better integration with McKesson is a key strategic move for CVS. CVS management sees significant potential for improving sales and margins through its enhanced pricing and promotional forecasting systems. Supply chain integration helps the retailer move from pull to push promotions by allowing category managers to plan promotions more effectively using item history taken from historical point-of-sale data on a store-by-store basis. The integration with McKesson will substantially reduce the amount of time needed to plan and stock inventory for individual promotions.

Clearly, a major business objective in the CVS-McKesson chain is to improve performance through better supply chain integration. This requires much closer cooperation between McKesson and CVS, with McKesson even taking responsibility for stock levels. McKesson monitors CVS's store-level consumption and replenishes the inventory to meet the agreed-upon service levels—true supply chain integration. This cooperative process between supplier and customer can be achieved only through seamless interenterprise process integration and sophisticated apps that link the customer directly to the supplier's production department.

What can we learn from McKesson and CVS? That retail SCM is about interenterprise process integration. The objectives of interenterprise integration are improved customer responsiveness, strengthened supply chain partnerships, enhanced organizational flexibility, and improved decision-making capabilities. The CVS example also illustrates that to succeed in today's customer-dominated environment, companies must apply the same approaches to inter-corporate processes that they do to processes that reside within one company's boundaries.

Build-to-Order: Intel, Solectron, and Ingram Micro

Consider the build-to-order supply chain integration between Ingram Micro (the world's largest IT distributor) and Solectron (the leader in contract manu-facturing). By leveraging their complementary core strengths in logistics and or-der management (Ingram) and very efficient high-volume manufacturing (Solectron), the two companies provide build-to-order and configure-to-order assembly services, for PCs, servers, and peripherals.

What is all the hoopla about build-to-order? In a traditional SCM example like Starbucks, the demand plan is usually established, and the implications are embodied in a demand forecast. Supply plans are implemented to match the pro-file of the demand forecast. Since traditional supply chain planning assumes that demand is known, it focuses more on cost reduction than on profitability and meeting strategic objectives, such as market share growth. A supply plan is im-plemented to cost-effectively meet the demand forecast while meeting customer service targets such as order fill rate. Revenue is a given, so only costs are mini-mized. Traditional planning does not provide a mechanism for ensuring that the demand plan is profitable or even feasible. The demand plan may cause severe disruptions to the supply chain or even exceed its supply capabilities, resulting in lost sales or market share and unprofitable operations.

As customer demand becomes unpredictable, make-to-stock demand fore-casting scenarios become unrealistic. To be effective, companies need to align a cost-effective supply plan with an efficient demand plan that best achieves cor-porate goals, such as maximized profitability. This is the core concept behind build-to-order: Match supply with demand in real time. Contrary to traditional supply planning, the demand plan is not a given; hence, a demand forecast is the result of a finalized demand plan that was established during the planning process. Similarly, the supply plan is not developed primarily to meet the demand plan, but is the result of a holistic planning process.

The supply chain partnership works as follows (see Figure 8.10): Ingram re-ceives a PC order from one of its reseller customers. The order is transferred elec-tronically to one of nine worldwide manufacturing locations currently owned by

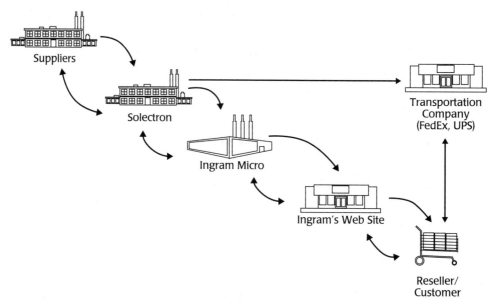

Figure 8.10: Build-to-Order Supply Chain with Zero Inventory

either Solectron or Ingram. The PC is produced to specification at the manufacturing facility (probably married at some point with the associated peripherals) and drop-shipped either to the reseller or end-user customer. The entire process takes less than seven days.

Intel, a supplier, is at the heart of the PC value chain. Hundreds of raw material suppliers, component manufacturers, assemblers, and resellers depend on its continued success. In the past, Intel's success was clearly attributable to its relentless product innovation, which remains paramount to PC industry prosperity. Lately, however, Intel's supply chain practices with both suppliers and customers have taken a much more conspicuous role in the PC value chain.

Customers have begun to demand just-in-time delivery. This trend is forcing PC makers to aggressively eliminate slack and excess inventory from the supply chain. Making PCs to order eliminates unwanted stockpiles of components and finished product. But it also requires all participants in the PC supply chain—including Intel—to coordinate and integrate supply levels, manufacturing capacity, inventory, and logistics data.

The enemy of an efficient supply chain is excess inventory, and in the fast-changing PC market almost any inventory seems like too much. A PC maker's worst nightmare is an overstock of yesterday's PC *du jour* languishing on warehouse shelves. Such situations force PC makers to sell their dated models at discount prices and forfeit profits. Aiming to accelerate delivery speed while reducing inventory and costs in the PC supply chain, Intel established an extranet, a private Internet, to communicate real-time inventory levels and demand to suppliers and customers. The chipmaker also implemented an enterprise resource planning system to improve inventory control, product delivery, and business integration, setting up an intranet to speed procurement cycles.

The Ingram-Solectron-reseller interenterprise supply chain should benefit all parties involved since it allows for time and cost savings by eliminating stops along the supply chain and the associated handling costs, reducing shipping costs. It improves inventory management through the use of a more efficient pull-driven production strategy. Perhaps more important, it should help further drive industry consolidation, particularly within the distribution category.

Supply Chain Management: A Manager's Roadmap

SCM is a complex subject involving the flow of goods from upstream suppliers to manufacturers, distributors, and end customers. It involves many disciplines, from procurement and supplier management to multisite manufacturing, customer management, order processing, distribution planning, forecasting, demand management, warehousing, transportation, and managing final points of sale. Integrating all this is not easy, nor can it be executed quickly.

It's a safe bet that at this very moment your company is either thinking about or struggling to design and implement a multicompany supply chain while gaining greater control over order fulfillment—the path to generating customer loyalty and increasing market share. Some questions your company might be wrestling with are as follows:

- *How do we define the interenterprise supply chain problem and scope of issues (i.e., what is our supply chain, where is it broken, how do we fix it)?*

- *How do we make a business case for the reengineering of an interenterprise process that no one owns or fully understands?*

- *Where do we start? Should we start with a clean-slate approach or are we better off with an incremental-improvement approach?*

- *Should we build or buy? Which vendors (and technologies) should we consider? Should we consider best-of-breed applications or a single-vendor, integrated solution?*

• *What will the impact of each choice be on our legacy systems? (Lack of integration of various legacy systems along the supply chain leads to redundancy and a high degree of variability.) How can we avoid this?*

What is the focus in your company? How are you forging a one-of-a-kind e-supply chain from your customers, distributors, suppliers, and outsourcing partners? Each company must cope with a confusing array of demands and choices as it develops a vision for the optimal supply chain. So, what can companies do now to prepare for this brave new world? Eight steps are crucial to turning tomorrow's promise into today's reality.

1. **Clarify your supply chain goals.** Companies must examine their SCM strategies as essential elements of overall business design. To what extent can your firm's integrated sourcing, production, and distribution capabilities be tuned to drive superior value and customer satisfaction? If the value is there, a company may choose to become an operations-intensive manufacturer. If the value lies elsewhere, the brand management/outsourced supply chain model may be appropriate.

2. **Conduct a supply chain readiness audit.** A readiness diagnostic is the logical first step. Are you ready for the consumer demands, globalization, and information needs of the coming age? What are you doing to promote supply chain coordination within the firm and with external partners? Are your performance metrics up to date? How do you compare with others inside and outside your industry? Such an assessment can provide a company-specific roadmap for supply chain development.

3. **Develop a business case.** CEOs and boards of most companies remain unconvinced that an integrated supply chain approach will pay hard-dollar dividends. Making the business case for supply chain integration thus becomes a high priority for managers. The case must be made on both the strategic and practical levels, combining a clear sense of direction with detailed examples of the gains in service and cost to be derived from closer horizontal integration.

4. **Establish a supply chain coordination unit.** Establish a hard-hitting but thinly staffed SCM team in your company. The objectives will be to provide corporate leadership in the analysis, design, and implementation of solutions that drive service and cost effectiveness to new levels across the organization and with external partners. Functioning almost as internal consultants with top management support, this team will work to take cost out and raise cus-

tomer satisfaction. The people involved must be trained in all aspects of the supply chain, from procurement through manufacturing to customer service; the latest decision-support tools; the best ways to establish win-win relationships with partners; and in the facilitation techniques essential to collaborative teamwork.

5. **Begin supplier integration.** A supply chain isn't any good if you're the only one playing. It's imperative that you convince, cajole, even threaten your upstream suppliers and downstream distributors/customers to join the game. Partners are needed to support the new virtual organization. Get your partners to plan now for Internet-driven supply chains. You say your industry isn't ready yet? Either you're missing key initiatives your competitors are already taking advantage of or you're sitting on a great opportunity to be first in your field. Get your marketing folks talking to your supply chain people to see how Internet orders can help drive distribution efficiencies.

6. **Develop a performance scorecard.** Don't rush to implementation without understanding supply chain measurement issues. Work with your chosen suppliers to come to a common understanding of how the supply chain performance is to be measured and what performance incentives and penalties should be put into place.

7. **Educate, educate, educate.** Invest in educating and reorienting employees, vendors, and other members of the supply chain on the practices needed to optimize business processes. No person, team, process, or company ever knows enough. Make a companywide commitment to creating and managing a more complex organization capable of tackling global business issues. Organizations must invest in ongoing training, mentoring, education, and feedback systems to keep their people current with the latest thinking.

8. **Learn to manage failure.** According to the law of averages, many supply chain projects are destined to fail in the coming decade. All too often project failures are blamed on not involving users, and on vendors promising more than they can deliver. Whatever the reason, managers must become adept at identifying brushfires before they become full-fledged infernos. The first step in turning around a problem project is to admit the project is in trouble. This is simple in theory but hard to do because egos, pride, and careers are at stake. But the facts must be faced. You're in trouble if you're behind schedule, over budget, or everyone is pointing fingers. This failure management can get quite complex in an interenterprise setting.

Supply chain excellence requires effective strategies, sustained management commitment, and changes in attitude, culture, and organization. Often all these actions must be taken simultaneously, making it even harder and more stressful. The ability to integrate and deploy SCM solutions is critical to remaining competitive. Most managers are perplexed by the bewildering rate of technology change, often throwing wrenches into supply chain initiatives. As a result, there's a lot of soul searching among manufacturers, distributors, retailers, and consumers as they scrutinize their roles within the supply chain. But technology is not the only variable changing. There are also the usual suspects: competitive pressures, regulatory issues, pricing, and promotions, as well as causal factors ranging from seasonal restrictions to channel constraints. In fact, we're willing to boldly state that we're seeing only the tip of the iceberg regarding how technology and other variables are affecting the structure of the supply chain process. Stay tuned for more supply chain drama in the next decade.

Memo to the CEO

Supply chain management results in major structural changes in the way industries operate. Traditional supply chains have undergone a major metamorphosis in the last decade. In an effort to improve their competitive positioning through lower costs and accelerated time to market, many companies are reexamining and restructuring the way in which products are designed, manufactured, warehoused, transported, and sold. Innovative companies within the supply chain, such as CVS and McKesson, are adapting their business models to capitalize on these changes. Importantly, as these changes occur, the old paradigm of company vs. company competition is becoming less relevant. As highlighted by the success of revolutionary companies such as Cisco and Dell, success is often measured in terms of supply chain vs. supply chain.

The current efforts by companies to streamline their supply chains are driven by several accelerating trends. These trends include ongoing advancements in technology, the globalization of the economy, an acceleration in corporate outsourcing, the standardization of enterprise apps, and the strong success of companies in the high-tech industry that have adopted nontraditional supply chain models. Importantly, the convergence of these trends is causing several major changes to occur in the underlying structure of the traditional technology supply chain.

First, sales are becoming customer driven (as opposed to vendor driven) as demand generation shifts from push to pull models such as build-to-order. Importantly, these strategies require significantly less inventory to be carried within the supply chain. While reductions in inventory levels are currently causing hiccups at a number of component and manufacturing companies, reduced inventory levels should in the long run lead to lower pricing, more stable product supply, and an eventual reduction in the severity of the traditional boom-bust cycles of many industries.

Second, consolidation is accelerating within each segment of the technology supply chain to reduce the number of suppliers with which they interact and establish a few key strategic supplier-partner relationships. As companies become increasingly dependent on these strategic relationships, the value assigned to selected strategic supply chain companies should rise.

Third, as companies work to improve their competitive positioning, they're broadening the range of services they offer; in fact, similar services are now offered at several different points in the supply chain. While this increasing overlap of service offerings creates the potential for tension between segments in the supply chain, it also creates the opportunity for a number of interesting channel partnerships and mergers over the next few years.

Supply chain efficiency will be one of the major competitive battlegrounds for a wide range of companies over the next several years. As companies work to lower costs and improve time to market, a number of changes are occurring within the underlying structure. As a result, there is a significant opportunity for innovative companies within the supply chain to capitalize on these changes to strengthen their competitive position.

The dynamics of transferring information between trading partners have been irrevocably changed. As a result, companies have to pay close attention to the world of interenterprise computing as the next foundation for growth. The next century is just around the corner. Major changes in the business environment are already under way. Progressive managers must act now to ensure they are driving winning supply chains into the brave new world of the twenty-first century.

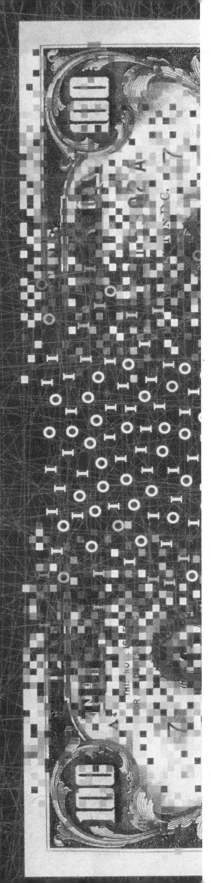

e-Procurement: The Next Wave of Cost Reduction

What to Expect

Inefficient buying, redundant processes, nonstrategic sourcing, and maverick buying are symptoms of poor procurement practices. As today's industrial-age companies change to tomorrow's e-business trailblazers, the ability to tie efficient procurement strategies and business workflow together with robust technology implementation truly differentiates market leaders. Plus, it frees employees to do their real jobs instead of wasting time doing paperwork.

This chapter illustrates a new wave of e-procurement automation that companies are deploying. It explains the concepts behind e-procurement so that you are not intimidated by the jargon. The chapter also provides an easy-to-follow roadmap for managers to take with them on their journey to e-procurement.

Large companies spend more than 5 to 10 percent of revenue on office equipment, supplies, software, computers, peripherals, and other so-called nonproduction goods. This business-to-business e-commerce comprises a significant market, exceeding $500 billion a year. Buyers and sellers recognize that by creating a more efficient method of exchange, they can realize business benefits such as additional revenue and lower costs.

Before solutions can be deployed, however, major procurement process surgery is needed. Typically, every time an employee orders something, he or she goes through the process of filling out a requisition form, waiting for approval, and finally getting a purchase order (PO). Sound familiar? *Are there many guidelines and rules that your organization wants employees to follow?* Is there little help available from the purchasing department, and does it takes weeks before the order is fulfilled?

Procurement inefficiencies are astounding. Nonproduction goods account for a third or more of corporate expenditures, and nearly 95 percent of them are acquired using paper-based processes. Consider, for instance, a high-tech manufacturer, which figures it spends $100 to process each purchase order. The company knows exactly how much it spends on the material used in production. But don't ask the company how it spends approximately $1 billion a year on computers, office products, furniture, and other nonproduction supplies. *Does this remind you of your company?*

Don't despair. With the increasing use of e-commerce, procurement is going through a revolution. We're entering a new era of a self-service approach to requisitioning. Help is just around the corner, with a new breed of integrated procurement applications whereby everyday employee business tasks can be efficiently completed through easy-to-use Web-based applications.

Structural Transition: From Isolated Purchasing to Real-Time Process Integration

Corporate purchasing is undergoing a structural transition, a process metamorphosis. For a majority of corporations, many of which are just getting used to the idea of office e-mail systems, the concept of employee self-service apps might sound futuristic and pretty far away. But believe it or not, next-generation procurement applications are rapidly taking hold in major corporations.

Consider the following scenarios:

• A machine goes down and a $100 part is needed immediately. The manufacturing company loses $100,000 for every hour the machine is not operational.

Jim, the factory foreman, uses the e-procurement system to expedite the replacement part order. The system automatically routes the purchase order to the supplier that has the part. The part is delivered to the shop floor within four hours. This is a maintenance, repairs, and operations (MRO) scenario.

- Ann used to fill out requests for miscellaneous office supplies and wait weeks for delivery. She now uses the new e-procurement system, browses the catalog from the approved vendor list, makes selections, and drops them in her shopping basket. The system automatically gets purchase order approval and ships the products overnight to arrive at her desk the next day.

- Alan's boss calls at 7 P.M. to ask him to take his place at an important meeting in Chicago. Alan logs into the e-procurement system, goes to the American Express corporate travel Web site, and books an airline ticket, car, and hotel accommodations in less than five minutes. The e-procurement system automatically checks his profile and authorizes the purchase.

- Lynn has just come back from a three-month consulting engagement in Italy. To do her expense report, she logs into an internal system for travel expenses. Instead of having to key in credit card expenses, the totals are already tallied in the expense report. Lynn simply adds out-of-pocket expenses and submits the report electronically. The report is cleared because it conforms to company rules.

Companies have talked about improving transactional services like office supplies procurement, travel, and expense-reporting processes for years. Why? Because the purchase of goods and services represents the single largest cost item for an enterprise. It's estimated that for each dollar a company earns on the sale of a product, it spends about 50 to 60 cents on goods and services. More capital is spent on the purchase of materials and services than all other expense items combined. Billions of dollars are wasted every year in inefficient procurement practices.

You Say "Purchasing" and I Say "Procurement"

Before going any further, it's important to clarify the difference between purchasing and procurement. These terms are often used interchangeably, but they differ in scope. *Purchasing* refers to the actual buying of materials and those activities associated with the buying process. Electronic purchasing addresses only part of the problem and represents only the tip of the iceberg.

Procurement, on the other hand, has a broader meaning and includes purchasing, transportation, warehousing, and inbound receiving. Procurement is a closed-loop process that begins with the requisition and ends with payment. Integrated procurement remains one of the truly significant business strategies to be developed in this century. But it's been hampered by technological limitations.

The initial goal of integrating the procurement supply chain was to take apart some traditional, hierarchically structured purchasing organizations. Many had layer upon layer of approval procedures that slowed the process down. What's emerging is an emphasis on order-to-delivery processes rather than tasks. The focus is moving quickly toward integrated procurement chain management (see Figure 9.1).

At the same time, procurement is migrating from traditional paper-based processes to e-procurement. The benefits of e-procurement fall into two major categories: efficiency and effectiveness. Efficiency includes lower procurement costs, faster cycle times, reduced maverick or unauthorized buying, more highly organized information, and tighter integration of the procurement function with key back-office systems. Effectiveness includes increased control over the supply chain, proactive management of key procurement data, and higher-quality purchasing decisions within organizations.

So, what's new? Procurement models of the industrial era are being replaced by the information era's more effective practices, which enable firms to reap benefits at both ends of the supplier-to-customer chain. This is thanks to the nearly

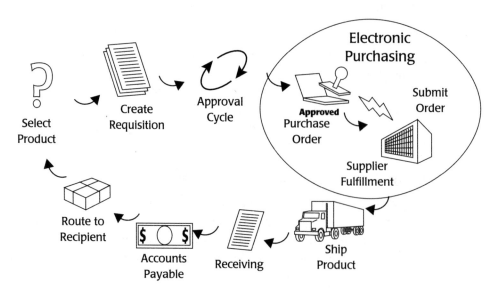

Figure 9.1: The e-Procurement Chain

ideal combination of volume advantages, flexible contracts, and valuable supplier alliances, along with decentralized, user-initiated and user-responsive purchases.

However, for many companies, development of a truly effective integrated procurement strategy is still a long way off. For all but a relative few, there is no clear vision of what needs to be achieved through reengineering and integrating the procurement process, nor is there a good roadmap of how to get there—or even an idea of what "there" should look like. Managers need a detailed understanding of how the next generation of e-procurement applications is being developed.

OK, managers, let's start by asking some key questions:

- *What is operating resource procurement and why is it important to top management? What functions within an organization do these solutions address?*

- *How did e-procurement systems restructure such companies as Microsoft?*

- *What are the primary e-procurement concepts on the buy and sell sides?*

- *What benefits will e-procurement bring to your organization? Is it worth the cost?*

- *What are the management pitfalls in moving toward an e-procurement solution? How does this redefine procurement chain relationships across different industries?*

Why Is Procurement a Top-Management Issue?

Procurement is evolving from a support function to a weapon in a corporation's competitive arsenal. Companies are looking for solutions that combat high procurement costs and lengthy cycle times and ensure smooth receipt and delivery of materials or services. They are seeking to automate the day-to-day purchasing tasks, such as catalog searching, authorization, and processing purchase orders. The goal is to free professional buyers so they can focus on more strategic issues such as managing supplier relations, reducing inventory, and improving the quality of the parts coming in the door.

Chief procurement officers are looking to solve the five biggest challenges faced by corporate procurement today:

1. Reducing order processing costs and cycle times

2. Providing enterprisewide access to corporate procurement capabilities

3. Empowering desktop requisitioning through self-service

4. Achieving integration with key back-office systems

5. Elevating procurement to a position of strategic importance within the organization

One of the most pressing challenges confronting purchasing is cycle-time reduction. Consequently, it would be impossible to find a CFO or a chief procurement officer who is not attempting to push requisitioning to the desktop. They want to provide employees the self-service ability to make routine purchases such as travel, office supplies, and computer supplies. Employees have been desperately waiting for streamlined procurement processes for years. Web-based self-service solutions are opening doors to unlimited possibilities.

Roy Anderson, director of purchasing at John Hancock Mutual Life Insurance, outlined the following bottom-line results of e-procurement:[1]

- $1,000 in savings = An agent generating $18,000 in insurance premium dollars.

- $1,000 in savings = $550,000 in mutual fund sales.

- $1,000 in savings = An agent selling a $1 million whole-life insurance policy.

Operational cost management is a central objective of e-procurement. As companies aggressively look at improving margins, remaining nimble, and maximizing profits, there is unprecedented pressure to manage operating expenses as intelligently and efficiently as possible. The dollar-for-dollar, bottom-line impact of the margin enhancement afforded by operational cost management is startling—especially when compared with only fractional increases in profits realized through revenue-focused initiatives. For example, according to *CFO Magazine*'s annual Sales General and Administrative Costs (SG&A) survey, "slicing SG&A by $1 has the same bottom-line effect as boosting sales by $13," and "cutting 1 percent from SG&A will tweak earnings by 2.3 percent."[2] Clearly, there are few actions a CFO can take to deliver such disproportionate dividends.

Now ask yourself whether your management is actively pursuing a strategy of operational cost reduction. *Do they think of the procurement process as a potential opportunity? If so, does your company have an e-procurement application framework that allows the development of various integrated procurement applications? Is your management's emphasis on developing a suite of applications that are capable of best-in-class procurement and financial practices?*

Now that you understand why this subject is important to top management and have done a quick assessment of your company, let's look more closely at what constitutes operating resource procurement.

What Exactly Is Operating Resource Procurement?

There are two types of corporate procurement: production-related goods and nonproduction-related goods (see Table 9.1). Production goods include raw materials, components, assemblies, and other items needed to produce a finished good. Nonproduction goods are items that businesses need to run day-to-day business operations: capital equipment; MRO products; office, computer, scientific, and industrial supplies; and travel and entertainment.

Nonproduction goods, the stepchildren of purchasing, are increasingly taking center stage. Consider the case of Ford Motor Company. In its continuing quest to cut costs, Ford is using e-procurement solutions from Intelisys in an attempt to slice billions of dollars from such mundane tasks as purchasing office supplies and filing expense reports. Ford spends an estimated $15.5 billion each year on nonproduction goods and services, making it one of the biggest purchasers of such goods worldwide.

Ford revamped its purchasing process. Instead of receiving catalogs and having employees fill out purchase orders that must be cleared by the boss (which often takes days or weeks), employees now log on to an Internet system. They browse manufacturers' catalogs, order from a preapproved group of suppliers, and get purchase approval in minutes. By using e-commerce to order goods from

Table 9.1: Production vs. Nonproduction Related Items

Characteristics of Production-Related Procurement	Characteristics of Nonproduction-Related Procurement
Production items: Raw materials, components	Operating resources: Office and computer supplies; maintenance, repairs, and operations (MRO) supplies; travel
Scheduled by production runs	Ad hoc, not scheduled
Locus of operation: Professional buyer's desktop	Locus of operation: Employee desktop
No approvals required	Approval required
High degree of automation	Almost no automation
Design-specification Driven	Catalog driven

online catalogs, Ford expects to cut spending and transaction costs by as much as 30 percent.[3]

Ford is also using procurement applications for processing the more than 1 million travel and expense accounts that employees submit each year. It's estimated that large corporations spend about $36 on processing each expense report. With the Internet and electronic downloading of credit card receipts, the cost drops to about $8—an approximate savings of $28 million annually. *Are you salivating yet?*

As the example of Ford illustrates, the focus of procurement automation is not so much on production-related raw materials but on nonproduction goods. Since so much emphasis is placed on nonproduction-related goods, let's take a closer look at the different types of operating resources.

Types of Nonproduction or Operating Resource Products

The procurement of nonproduction goods, known as operating resource management (ORM), is defined as the strategic purchase of nonproduction goods through the effective use of aggregate buying, volume discounts, lowered transaction costs, and decision support techniques to identify vendor discount operations.

Of all the types of operating resources referenced in Table 9.2, the most significant category encompasses the mission-critical purchases without which a company cannot operate: maintenance, repairs, and operations. It's estimated that the size of the market for industrial MRO products is approximately $300 to $400 billion annually. This category includes electrical supplies, PVF (pipes, valves, and fittings), power transmission, and other product classes. Table 9.3 illustrates the various types of MRO products.

The overall MRO market is highly fragmented, with the 50 largest distributors (all of which have annual sales of more than $90 million) accounting for less than 15 percent of the market. As a result, most industrial customers currently purchase their supplies through numerous local distribution and supply companies. These distributors generally provide the customer with repair and maintenance services, technical support, and application expertise with respect to one product category.

Products typically are purchased by the distributor for resale directly from the manufacturer and warehoused at branch distribution facilities until sold to the customer. The customer normally purchases an amount of product inventory for near-term anticipated needs and warehouses them at its industrial site until the products are needed.

While growth in the industrial distribution market is generally related to the expansion of the economy, revenues attributable to the outsourcing of MRO supply procurement, inventory control, and warehouse management, known as *inte-*

Table 9.2: Types of Operating Resources

Types of Operating Resources	Characteristics
General and Administrative	Low dollar value/high transaction volume
Office supplies and books	Commodity products
Furniture	Minimal tracking required
Professional services and education/training	Large pool of requisitioners
Computer-Related Capital Equipment	Inventoried assets must be closely tracked
Computer hardware and software	Medium to high dollar value
Computer supplies	Technical product specifications
Networking supplies	Budget constraints
Copiers, fax machines, telephones	Hidden inventories difficult to track
MRO: Maintenance, Repairs, and Operations	Critical to plant maintenance
	Critical to factory and production operations
Machine parts	Off-site, distributed regions
Electrical controls	Significant dollar volume
Tooling	Careful tracking needed
Shop supplies	
Travel Services and Entertainment (T+E)	High dollar value
Travel management	Budget constraints—expense tracking
Hotel management	Multilevel approval process—spending analysis
Catering	

Table 9.3: Types of MRO Products

Electrical and mechanical	Fluid-handling equipment
	Bearings and power transmission equipment
	Pipes, valves, and fittings
Electronic	Networking equipment and cables
	Computers and peripherals
Laboratory equipment and supplies	Instruments, equipment, chemicals, and other laboratory products
Industrial supplies	General maintenance supplies, safety products, and production consumables, including cutting tools and abrasives
Service and sanitary establishment equipment, parts, and supplies	General mill and safety supplies
Machine shop supplies	Industrial machinery, equipment, and tools
Office supplies and equipment	General supplies
Construction and building supplies	Lighting, plumbing, appliance, and HVAC products

grated supply, are expected to grow at an annualized rate of 40 percent, from $1.8 billion in 1995 to $10 billion in 2000.[4]

Operating Resource Procurement Processes: Controlled Chaos

Inefficient buying, redundant processes, nonstrategic sourcing, and maverick buying are all symptoms of poor operating resource procurement practices. For example, a large semiconductor manufacturer requires employees to fill out a paper form that has three copies. Employees keep a copy and give one to the purchasing department, which faxes a copy to the supplier. The supplier fills the order and ships it back. The supplier collects the forms periodically, aggregates the charges, and bills the manufacturer. This process is neither efficient nor cheap for either party.

Clearly, even though operating resources are a leading corporate expenditure, most procurement processes are paper intensive. *How much does it cost your company to buy something?* Chances are, your company spends far more on managing the procurement cycle than it does on the goods it actually purchases. Every purchase—from paper clips to spare parts for shop equipment—costs the company anywhere from $70 to $300 in administrative overhead in a paper-based procurement cycle.

Is maverick buying a problem in your company? Maverick buying happens when employees buy products on their own, often charging items to corporate credit cards and missing out on volume discounts that large companies arrange with preferred providers of products and services. This costs organizations incredible overhead in terms of additional administrative effort.

Purchasing managers have a growing awareness of how they can reduce maverick buying and improve profits: Reduce the need to service small-dollar orders (focus on new, better contracts), and obtain better purchasing information for contract negotiations (negotiate with the knowledge of what has been purchased). Electronic procurement will not only immediately reduce off-contract buying, but will also free purchasing professionals to concentrate on more strategic activities that will make the company more competitive in the global business climate.

Now that we have identified the problems, let's look at the size of the market opportunity.

How Big Is the Operating Resource Market?

Automating operating resource procurement is definitely a big market opportunity. But while the area of production-related procurement is mostly automated with enterprise resource planning applications (see Chapter 7), non-production-related procurement has seen very limited automation.

It's estimated that even though operating resources account for at least 30 percent of company spending, such spending is managed via a maze of paper-based processes. This method allows for very little leveraged buying and savings across the enterprise. Therein lies opportunities for automation, control, and leverage. For example, automation in travel and entertainment not only reduces the cost of processing expense reports (from more than $36 to less than $8, as we have seen), but also shortens the cycle time, from 22 to 3 days.[5]

America's top 2,000 corporations currently purchase more than an estimated $400 billion of nonproduction goods annually. Many of the orders are for less than $1,000 of merchandise, a large percentage of which is now bought outside of the preferred buying channels, or off contract. As a result, the level of purchase detail available for negotiating supplier contracts is inadequate.

Procurement enterprise applications must support internal processes, e-commerce capabilities, and sharing information in real time. Firms not pushing ahead at a fast rate on information systems tend to plateau. At some point, they will no longer be able to make significant efficiency jumps in their integrated procurement chains.

Let's look at a best-practice company—Microsoft—and the advantages it gained from an integrated procurement application called MS Market.

Operating Resource Procurement at Microsoft: MS Market

In recent years a number of businesses have sought to extend the benefits of automation to employees, corporate partners, and key suppliers. In summer 1996, the Microsoft Corporate Procurement Group implemented an innovative new tool called MS Market, an online ordering system that works on Microsoft's intranet. MS Market reduced the personnel required to manage low-cost requisitions and gives employees a quick, easy way to order materials without being burdened with paperwork and bureaucratic processes.

Internet Week quoted Bob Herbold, executive vice president of Microsoft, as saying that MS Market was spurred by Microsoft's goal of eliminating all paperwork companywide to gain new efficiencies. In its first year, MS Market was used to purchase more than $1 billion in supplies. Some 6,000 Microsoft employees worldwide have used the system, in which the company invested $1.1 million.[6]

In a case study published on Microsoft's Web site, Clayton Fleming, senior manager of the Corporate Procurement Group, elaborates on the procurement scenario: "We have a lot of dollars flowing into marketing and R&D. Unlike manufacturing companies, ours is a very distributed procurement environment. We get thousands of requests every week from all over the company for small purchases, from office supplies to business cards to catering services. The bottom line is that the majority of purchase requests from Microsoft employees involve relatively small amounts of money."[7]

Fleming points out that these "high-volume, low-dollar transactions" represent about 70 percent of total volume, but only 3 percent of accounts payable. Clearly, many employees were wasting time turning requisitions into POs, trying to follow business rules and processes—one of the biggest drawbacks to using traditional procurement procedures. Managers wanted to streamline this process, so the decision was made to create a requisitioning tool that would take all the controls and validations relegated to requisition personnel and push them onto the Web. Employees wanted an easy-to-use online form for ordering supplies that included interfaces to procurement partners, such as Boise Cascade and Marriott. The result is MS Market.

How does this system work? Let's say a Microsoft employee wants a book about Bill Gates. He goes to the MS Market site on Microsoft's intranet, and MS Market immediately identifies his preferences and approval code through his log-on ID. The employee selects the Barnes & Noble link, which brings up a catalog, order form, and a list of hundreds of books with titles and prices that have been negotiated between Microsoft buyers and Barnes & Noble. He selects a book, puts it in the order form, and completes the order by verifying his group's cost center number and manager's name.

The order is transmitted immediately to the supplier, cutting down on delivery time as well as accounting for the payment of the supplies. Upon submission of the order, MS Market generates an order tracking number for reference, sends notification via e-mail to the employee's manager, and transmits the order over the Internet to Barnes & Noble for fulfillment. In this case, since the purchase total is only $20, the manager's specific approval is not required. Two days later, the book arrives at the employee's office. MS Market lets employees easily order low-cost items in a controlled fashion at a low cost, without going through a complicated PO approval process (see Figure 9.2).

The business benefits were profound. The people in charge of processing POs were redeployed so that they could concentrate on higher-level procurement functions, such as analyzing procurement data and cutting deals with vendors. The use of MS Market has climbed exponentially since implementation. It's estimated that more than $3 billion annually flows through MS Market.

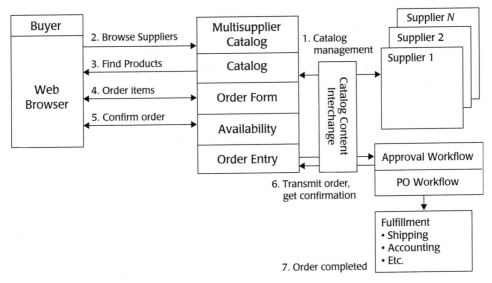

Figure 9.2: MS Market in Action

The biggest benefit of e-procurement apps is that they eliminate the rules, paperwork, hidden procedures, and other obstacles that keep employees from doing their jobs. Instead of dealing with the process, employees focus on completing their work. As seen in Table 9.4, the business benefits that accrue from an e-procurement implementation can be quite substantial.

Procurement Business Problem: Lack of Process Integration

Operational resource management is a discipline requiring a comprehensive and consolidated solution. It must be extended in stages to encompass all of a com-

Table 9.4: Business Benefits of MS Market

MS Market Solution	Business Benefits
User-friendly catalog for employees worldwide	Control and tracking of orders with direct vendors
Integration with SAP R/3	Automate $3 billion annual spending
Components: Windows NT Server 4.0, Internet Information Server 3.0, SQL Server 6.5, Site Server Enterprise 2.0, Microsoft Exchange Server for e-mail approval	Reduce purchase cycle from 8 to 3 days
	Reduce employee overhead from 14 to 1.5 full-time employees
	Average 1,000 orders per day; 6,000 transactions

pany's major cost areas, while augmenting existing investments in accounting, financial planning, and human resources systems. Thus, while it's easy to automate distinct procurement areas, current stand-alone or "point solutions" address each segment of the procurement life cycle individually and miss the point entirely. The need for an integrated solution—e-procurement chain management—is evident (see Figure 9.3).

In managing the movement of resources—materials, services, knowledge, or labor—through the procurement chain, successful firms have created direct linkages between suppliers and employees. This method obliterates rigid intra-organizational and intercompany barriers that tend to dominate outmoded procurement practices.

The big challenge is structural migration—how to get from the current state to the next generation of an integrated framework. Integrated e-procurement becomes critical as companies adapt *strategic sourcing,* a model by which purchasing's efforts are focused on value-added portions of the business and away from day-to-day transactional activities. The strategy is aimed at giving purchasing as much control as possible over what the company spends, including several areas not traditionally under their command.

What are the integrated solution requirements? A successful system must be designed for casual use by untrained employees. If users don't like the system, then the whole application will fail. Even if users love the system for various reasons, such as ease of use, it must also meet the needs of purchasing managers. Be-

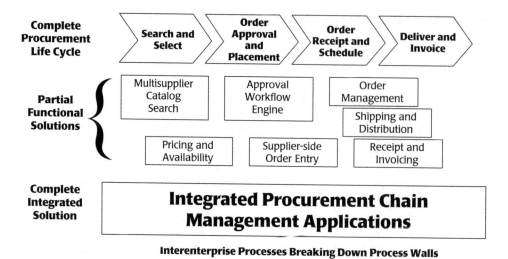

Figure 9.3: e-Procurement Chain Management

hind the scenes, it must provide extensive support for the professional buyers, including management controls, reporting, and integration with existing systems. Evaluate your integration alternatives using the following guidelines.

- **Management control.** First and foremost, purchasing managers should have control over which products are available to employees, where they can be purchased, and who needs to approve an order. With these controls available, managers can then choose which level of empowerment makes sense for different employees, commodities, and projects.

- **Online product selection.** Online catalogs save time and reduce errors by catching mistakes earlier, but managing these catalogs can be the most challenging aspect of the system. All suppliers should be accessible from the system, and they should have control over how products are presented. Employees should be able to quickly find what they need (even if they do not know the supplier), place an order, and return to work.

- **Electronic ordering.** In addition to the ability to place orders with suppliers via electronic data input, fax, or e-mail, a procurement system should provide a seamless transition from requisition to purchase order with no rekeying.

- **Application integration.** Procurement touches virtually every aspect of an organization and the systems used to run it. Unless a procurement system can seamlessly integrate with existing applications, such as general ledger, accounts payable, purchasing, and human resources applications, duplicate efforts will be required to maintain multiple systems.

- **Information and reporting.** Solid information is the key to process optimization and cost reduction. A good procurement system should track what was purchased, by whom, from whom, at what price, and how long it took to complete each step of the cycle. This information is invaluable for supplier negotiation and month-end reconciliation.

Next-Generation Integrated Procurement Applications

Broadly speaking, e-procurement applications can be further divided into three categories: buy-side desktop requisitioning, buy-side centralized procurement management, and sell-side applications.

- Buy-side desktop requisitioning software enables employees to buy online while the company maintains approval routing and purchasing processes. By hooking up the corporate intranet to suppliers' Web-based commerce sites, buy-side software routes employee purchase requests internally before turning them into orders.

- Buy-side centralized procurement solutions allow procurement managers and professional buyers to manage the process, analyze transactional data, and perform supplier management.

- Sell-side applications are solutions that help distributors or manufacturers sell products over the Web. These applications often include tools for creating and maintaining electronic product catalogs, as well as transactional support for order entry from customers.

Table 9.5 captures the key differences between buy-side and sell-side applications.

Elements of Buy-Side e-Procurement Solutions

A buy-side application is an intranet application that streamlines and integrates the entire procurement process—from point of need to final settlement of transactions and the delivery of goods. The system leverages existing application investments, linking the buying organization directly with suppliers on the Internet and delivering product availability and customized pricing data directly to the desktop.

Table 9.5: Comparing Buy-Side and Sell-Side Applications

Requisitioning applications (buy side)	Make buying fast and hassle-free for employees
	Automate approval routing; standardization
	Provide supplier management tools for the professional buyer
Centralized procurement management applications (buy side)	Spending analysis and multisupplier catalog management
	Centralized multisupplier contract management
	Approval controls
Supplier applications (sell side)	Create a new sales channel for distributors and manufacturers
	Build Web storefronts and transaction processing systems

A good buy-side application

- Automates the selection and purchase of goods right from the desktop

- Cuts the administrative overhead involved in purchasing goods throughout the organization

- Integrates the sourcing, ordering, and payment processes into one standard end-to-end solution that takes advantage of current buyer/supplier relationships

- Electronically sends and receives the full range of requisition documents from buyers—purchase orders and requisitions, invoices, advance shipping notices, and acknowledgments

- Reports quickly and accurately about organizationwide purchasing patterns

- Controls the number of preferred suppliers, eliminating unauthorized purchasing by employees

Many startup companies are realizing that the buy side of operating-resources-related procurement represents a great, untapped opportunity for automation. Now let's examine the buy-side process in greater detail.

The Buy-Side Requisitioning Process

Using an easy point-and-click interface, employees can create, submit, and track many types of requisitions, including catalog, off-catalog, blanket, and preauthorized purchases, right from their desktops. Preapproved shopping lists speed ordering supplies for new employees or for repeat purchases.

Let's look at the requisitioning process, depicted in Figure 9.4, in greater detail.

Secure Personal Log-in. Each requisitioner is given a secure personal log-in code that contains a user profile (job title, default department, accounting codes, and default ship-to and bill-to information). Profiles are also used to customize the presentation so requisitioners can access and order only those catalog items he or she is authorized to purchase.

Browse Authorized Supplier Catalogs. Requisitioners can use powerful search and browse capabilities to peruse multiple supplier catalogs. Catalogs can be viewed by specific supplier or by functional category of products across all suppliers. Only contracted products and prices are shown. Purchasing administrators can add product detail to help steer requisitioners to preferred products or to

Figure 9.4: The Buy-Side Requisitioning Process

indicate which products require approval prior to purchasing. Requisitioners can also order services and place requests for nonstandard product sourcing.

Requisition/Order Creation. Requisitions are created in real time and can include products from one or more suppliers. Requisitioners can then add products to a requisition by searching the product catalog or by adding products from their personal "favorite product" list. In addition, requisitioners can copy existing orders and modify them for requisitions that approximate past purchases, further speeding the process.

Requisition/Order Submission. Payment options supported include a blanket purchase order, a new purchase order number, or procurement/credit card, limited by what each supplier accepts. Requisitions that fall within purchase controls are broken out into one purchase order per supplier and sent to the appropriate supplier for fulfillment.

Purchase Controls. Embedded purchase controls ensure that requisitioners cannot purchase restricted items or place orders beyond limits such as a specified dollar amount per order or dollar amount per period. Requisitions that violate purchase controls are required to be routed for approval, either to an individual or a group (such as the purchasing department).

Workflow and Approval Routing. Once a requisition is submitted, it's routed for approval based on an organization's business rules. Approvers are notified of pending approval requests via e-mail and can choose to approve, reject, or forward the request to another approver. Approver limits are also enforced, minimizing fraud in approval routing.

Order Dispatch and Fulfillment. Cross-supplier requisitions are broken down into one purchase order per supplier and sent to each supplier via a range of order formats to match the supplier's preferred method of receipt. Copies of the purchase orders are sent to the purchasing system for reporting and tracking. As the orders are fulfilled, suppliers send back order acknowledgment, order status, and shipment notifications.

Order Status Tracking. Requisitioners are notified via e-mail of order status, including approval status, order acknowledgment from the supplier, and shipment status. Requisitioners can also access online order status information to review detailed order and line-item status histories.

In the next section we'll look at an example to better understand opportunities for buy-side requisitioning.

Ariba Technologies: Spotting a Buy-Side Opportunity

Ariba was first to market with an operating resource management system (ORMS). Ariba began by asking, How can firms automate the purchasing of non-production-related items such as office supplies?[8] The motivation behind their curiosity was clear. While firms have a well-established procedure for production-related purchasing, there has been little innovation over the last 50 years in reducing the cost of operating-resource-related purchasing.

Ariba's goal is to help companies save by eliminating the internal paper chase of purchase orders. Savings come from consolidating purchasing with a few key suppliers that can provide volume discounts and specialized products. Unlike others who concentrate on automating the purchasing process, Ariba followed a different logic. The company set out not to make the purchasing experience better than the competition, but completely different, irresistible, and easy to use. In order to give employees of large companies a package they would value highly,

Ariba put aside conventional thinking about what a purchasing process is supposed to look like. Ariba sought to reach the customer—masses of corporate employees—by focusing on widely shared needs.

Ariba's software works like this: Sharon launches her Web browser and logs into the procurement site on her company's intranet. She then clicks on "Create" to get a requisition form and navigates through a customized electronic catalog to find the item she is looking for. Ariba has convinced several suppliers—including Dell Computer, Boise Cascade, and Corporate Express—to make their electronic catalogs accessible to users of the Ariba software. Sharon finds an item she wants to know more about. She clicks on her choice and is immediately transported to the manufacturer's Web site for a more detailed description and photograph.

Sharon decides that she likes what she sees, so she completes the form, specifying that she wants the product delivered to her desk. She also specifies why she needs this item as justification for the purchase. The form is automatically routed to her boss for an electronic signature, then to the preferred supplier with whom the company has a negotiated contract. The purchase order finds its way automatically into the accounting system. The supplier responds with a confirmation and a delivery date. Sharon comes to work the next day and the order is sitting on her desk. Talk about convenience.

But convenience doesn't come cheap. Ariba's ORMS, for example, costs several million dollars. Ariba provides its customers with a server that can be accessed by as many as several thousand end users. Users can buy their own supplies from preapproved lists or clear requests through managers in a workflow process. Ariba's catalog server contains aggregated information from as many suppliers as the company wants. The suppliers link to the site and automatically update their product lists through a free set of publishing tools provided by Ariba.

Ariba has been first to market with an integrated suite of applications that manages all the goods and services companies need to acquire to run their day-to-day business operations. Ariba did a very smart thing. They did not write a single line of code until they understood what the value proposition was for the user. Ariba focused on customer need, conducting interviews with more than 55 prospective customers and gathering feedback from several Fortune 1000 companies. They did not fall into the trap many businesses do when executing an application design strategy. Too often, companies fail to see that innovation is not in the eye of the manager or inventor; it's in the eye of the user.

The big question is whether Ariba can keep its lead in the ORMS market. Challengers such as SAP are enhancing their lineups to incorporate sophisticated buy-side capabilities under the business-to-business e-commerce application category. This duel will be interesting to watch.

Buy-Side Requisitioning Integration Issues

The buy-side e-procurement solutions are only viable if they enable a broad range of users, existing management systems, and suppliers to work together easily and seamlessly, not only within the company, but also across the supply chain. Solutions need to connect people and systems to meet the dynamic requirements of the entire procurement process.

The types of integration in buy-side applications include the following:

- **Employee connectivity.** e-Procurement solutions, with their intuitive, graphical Web browser interfaces, enable employees to increase their productivity immediately by connecting with suppliers right from their desktops. The interface must be powerful enough to meet the needs of a broad range of users, including casual users, purchasing professionals, and system administrators.

- **Back-end systems connectivity.** Leverage the enterprise resource planning (ERP) investments already made in your organization's information technology (IT) infrastructure by integrating existing financial applications. Consider the case of Canadian Imperial Bank of Commerce (CIBC), estimated to have operating resource spending of more than $1.3 billion (CDN). Their business objective is to simplify and streamline procurement. CIBC is attempting to integrate the buy-side ORMS solution from Ariba with PeopleSoft financial systems, their ERP back-office system. The goal is to use data from the ERP applications to create a seamless flow of information from one process to another. A good buy-side solution must be linked to the ERP backbone.

- **Supplier connectivity.** Buy-side applications must streamline and automate all interactions between the enterprise and suppliers, from creating and updating catalog pages to issuing purchase orders directly to the suppliers' systems, while giving the professional buyer complete control over the entire process. If everything works according to plan, it all adds up to substantial efficiencies for the company and suppliers.

Connectivity by itself isn't enough, however. Sophisticated capabilities for the procurement professional are needed to increase effectiveness.

Buy-Side Applications for the Procurement Professional

Typically, purchasing has little control beyond direct production materials and shop-floor MRO spending. Limited control minimizes the purchasing professional's effectiveness. Figure 9.5 provides a detailed view of the requirements of a procurement professional. The key to successfully achieving procurement effectiveness is the application of spending analysis and planning across the entire spectrum of procurement.

If you don't know where the money goes, you can't have any influence over it. Transaction automation alone does not provide the depth in data collection, reporting, analysis, and controls required to implement best practices across the global enterprise. Without the ability to measure, control, and provide continuous feedback to the procurement process, it's extremely difficult to measure returns from such systems.

Spending analysis and planning can give procurement professionals the information they need to purchase wisely and measure the savings. Spending analysis and planning includes the following functions: data collection, multidimensional analysis, supplier management decisions, configuration of spending controls, and continuous feedback.

Data Collection. Professional buyers need to collect and generate comprehensive data on all purchasing activities, including spending to date against budget; spending pending approval; activity by geography; supplier on-time delivery compliance; items received; and weekly, monthly, quarterly, and annual historical spending data.

Multidimensional Analysis. Analysis is critical to strategic sourcing. It is a very defined process that helps buyers better understand their spending, requirements, and market. Procurement professionals use predefined, procurement-

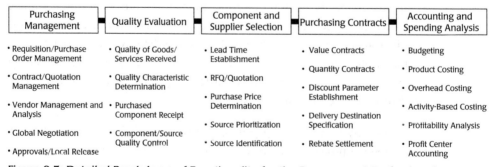

Figure 9.5: Detailed Breakdown of Functionality for the Procurement Professional

centric online analytic processing (OLAP) reports to view the vast amount of data collected for forecasting and trend and what-if analysis. These reports, designed in concert with procurement and management consulting professionals, give organizations the ability to make sense of the data in a way that is most productive for them. Figure 9.6 shows the objectives of multidimensional analysis.

Supplier Management Decisions. Management can use various decision criteria to analyze data in useful ways and make informed procurement decisions based on best practices. These decisions include what products to include in a given catalog, restricting the procurement of certain goods to meet fiscal and business imperatives, or renegotiating volume contracts for more favorable discounts. Without this native procurement intelligence, purchasing professionals may have a much more difficult task making sense of the data and making decisions that benefit the company.

Configuration of Spending Controls. All of the data, analysis, and decisions available would not be useful if procurement professionals could not actually reconfigure spending controls in real time. Because the horizon for completing purchasing transactions is relatively short (one to two weeks), the ability to enact controls quickly is paramount. Procurement buyers must be allowed to make real-time changes to catalogs and workflow so that spending patterns can be al-

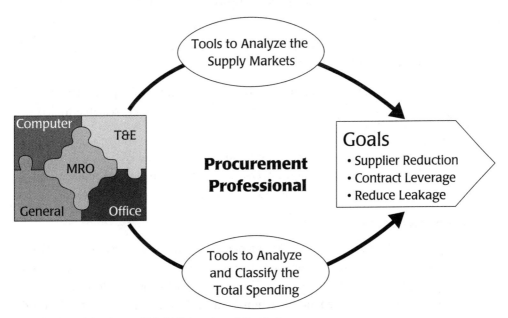

Figure 9.6: Objectives of Multidimensional Analysis

tered to meet spending and business imperatives. In other words, buyers—not IT—must control the process.

Continuous Feedback. To close the spending-analysis loop, procurement professionals need to quickly see the results of their controls through subsequent data collection and analysis. This feedback allows them to further refine controls, if necessary.

Elements of Sell-Side e-Procurement Solutions

What is sell-side functionality? In the second generation of e-commerce, companies are moving beyond the business-to-supplier model and are moving toward trading communities. Here's how the community model works. The content from many suppliers' product catalogs is aggregated into one entity, which resides in a secure, online trading "community." Note that these are vertical, specialized trading communities for specific markets, not broad horizontal shopping malls. Buyers can then access this megacatalog and comparison shop for the best prices. This system also pares down the number of suppliers. Both comparison shopping and limiting suppliers have proved to cut costs in conventional procurement systems.

Three factors must be addressed to ensure success with this model:

1. **Supplier integration.** Suppliers' networks must be seamlessly integrated into the extranet.

2. **Supplier content.** Product information from suppliers' catalogs must be maintained religiously.

3. **Customer internal rollout.** The user interface for this community must be browser based, and the infrastructure must be infinitely scalable to accommodate changing product and user volume.

So what's in it for the suppliers? Suppliers can use the Web to reduce the acquisition cost they must charge buyers, and they can start to compete with much larger suppliers. Let's look at the example of Maintenance Warehouse.

Maintenance Warehouse

A subsidiary of Home Depot, Maintenance Warehouse is a leading supplier of building repair and replacement products to owners and managers of multihousing, lodging, and commercial properties, such as apartment complexes, hotels, and office buildings. Maintenance Warehouse currently offers more than 10,000 products, including hardware, electrical, lighting, plumbing, appliance, and HVAC products. Published and mailed twice a year, the company's catalog is unique in the industry for the way it provides easy-to-identify, 3-D technical illustrations, plus published, three-tier pricing that's guaranteed for the catalog's six-month lifetime.

Maintenance Warehouse customers want to be able to search for and order products easily, compare prices, and review order status via the Internet 24 hours a day. Customers currently search manually through Maintenance Warehouse's 1,500-page, 10,000-product catalog and place orders by phone or fax. Web-based ordering capabilities will allow Maintenance Warehouse to establish an alternate sales and marketing channel. The Internet sales site will enable customers to shop 24×7, and will make the ordering process easier with such valuable services as a catalog search engine, customized order templates, workflow approval processes, and order-status history.

With its Internet-based sales solution, Maintenance Warehouse will be able to update its catalog as new products or pricing become available. And an electronic catalog can proactively inform customers when they approach volume discounts, track previous orders, and offer cost-saving suggestions based on established buying patterns. Customers can also minimize unauthorized purchases and can work with Maintenance Warehouse to determine purchase limits for designated employees.

Vertical Procurement Portals

A *vertical portal* is a sell-side destination site. Vertical procurement portals are also called *infomediaries*—online exchanges that link buyers and sellers by efficiently distributing market information. Infomediaries are a cross between electronic catalogs, efficient marketplaces that greatly reduce transaction costs, and content libraries, which help companies make purchasing decisions.

These vertically oriented sites license or produce content that is tied closely to the products each vertical or industry niche needs. For example, Chemdex.com is one of the largest online sources of biological and chemical reagents, featuring over 150,000 products from various suppliers. Chemdex.com enables lab personnel to search, locate, and instantly order everything they need—24 hours a day, seven days a week.

A key difference between a portal like Yahoo! and a sell-side vertical portal is that a portal is something you go through to get somewhere else, whereas a sell-side destination like Chemdex.com or SciQuest.com is where you go to satisfy industry-specific needs. Since different industries have different needs, focus seems to be key. Industry exchanges are appearing for steel, paper, research chemicals, hospital supplies, marine equipment, home equity loans, and transportation.

Vertical portals have the ability to lower transaction costs, especially in fragmented markets where prices are difficult to compare. For instance, information on laboratory chemicals is so hard to find that a chemist can spend five hours a week thumbing through thick paper catalogs. The price of a single chemical can vary by more than 200 percent. Now pharmaceutical industry and university scientists can search electronically through multiple suppliers' products on Chemdex.com or SciQuest.com and cut their research time to an hour a week. The cost of processing a transaction has dropped too, since scientists can place orders directly from their desktops.[9]

Vertical procurement portals are an important trend that deserves attention. The appeal of a vertical portal is that it is Web based and easy to use. The vertical portals figure that if their content, services, and products are vertically organized, it's easier to sell their own products, keep customers on the site, and—most important—offer advertisers a more focused demographic.

The e-Procurement Manager's Roadmap

Managing a procurement chain is a little like playing chess. There are many components on your procurement chain chessboard, and you must move all of the pieces strategically to win. In this section, we look at the key pieces in the procurement chess game.

Chief procurement officers (CPOs) are looking to deliver the maximum business impact at the lowest possible cost. The business objectives of CPOs are fourfold: (1) leveraging enterprisewide buying power, (2) quick results, low risk, (3) supplier rationalization, and (4) cost reduction by automating best practices in strategic procurement. To achieve these goals, CPOs are coming to the conclusion that e-procurement is where the action is. Simple in concept, e-procurement applications are powerful when applied to the large number of products and services that companies buy. Consolidating the buying of these items and rationalizing the procurement chain can add tens to hundreds of millions of dollars directly to the bottom line.

Take this systematic roadmap with you on your journey to e-procurement.

 ## Step 1: Clarify Your e-Procurement Chain Goals

Every company wants to improve its procurement chain, but you can't get there if you don't know where you're going! The critical first step in designing, reengineering, or optimizing your procurement chain is to assemble your team to define precisely what goals you want to achieve. The typical goals of e-procurement include:

- Automating the selection and purchase of goods

- Cutting costs significantly throughout the organization

- Quickly and accurately reporting companywide purchasing patterns

- Eliminating purchasing by unauthorized employees

What is your company's specific e-procurement goal? It can be to increase employee self-service capabilities. Most purchasing and finance organizations recognize the value of moving routine purchasing activities directly to the employee. Hassle is reduced, costs are lowered, and purchasing professionals have more time to focus on complex acquisitions and supplier negotiations. This form of employee empowerment introduces requirements beyond the scope of traditional purchasing systems. Because the average employee will use the system only occasionally, operation must be simple and intuitive. And because purchasing is not their primary function, employees should be able to quickly find what they need so they can return to their regular duties.

At some point, it's important to set numerical targets for the processes you are implementing. It's not uncommon, for example, to take 10 to 15 percent of your procurement chain cost out of the system by process reengineering. This is tangible, hard capital that can be saved and deployed toward other strategic projects. The key is to examine the procurement chain elements essential to your company and set achievable goals that are in harmony with the organization's overall objectives.

 ## Step 2: Construct a Procurement Process Audit

With strategic goals in place, it's important to understand your current procurement process and the global factors that affect, impede, and interact with it. Do you truly understand all aspects of your current process? Is all the information in one location? Is it easily accessible? Accurate? Complete?

Take time for a procurement chain audit to ensure that you have an accurate big-picture model. This audit is a critical first step in the process of moving from where you are today to where you want to be tomorrow. The first phase of the procurement chain audit consists of collecting data. Where is the data located?

How is it created? Who interacts with it? Remember, the collected data isn't only numbers but also information about people, procedures, and processes.

Once the data is collected and analyzed for consistency and accuracy, it can be compiled into a model representing the current procurement chain. This model represents a baseline that is used to drill down to the next level of analysis, during which key areas can be studied to ensure that

- Current processes are consistent with the organization's strategic goals and objectives.

- The procurement chain processes meet customers' needs.

- Current procurement chain processes promote efficiency.

Through these analyses, you will identify critical success factors and key performance indicators. You will also assess problem areas and areas of vulnerability. The results of these assessments can then be inserted into the mix (let's call it the "global procurement chain optimizer") to help determine the proper direction for the design phase.

 ## Step 3: Create a Business Case for e-Procurement

Putting a return on assets (ROA) business case together for e-procurement can be useful because it forces you to systematically analyze your business. If you don't understand your environment, you can do very little to fix it. The process of putting a business case together forces you to articulate hidden assumptions. One widely used technique in creating an e-procurement business case is ROA, which uses the following formula:

$$ROA = (Revenues - Expenses)/Assets$$

To increase ROA, you either need to increase revenues, decrease expenses, or keep the asset base as small as possible.

Whereas increasing profitability by generating revenue requires substantial investment in capital equipment, marketing, and sales, increasing profitability through e-procurement requires only a relatively limited additional investment. Implementing an e-procurement solution commonly saves at least 5 percent of operating resource costs.

Decreasing expenses can be accomplished by identifying inefficiencies in the procurement chain, which enables companies to reduce expenditures such as inventory carrying costs. Reducing the amount of captive capital in the procurement chain means a company becomes profitable faster. Cost improvements are not just cutbacks. Enhancements are often made through better coordination and communication. For instance, many companies have to expedite operating resources by shipping "premium freight" in order to get an order to an employee on time. With proper planning, this cost can be avoided.

Improving asset utilization can be accomplished by reducing working capital. The amount of assets companies have captive in the procurement chain affects the profitability of the company directly. Working capital can be reduced in two ways: Eliminate warehouses to maximize stock availability and minimize inventory holdings; and eliminate excess inventory to reduce leakage or hidden inventory.

Companies are beginning to move from optimizing within the four walls of the enterprise to optimizing the entire procurement chain. The goal is not just to support an integrated business process that connects the customer's customer to the supplier's supplier, but to increase the velocity at which the virtual enterprise operates.

 ## Step 4: Develop a Supplier Integration Matrix

In today's world with its ever-increasing velocity of change, few organizations want to commit to long-term relationships. Conventional wisdom says that if a company encumbers itself with long-term agreements, it will lose the flexibility to react to new opportunities. What if something better comes along tomorrow? But the reality is that this approach may be costing your organization money.

What's needed is a supplier integration matrix (SIM). A SIM helps determine the best type of relationship to have with individual vendors. In the complex procurement environment, a company must define favorable relationships to have with vendors in order to optimize the procurement chain. Any organization that applies only one relationship structure to all vendors, either consciously or unconsciously, is shortchanging itself.

A SIM helps evaluate suppliers according to how each contributes to the current or future success of the company, classifying suppliers into four categories.

- **Strategic-Collaborative.** A supplier offering a unique or scarce product or service is a candidate for a collaborative relationship. This relationship might entail long-term commitments by both parties to procure future production or investment. These suppliers become strategic partners, and the technological systems set up to share information with them are often critical components. Examples are MRO suppliers.

- **Strategic-Cooperative.** A supplier that offers a strategic product (but not a unique or scarce product) is a candidate for a cooperative relationship. This might entail incentives for the supplier to invest in improving the procurement chain, such as reducing the number of suppliers to increase the volume of business you give to each. Cooperative relationships may be short-, medium-, or long-term relationships. Examples are computer suppliers.

- **Nonstrategic-Limited.** A supplier who provides products or services that are not strategic to your organization's success and are limited in supply is a candidate for a short-term, nonstrategic, limited relationship. In this situation, you look at the quality and value provided by the supplier versus the availability of similar products and services from other suppliers. Examples are administrative and professional services such as temp agency services.

- **Nonstrategic-Commodity.** A supplier offering a nonstrategic product that is in plentiful supply will have a nonstrategic, commodity relationship with your company. With these kinds of products or services, you can tolerate price variations without feeling a critical impact on your strategic products or services. These relationships are usually short term, with minimal commitment. Examples are office and book suppliers.

When using a SIM, review your supplier set on a periodic basis to determine if external or internal factors have changed enough to require moving suppliers to a different classification. A good SIM model can prevent roadblocks in the procurement process.

 ## Step 5: Select an e-Procurement Application

Obviously there is much to consider in selecting an e-procurement application. However, many of these issues can be addressed by asking four questions:

- **Will it support my procurement process?** Optimization of the business process is the goal. The application choice must support that goal. For instance, a proprietary catalog system might create more problems than it solves. Careful evaluation of the application support for the buy-side process must be done.

- **Does it leverage my other application investments?** You've probably already made multimillion-dollar investments in enterprise resource management systems. Therefore it is imperative that the procurement solution build on these investments rather than recreating the same functionality.

- **Will it work seamlessly with other applications?** Procurement is a complex chain of events. The solution must interface with the various integration points along the procurement chain. For example, it must exchange accounting information with the general ledger system. Likewise, the receiving function must feed accounts payable and asset management systems.

- **Is it extendable?** Can it accommodate technology from other vendors? With technology innovation being quite unpredictable, it is important that the solution be scalable and extendable in new directions. For instance, can the solution leverage new best practices as they emerge? The solution must keep the door open to take advantage of new twists and turns in technology.

Table 9.6 presents a quick checklist to help evaluate various solutions.

 ## Step 6: Don't Forget—Integration Is Everything

We can't stress strongly enough how critical it is to the success of your e-procurement chain that you not take an exclusive buy-side or sell-side viewpoint. Companies implementing ORM solutions often choose one or the other.

Table 9.6: Evaluation Checklist

Catalog management	Does it provide multisupplier search capability? Can it access supplier-maintained, Web-based catalogs?
Requisition management	Can requisitions be created without data entry? Can users pick from "noncataloged" items?
Transaction management	Are requisitions seamlessly converted into purchase orders? Is there a log of every activity associated with the order? Is the approval process easy to navigate?
Interenterprise management	Is there seamless flow from the employee to the supplier and back? Is there real-time connectivity to check for product availability?
Back-office integration	Does the system easily interface with other applications? Does the system provide easy administrative tools for management?

In our experience, we've found that this does not lead to good integrated solutions. You must collaborate with the supplier. Collaboration means both the buy-side and sell-side applications must dance cheek to cheek for effective procurement. The ideal goal for managers should be to target—and hit—the integration sweet spot (see Figure 9.7). By focusing on each of the areas of ORM, none will be left out of the integration effort. This will ensure that the requirements of employees, suppliers, and buyers are considered when you are building your integrated ORM application.

 ## Step 7: Educate, Educate, Educate

Failure to take care of the people part may be the most common reason why projects don't succeed. Why do companies let this happen? Why don't they work on the soft stuff? Because it's hard. It's so much easier to get all wrapped up in the software modules and the transaction and processing speeds of the new computers. We see this frequently when companies are implementing ERP systems.

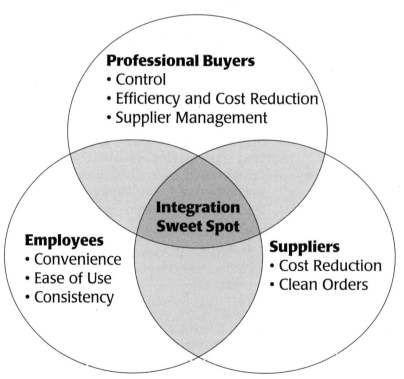

Figure 9.7: The Three Faces of Operating Resource Management Applications

Enormous amounts of staff time, mental energy, and dollars are devoted to working on the software, and relatively little time is devoted to people. The result: frustration, subpar results, and a lot of money spent for not much payback.

The soft stuff is also about improvement along the procurement chain, and change often generates opposition. If opposition slows the e-procurement project down or alters its direction, major problems occur, among them schedule slippage, higher costs, and poor morale. Senior management must deal with this problem by listening, communicating, selling, and, when all else fails, firing. If senior management can't do this, the project will fail. The opposition will grind down the project team to an expensive crowd of people wandering around accomplishing nothing.

Remember that your procurement chain is a dynamic, living organism. It consists of people, information, technology, and systems. The key point here is that it never stops changing. At today's maddening pace, it is critical that we keep in mind that procurement is a continuous process and not merely discrete elements. To be successful, we must improve continuously.

Memo to the CEO

Regardless of the industry, today's competitive pressures and unrelenting focus on profits mean that operational cost management is more than just a nicety. A new suite of applications provides the fastest and surest way to benefit from what is now an absolute business necessity.

To improve procurement, companies are doing the following:

- Focusing purchasing on strategic, value-added upstream portions of the business rather than on transactional, downstream activities

- Increasing purchasing's role in the company's total spending, including such nontraditional areas as operating resource procurement

- Centralizing procurement activities to concentrate the total spending and improve negotiating power

Today, a spotlight is being placed on operating resources—nonproduction goods and services that businesses acquire and manage to run their day-to-day business operations. They include capital equipment; maintenance, repair, and operating (MRO) supplies; and travel and entertainment. For example, communications and computer equipment, software, advertising and corporate expenses, office supplies, travel and entertainment expenses, facilities and services, and scientific and industrial supplies are all operating resources. Although these operating resources often account for more than 30 percent of spending, they are typically managed through paper-based processes, providing few opportunities for automation, control, or leverage.

The e-procurement suite of Web-based operational cost management solutions provides purchasing professionals with an opportunity to deliver cost savings and increase bottom-line results. By directly reducing your operating resource costs, e-procurement affects your bottom line. e-Procurement also decreases cycle time by focusing on enterprise processes currently untouched by automation. It streamlines the costly, time-consuming, paper-based processes currently associated with acquiring most goods and services, and replaces them with an automated, easy-to-use system.

By providing improved visibility into the process flow, e-procurement can strengthen management control. e-Procurement reduces maverick buying, ensures compliance with corporate policies, and institutionalizes a company's best business practices. While improving accountability and control, implementing e-procurement can improve productivity. End users know the status of requests and receive approval sooner, so they get the goods and services they need faster. e-Procurement can build strategic supplier relationships and use aggregate buying to gain volume discounts from suppliers.

e-Procurement reduces operating resource costs by providing an easy-to-use system that is flexible enough to adapt to changing business environments. Traditionally, most enterprise software systems have provided few options to truly optimize these processes. Consequently, most companies have little or no control over their operating resource suppliers and no centralized collection of data about operating resource spending.

The advances in e-procurement solutions are promising, with the potential to turn the management of operating resources into a strategic weapon. Most important, the savings gained from procurement automation drop directly to the bottom line to deliver a substantial boost to profitability.

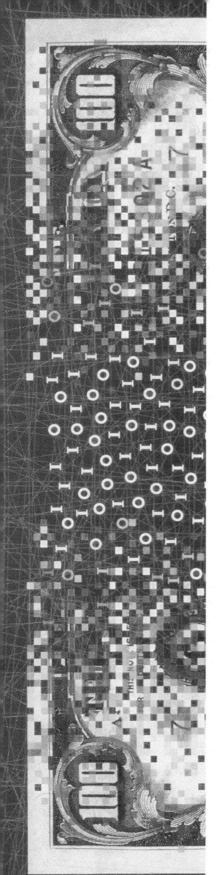

CHAPTER TEN

Knowledge-Tone Applications: The Next Generation of Decision Support Systems

What to Expect

Conventional wisdom says knowledge is power, but knowledge harvesting without focus can render you powerless. As companies migrate toward responsive e-business models, they are investing in new data-driven application frameworks that help them respond rapidly to changing market conditions and customer needs.

Another aspect of knowledge harvesting is customer-centric personalization and customization, which implies having the capabilities to tailor the content, format, and medium of key decision-support information to the needs of individual users. This trend utilizes technology to enable the delivery of personalized information to large numbers of end users through a variety of channels, such as e-mail, pager, fax, or Web pages.

We call this emerging class of applications knowledge-tone apps. These applications focus on personalized decision support, modeling, information retrieval, data warehousing, what-if scenarios, and reporting. In this chapter, we'll dissect knowledge tone to see how it works. We also provide an easy-to-follow guide to how managers should be setting up their company's knowledge-tone framework.

The main objective in war, as in life, is to deduce what you do not know from what you do know.

—The Duke of Wellington

An international credit card company differentiates itself by offering customers the ability to access and analyze credit card transaction activity online. The company's travel analysis application enables its customers to reduce their travel expenses by giving them the ability to analyze various carriers' flight patterns, airfares, city pairs, and other information. Corporate customers use this information to select the airlines and routes suited to their needs for the lowest possible cost.

A multibillion-dollar retailer of electronics with more than 5,000 retail stores nationwide delivers an online weekly sales report to managers so they can identify opportunities—"hot spot" areas where products are selling at a faster rate compared with the rest of the country. By identifying these hot spots, the retailer can inform manufacturing partners what products are in demand in which regions, enabling them to stay abreast of changes in inventory levels as they happen. The retailer's executives can also use the information to analyze store performance, improve inventory controls, and target promotional mailings.

A provider of insurance claim software offers more than 200 auto insurance companies the ability to access and analyze insurance claim data via the Web. Its consumer database alone includes profiles of more than a million consumers. Auto insurance companies access and analyze nationwide insurance claim data, including repair cycle times and amounts paid for vehicle parts, and compare their claim-resolution performance against industry averages and historical trends.

These companies and many more like them are running "about the business" applications. While the first generation of e-commerce focused on buying and selling goods via the Internet, the second generation focuses on organizations gaining insight from data collected with each transaction, then using this insight to more effectively produce and market products and services to develop customer loyalty and enhance profitability. In other words, these applications analyze the business and optimize customer relationships. They aid both in interpreting what has happened and in deciding where to go next.

So, what makes "about the business" knowledge apps different? Although enterprise resource planning (ERP), customer relationship management (CRM), and other software applications amass piles of data on operations and customers, most of it ends up unused in data warehouses. To turn that stored data into valuable information, companies are now in quest of knowledge applications. The business advantage lies in the ability to analyze large amounts of data from any business model, determine the personalized preferences of all people, then reach these people with the relevant information, wherever they may be. These serve as the driving force for the new generation of "about the business" applications.

The intersection of e-commerce and traditional knowledge apps is creating a new area: personalization. Personalization includes employing user-defined information filters and specifying events as triggers for information delivery. Time-sensitive information such as stock quotes can be personalized in a number of ways. By supporting multiple output devices (e-mail, Web page, fax, pager, cell phone) with appropriate device-specific formatting, data can be sent to specific end users based on their needs. Personalization also includes delivering information using natural-language sentences rather than traditional report formats. Personalization is a very important category of e-business, and every manager should pay extra attention to make sure that his or her infrastructure can support it.

As the world moves from mass production to mass customization, the traditional decision support applications are not quite up to the task. Mass customization requires new decision support capabilities, new personalization capabilities, and new distribution capabilities. An example of this trend can already be seen in MicroStrategy's DSS Broadcaster, a database add-on that uses push technology to send subscribers information based on predefined parameters.

These new applications flip the paradigm of decision support on its head. Traditionally, we have lived in a query-and-response paradigm. With the new generation of applications, the logic is reversed: What if the system didn't wait for the end user to have the question? What if the system just asked the question for them and sent them the answer? One could anticipate a whole set of questions. For instance, take a credit card company that has 25 million customers; all their customers want to know what their balances are, what new transactions were charged to their accounts, what unusual transactions were conducted, and how much interest they paid on balances over the last 12 months.

This new class of applications allows firms not only to collect but to slice and dice data in order to forge better supplier and customer relationships. It is aimed at increasing profitability through revenue growth. This revenue-enhancing framework, which we call *knowledge tone,* focuses on an interesting mix of decision support, modeling, information retrieval, ad hoc reporting and analysis, what-if scenarios, and data warehouses. Let's take a brief look at why this application framework is important.

Knowledge Apps: Why They Are Important

The extensive deployment of PCs and connected servers has fueled the demand for graphical, easy-to-use applications and for access over the network to key corporate data previously locked away in the company's mainframe. New knowledge apps are now freeing the data assets and making them accessible to large audiences. This is the opportunity in enterprise knowledge software—to deliver the long-promised efficiency gains by making the information assets open and visible.

Why do we need "about the business" knowledge apps? There are several drivers for the growth of knowledge apps. First, to compete in today's real-time economy, businesses must be able to quickly identify and respond to changing market conditions and customer needs. Today's business runs 24×7, creating a new business need: applications that work nonstop to collect a real-time flow of information, a river of data that never stops. To do that, applications must be able to collect, organize, access, and analyze large amounts of data—fast.

Another reason is one-to-one marketing. In order to deliver on the promise of one-to-one marketing, companies have to differentiate the value of customers to the company and what their needs are. This strategy requires a lot more information about customer behavior and preferences. Until recently companies didn't capture detailed customer behavior information. Even if they did, it was not easily accessible from one source. The new generation of knowledge apps is addressing these deficiencies.

Another important factor is the growth of the "information at employee fingertips" revolution. The universe of connected employees has ballooned. Many companies have flattened their organizational structures, plucking out layers to empower employees at all levels to make decisions. This change has created two requirements:

1. Companies want employees to spend less time compiling data, and more time analyzing it to identify key customer trends and preferences.

2. Employees expect high-quality information, around-the-clock access, and lightning-fast performance.

A final driver is return on information investment. Management expects a significant return on their data warehouse and other technology investments. The data warehouse investments have resulted in a vast trove of internal financial and operational data—the bread and butter of business—and large amounts of historical data on customers, projects, suppliers, and more. However, this data is sitting in a database gathering silicon dust. Most of it is not being used effectively in managing companies.

These factors combine to create a need for proactive decision support tools for reacting to changing business conditions. It is important to note that while data analysis is important, the real value comes from data delivery. Real-time delivery of information has become easier with the advent of Web and wireless delivery. Companies are looking for solutions to help make sense of the data deluge. We are thus in the midst of a structural migration from data access applications to more proactive enterprise decision support systems (DSSs).

What does all this mean? The integration of data analysis and knowledge delivery is making new functionality possible. The convergence of the Web, decision support systems, databases, and integrated back-office infrastructure is leading to a knowledge renaissance. The Web browser has become the de facto interface for the "information at your fingertips" paradigm. Development of the knowledge-tone framework requires serious management attention.

Knowledge Tone Is an Application Framework

Knowledge tone is neither a product nor a capability. It's a framework of a fully evolved knowledge economy.

Knowledge tone's objective is to make effective use of tremendous stores of data. Now you can go online to access and analyze the business information you need for making timely, sound business decisions. Take, for instance, a leading retailer. Where it used to take nine months to profile customers and reasonably predict their purchasing behavior, new DSS applications take less than half that time. This speed enables the retailer to direct services to its most valued customers much more aggressively in a highly competitive marketplace.

Companies are demanding more than access to data; they want processed and refined information that will help them make tactical decisions. Consider the example of Federal Express. FedEx reengineered its database marketing process from marketing and campaign planning to customer segmentation, evaluation, and refinement. A knowledge-tone application has been instrumental in FedEx's efforts to automate its database marketing process. FedEx reports a time reduction in direct-marketing campaign cycles and a major improvement in "prospecting" campaigns.[1]

Knowledge tone is the business of information sorting, extraction, packaging, and dissemination. Retailers, manufacturers, and financial institutions have spent millions of dollars to build data warehouses containing masses of information about their customers and transactions. Managers sit at headquarters and use a query engine and tools to try to extract insights from these huge databases. Slowly but surely, the reactive, data-centric world of today is migrating to the proactive, query-driven knowledge-tone world of tomorrow.

Knowledge tone is a natural extension of today's Web tone. Just as a telephone dial tone signals that a conversation with nearly anyone in the world is possible, Web tone signals users that information of any type and in any place is available in a standard, accessible way. Web-tone enabled data access is no longer enough. As a result, there is a migration from the data-intensive Web tone to information-intensive knowledge tone (see Figure 10.1).[2]

The Rise of Knowledge Tone: Any Time, Any Where, and Any Place DSS

Knowledge tone is a prerequisite to creating a responsive business model, the dominant form of marketplace warfare in the next millennium. The knowledge-tone paradigm is based on the premise that corporations will shift capital priorities to invest in a "sense and respond" infrastructure to serve customers better.

Consider Home Depot, the do-it-yourself building supplies retailing giant, which is pushing knowledge to its employees. Home Depot carries a diverse inventory in its more than 500 stores. Most stores have installed a radio-frequency-transmitted data warehouse link, which Home Depot calls its Mobile Ordering platform. The system uses Windows-based devices mounted on carts that let floor clerks and department managers access data analyses of the store's past and present inventory. They use this information to make order decisions while standing in front of the merchandise.[3]

As this example illustrates, knowledge-tone applications streamline the process of turning decisions into actions. The objective is to help users address critical uncertainties affecting their businesses by answering highly focused management questions, which vary by industry.

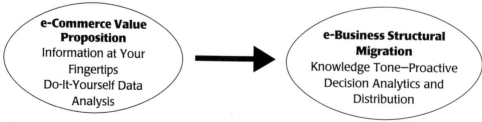

Figure 10.1: Structural Migration Toward Knowledge-Tone Infrastructure

- **Retail.** What products or groups of products should be sold? Where? At what price? How much shelf space should be allocated for specific products? How much promotion should each product receive? Which products sell well together? How much inventory should be carried? What was the in-stock position and stock-to-sales ratio of the ten most profitable and ten least profitable items in ladies departments of my Atlanta-area stores last week?

- **Banking and Finance.** Show me the 100 most profitable customers by branch and determine how they are contributing to income. What portion comes from fees? Interest income? Overdraft charges? Whom should I target for direct-marketing efforts? What is the proper pricing strategy for a given set of financial products? How efficiently are underwriters and credit officers performing? Which customer groups are credit risks? How much fraudulent activity is occurring?

- **Telecommunications.** Of the customers who have switched carriers in the last month, show me their average call volumes and dollars spent since they signed up with my company. Calculate the same metrics for the three months before they quit.

- **Health care.** What is the range of outcomes for a given treatment? How frequently is this treatment prescribed? Which drugs, hospitals, doctors, health plans are most effective? Which patient groups are most at risk? How efficient and effective is a given technique for treating a specific illness?

The promise of knowledge tone is to offer decision makers across a broad range of industries the opportunity to ask and answer mission-critical questions about their businesses using transactional data assets that have been captured but not exploited to their fullest extent.

The Second Wave: e-Commerce-Driven Decision Support

So, what does decision support have to do with e-commerce? A lot. Knowledge tone uses e-commerce technology to open the world of data warehouses to consumer devices. Data warehousing, the highly evolved technology for the capture, organization, and delivery of information, now promises to find a place in the lifestyle of millions of people alongside their pagers, phones, e-mail systems, and fax machines. Using exception conditions and recurring schedules as triggers, knowledge tone automates the delivery of critical information to end users in an efficient and unobtrusive fashion.

An example is the MicroStrategy application DSS Broadcaster, a push-technology product. Preset queries are run against the data warehouse. Users can either receive all reports or receive an alert through e-mail, fax, or pager when there's an exception. For instance, a customer deposits $50,000 in a direct deposit account. A message is automatically sent to a marketing representative so that he or she can act on a potential cross-sell opportunity. Success in competitive markets requires that businesses accelerate the rate at which they identify and respond to opportunities.

A DSS Broadcaster customer is Sabre Group, which books $66 billion of travel reservations a year. Sabre has built a 2-terabyte (TB) (2,000-gigabyte) warehouse of airline bookings, which will grow to 4TB when hotel and rental car bookings are added. About 1,000 Sabre employees will eventually have access to at least some of the data, as will the airlines that presently buy tapes of Sabre's raw booking data. Using Broadcaster, Sabre plans to sell e-mailed reports to travel agents and companies that want control of their travel costs. A company could also buy Web access to extract such information as which departments book an inordinate number of expensive, last-minute fares.[4]

Sabre's market agility and ultimate success depends on its ability to rapidly collect, organize, and analyze data. Many organizations are implementing initiatives to improve planning, analysis, and decision making. Consequently, they've made substantial investments in information systems to automate activities that generate large quantities of data. Spreadsheets, data warehouses, and query and reporting tools are used to store, manipulate, and review this data. Each performs specific functions but none fully addresses the need to transform data into the kind of information upon which decisions can be based.

Hence, for information-based business models like Sabre to function well, there is a clear need for an integration framework that can tie together the various classes of knowledge-tone applications. Without an integration framework, organizations may not reap the benefits they are looking for from knowledge-tone investments. To understand what these investments are, let's look at some emerging classes of knowledge-tone applications.

Emerging Classes of Knowledge-Tone Applications

Knowledge tone has the potential to expand the audience for information by transforming a data jungle into a revenue-generating asset. Let's first look in more detail at the different classes of knowledge-tone applications: customer relationship, supply chain, remote performance monitoring, simulation or what-if scenario analysis, and innovation management (see Figure 10.2).

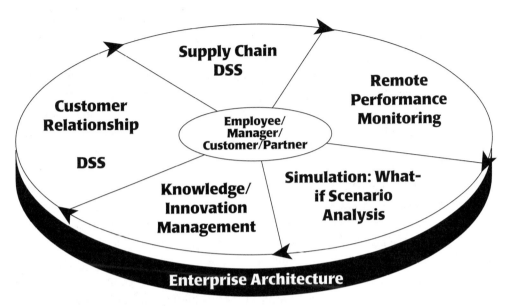

Figure 10.2: Knowledge-Tone Applications

Customer Relationship Management Decision Support Systems

Customer relationship DSS apps offer companies tools for mining customer data. The desired outcome of this data mining process is improved pricing, greater market share, longer customer retention, or a new revenue stream.

Consider the case of BC Telecom, Canada's second largest telecommunications company. BC Telecom faced many challenges in marketing its services, including a need to shift its focus from product marketing to customer-centric marketing. The company also lacked automation in managing customer relationships across their life cycles and had limited capabilities to allocate marketing dollars to customers with the greatest potential value. Although BC Telecom had made a major investment in a multiterabyte data warehouse, it believed that its business processes and marketing systems were not sufficiently linked to the information available and that its large investment was therefore not generating optimal returns. To solve the integration problems, BC Telecom implemented a customer optimization service. Within three months, BC Telecom achieved significant results from highly targeted marketing campaigns aimed at its 1.7 million residential customers.

As the example of BC Telecom illustrates, CRM begins with developing a clear picture of customer behavior. The challenge is to spot the clues, piece together the story, and then act on the evidence. For instance, in banking, the history of a customer's transactions offers significant insight into his or her lifestyle. Analyzing customer information is not simple. Information is scattered throughout different parts of the bank and stored according to different rules. Even when customer data is gathered in one place, it's still a huge challenge to turn that information into knowledge that can be used to build profitable, long-term relationships with customers. Data warehousing has been promising this for some time, but it has been focused primarily on the technology, rather than on the value of the knowledge that can be extracted from information. Executives are looking beyond data warehousing for solutions that address the question: how to extract customer knowledge and use it to make decisions (see Figure 10.3).

Several industries are racing to exploit the opportunities of CRM DSS, including the health care industry. The industry is attempting to turn health care into an experience, to create differentiation by making customers feel valued, recognized, and special. A few managed-care companies have begun moving into the top tier of the customer relationship curve by building true knowledge-tone processing capabilities. Companies like Aetna US Healthcare and Healtheon have rolled out Web-based benefit management programs. For group customers, these

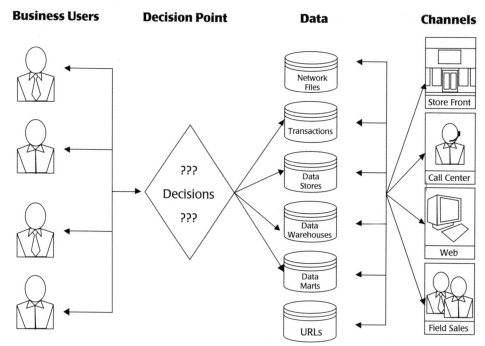

Figure 10.3: Customer Decision Support Systems

programs streamline the annual enrollment process and the ongoing maintenance of member enrollment and eligibility. We anticipate that the availability and sophistication of Web-based benefit management programs from several managed-care companies will grow quickly.

Personalization Apps

Not all CRM DSS activities are based on analyzing stored data. e-Commerce is pushing companies to do more real-time relationship management. This trend is broadly known as *personalization*. Personalization capabilities help companies better understand and respond to each customer's needs, behaviors, and intentions, ensuring that customers get exactly what they need—when they need it.

Why personalization? Customers increasingly want to interact with companies that customize products and services to fit their needs. They don't want to be treated as part of a crowd. Therefore, a new breed of personalization applications is emerging that aims to meet the following customer needs: a business that is responsive to customers, shows interest—knows who they are, keeps them informed—knows their needs, appreciates their business, and makes them feel special and valued.

To achieve the above objectives, personalization apps allow you to do the following.

- Give each customer a personalized Web page—a portal to the enterprise—that serves as a launching pad for the customer to interact, transact, and collaborate with the organization. For instance, provide customers one-click access to all activity with your company—from support requests and credit checking to sales questions and order status.

- Display only the information you want individual customers to see. For example, all customer cases (inquiries, trouble tickets, purchases, etc.) can be stored in the same database, but each customer sees only his own cases.

- Automatically and proactively notify customers of product improvements and upgrades, promotions, and service enhancements that are relevant to them individually.

- Tailor information and recommendations according to each customer's individual preferences; for instance, prefill service or sales requests with customer information, saving them time and saving you from having to repeatedly ask the customer the same information.

- Deliver information based on products that customers own, information that is personally relevant. Avoid overwhelming customers with unrelated information. For instance, structure workflow interactions and transactions based on profile or service-level agreement—so Gold customers, for example, are automatically escalated and managed in a distinct business process.

A key component of the next wave of e-commerce is personalization. Personalization increases customer efficiency in interacting with the enterprise and creates enthusiasm for transacting with you. *Is your company thinking about personalization and laying the foundation for it?*

Supply Chain Decision Support Systems

The manipulation of knowledge along the supply chain is one of the least understood areas of business. Supply chain DSS applications encourage trading partners to improve profits by managing inventories in the supply chain. In order to obtain the information that enables visibility and certainty, partners may want to offer more favorable terms, invest more in co-marketing, make available increased levels of supplies, provide more shelf space, or pay higher prices. The business objective is to give preferential treatment to one another in exchange for detailed ordering and inventory information that provides greater certainty and visibility up and down the supply chains.

Consider the case of Lexmark International, which develops, manufactures, and supplies laser and inkjet printers and associated supplies for the office and home markets. Lexmark is using supply DSS solutions from Microstrategy to help customers manage their inventories. Through Lexmark's data warehouse and an inventory management application called the Retail Management System (RMS), Lexmark aims to help dozens of large retailers manage their inventories of printers. It's using an approach called vendor-managed inventory (VMI), which is used by the retail packaged goods industry to track inventory. VMI helps replenish inventory before it's depleted. In contrast, stores without VMI often don't order inventory until after it runs out because they're too busy to act in advance.[5]

Potential users of Lexmark's RMS application include a firm's vendors, distributors, partners, outsourcers, resellers, and financing sources. Initially, the RMS project was used to provide customer inventory information to about 35 field salespeople. It later was expanded to provide management reports to about 75 top executives and line managers at headquarters. The number of potential supply chain DSS users can range from hundreds to tens of thousands.

In addition to boosting sales, the RMS gives Lexmark a better idea of where its customers are and what are the best locations for the products they sell. The data warehouse replaces a system in which inventory figures were compiled by paper. Using the data warehouse, sales and inventory information that used to take four or five days to turn around is now compiled in half a day.

Clearly, Lexmark's RMS application—an example of supply chain DSS—provides access to valuable retail sales information that can be used to design new products, refine marketing campaigns, develop optimal pricing schemes, rationally allocate inventory, and proactively schedule factory production.

Remote Performance Monitoring

Remote performance-monitoring applications provide information to operating managers throughout an enterprise that enables them to improve performance on a routine basis. Performance monitoring is the process that bridges operations and strategy. Using key performance indicators (KPIs) linked to a balanced scorecard, companies can continuously monitor actual performance at all levels in the business against strategic targets. An effective monitoring system is the best way to translate strategy into action.

For companies like British Telecom (BT), dormant information is worthless. Consider the case of BT's Interactive and Reporting Information System (IRIS). IRIS permits BT to track the costs of more than 10,000 ongoing development projects. BT desperately needs IRIS to become smarter and faster as the competitive environment in Europe becomes deregulated. That means having up-to-the-minute project information and being confident about information integrity and consistency, so that accurate spending and management decisions can be made. IRIS enables BT to perform program management that groups together projects with a common business theme. However, IRIS requires a new business analysis framework that includes more sophisticated analysis and reporting capabilities. This framework needs to provide precanned reporting, data analysis, modeling, and forecasting—knowledge-oriented functionality.[6]

What applications do companies like BT turn to? Application frameworks such as SAP's Strategic Enterprise Management (SEM). SEM is a set of applications that enables executives to make informed decisions about the future in a corporate war-room environment. Core to this system is the Management Cockpit, in which key performance monitors are shown graphically on huge color-coded screens mounted on the walls of a specially designed room. The cockpit notion is similar to military war rooms, in which a tremendous amount of battlefield information is processed for decision making.

SEM generates easily digestible information that helps executives make rapid decisions. The SAP Business Warehouse feeds the Management Cockpit with all relevant data, including information from transaction systems and external sources, providing executive teams with up-to-the-minute corporate data in view at all times. Executives can immediately see external market trends and interrelationships in cross-functional business data and receive early warnings of missed targets.[7]

Potential users include senior executives and other managers throughout the sales, marketing, manufacturing, logistics, finance, and human resources functions, regardless of their geographic location. Although an enterprise rarely has more than a few hundred centralized analysts and executives for any performance-monitoring application, the same enterprise may have thousands of remote enterprise users spread across dozens, hundreds, even thousands of locations. For example, a remote performance-monitoring application that profiles customers and provides relevant sales information allows account executives located across a business organization to identify problem accounts, discern abnormal trends in their territories, and proactively manage sales calls. *What is your company doing with respect to Web-enabled performance monitoring and measurement?*

Business Simulation: Interactive What-if Scenario Analysis

A leading packaged goods manufacturer, with more than 200 brands and 1,000 products, provides better and faster point-of-sale and product information to its sales representatives by giving them access to online product sales. The reps use the information to analyze sales based on such variables as location, seasonal patterns, and style trends. The mangers use the information to create simulation models that allow them to anticipate inventory fluctuations, thereby improving inventory controls.

For instance, what should the inventory levels of various merchandise mix be due to the *El Niño* weather effect? In retail, the unpredictable nature of weather often plays havoc with inventory policies, resulting in managers having to scramble to have the right product mix. What-if scenario analysis provides the managers with timely information for decision making, such as which products are likely to sell and when.

The what-if class of applications encompasses advanced simulation and scenario modeling. Based on information from diverse internal and external sources, what-if scenario analysis helps support managers in decision making. The goal is to enable management to participate in developing strategy and learn risk management. These apps also allow modeling of future risks and returns.

Business simulation applications are especially important in an overheated mergers and acquisitions environment. Because of the complexity of modern companies—with their globalization and penchant for merging, divesting, and acquiring—the need for complex decision support or business analytic applications has also increased manyfold. *Is your company developing simulation capabilities to support decision making and scenario planning?*

Innovation or Knowledge Management

Today, e-business corporations are pushing technology further, giving their employees instant access to data and reports that previously took days or weeks to obtain. Consider Intraspect, an innovative startup in this area. Intraspect's knowledge-enabled applications integrate collaboration, organization, searching, and subscription into a single place called a "group memory." Contribution and subscription to the group memory is made easy via tight integration with e-mail and desktop applications. Powerful search technology facilitates discovery and reuse of information in the group memory, Web servers, or legacy databases.

Intraspect applications deliver significant return on investment by improving organizational learning and by reducing the costs associated with supporting existing applications. Intraspect applications form the core of so-called knowledge management. At its core, knowledge management (KM) enables companies to use their data to determine best practices, retain the tacit knowledge of individuals, and classify expertise. KM also makes it easier for corporations to react more quickly and decisively to problems, as well as to competitors. Methods and combinations of products needed for implementing a KM application, however, vary widely.

Knowledge management has become the buzzword of the 1990s, and it's often failed to live up to the hype. It's been long on cost and short on results. Consequently, a major backlash is forming against KM, chiefly for three reasons:[8]

1. **Few can define it.** Vendors of document management systems, data warehousing apps, and push technology all claim to provide KM tools, and some consulting firms help clients indiscriminately develop knowledge-based strategies for virtually any process. The result is a deluge of contradictory and confusing messages.

2. **Software vendors are distancing themselves from it.** Riding the KM wave is not the in thing anymore. KM is to the late 1990s what reengineering was to the early part of this decade—a fad spawned by consultants and vendors to generate demand for their products and services.

3. **Costly knowledge management efforts aren't delivering expected returns on investment.** The efforts of one company have produced a number of knowledge databases using Lotus Notes. The most widely used one is the "gossip and rumors" database. In fact, KM is being called the "knowledge scam" due to the miniscule payback that firms receive from their KM efforts.

Unfortunately, KM's pop icon status is causing business to throw the baby out with the bath water. However, when this happens the idea usually reappears in new incarnations. *Does your company have a KM effort? What are the results?*

Knowledge-Tone Usage in the Real World

Knowledge-tone applications help organizations understand customer buying patterns, identify sales and profit growth opportunities, and improve overall decision making. Let's look at some examples in three different industries: telecommunications, retail, and health care benefits management.

Knowledge Tone in Telecommunications: Combating Customer Churn

In the telecommunications industry, there is competition on every front to offer services that to consumers seem nearly identical. Not surprisingly, consumers have tended to accept one best offer after another, switching carriers for a better price or for more convenience. Telecom providers have dubbed this constant hopping around the *churn factor,* an expensive form of customer turbulence that forces providers to process a steady stream of service starts and stops.

Customer churn is a challenge in any industry, but in the ultracompetitive wireless industry, the problem is more acute. Take, for instance, 360 Communications, which provides wireless voice and data service to 2.4 million customers in more than 100 markets in 15 states. 360 Communications identifies its business information requirements as needing to improve information quality, accuracy, and timeliness for its marketing and product management users.[9] The company uses its data warehouse to serve multiple sites, rather than having individual data marts, and authorized employees in each location can access it. The warehouse is used primarily by marketing and sales to understand customer usage and spending patterns.

360 Communications also applies data warehousing to cross-selling cellular and long-distance services, credit analysis, and churn-factor analysis and reduction. In the credit analysis application, the company determines the profile of a

customer who is likely to default, then uses that profile to predict future default-ers. Profile anaysis is done by proprietary tools that rate a customer's level of credit and churn risk. Wireless and wireline carriers use these techniques to gain a critical mass of customers and reduce costs when entering new markets or deploying new services.

Carriers like 360 Communications are focusing on customer retention, acquisition, and win-back; data warehouses and information mining are strategic weapons in this arsenal. Why? Because it's estimated that it costs $300 for a wireline carrier and at least $500 for wireless carriers to acquire a new customer, and $50 per year to retain that customer.

All carriers need to market to and attract customers by unique features or services, not just the lowest price. Data mining crunches call-detail records and other customer data to reveal hot prospects. With an average annual churn rate of 20 to 25 percent, a 1-percent reduction in churn can amount to millions of dollars, quickly returning the data warehouse investment. The warehouse also enables easy access to customer profile information that managers can use to understand customers better. Based on customer profiles, companies can design new promotions to help retain existing customers and to cost-effectively attract new customers. They can also build accurate predictive models to determine which customers are most likely to switch to a competitor, and take appropriate action to fix internal problems that contribute to the churn factor.

With deregulation and the explosion of new technologies, service providers must clearly differentiate themselves in what is quickly becoming a commodity business. To become total telecommunications providers, companies need knowledge tone to help them deliver a better variety of services now and in the future (see Table 10.1). These decision support solutions will help providers react to changing market conditions and overcome the revenue-sapping effects of customer churn.

Table 10.1: Uses of Knowledge Tone in the Telecommunications Industry

Uses	Representative Companies
Analysis of scanner check-out data	AT&T
Analysis of call volumes	Ameritech
Analysis of equipment sales	Belgacom
Analysis of customer profitability	British Telecom
Analysis of costs and inventory	Telestra Australia
Purchasing leverage with suppliers	Telecom Ireland
Frequent-buyer program management	Telecom Italia

Knowledge Tone in Retail: Sears' SPRS Application

The largest department store chain and third-largest retailer, Sears, Roebuck and Co., has clung tenaciously to its industry lead despite the encroachment of discount mass merchandisers. Founded in 1886, Sears became synonymous with American retailing over the next century, only to be caught by surprise in the 1980s as shoppers defected to specialty stores and discount mass merchandisers.

Sears needed the right technology to support its reinvention into a more agile, responsive company. In the early 1990s, Sears operated with 10- to 20-year-old sales information systems packed with redundant, conflicting, and sometimes obsolete data. For example, a system setup based on ten geographic regions didn't reflect closed locations or Sears' current operations, which are divided into seven regions. Sears' finance, marketing, and merchandising departments had their own systems, which meant a manager might come up with a different sales figure than the accounting department for the same region. Even within departments, information was scattered among numerous databases, forcing users to query multiple systems even for simple questions.

To survive, Sears had to embrace information technology on a dramatic scale. Sears' executives decided that a single data source for its key performance indicators—sales, inventory, and margin—was a strategic imperative. The vision: Generate reliable reporting of sales. Dubbed the Strategic Performance Reporting System, or SPRS, the resulting system includes comprehensive sales data; information on inventory in stores, in transit, and in distribution centers; and cost per item, which enables users to determine margin daily by item and location. See Table 10.2 for additional knowledge-tone uses.

Among Sears' most significant initiatives was constructing a sales knowledge-tone application in less than one year. This application is built on a massive, 1.7TB data warehouse that replaces 18 major databases, each of which previously ran on separate systems. This new application tracks sales by individual item and location on a daily basis to fine-tune buying, merchandising, and marketing strategies with previously unattainable precision. The benefits are measurable. Managers use the knowledge-tone application every morning to check the previous day's sales—nationally and by region, district, store, line, and stock-keeping unit, which is the equivalent of individual items.

Today, managers monitor the precise impact of advertising, weather, and other factors on sales. Meanwhile, the ability to monitor sales by store is enabling Sears to fulfill the strategic goal of creating a sharp local market focus. Sears also has freshened the merchandise mix in its mall-based stores. Long viewed as male oriented, Sears acted decisively when market research revealed that a large portion of buyers for its merchandise were actually women shopping for their families. The retailer began reconfiguring stores to emphasize women's apparel, rolling out the "Softer Side of Sears." The transformation of Sears is not over. They have to address the rapid rise of e-commerce and ask: How can they use the knowledge-tone applications to provide competitive advantage?

Knowledge Tone in Health Care: Employee Benefits Management

Every company seeks new ways to streamline business functions and use them to gain an advantage. One such area is employee benefits management. Companies have done an extensive job catering to employee needs with more flexible benefits, new disability products, efficient HMOs, and 401K programs. There has been a transformation from paper-based to automated systems. This is a logical transformation, as the human cost is often the biggest a company incurs.

Unfortunately, new features often have made the administration of a comprehensive benefits program very difficult and time-consuming for employees. To make benefit management more easy, human resources (HR) departments are moving toward self-service knowledge-tone applications. To illustrate this trend, let's look at startups Healtheon and WebMD, that are attempting to replace costly, labor-intensive, paper-based processes with self-service benefits management processes.

What is the business problem? In the benefits management area, employees face multiple choices, shoddy information, and limited access to resources. Consequently, employees are unable to make the right decisions about health care or obtain the information they need. Today, although some automation exists—in

Table 10.2: Uses of Knowledge Tone in the Retail Industry

Uses	Representative Companies
Analysis of scanner check-out data	Wal-Mart
Tracking, analysis, and tuning of sales promotions and coupons	Kmart
Inventory analysis and redeployment	Sears
Price reduction modeling to move products	Osco/Savon Drugs
Negotiating leverage with suppliers	Casino Supermarkets
Frequent-buyer program management	W. H. Smith Books
Profitability analysis	Otto Versand Mail Order
Product selections for granular market segmentation	

insurers' and hospitals' mainframe systems—information access is difficult, connectivity between participants is limited, and coordination of care across the continuum of services is poor. The result is inefficient benefits management, duplicative processes, poor service, high costs, and poor-quality care.

Employees and employers are demanding greater value, better service, demonstrated quality, and lower cost. To provide value, a core knowledge integration problem has to be solved. The problem is that there are numerous parties (see Figure 10.4) involved in benefits management that lack the ability to communicate with one another. An estimated $200+ billion is spent annually on administrative expenses (moving data around paper-based management systems) and on a morass of proprietary technology that makes it impossible for insurers, doctors, and patients to communicate easily.[10]

What is the solution? Integration of disparate parties into a seamless network. The Web makes integration possible. Health management networks are buying into Internet technology on one end, and corporations are extending their infrastructure on the other. Obviously the solution lies in a knowledge-centric business model that allows both service providers and employees to meet in the middle. The self-service architecture allows consumers to drive transactions such as plan analysis and claims processing. With the self-service architecture, employees can perform:

- Managed-care functions (membership management, network management, care management, premium billing, and claim/encounter processing)

- Historical tracking of employee and benefits information via access to a centralized HR system that maintains employee data

Figure 10.4: Fragmented Service Providers in Benefits Management Arena

- Eligibility checks, referral scheduling, and authorizations

- Claims submission, information access, and reporting

Clearly, the next generation of human resource systems will be sophisticated self-service apps. These apps provide a way to connect all entities (consumers, providers, payers, and employers) in a common end-to-end solution, independent of location and platform. By providing immediate access to information, supporting common transactions across business boundaries, and moving mission-critical functions out of the legacy environment and onto the Internet, information flows between entities can be vastly simplified and efficiency greatly enhanced. See Table 10.3 for knowledge-tone uses in the health care industry.

Tech Trends Driving Knowledge-Tone Framework Investments

Despite the significant promise of knowledge-tone applications, until recently a number of technical and cost constraints have impaired development of the market. An increase in electronically captured and stored transactional data and recent advances in software, hardware, and networking have helped resolve these issues. The convergence of many technology drivers is shaping the emergence of knowledge-tone solutions. Factors driving knowledge-tone development include the following.

- **Increased electronic capture of transactional data.** Electronically captured data is critical to knowledge tone. In retail, telecommunications, financial services, health care, and other industries, an increasing percentage of customer and supply chain transactions are captured and stored electronically in ERP applications such as SAP R/3. The rapid growth in the electronic capture of business transactions and the increased availability of related profiles are laying a solid data foundation for the growth of knowledge tone.

Table 10.3: Uses of Knowledge Tone in the Health Care Industry

Uses	Representative Companies
Customer profiles	Aetna
Relationship management	Cigna
Benefits management	Blue Cross–Blue Shield
Risk and credit analysis	Kaiser
Hospital and HMO performance analysis	Healtheon

- **New publish and subscribe models.** Improved publish and subscribe models enable decision support to become a real-time, personalized activity. They can automate decision making, integrating decision support systems with operational systems and shortening the time required to make business decisions and to implement them. How does publish and subscribe work? Publish and subscribe is a brokered approach to program-to-program communication. This communication involves three "parties": publishers, brokers, and subscribers. Publishers are programs that signal the occurrence of events. Subscribers are programs that are "interested" in their occurrence. Brokers mediate between publishers and subscribers. They "listen" for the occurrence of events from publishers and appropriately notify all interested subscribers. Prior to any event handling, subscribers enroll their subscriptions with the broker, and publishers register their events. Publish and subscribe is widely used in online publishing.

- **Improved RDBMS software.** Relational database management system (RDBMS) technology has become accepted as the primary data storage and access platform for knowledge-tone applications. Traditionally optimized for only transaction applications, RDBMS technology has been improved specifically for DSS applications. Improvements have removed many of the database size, manageability, and query performance constraints that have made developing DSS difficult.

- **Improved price and performance of computing and storage hardware.** The widespread availability of scalable hardware from a variety of server vendors has produced significant improvements in server price and performance. In the early 1990s, building and managing databases of 1GB to 5GB of stored data was considered typical. In 1997, the average data warehouse was 132GB, and by 2000, it's expected to grow to 259GB.[11]

- **Improved infrastructure of the Web.** The maturation of the Web infrastructure combined with commercially available servers and browsers, expanded bandwidth, security products, authoring tools, administrative suites, access devices, and third-party expertise have substantially decreased the cost of deploying multiuser knowledge-tone applications. The corresponding advances in usability, reliability, maintainability, and connectivity have accelerated the commercial acceptance of knowledge-tone applications by making such deployment less risky, less expensive, and less time-consuming for organizations.

Clearly, synergies produced by the combination of improved database software, abundant computing power, and efficiently connected networks are resulting in a dramatic increase in the knowledge-tone market. However, several tricky issues have to be resolved before knowledge-tone applications become widespread. Most involve the integration of Internet e-commerce with internal systems and data. The issues may include any or all of the following:

- Inability to accommodate additional—or even any—online activity due to performance, capacity, or infrastructure issues at the core of the processing environment

- Multiple fragmented processing platforms (born out of mergers and acquisitions)

- Poor quality of core data and applications

- Lack of knowledgeable Internet/Web development resources

Solutions (or compromises) to any of these issues are available to most organizations by using internal or external resources. These issues do not present insurmountable technical barriers. In many cases they present only a financial or resource hurdle. Thus, the real issue boils down to whether the cost of implementing Web-based applications can be offset by the benefits. All we can say is that potential benefits are driven by the use of a Web-based facility.

Elements of the Knowledge-Tone Architectural Framework

To meet the challenge of creating an integrated decision framework, organizations have to implement a number of decision support applications under the framework of knowledge tone. The knowledge-tone architecture is built on a platform composed of three layers (see Figure 10.5):

- **e-Business decision-support solutions.** This layer includes the ability to deliver informational views and querying, reporting, and modeling capabilities that go way beyond current offerings.

- **Enabling technologies—data mining, query processing, and result distribution infrastructure.** This layer includes the ability to store data in a multidimensional cube format (online analytical processing, or OLAP) to enable rapid data aggregation and drill-down analysis.

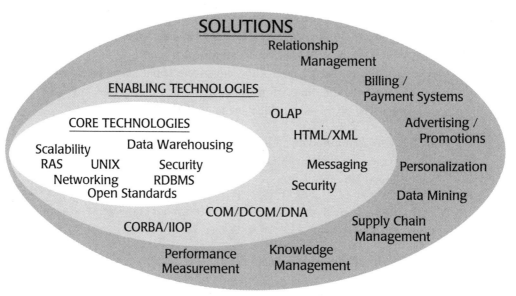

Figure 10.5: Knowledge-Tone Architecture

> • **Core technologies—data warehouses and data marts.** This layer includes the ability to extract, cleanse, and aggregate data from multiple operational systems into a separate data mart or warehouse.

In the previous sections, we talked extensively about various solutions. Let's now address the core technologies layer, followed by the enabling technologies layer.

Core Technologies: Data Warehousing

What is a data warehouse? A data warehouse is, well, a warehouse of data. Today, a majority of Fortune 2000 enterprises have constructed or are constructing data warehouses to serve as a "networked information service hub" for optimizing their business operations. Data warehouses are electronic repositories of summarized historical data, often extracted from disparate departmental or enterprise databases. The idea behind data warehousing is simple: Get all company data working together so users can see more, learn more, and make the organization work better.

Business Rationale

The business goal is to simplify integration issues by having a one-stop source for enterprise data. Companies of every size are finding that data warehouses are essential for running their business. Consider the case of General Motors (GM). Over the last 30 years, GM installed centralized databases that were "best in class" in their day, but are now considered legacy—old and decrepit. Too often the high volumes and the complexities of day-to-day operations have brought these systems to their virtual knees. Moreover, the data access tools that came with these old databases were either too unsophisticated for detailed data analysis or too difficult for the average end user to use. These information systems also segregated the company's operational data and data query activities from the production databases.

The goal of data warehousing is to help users identify trends, find answers to business questions, and derive meaning from historical and operational data, all of which enhances decision support in the enterprise. For instance, in the early 1990s, GM began aggregating all of its data regarding vehicles and vehicle orders into data warehouses. The result is a common, comprehensive view of all the information. GM users can surf through, aggregate, and manipulate the data as they see fit. Data access is easier and less costly, regardless of the source data's location. Plus, decision support solutions, such as analyzing how warranty claims vary by car model, run faster and are more accurate.[12]

How It Works

A data warehouse takes production data such as customer transactions, scrubs it up, organizes it, and puts it in a place appropriate for browsing, analyzing, and decision making. The practice of data warehousing usually involves centralizing a variety of data sources or extending the value of a central repository so more can be done with the stored data, such as mining, transforming, or analyzing it and depicting it visually. The result: practical access to critical data and decision support. This is a big deal when you consider the fact that companies have always had to go out and find the data each time they wanted to write a new decision support application.

Data warehouses store data in a format optimized for analysis and are frequently used in conjunction with query and reporting tools designed to perform some predefined queries and simple calculations. This level of analysis, however, is limited. For example, query and reporting tools generally are not designed to perform time-series analyses such as calculations of the weekly changes in market share by region. Tools that can do those types of tasks often require users to understand the technical aspects of data storage and data structures. As a result, the use of data query and reporting tools is often limited to highly trained technical users.

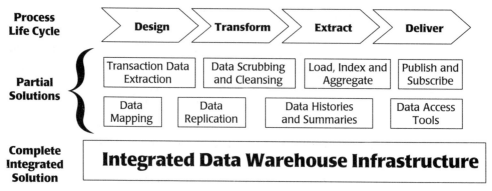

Figure 10.6: The Data Warehousing Process

Data Warehouse Components

Figure 10.6 provides a complete picture of the data warehousing process. Here's a breakdown of the components.

- Transactional applications ensure that source data can be stored in any format, from modern relational databases to traditional legacy sources.

- Data extraction and transformation tools read data from transactional systems, transform the data for consistency, and write it to an intermediate file.

- Data scrubbing tools are needed to further cleanse raw data.

- Data movement tools move data from the intermediate files to the data warehouse, while automatically managing data volume and cross-platform issues. The key elements in data movement are data transformation and routing services as well as business rule sequencing and management.

- Data repository tools maintain the metadata (information about data), which points to the data in the warehouse. Repository tools monitor transactional applications so that if a data record changes, the data extraction and transformation tools will be updated.

- Data access tools retrieve, view, manipulate, analyze, and present data. On the desktop, these tools include spreadsheets, query engines, report writers, and even Web browsers.

- Data delivery includes ubiquitous end-user access; that is, instant messaging between all manner of devices (e.g., browsers, e-mail, pagers, fax, Palm Pilot, Windows CE, and wireless), regardless of the communications medium.

Enabling Technologies: Online Analytical Processing

Historically, building, using, and managing decision-support solutions required a variety of specialized tools and multidimensional databases. To meet these challenges, organizations implemented a number of technology solutions, including data warehouses and data marts, query and reporting tools, and online analytical processing (OLAP) applications.

OLAP solutions provide a means to analyze complex data along a more intuitive set of business rules and dimensions (for example, profitability analysis by product, channel, geography, customer, or fiscal period). In addition, by insulating the user from the technical aspects of data storage and data structures, OLAP solutions enable less technically sophisticated users within an organization to perform their own analyses.

Typically, OLAP solutions provide complex computational capabilities, including sophisticated time-series analysis, as well as ad hoc, drill-down, and interactive analysis (for example, a marketing manager identifying a market share reduction can drill down to isolate the problem to a specific product at a specific store).

Defining the OLAP Terminology

Most decision support applications are limited in their ability to answer complex questions due to a lack of analytical sophistication, schema limitations, or the inability to handle large amounts of data. This is changing with the advent of OLAP applications. In assessing this market, we see vendors, market analysts, and investors quickly becoming needlessly entangled in the terminology and positioning nuances of the many products and vendors.

Table 10.4 is a quick introduction to the terminology underlying some of the more widely known decision support products. We must note, however, that there is little consistency in the application of these terms; unfortunately, vendors are combining and extending their approaches in so many ways that distinctions across product categories will continue to blur. However, details of product implementation matter less than the fit of the product design to the target applications and markets.

Online analytical processing is an umbrella term for a range of decision support approaches. Typically, data that is entered into a transactional relational database system is offloaded, reformatted, or accessed in specialized ways to enhance the processing of complex queries that are beyond the capabilities of the standard database.

Table 10.4: OLAP Types and Terminology

Definition	Sample Products	Uses	Best Fit
Desktop OLAP: Also called client-side OLAP. Products that pass data from a server to a desktop client to perform most of the processing locally. Often linked to query and reporting tools that create specialized views from within larger data sets for particular end-user needs.	Business Objects, Brio, Cognos	End-user report viewing and drill-down analysis	Small, customized data sets; offline usage on laptops or portable devices
Relational OLAP (ROLAP): Places the emphasis of data query processing and delivery within the source relational database. Data access, query processing, and data storage are all managed by the foundation data warehouse platform. The ROLAP engine submits automated, highly specialized, iterated queries to the database and handles the return of the information to the users.	MicroStrategy DSS Products Server; Information Advantage, Platinum Technology (Prodea)	Retail market analysis, health care information processing, customer relationship analysis, Web-based information stores	Data warehouse analysis, analysis of transaction records, rapidly changing data or very large data sets
Multidimensional OLAP (MOLAP): A specialized server-based database that takes relational data from a transactional system and physically stores it in a unique format to enhance query access. Typically, data is summary level and contains defined dimensions or data characteristics. MOLAP storage is often visualized as a cube of multiple dimensions, each corresponding to a particular data characteristic.	Arbor Essbase, Oracle Express, Seagate (Holos), and SAS	Financial budgeting and forecasting	Fast response times on consolidated data records; data analysis needs combined with data updates
Hybrid OLAP: Products that combine the characteristics of MOLAP and ROLAP approaches. For example, supporting both server- and client-based processing, or processing both within the standard relational format and in special data storage structures.	IBM DB2 OLAP Server, Microsoft Plato	Emerging range of selected MOLAP and ROLAP uses	Data center or LAN processing of operational data stores

As Table 10.4 shows, OLAP is evolving into several distinct areas: desktop OLAP, relational OLAP, multidimensional OLAP, and hybrid OLAP. Organizations are seeking ways to extend the benefits of OLAP in order to empower employees at all levels to make better business decisions and react faster to market opportunities. To effectively deliver OLAP throughout the enterprise, the solution must support large data sets and thousands of users and offer simple as well as complex analyses.

A Roadmap to Knowledge-Tone Framework

Figure 10.7 depicts the four elements of the knowledge-tone framework: users, applications, analytic tools, and data sources. To set up your company's knowledge-tone framework, use the following steps as a series of guideposts.

1. **Identify the goals of the knowledge-tone project.** Once you've established what you want to achieve, make sure that goals are actionable and that the business can put newly discovered knowledge to use.

2. **Determine where knowledge resides in the company.** Part of what makes knowledge tone such a difficult concept to grasp and put into practice is that knowledge is ubiquitous. It can live inside myriad databases, which explains why data warehousing is such a crucial component of business today. Some knowledge is difficult to find because it often lies hidden and undervalued in the minds of employees. Or it might dwell in the relationships your colleagues have with people at other companies.

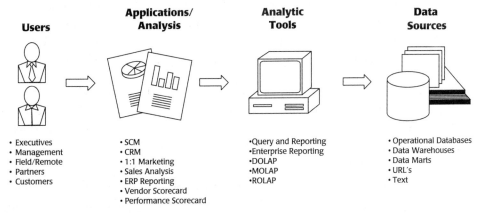

| Users | Applications/ Analysis | Analytic Tools | Data Sources |

• Executives
• Management
• Field/Remote
• Partners
• Customers

• SCM
• CRM
• 1:1 Marketing
• Sales Analysis
• ERP Reporting
• Vendor Scorecard
• Performance Scorecard

•Query and Reporting
•Enterprise Reporting
•DOLAP
•MOLAP
•ROLAP

• Operational Databases
• Data Warehouses
• Data Marts
• URL's
• Text

Figure 10.7: Knowledge-Tone Blueprint

3. **Determine what information the company needs to capture.** Despite what you might have read, knowledge isn't just about "knowing what you know." It's more important to learn what you need to know. Help employees capture information by employing "journalists"—analysts with knowledge of or experience in business operations—to help determine what information needs to be captured. They can also teach you how to apply knowledge already captured to improve specific business processes.

4. **Collect, clean, and prepare data.** Obtain necessary data from various internal and external sources. Resolve representation and encoding differences. Check and resolve data conflicts, outliers (unusual or exception values), missing data, and ambiguity. Use conversions and combinations to generate new data fields such as ratios or rolled-up summaries. These steps require considerable effort, often as much as 70 percent or more of the total effort. If you already have a data warehouse (especially one that contains detailed transaction data), you probably have a head start on the data collection, integration, and cleaning that is needed.

5. **Balance outward and inward data.** In the majority of data warehousing efforts, enterprises focus inward. As markets become turbulent, the traditional way of doing business becomes less viable. Therefore, data from internal operational systems becomes less relevant to managing your business and planning for its future. Instead of focusing inward, the enterprise should be keenly alert to outside sources. Many people think that external data has little value because internal operational systems contain all the required data. But business experts such as Peter Drucker think differently. Drucker admonishes IT executives to look outside their enterprises for information, pointing out that the single biggest challenge is to "organize outside data because change occurs from the outside." He predicts that the obsession with internal data will lead to organizations being blindsided by external forces.[13]

6. **Develop new approaches to categorizing information.** Several startups, such as Intraspect and Plumtree, are developing capabilities to categorize information across core business apps such as SAP. One key to success is to create a categorization scheme with business relevance. IMS Health, a health care data provider, reorganized its intranet around business issues, such as recruiting and employee skills availability, instead of organizational structure. By doing so, the company improved users' ability to find critical information.

Use librarians to help develop and manage the categorization schemes that will spring up across the company.

7. **Learn how to mine data.** The model-building step involves selecting data-mining tools; transforming data if the tools require it; generating samples (as necessary) for training, testing, and validating the model; and using the tools to build, test, and select models.

8. **Validate the model.** Test the model for accuracy on an independent data set, one that has not been used to create the model. Assess the model's sensitivity, and conduct a pilot test on the model to ensure usability. For example, if you are using a model to predict customer response, make a prediction and do a test mailing to a subset. See how closely the responses match your predictions.

9. **Deploy the model.** For a predictive model, use the model to predict results for new cases, then use the prediction to alter organizational behavior. Deployment may require building computerized systems that capture the data and generate a prediction in real time so that a decision maker can apply the prediction. For example, a model can determine if a credit card transaction is likely to be fraudulent.

10. **Monitor the model.** As the environment changes, so must models. Changes in the economy, products, or competition must be reflected in the models. Any of these forces will alter customer behavior, making the model that's correct today useless tomorrow. Monitoring models requires constant revalidation of the model on new data to assess if it's still appropriate.

11. **Measure the ROI of knowledge tone.** Quantifying a return on knowledge tone is definitely hard to do. Although a slew of companies are coming to market with new software to help, it's still hard to put exact numbers on the value of information. Companies that fail to exploit their knowledge tend to come up with ideas and decisions haphazardly rather than through a carefully organized method that takes advantage of all available information. But in the knowledge-based world of today and tomorrow, happenstance won't cut it. It's not what knowledge you have that's important, it's whether you can find it and what you do with it.

The knowledge discovery process is iterative. For example, while cleaning and preparing data, you might discover that data from one source is unusable or that you need data from a previously unidentified source to be merged with other data. Often, the first time through the data-mining step reveals that additional data cleaning is required.

Memo to the CEO

Companies are drowning in data. It's widely reported that companies such as Wal-Mart have more than 50TB of transactional data. In the wake of this information deluge, workers and consumers are feeling both empowered and powerless, and they're trying to find ways to control its benefits and risks.

Clearly, dumping reams of information on employees' desktops isn't effective. Key information should be disbursed when it's needed. For example, a large software company improved its sales close ratio when it tracked the sales force's progress in the sales cycle, then disseminated information (such as competitor intelligence or industry-specific data) only if it was relevant at that stage in the sales cycle.

Increasingly, information access and control drive business competition. This is obvious when you consider the lack of boundaries in modern businesses. Corporations and consumers are becoming more interconnected via private networks and the Internet. These interconnections are facilitating the rollout of knowledge-tone applications in three phases.

Phase 1: Corporate Intranets. In this phase, companies seek to create more complete and uniform linkage of information resources scattered throughout the organization. For knowledge creation to occur, data aggregation needs to be complemented with data analysis. With data warehouses burgeoning in size and the time available for in-depth analysis shrinking, it's clear that automating the predictable components of a decision maker's routine makes a lot of sense. The technology for enabling this is the corporate intranet. Moving from departmental solutions, in which data and reports are developed for small, specialized communities of users, to a corporate intranet opens up data resources to a broader base of users by using the browser as a standard interface.

Phase 2: Extranets. This phase focuses on supply chain partners. Companies begin to move select parts of the internal corporate information infrastructure outside the firewall so that suppliers and trading partners can access them. Fast information access, customized data, and responsiveness are key business drivers. Standardized reports and interfaces are crucial to eliminating the need for training and minimizing service requirements. Interenterprise linkages create new requirements: the ability to manage huge data volumes (or data size scalability), data breadth coverage, cross-platform support, response time speed, and a broad range of interface choices. Cross-platform capabilities are crucial because inter-enterprise data sets are quite huge and the number of users is also quite large.

Phase 3: Commercial Internet Applications. This phase focuses on new business models. As companies gather information from their own activities, they also seek to syndicate and resell that information for a broader range of uses. For instance, credit card companies are not restricting themselves to processing individual sales transactions. They are actively packaging the transaction information to create new forms of value. In this rush to commercialize transactional data, privacy issues, intellectual property rights, and pricing issues will predominate as new business models emerge for capturing, consolidating, and reselling consumer information, business transaction records, and financial data.

Today, most corporate strategy is in phase 1. The emphasis is on creating the ability to initiate decision making throughout all levels of an organization. For this purpose, vast amounts of data must be collected daily and distributed to more people than ever before. Organizations also face the challenges of performing complex computational analyses on collected data and of disseminating the information not only to employees, but also to customers, suppliers, and business partners.

In short, managing a company's information network can make or break a business. That's why knowledge tone—the harnessing and organizing of information assets—has become such a critical part of doing business.

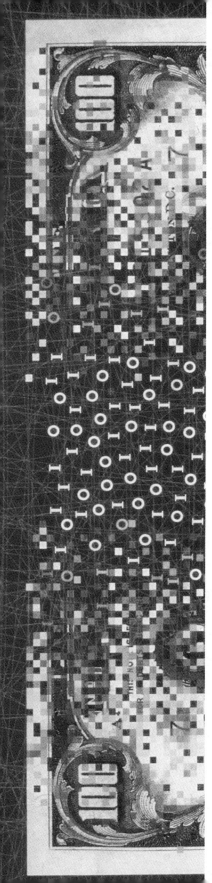

CHAPTER ELEVEN

Developing the e-Business Design

What to Expect

e-Business technology has created a seismic shift in the way companies do business. Just knowing the importance and structure of e-business is not enough. You need to create and implement an action plan that allows you to make the transition from an old business design to a new e-business design.

The e-business planning process may sound like so much common sense, but doing it right requires an ongoing commitment of time and energy that could be spent on day-to-day operations. Many, if not most, companies are unwilling to make the commitment. Yet in a dynamic marketplace, that's a perilous strategy because the distance from hero to zero is rather short. Use this chapter's step-by-step roadmap to initiate a highly focused e-business blueprint strategy that aligns with your goals.

The monster was upon him. One of the snake-like heads darted out at him.
Swinging his sword, Hercules cut it off. Immediately two new heads grew from
the Hydra's bloody neck. Hercules cut them off also—but four new heads grew
in their places. Hercules gasped, "I fear that before I am finished it will have
nine hundred heads!"

—The Twelve Labors of Hercules

Working to create an e-business design strategy may seem like fighting a multi-headed monster: The number of challenges you encounter multiplies rapidly. Creating business solutions requires simultaneously molding multiple disciplines—business strategy, enterprise applications, and technology implementation. Having only the pieces isn't enough. Creating a synergy of these business disciplines is the only way to create sophisticated digital solutions.

The business strategy questions confounding managers are *how to transform the old company to the new company design* and *how to bridge the capability gap between the "needs of physical today" and the "needs of digital tomorrow."* The "needs of physical today" are anchored in cost-cutting back-office software that aids process reengineering and helps save money by streamlining operations. The "needs of digital tomorrow" are tied to revenue-enhancing front-office software that helps spur profit growth by making it easier for businesses to sell products via the Web, to get the most out of customer data, and to manage relationships with suppliers and consumers.

In the e-business world, companies must anticipate the need for transformation and be ready to reexamine their organizations to their cores. One company that understands the transformation issues is OfficeMax. It's making the right moves to evolve from a legacy infrastructure to an e-business infrastructure.

Moving Physical to Digital: The Case of OfficeMax

OfficeMax, one of the largest high-volume, deep-discount office products superstores, operates more than 780 full-size stores that feature more than 8,000 office products, computers, and related items in more than 330 markets. The company also operates CopyMax and FurnitureMax, store-within-a-store modules devoted exclusively to print-for-pay services and office furniture, respectively.

With the launch of OfficeMax Online in 1995, OfficeMax became the first office products retailer to sell products over the Internet. In addition to a vast assortment of products, OfficeMax.com offers search and browse features, order and usage reports, and customized express order templates. The e-commerce channel is supported by call centers seven days a week, 24 hours a day, and there are 17 delivery centers around the country that guarantee next-day delivery.

OfficeMax has invested more than $50 million to upgrade systems and controls, and the company intends to continue investing aggressively in infrastructure to support growth. It has initiated a replatforming project, FutureMax, that will provide integrated, state-of-the-art applications and technology. FutureMax comprises three major application suites: merchandising, inventory management, and financial systems. These suites are integrated to provide seamless connectivity to a number of special-purpose applications that provide information required to make timely, informed decisions.[1]

Like OfficeMax, you're probably in the early stages of the transition to a digital tomorrow. So, here you are at the beginning of the twenty-first century searching for a place to start, a path to follow, and a destination to reach. The question you're struggling with is, *What makes a good e-business strategy in highly uncertain business environments?* Some executives seek to shape the future of their companies with high-risk, high-return investments. More conservative executives hedge their bets by making a number of smaller investments. Alternatively, some executives favor investments in flexibility, which allows their companies to adapt quickly as markets evolve. *Which strategy is right for you?* First, figure out which strategy creation process is right for you.

The Challenges of e-Business Strategy Creation

According to Niccolo Machiavelli, the sixteenth-century Florentine philosopher, "There is nothing more difficult to take in hand, more perilous to conduct, or more uncertain in its success, than to take the lead in the introduction of a new order of things."

e-Business strategy is about the uncertain future and therefore tends to be based on assumptions, premises, and beliefs about customer priorities, technology evolution, competition, and the core competencies that will be needed to compete. There are two types of e-business strategy planning: top-down, analytic planning and bottom-up, "just do it" tactical planning. Top-down planning takes a broad view of the environment, identifies options, and then defines the organization's mission and direction. A tactical operation takes a more focused or narrow view of the environment and performs the necessary activities required to produce short-term results.

Top-down Analytic Planning

The top-down method attempts to systematically lay out a vision of the future precise enough for some capital budgeting technique. It's often data rich, numbers driven, and analytically based. Of course, managers discuss alternative scenarios and test how sensitive their predictions are to changes in key variables, but the goal of such analysis is to find the most likely outcome and create a strategy based on it. That approach serves companies well in stable business conditions. But when there is greater uncertainty about the future, top-down planning is only marginally helpful, and at times downright dangerous.

The biggest problem with top-down planning is the separation of strategy formulation (analysis) and implementation (execution) (see Figure 11.1), which can lead to the following flawed plans.

- **The never-seen-again strategic plan.** Once-a-year top-down strategic planning is often a joke, a "paralysis by analysis" bureaucratic nightmare. Too many businesses invest countless hours of their top managers' valuable time in endless meetings and spend thousands of dollars creating a plan only to file it away and never use it.

- **The no-goals strategic plan.** A strategic plan that isn't used to set targets and goals is worthless! Strategic plans need to include specific performance goals that the company must meet and use as a measure the following year. A strategic plan is simply a wish list unless you identify the applications needed to meet goals. What resources are needed to develop those applications? Who's going to be responsible for building them? Many companies are great at top-down planning but falter when it comes to execution.

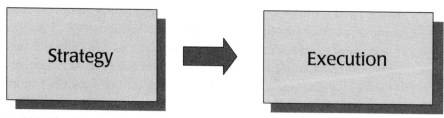

Top-Down Strategic Planning

Figure 11.1: The Chasm between Strategy and Implementation

- **The no-feedback strategic plan.** Lack of feedback leads to disaster in innovative environments. Traveling on the wrong road never leads to the right destination. Feedback signals if you're headed in the wrong direction. Because e-business deals with future events and opportunities, much of the information—market and technical—required to make strategic decisions is at best uncertain and at worst unreliable. What looked like an excellent project six months ago can suddenly be not so promising. At the same time, customer requirements are constantly changing and new opportunities are always being discovered. In the e-business environment, continuous feedback is essential so that the strategic plan can be adjusted.

Another problem with the top-down approach is that no matter how many smart managers work together on the big picture, getting it right in the face of continuous change is very difficult. Today, organizations and industries face tremendous structural change, uncertainty, and decisions with huge opportunities and risks. Making smart choices in this volatile environment calls for more than systematic analysis. It also demands creativity, insight, and intuition.

Bottom-up, "Just Do It" Planning

Today, business stability simply doesn't exist. In this chaotic environment, it's no wonder that faith in traditional strategic planning has eroded. The idea of planning as an ordered process rested on assumptions that the future would be a continuation of the present, or at least that it would be a slow, predictable shift, with plenty of time to adapt. In many industries, those assumptions are no longer true.

In an environment in which change is the norm, the insights of those on the front line take on new importance. Those close to the action—salespeople and others who deal directly with outside clients—are first to get wind of changes in customer needs. Organizations with hierarchical decision-making structures have few mechanisms for ensuring that the insights of frontline people reach strategy makers. This limitation makes it nearly impossible to respond quickly to the demands of the marketplace.[2]

As a result, bottom-up, "just do it" planning is flourishing. Managers are abandoning the analytical rigor of traditional planning processes and basing their strategic decisions on solving immediate needs. Often, many individual projects are heroically executed. Frequently, however, there are no integrated plans that link individual projects into a cohesive whole.

This "just do it" strategy can lead to misinformed decisions that result in a fractured pattern of authority, which impedes comprehensive planning and integration. Banks that invested in Web banking in the mid-1990s without carefully integrating their existing channel strategies are a good example.

In many Fortune 1000 corporations, there's growing dissatisfaction with the first generation of applications that came out of the "just do it" phase of e-commerce. These applications were not integrated with the rest of the service/ delivery infrastructure (see Figure 11.2). We're beginning to see many companies hit the pause button, take a step back, and ask how e-commerce fits with the rest of the corporate strategy.

Continuous Planning with Feedback

So, what is the right approach? Continuous planning with feedback. In a fluid, volatile environment, the best approach may be to allow strategy to evolve through the discovery of what works and what doesn't. As a result, the distinctions that characterized strategic planning—formulation and implementation— will blur. Planning cycles not only become shorter, but also become more organic as planning segues into implementation. The perceived distinction between strategy and tactics also blurs, especially since conditions often require such quick response that tactics will dictate or at least shape strategy.

However, this approach is much easier described than done. The structural requirements of continuous planning are quite different from hierarchically structured models. The former involves the use of "e-business councils"—cross-functional teams that are adept at translating the strategy blueprint into implementation. This method is built on four steps (see Figure 11.3).

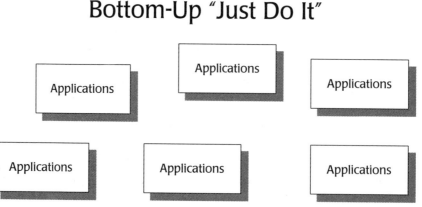

Figure 11.2: A Collection of Nonintegrated Applications

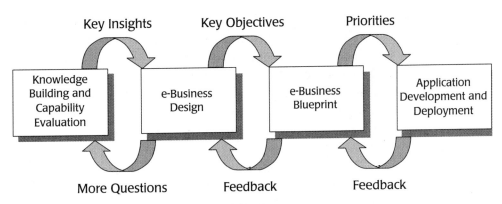

Figure 11.3: Continuous Planning with Feedback

1. **Knowledge building and capability evaluation.** Develop a clear vision of what the customer needs are. Develop a clear understanding of what capabilities you need in order to address the customer needs. The last thing you want to do is fight a high-tech war with sledgehammers. This vision must be communicated in a way that every employee understands.

2. **e-Business design.** Develop a coherent design that lays the foundation to address the new customer needs. If the customer wants self-service, then your business design must facilitate that. The e-business design is the foundation that helps the company get where it needs to go.

3. **e-Business blueprint.** Create a link between the e-business design—the business goals—and the technology foundation. If you want to provide a self-service business model, determine what application framework you need. Clearly define the projects and key milestones that must be achieved.

4. **Application development and deployment.** Translate these key milestones and projects into integrated applications. Make sure that employees know how performing their jobs helps corporate objectives. Get periodic feedback about what's going well and what isn't so that the plan can be refined.

This process of defining the vision, stating the objectives, and communicating them throughout the organization is what we call "continuous planning with feedback." Many companies are already doing this. For some, it's become an important management tool, allowing the organization to set clear priorities, establish target areas for improvement activities, and allocate resources for the most important projects.

The new element in the continuous planning model is the blueprint piece. This is the integration traffic cop that ensures that a project integrates with the company's strategies and goals. The big question these days is how to integrate diverse applications. Integration has to occur internally first before it can make a favorable impact on the customer.

Continuous planning success depends on feedback. A good e-business strategy must evolve as innovative infrastructure emerges and new customer needs are spotted. Most companies are uncomfortable with this feedback-driven revision. They want to hear about sure things. They want guarantees concerning their return on investment (ROI). It's very hard to guarantee ROI in e-business, because tomorrow is unpredictable. In fact, it's the requirement of quick success and maximum return that often derails established companies. Due to the pressures of profit growth from Wall Street, companies are so concerned with short-term ROI that they don't pay enough attention to long-term payoffs.

Continuous planning is also practiced in the form of trigger-point planning. Trigger-point planning is one of the emerging methods for making decisions in a rapidly changing environment. In the absence of clear long-range plans, companies establish contingencies based on multiple visions of the future. They then determine the trigger points—a competitor's decision to extend its product line, for example—that will signal which of the contingencies should be put into action. Finland's Nokia Corporation used such a trigger-point model in the timing of its successful decision to become the first major wireless company to adopt code division multiple access (CDMA) as a standard for digital wireless communication technology.[3]

Trigger-point planning is becoming more widely used as the technology becomes more readily available to keep up with triggering events. Companies like Lucent, Xerox, and Ericsson routinely use the Web to monitor real-time data from customers, suppliers, and channel partners to help them know when to pull the trigger. The trigger-point process also requires a more constant sharing of information throughout the corporation. Compaq's cross-functional strategy team meets weekly to pore over updated information and, if necessary, realign strategy.

To be effective, trigger-point planning must be used as a tool, a means to an end, and not as the goal itself. It must be a venture that involves people throughout the organization. It must capture existing activities, not just add more activities to overflowing plates. Finally, it must help senior managers face difficult decisions, set priorities, and eliminate many activities, rather than start new ones.

Roadmap to Moving Your Company into e-Business

e-Business strategy appears mystical. However, there are a few guidelines that managers can use to reduce the mystique. These guidelines are presented here in the form of strategic questions. These questions are not to be the skimmed. Spend a few quiet hours contemplating and answering them. The answers will form the foundation of your e-business initiatives. Once you have worked through the questions, meet with other senior executives and compare answers. This meeting will reveal gaps—the closing of which is your starting point on the e-business journey.

Getting Started on Your Journey

Making e-business a reality involves two key elements: the business strategy formulation and the application framework strategy (see Figure 11.4). Business strategy helps figure out the why and what of customer value creation. *e-Business strategy formulation* includes the following phases.

- **Knowledge building** helps the company understand what the customer is looking for and where the industry is going. It opens a window on the future and provides an opportunity to really understand what customers value.

- **Capability evaluation** defines the existing business and identifies what capabilities it has today and what capabilities it needs to have tomorrow. It allows companies to question if they have what it takes to serve customers' changing priorities.

- **e-Business design** asks what value proposition a business must provide to take advantage of digital capabilities. How is this value going to be packaged into products, services, or experiences?

The e-business blueprint, or application framework strategy, helps take the "what to do" and convert it into the "how to" of value creation. Among the deci-

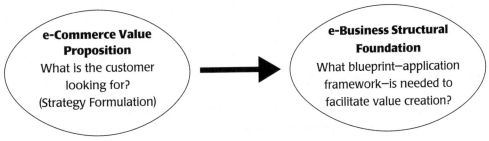

Figure 11.4: Linking Value to Structure

sions that should be made up front are how the business will be integrated, what the measures of success will be, how much will be committed to resources, what the depth and breadth of implementation will be, and what transition methods will be used. The e-business blueprint includes the following phases.

- **Blueprint design** involves translating strategy into action. This phase includes drafting a blueprint composed of software building blocks that will allow a company to seize the opportunities created by changing customer priorities.

- **Business case creation** must convince management to invest in enterprise software, which is what makes e-business tick. These programs aren't cheap. Installing a full-fledged enterprise software system often costs from $10 million to $30 million in licensing fees and from $50 million to $200 million in consulting fees.

- **Blueprint execution** brings the blueprint to life. It helps implement the necessary enterprise software that will facilitate creating the e-business design. This phase is where the rubber hits the road.

Our objective in this chapter is to provide a roadmap to creating an e-business strategy. In the next chapter, we turn strategy into action.

Even in a technology-crazed world, a good business strategy comes first. Many organizations fail to create an effective e-business strategy before they rush into the blueprint phase. As a result, they risk pouring time and dollars into an initiative that will eventually collapse. And if you don't know where you're going, you may not like getting there.

Let's not kid ourselves. Talking about e-business is easy; actually making it happen is the hard part. The methods for achieving e-business success are simple to grasp. After all, isn't it obvious that you should serve your customers better? However, implementing e-business methods is extremely difficult because it requires you to ask, *Why do we do things the way we do them?* You have to look at what you do in a different way. Throw out traditional methods and acquire new skills. In short, you don't buy e-business: You strategize, design, and build it into your everyday business.

Phase 1: Knowledge Building

The first step in any e-business transformation journey is knowledge building. Knowledge building enables managers to understand their customers' priorities.

Most managers don't really understand their customers or the relationship between customer and profit. Today, powerful management insights can be gained by asking how customers have changed. Only those business leaders who can properly ascertain customers' present (and future) priorities can design their businesses to align with those priorities and grow market share.

Knowledge building is difficult. The first mistake many companies make is underestimating the amount of knowledge and data needed to make effective strategy. Strategy must be based on fact, not opinion, but it usually isn't. Most strategy sessions are conducted in intense two- or three-day off-site planning meetings where opinions rather than facts dominate. Now ask yourself, *How does my company develop strategy? Do we use data and facts to support decisions?*

Why are data and facts important? Without understanding the surrounding environment and developing an internal frame of reference that serves as a roadmap, managers often develop the right strategy for the wrong problem.[4] The best-laid strategies go awry when the roadmap fails to chart the realities of a business situation, when one or more of management's assumptions, premises, or beliefs are incorrect, or when internal inconsistencies make the overall business design invalid.

Every company has its own set of data for planning, but in general data should address the following key areas: (1) understanding the customer, (2) customer value and relationship trends, (3) technology trends, (4) supply chain trends, and (5) competition and predicted moves. Data from each area should be segmented and analyzed until it's obvious to everyone what the key opportunities are. The focus on data helps remove personalities from the decision-making process. It also improves buy-in because decisions are supported with data.

This chapter has been arranged to help you gather data to move your company into the e-business world. By answering the questions posed here, you are positioning yourself to make better decisions. Suffice it to say that failure to answer these questions and research the marketplace before committing to a strategy is asking for trouble.

The intelligence-gathering process involves answering a sequence of questions (see Table 11.1). As you can see from the questions, we think it's a good idea to begin "outside in" rather than "inside out." This approach forces managers to take a broader perspective and answer such questions as these: How are my customers changing and how will that affect me? What are the new trends that will make me obsolete in five years? What are the decisions that have to be made to sustain the growth of the company?

Table 11.1: Questions to Ask to Get into e-Business

Understanding the customer	*Who are my customers?*
	How are my customers' priorities shifting?
	Who should be my target customer? How will the e-business help reach my target customer segments?
Customer value and relationship trends	*How can I add value for the customer?*
	How can I become the customer's first choice?
	How does my product reach customers?
Technology trends	*Do we understand the environment and industry trends?*
	Do we understand technology trends?
Supply chain trends	*What are the priorities in the supply chain?*
Competition	*Who are my real competitors? What is my toughest competitor's business model? What are they doing really well?*

Who Are My Customers?

Managers often think they know who their customers are because they are selling products or services to them. However, understanding customers really means being able to categorize them into distinct groups whose behavior can be analyzed systematically. As a model, look at the customer segmentation devised by Charles Schwab, the discount brokerage powerhouse.

- **Life-goal planner.** An investor who is interested in trading mutual funds for long-term growth and wants tools for financial planning and portfolio optimization. A stable financial service provider is more important to him than the latest in technical analysis.

- **Serious investor.** This data-hungry investor is an active trader who values high-quality information, investment tools, and research. She or he wants one, integrated, easily accessible place to get help in deciding what to buy.

- **Hyperactive trader.** Low-cost trading, a simple interface, and fast execution are keys to this market junkie. His or her trading is so frequent, he doesn't want to have to reenter his password on every order.

- **One-stop shopper.** This convenience-minded consumer wants a comprehensive package of financial products—stock trading, mutual funds, credit cards, bill payment, and checking. Breadth of offerings and ease of use are important to him or her.

By understanding its customer segments, Charles Schwab is able to focus its e-business strategy and tailor it to the needs of the distinct segments. **Now, write down your customer segments.**

Now that you understand customer segments, answer these questions: *What is important to each customer segment? How do you go about doing customer analysis?* Customers who buy from you also buy many other products and services. By extrapolating customer behavior in complementary markets, you can apply this information to your industry. Your answers to the following questions will help you figure out what is important to your customers: *What are five new products or services in your industry that have become popular in the last five years? What customer segments are buying these products or services? Why do these customer segments like these products or services?*

Answers to these questions will help you assess your customers' needs. Typically, customers have two sets of needs: spoken (explicit) and unspoken (implicit). The most difficult challenge in customer analyses is understanding the unspoken needs of the customer. **Now, write down the spoken and unspoken needs of your customers.**

Finally, answering the question "Who are my customers?" will influence how performance ought to be measured. If you believe that distributors are your customers, then you might measure performance based on only the things distributors care about. Are products in stock? What are the discounts and payment terms? In short, you have to understand who your real customers are, what they expect, and what they value. **Write down the performance indicators that you think each of your customer segments cares about.**

How Are My Customers' Priorities Shifting

Understanding customer needs is priority one. Those companies content with where they are won't be there long. Customer priorities have a natural tendency to change, often catching firms off guard. Companies resist change because their operating models tend to be fairly static. This dichotomy creates tension and opens the door for innovative upstarts that can easily shift to satisfy customers' needs.

To understand customer priorities, you must listen to your customers. Many companies find that the absolute best place to start is by improving those things that your customers would like you to improve. Collecting these ideas and acting on them has been an unexpected gold mine for many companies. **Now, write down the five things your customers ask for.**

A company that doesn't understand customer priorities is running blind.

The scene in Lewis Carroll's *Alice's Adventures in Wonderland* in which Alice asks the Cheshire Cat for directions speaks volumes about business today:

> "Would you tell me, please, which way I ought to go from here?"
> "That depends a good deal on where you want to get to," said the Cat.
> "I don't much care where—" said Alice.
> "Then, it doesn't matter which way you go," said the Cat.

It's the classic planning conundrum: Until you know what your customers' priorities are (where you want to go), you can't fashion a way to meet them (get to your destination). Often, the organization knows it wants to go somewhere, but that "somewhere" has never been clearly defined or communicated. *Is your company in a similar situation?*

First, ask yourself who your customers will be three to five years from now. What will their needs be? How will you add value for them? Then work your way back. Remember, you must intuit how technology can and will change customers' needs and alter markets. For instance, Jeff Bezos, CEO of Amazon.com, believed that once bibliophiles and time-starved business people were comfortable using the Internet, they would be interested in buying books online. Everyone, even die-hard e-commerce visionaries, was surprised at how big this unspoken need was and how fast it has transformed the dynamics of book retailing.

Changing customer priorities (see Figure 11.5) create opportunities for new e-business models and render old models vulnerable. Discovering customers' unspoken needs and meeting them faster and better than anyone else is key to developing a competitive advantage. Management cannot build the framework for an effective strategic plan if it does not know where the customer value proposi-

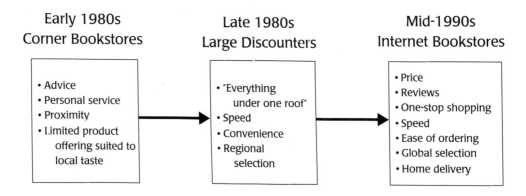

Figure 11.5: Needs Migration in Book Retailing Market Supported by Structural Migration

tion is or where it's going. Without a clear vision of where the enterprise needs to be—based on business drivers and other factors specific to the organization—the notion of an enterprise architecture is nothing more than a game played by business units. Now, answer this question: *How has your customer changed in the past five years and how do you think the customer will change in the next five?*

Who Is My Target Customer?

Once you understand who your current customers are, what their priorities are, and how their priorities are changing, think about how you might expand the boundaries of your customer set. Are there new groups who value what you do? Can you jump a step along the value chain and serve your customer's customers?

Creative customer selection is a central element of value reinvention. Amazon.com's affiliate program, Digital Associates, is an interesting variant of creative customer selection. The Associates program, estimated to include more than 100,000 commercial and amateur Web sites, attempts to lure first-time cybershoppers, consumers who might not otherwise seek out or stumble upon member companies' Web sites. For member sites, there seems to be nothing to lose by being part of the program since there are no joining fees and the only cost is maintaining banner ads and product information on their own sites. And there's a bonus: Each affiliate earns commissions of up to 15 percent just for enticing online shoppers to click over to Amazon.com's online superstore and buy something.[5]

In 1998, Dell was encroaching on Compaq Computer's market share in the desktop computer marketplace because Dell was using a direct delivery model to reach customers. Compaq's customer was the reseller. However, vendors such as Compaq can no longer afford to support multiple sets of hands between their operations and end users. Compaq was forced into a strategic decision that their target customer is the end user, not the reseller. Clearly, with the advent of the Internet, the structure of the channel is not so clear anymore for some companies.

Now, answer these questions: *Who are my top ten customers today? In order to grow my company, whom should I be targeting? What are the needs of this new target customer base?*

How Can I Add Value for My Target Customer?

Customers want innovation, value, and savings. *Which one do you offer?* Now write down the answer to this question: *How do I currently add value to my target customer base? Do I save money? Offer convenience? Offer new forms of value?*

The *"how do I add value?"* question is especially important in transition moments, when a company tries to migrate from its bread-and-butter business to another technology or service channel. How can managers stimulate value creation that results in the simultaneous pursuit of radically superior value for customers and lower costs for companies?

One way is to refuse to allow industry assumptions to become a barrier to innovative thinking. Take, for instance, palm computing. Venture capitalists and most consumer electronics outfits had written off the handheld computing market as unprofitable. But in 1998 alone, 3Com, which acquired the pioneer Palm Computing in June 1997, had sold 3 million Palm Pilots. The Palm Pilot has become the fastest-selling computer product in technology history.

Another method is to avoid focusing too much on the competition. In short, rule breakers must be creative. Often rule breakers such as Starbucks and Amazon.com lead the creation of value. In the process they are often ridiculed. Wal-Mart went through this phase in the 1970s and 1980s, when most analysts thought that it would not make it.

In e-commerce, the number one question to ask is, How can I use the new technologies to create new forms of value for my target customer? If you are having difficulty answering this question, then your e-business efforts are not well grounded. The structure must be built to support value, not the other way around.

How Do I Become My Customer's First Choice?

You can be first choice if you dazzle customers with unexpected service. The Ritz-Carlton hotels are a good example. At the Ritz-Carlton, quality service is a way of life. But it's no longer enough to just offer mints on the pillow. They've created ways to continually surprise guests with quality, build customer loyalty, and ensure repeat business.

It all starts at registration. Guests' preferences, noted in a central computer, can be recalled when they visit any Ritz-Carlton hotel: preferred room types, favorite newspapers, even what radio stations they like. It's become clear that companies that continually surprise and dazzle customers with quality can build customer loyalty that is difficult, if not impossible, for competitors to challenge.[6]

In order to become your customer's first choice you have to offer incentives. Consider airline loyalty programs. What started in the early 1980s as a simple way for airlines to build loyalty by rewarding repeat customers with free flights, upgrades, and other incentives has snowballed into a major battle for business over the years. All the large carriers now offer various gimmicks, sign-up bonuses, and reciprocal partnership perks in an effort to win clients' bookings. *What incentives are you offering your best customers?*

Now answer these questions: How does the customer make decisions about buying my product or service? *What have I done to retain customers and deepen the customer relationship?* Understanding the customer choice process means knowing who will buy the service or product, when, in what form, and how. That knowledge can often be the foundation of improvement.

How Does My Product Reach the Customer?

Equally important is delivery/distribution and marketing of the product or service. Understanding distribution is crucial to business success because a good product that doesn't reach its intended customer will flounder or fail as surely as a business with a bad product.

The procedure for sending flowers from one city to another seems reasonably straightforward. Most likely everyone is familiar with the flower delivery process. But when you look behind the scenes you see how involved the process is. You call your local florist, who places a call to another participating florist that selects and delivers the flowers. Note that the participating florist has ordered these flowers from a distributor, which got its flowers from a wholesaler, which bought its flowers from a farmer. By the time the flowers are delivered, they're eight, nine, or even ten days old. Enter Ruth Owades, CEO of Calyx & Corolla, who asked a simple question: Is it possible to bring the experience of the catalog business to the flower industry, even though the product is perishable?

Before Owades, everyone simply accepted this traditional, time-consuming process as a given. The secret of her success was looking at an existing process from an entirely different perspective and knowing when and how to break the rules. She reengineered the process to remove nonessential steps. Calyx & Corolla customers call a toll-free number and order flowers from a catalog. The order is transmitted by computer directly to the farmer, who has a talented flower arranger right on the farm. The order is packed in special containers and delivered the next day by Federal Express. In reengineering the process, Ruth eliminated three unnecessary steps and the associated costs, and the recipient has flowers that are up to nine days fresher.[7]

Now ask yourself: *How are my products delivered? How many steps do they go through before they reach the customer? How many of these can be eliminated? How much can be streamlined by using the Internet?*

Do We Understand the Environment and Industry Trends?

Technology alone isn't what's driving most companies toward investments in e-business. Rapid business change is. To build an effective structural foundation, managers need to very carefully evaluate the environment they are in. Given all the demands on their time, managers often lose sight of the big picture. When it comes time for strategic planning and long-term decision making, developing this broader perspective is the starting point, which is achieved through an environmental analysis.

Why environmental analysis? It makes no sense for a business to set its future direction without first reconnoitering the landscape. Environmental analysis enables a business to:

1. Take a fresh look at its environment and how it's changing.

2. Define critical industry and customer issues so that decisions can be made against the backdrop of a broader context.

3. Correctly position the firm within the industry and identify those issues most crucial to them.

Environmental scanning provides invaluable insights. It's a golden opportunity to take the blinders off and look at trends in business and society in general and to assess the impact of these trends. Equally as valuable is the comprehensive internal inventory that provides a clear snapshot of where the industry is at all times. Generally speaking, it's best for an enterprise to undertake an environmental analysis every couple of years to spot major discontinuities.

How do you do environmental analysis? A typical method is to arrange a series of meetings with a qualified consultant or expert who understands the landscape. The identification of trends—in technology, competition, customers, demographics, legal and regulatory developments, and local, regional, and national economic conditions—benefits the participants immensely. They walk away with a deeper understanding of industry issues, a shared vision for the future as a result of shared experiences with colleagues, and the assurance that all parties understand the ramifications of the issues at hand.

An environmental trends analysis can serve as a useful foundation. By identifying key economic, political, social, and technological trends, strategies for the future of the company or business unit can be developed. However, if not controlled, an environmental analysis can be the worst time sink. When managers describe future scenarios in which they will compete, they believe they are involved in a strategic decision-making activity. They are not. They are developing a context within which strategic decision making can occur.

Do We Understand Technology Trends?

It's hard to predict which technology will capture the market. To hedge their technology bets, some companies are active in many new e-business ventures, embracing e-commerce 100 percent, because if they don't experiment, they're dead.

Take an example from the '90s —the 1890s, that is. Mark Twain knew a thing or two about the book business. He observed that authors were writing books faster than they could be printed. So, Twain sank his entire life savings into a new technology for typesetting. Twain was right about the revolution that was to come; however, he put his money into the wrong technology. A year later, an inventor came up with a process to set type a line at a time. Linotype became the technology of choice and Twain went broke. Shortly thereafter, he picked up his pen and went back to being a writer. Twain's story is similar to what's happening today. We're all making bets about the technologies that will transform our future. But as Twain found out, problems come when you bet everything on a single technology and spin the wheel.

Now consider the case of CompuServe, one of the original Internet online pioneers. CompuServe was founded in 1969 as a computer timesharing service and introduced its first online service in 1979. In 1994, CompuServe was the largest online service, with double the number of customers America Online had. The management of CompuServe failed to react to the emergence of the Web as a competitive threat. According to Scott Kurnit, formerly second in command at Prodigy, the rise of the Internet "turned the model of the online services industry upside down."[8] CompuServe floundered by trying to cling to the vestiges of the past and watched helplessly as the number of its subscribers fell and as competition escalated. The ultimate indignity was its acquisition by America Online. What went wrong? Why didn't management react to the threat from technology changes?

Write down the core technology on which you are betting your future. *Is it going through a transition? If so, do you have a transition plan? Are you putting all your eggs in one basket or have you diversified?*

What Are the Priorities in the Supply Chain?

Orchestrating all the players across the supply chain requires detailed understanding of partners. What are upstream suppliers looking for? What capabilities do my suppliers have today? How can we partner with them better to deliver value more effectively? For instance, can we deliver products in two days if it takes the competition three weeks?

Now, write down what your supply chain looks like. It's quite possible that you have several supply chains in your company. Draw the three most important ones that you think significantly affect customer value. For each of these supply chains, answer the following questions:

- What's our cycle time? How does it compare with our closest competitor? How can we compress it? How can we streamline our supplier and transportation relationships to respond to customer demand faster than anyone in our industry can?

- What's our lead time? How does it compare with our closest competitor? How can we reduce lead time yet increase the time spent adding value to products?

- What's our average inventory level for finished goods? Work in progress? Raw materials? What would it take to increase inventory turns?

- How effectively do we use our warehouses? Our equipment? What would it take to increase throughput by 20 percent?

- What channels are ideal for selling and marketing our products, and to whom should we sell them? How should we support these products to keep our customers happy?

You have to carefully think through these questions in order to shape a high-velocity business model. The high-velocity model delivers the right product at the right time, while making rapid course corrections as needed. Four undeniable phenomena complicate next-generation supply chain design: mass customization, shrinking product life cycles, intensified competition, and frictionless flow of information. In this environment, being ahead of the supply chain curve becomes an absolute necessity to remain competitive.[9]

Who Are My Competitors?

Now write down who your competitors are. It's not easy. Competitors aren't just the other companies doing the same thing you're doing. If those are the only companies on your list, you're making the same mistake the telephone industry made when it was unconcerned about an emerging technology called Internet telephony.

Somewhere out there lurking in the shadows is a competitor that will attempt to render your business model obsolete. Take, for instance, the changes in the retailing world: Main Street in the 1950s, malls in the 1970s, superstores in the early 1990s, and e-commerce in the late 1990s. In the last 40 years, we've seen a fundamental shift in the retailing paradigm with each new generation. It's worth noting that each time the business model changed, a new group of leaders emerged. Woolworth never really escaped Main Street. Sears, for the most part, remains stuck in the mall. Again and again, incumbents missed the early warning signs. Who was paying attention when Sam Walton opened the first Wal-Mart Discount City in 1962? Who really understood the impact that Wal-Mart would have on the distribution chain? Likewise, everyone initially dismissed Amazon. com, and now it's a category killer.[10]

Companies often have blind spots in competitor analysis. They frequently miscalculate the boundaries of their industries, do a poor job of spotting competition, and make erroneous assumptions about competitors. By focusing on the most visible aspects of a competitor's operations, strategists often end up with an incomplete assessment of the competitors' capabilities. They anticipate competitors' moves based on past behavior. In other words, they simplify the situation, assuming that the competitor's actions will follow historical patterns of behavior or that the competitor shares the same view of the world and will behave in accordance. When simplified assumptions are substituted for clear understanding, a variety of strategic errors occur.[11]

Now ask yourself: *Who are my five top competitors today? Who are the five upstarts that will become fierce competitors in five years? Are you sure you really understand your competitors?*

Phase 2: Capability Evaluation

It makes no sense for a business to select its future direction without first assessing its capabilities. The old adage "Know thyself" is vitally important in plotting a course for the future. Assessing core competencies involves asking two questions: *What capabilities do we have today? What capabilities and resources do we need to acquire quickly?*

What Internal Capabilities Do We Have Today?

One of the most critical elements of self-examination is a review of strengths and weaknesses (see Table 11.2). This assessment can be an extraordinarily useful exercise if the business takes it seriously. The idea is to challenge long-held beliefs. Because strength and weakness are relative concepts—relative to the competition

Table 11.2: Areas of Assessment

Customer Interactions	Production and Fulfillment	People	Technology	Core Infrastructure
Sales	Manufacturing	Culture	ERP systems	Financial systems
Electronic commerce	Distribution	Skill sets	Legacy apps	Research and development
Marketing	Supply chain management	Training	Networks	Human resources
Customer service	Production scheduling	Knowledge management	Web site and intranets	
Call centers	Inventory management	Executive commitment	Security	
Distribution channels			IT skill sets	
			Help desk	

and to customers' expectations—yesterday's strengths may have become today's weaknesses without anyone at the helm noticing. After a thorough assessment, you should know your readiness in each area, your existing e-business environment, and your vulnerabilities and risks.

When assessing your company's infrastructure, remember that technology implementation can either accelerate or impede an organization's ability to adapt to changing business conditions. Today's solutions must fully meet business requirements. The underlying design must be flexible enough to integrate new and emerging technologies without compromising the existing enterprise architecture.

Now ask yourself, *Does my organization have a different business philosophy than my information technology (IT) department?* This is probably the biggest cause of failure in companies in which the application infrastructure isn't aligned with the business objectives. Another key assessment question: *Is the infrastructure of my company organized around application stovepipes due to political reasons?*

What Capabilities and Resources Do We Need to Execute Quickly?

Capabilities assessment identifies what you need to acquire, improve, or build to make your vision a reality. Alignment between a firm's vision and capabilities is a precondition for sustainable success. With the strategic direction formulated, each function will need to specify the capabilities it needs in order to deliver the targeted benefits.

Plans for linkages across functions must also be developed. Transition plans describing how each function must change or expand in order to execute the required activities should mesh with the final functional strategies. This ensures that a coherent face will be presented to the market during the transition.

You must develop skills for developing an enterprise architecture. A solid enterprise architecture provides a logical, consistent plan of activities and coordinated projects that guide the progression of an organization's application systems and infrastructure from its current state to a desired future state. Most large organizations claim to have an enterprise architecture in place. What they often have, however, is a bunch of stand-alone solutions that don't talk to each other. To exacerbate the situation, unsubstantiated, or cool, technologies or application features are frequently brought into the environment, destabilizing the architecture. This habit in turn causes other application systems or technologies that could significantly improve operations to suffer because the environment is too chaotic to introduce them effectively. Organizations must specify the overall strategy and migration steps, as well as provide guidelines on how individual project teams should integrate to achieve IT goals.

Phase 3: e-Business Design

Once you gather all the data, the next step is to tackle the question of defining your e-business design. This may seem so straightforward that it's hardly worth spending any time pondering; obviously, the business is trying to maximize customer value and, in the process, make profits. But this answer is so general that it does nothing to advance the process. It's like telling a military unit that its mission is to help win the war: It provides no meaningful direction.

Select an e-Business Design

Which of these e-business designs comes close to what you're trying to accomplish? Some large companies may be trying to accomplish several of these at the same time.

- **Category killer.** Use the Internet to define a new market by identifying a unique customer need. This model requires you to be among the first to market and to remain ahead of competition by continuously innovating. Examples: Amazon.com and E*TRADE.

- **Channel reconfiguration.** Use the Internet as a new channel to directly access customers, make sales, and fulfill orders. This model supplements, rather than replaces, physical distribution and marketing channels. Examples: Cisco and Dell.

- **Transaction intermediary.** Use the Internet to process purchases. This transactional model includes the end-to-end process of searching, comparing, selecting, and paying online. Examples: Microsoft Expedia and eBay.

- **Infomediary.** Use the Internet to reduce the search cost. Offer the customer a unified process for collecting information necessary to make a large purchase. Examples: HomeAdvisor and Auto-By-Tel.

- **Self-service innovator.** Use the Internet to provide a comprehensive suite of services that the customer's employees can use directly. Self-service affords employees a direct, personalized relationship. Examples: Employease and Healtheon.

- **Supply chain innovator.** Use the Internet to streamline the interactions among all parties in the supply chain to improve operating efficiency. Examples: McKesson and Ingram Micro.

- **Channel mastery.** Use the Internet as a sales and service channel. This model supplements, rather than replaces, the existing physical call centers. Example: Charles Schwab.

e-Business Design Refinement

Once you choose an e-business design, such as self-service, you need to revisit the questions raised in the knowledge-building and capability phases. The objective is to create a precise and detailed understanding that is relevant to the chosen e-business design. Some of the critical questions to consider are listed here.

- **Customer selection.** Which customer segment do I serve? What features are these customers looking for? What capabilities do I need in order to provide these features?

- **Customer experience.** Are there unique experiences that I can offer my customers that competitors would be hard pressed to match?

- **Customer capture.** How will I retain my customers so that they don't migrate to more powerful competitors? What features do I need to attract and retain customers?

- **Scope of design.** What are the critical activities and product/service offerings? Which activities will I perform in-house and which ones will I outsource?

- **Ease of doing business.** What process design should I embed in the applications to make it easy to do business with my company? Ease of doing business is a key driver in changing industry rules.

- **Organizational systems.** What organizational capabilities are critical to my translating the answers to these questions into marketplace success?

Clarify the Differentiation Levers

Ask yourself, What is my market positioning and differentiation strategy? Market positioning identifies how you want to compete for customers in the marketplace. Identifying a company's center of gravity in the market is important because it determines the capabilities needed to achieve market position. Market positioning hinges on the firm's superiority along at least one of the following major dimensions of differentiation:

- Product features that are aesthetically appealing or functionally superior

- Marketing channels that provide desired levels of responsiveness, convenience, variety, and information

- Service and support tailored to end-user and channel-member sophistication and urgency of need

- Brand or image positioning that imbues the company's offerings with greater appeal on critical selection criteria

- Price, including both net purchase price and cost savings available to the customer through the use of the product or service

Some companies have become successful by leaning heavily on one or two dimensions. Which ones are your company focusing on? Things change. Periodically—at least every few years—you must reexamine every dimension of differentiation to see if it still makes sense.

Next question: *What kinds of applications are required to support a modern, flexible e-business design?* We will address this question in the next chapter. Finally, revisit the business design frequently. Even if it appears to be solid, constantly ask yourself what can derail it. After all, the *Titanic* was introduced as an unsinkable ship. It wasn't the collision with the tip of the iceberg that sank it, but unseen shards of ice beneath the water that sheared rivets off the ship's hull. Corporations face similar danger. No company is unsinkable. There are many icebergs lurking in business waters, in the form of changing customer priorities, new technology, and competition. Better navigational systems, flexibility, and consistent examination of the business design enable companies to avoid a fate like the *Titanic*'s.

e-Business Design in Action: The Case of E*TRADE

To illustrate some of these dimensions, consider E*TRADE, a leading provider of cost-effective online financial services. E*TRADE is a self-service innovator. It's become synonymous with the term "online trading" by being one of the first to establish a leading, branded destination Web site that offers self-directed investors compelling prices and direct access to high-quality, real-time information.

E*TRADE presents an interesting side of e-business design, that is, the tension between incumbents and startups. Incumbents and new entrants have different sets of advantages. Incumbents, such as Merrill Lynch, have cash, financing, customers, production assets, and brand. New entrants, such as E*TRADE, have a clean-slate business design, entrepreneurial culture, and nimble decision making.

Table 11.3 captures the key differences in e-business strategic planning between successful large firms and innovative startups, where managers create change. Creative destruction—that's what it's about for category killers like

Table 11.3: Traditional versus Startup Planning

	Traditional and Widely Used Strategic Planning Framework	Entrepreneurial Innovator Framework
Phase 1	Analyze trends in industry. Analyze enterprise business processes to identify gaps between the firm and best-practice leaders.	Develop and build a working implementation that solves a critical customer problem.
Phase 2	Design fundamental organizational change.	Develop e-business infrastructure, services, and applications that bring efficiencies to business model. Acquire or merge with firms that provide complementary solutions in order to move from point solutions to integrated solutions.
Phase 3	Implement and execute plan to bring about organizational change.	Use electronic business architecture to attack new market segments. Constantly improve e-business architecture.

E*TRADE. It's about making things happen, getting the parade moving, and then jumping out ahead of it. It's not "ready, aim, fire"; it's "ready, fire, aim." In large companies, too often it's "ready, aim, appoint a committee." Another difference between the startups and established companies is the payback period. In most traditional planning models, payback is often five to ten years, with a conservative ROI of 10 to 15 percent. Startup companies often aim for a payback of two to three years, with an exponential ROI in excess of 100 percent.

In many industries, we see up-and-coming companies that are capable of a faster time to market taking the lead. This parallels what happened in the 1970s with the quality revolution. Quality dramatically changed the way many organizations conducted business. For instance, Xerox watched its share of the U.S. copier market drop from a dominant 85 percent in the early 1970s to 13 percent in the early 1980s.[12] Other companies were experiencing similar crises. Business quickly realized that quality was a matter of life and death. In fact, some of the biggest casualties of the quality war were U.S. manufacturers of consumer electronics; many died before they could react. Today, a similar transition is happening as established companies attempt to revitalize their business to adapt to the new economy—the e-economy, or digital economy.

To understand why companies like E*TRADE have been successful, we need to look at why startups are so successful in creating e-business strategy. For startups, the logic of e-business differs along the five basic dimensions of strategy: assumptions about customers, customer segments, customer value, resources and capabilities, and product and service offerings.

Customer Assumptions

Customer assumptions determine which questions managers ask, what opportunities they pursue, and how they understand risk. As an online brokerage pioneer, E*TRADE did not take industry conditions as a given. E*TRADE added value to the traditional brokerage business by offering 24-hour service, a significant price discount due to cost advantages inherent to the Web (no bricks and mortar), and direct access to such information as stock quotes, news, and charts. E*TRADE's goal is to optimize the quality of the information it offers and break down barriers to information in the brokerage community.

The lesson: Many companies take their industry's conditions as a given and set strategy accordingly. e-Business innovators don't, because there usually is no precedent. No matter how the rest of the industry is faring, e-business innovators look for blockbuster ideas and quantum leaps in value.

Customer Segments

E*TRADE's customer base can be characterized as highly active. In fact, more than 25 percent of E*TRADE's customers go online every day and trade an average of 25 times per year! E*TRADE enjoys tremendous customer loyalty: The company's customer retention rate is 96 percent.

Many companies seek growth by retaining and expanding their customer bases. This approach often leads to finer segmentation and greater customization of offerings to meet specialized needs. e-Business innovators follow a different logic. Instead of focusing on the differences among customers, e-business innovators build on new qualities that a market niche values.

E*TRADE understands that customer service and product depth will become increasingly important as price premium deltas decline. Building customer loyalty is critical. The challenge is to create a situation in which the customer perceives the switching costs to be high. Strong front-end systems, automated data accumulation, and management are critical to success in this arena.

E*TRADE's success has not gone unnoticed. In the past year, the number of online investment funds and brokerage services has increased to more than 30, double the number online only a year ago. E*TRADE's fiercest competitor is Charles Schwab's eSchwab, which has a customer base of over 1 million online accounts.

The lesson: While e-business investment funds and brokerage services have developed business models focused exclusively on creating online service, traditional brokerage houses face the challenge of launching online services while continuing to support their existing business models. This situation presents an internal conflict vis-à-vis people and resources.

Customer Value

E*TRADE started with an ambition to dominate the market by offering a tremendous leap in value. The company didn't let competitors set the parameters of its strategic thinking. They compared their strengths and weaknesses with the competition's and focused on building advantages. E*TRADE realized early that although investing appeals to a broad audience, each investor has his or her investment objectives and risk tolerance, providing the opportunity to create unique one-to-one relationships at a lower cost than traditional full-service brokerages.

While full-service brokerages pride themselves on service, the cost model is dramatically higher due to both labor and brick-and-mortar expenditures. Many discount brokerage houses provide relatively low-cost trades but less service. E*TRADE can provide low cost and high service, enabling the company to gain market share from both brokerage segments. The lesson: e-Business innovators redefine core competencies needed to compete.

Resources and Capabilities

Many companies view business opportunities through the lens of existing assets and capabilities. They ask, "Given what we have, what is the best we can do?" In contrast, e-business innovators ask, "What if we start anew?"

E*TRADE has taken a clean-slate approach to the brokerage business. This is not to say that e-business innovators never leverage their existing assets and capabilities. They often do. But more important, innovators assess business opportunities without bias or constraint. This approach gives them insight into where to create value for customers (and adroitness at figuring out how value changes) and how to create value fast.

E*TRADE's first priority is to maintain the momentum by being a first-mover. Customer acquisition and retention get more expensive as competition intensifies. Therefore, E*TRADE is reinvesting a large portion of its revenue into sales and marketing, launching aggressive advertising campaigns aimed at full-service and discount brokerages.

E*TRADE's plan is to build a presence in the top 20 markets worldwide via partnerships. It believes that collaboration with online content companies with technology know-how will provide a significant first-mover advantage and reduce its risk. The company has already established franchise relationships in Canada and Australia. A typical international franchise deal with E*TRADE includes upfront fees of $2 million, plus participation in future revenue streams.

The lesson: To keep up with new entrants, traditional brokerage houses and banks are adjusting their business models to take advantage of online opportunities and invest heavily in technology development. In the meantime, E*TRADE is investing heavily in building brand-name recognition and adding products and services that go beyond basic trading capabilities to maintain customers.

Product and Service Offerings

Conventional competition takes place within clearly established boundaries defined by the products and services the industry offers. e-Business innovators often cross those boundaries. They think in terms of the total solution customers want. From there they brainstorm ways to overcome the chief compromises that the industry forces customers to make.

E*TRADE is expanding by forging relationships with other financial service providers in order to increase the depth of its products. For example, the company hopes to provide electronic bill payment as an option for its customers. New products and services serve the dual purpose of providing added value to customers while diversifying revenue streams and reducing the potential for volatility. E*TRADE has aggressively extended its services to include such services as the ability to purchase mutual funds online and make initial public offerings. It has also launched subscription services that provide consumers with valuable information, such as research by Wall Street analysts, sophisticated charting and modeling capabilities, and personalized investment advice.

The lesson: While competition is certainly on the horizon, E*TRADE is working diligently to maintain its advantage. Most of its research and development is focused on dramatically enhancing the front end via both customization and the addition of complementary financial services. Hence, while competing brokerage firms struggle to adjust their cost structures in order to support $15 to $20 trades, E*TRADE is developing product and service enhancements and marketing partnerships designed to create customer loyalty and increase perceived switching costs.

Future Opportunities: Rethinking Organizational Structure

Creating an e-business strategy means more than simply acting faster or creating a differentiated market offer. Companies must ensure that various parts of their operations—marketing, sales, manufacturing, product development, and finance—are tightly integrated so that when decisions are made, the parts come together quickly to form a cohesive whole that meets customer expectations in real time—easier said than done.

e-Business isn't limited to product development and distribution but can extend to organizational structure as well. For example, E*TRADE doesn't cross-sell new financial services to its highly proactive, self-directed customer base. The company doesn't take advantage of this opportunity because it's focused on gaining market share by scaling its back-end processing engine in order to dramatically lower its cost structure. In order to take advantage of cross-sell opportunities, E*TRADE must make a shift in its organizational structure.

The lesson: The forces of e-business are creating a structural upheaval in business processes, a social shift that rearranges consumers' lives more than mere hardware or software ever can. This new world has its own distinct opportunities and its own rules. Businesses that play by the new rules will prosper and become market leaders; those that ignore them won't.

Memo to the CEO

Peter Drucker noted, "A time of turbulence is a dangerous time, but its greatest danger is the temptation to deny reality."[13] Executives recognize that before they get to the twenty-first century, they must leave past practices behind. They recognize that there is a tollbooth at the entrance to the new millennium. Not all firms will be able to pay the toll, because it requires a new type of currency—e-business leadership. Admission will not be granted to firms that continue to use yesterday's assumptions and practices. To proceed, executives need to recognize that new realities call for new mental models, new approaches, and new ways to do business.

With large-scale technological and environmental change, companies in all business sectors are faced with the same basic questions: How should we compete in our industry? What are our important objectives? How do we achieve long-term focus in an increasingly competitive and sometimes downright hostile business and technology environment? Answering these questions is the essence of strategy planning. However, aligning innovation with strategy is the most significant way to create value. It's not hard to see why. By its very nature, innovation requires "out of the box" thinking. The challenge lies in nurturing this sort of thinking while ensuring that it does not conflict with the strategic goals of the company.

Some people use e-business strategic planning to create a written document that will only gather dust on a shelf somewhere. But strategic planning isn't a written scheme so much as it is a systematic way of figuring out what your company is trying to accomplish, identifying the best ways to accomplish those goals, and effectively communicating the specifics of accomplishing those goals throughout the hierarchy. Unfortunately, this straightforward process can be time-consuming, difficult, even unpleasant. As a result, most companies either don't execute strategic planning or they do something that passes for strategic planning, but really isn't. This is a myopic way to save time and ultimately results in more chaos and problems.

The difficulties of creating e-business strategy are often compounded by the fact that executives are too focused on the short term to pay attention to long-term progress. Because the stock market places great emphasis on the short term, companies concentrate on peripheral elements—financial management, penetrating new markets, growth through acquisition and consolidation. While these things are important, they don't advance the company's core value.

So, how do we turn the tide? The challenge is to create a planning process that is customized, results in collective organizational learning, and increases knowledge about your business. The case for devising an e-business blueprint strategy and creating a strategic plan is compelling, yet justifications for not doing it abound.

- Management and employees are too busy putting out today's fires to worry about tomorrow's problems or opportunities.

- Managers rationalize that their solid market niche protects them from the turbulence in the marketplace. Why waste time planning for a future that will be pretty much the same as it is today?

- Managers rationalize that because the future is inherently unpredictable, there's no way to prepare for it. In other words, what will be will be.

The logic behind these thoughts is fundamentally flawed. Any manager who believes that his or her business will be unaffected by the changes overtaking all industries is just asking to be blindsided or to miss golden opportunities. The unpredictability of the future is no excuse for failing to plan. A business can influence its own destiny in even the most changing environments; in fact, rapid, unpredictable change and disarray usually present unparalleled opportunities.

Thoughtful planning is hard to fit into today's busy schedule, but keep in mind that a common characteristic of virtually every successful business is disciplined planning and preparation. To paraphrase Bobby Knight, Indiana University's colorful basketball coach, businesses with the will to win are a dime a dozen. The truly successful businesses are those with the will to prepare to win. Preparing to win is what strategic planning is all about. There's real value in following a disciplined, step-by-step approach to the process.

CHAPTER TWELVE

Translating e-Business Strategy into Action

What to Expect

Many companies plan really well, yet few translate strategy into action, even though senior management consistently identifies e-business as an area of great opportunity and one in which the company needs stronger capabilities. If you ask these same managers how their organizations execute activities and to assess their ability to achieve desired targets, you'll hear a litany of frustrations and little optimism for success.

This prescriptive chapter shows how to cross the chasm between strategic planning and execution. We'll give you the steps to take in building an enterprise framework prioritization plan, a business case for e-business investments, and an execution project checklist. We'll also alert you to the top ten ways to fail at turning strategy into action.

Why is it that converting strategy into action is high on the priority list but not well understood? Could it be that top management underestimates the complexity involved? Is top management slow to realize that while designing a high-level e-business design (i.e., identifying the journey) might take a few months, building a comprehensive e-business architecture (i.e., getting to the destination) is a long, bumpy road? As noted in Chapter 11, many firms establish little connection between their business planning processes and the processes they use to identify and select individual projects. The e-business blueprint process illustrated in this chapter will help executives make the connection.

Why is a blueprint necessary? Imagine taking a caravan of thousands of people on a journey with no map, no plan, no one in charge, no logistical support, no way to keep everyone informed, no scouting reports to assess and update progress, and no navigational instruments. Sheer madness, yet that's how most companies are handling the transition to e-business. The purpose of the blueprint is to map a course for creating an integrated enterprise and to reduce the chaos that normally results from not having a roadmap.

Integration is the essence of e-business. Every company today, whether it knows it or not, is an information-driven company. So, how do you create the necessary information integration needed to deliver value to customers? You determine the strategic elements of application infrastructure and translate them into a unified foundation that is efficient and at the same time flexible. This process allows the company to adapt, change, grow, and innovate. The relationship between value creation and integration forms the core of e-business blueprint planning.

e-Business blueprint planning addresses two requirements. The first is balancing opportunities for improving application infrastructure by prioritizing correctly. The second is achieving the right project mix so that resources are allocated in ways that enhance the strategic direction. Often, there are too many projects, and many of the resources are devoted to patching short-term problems rather than building the foundation for long-term success. Short-term versus long-term planning leads to an interesting question: Should a company patch together a blueprint from existing applications or create a fresh one, that is, start with a clean slate? *Which path is your company taking?*

Figure 12.1 illustrates the process of translating strategy into action. In the previous chapter, we detailed the questions that managers need to ask before they can create an e-business design. However excellent a design may be, it will not succeed without effective execution. The purpose of this chapter is to add relevant detail to the e-business roadmap that can help bridge the chasm between

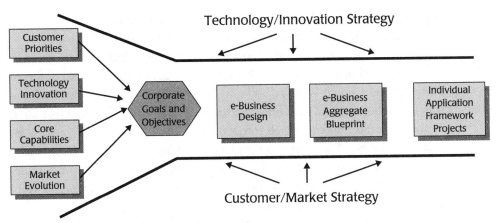

Figure 12.1: The Overall Process—Translating Strategy to Action

high-level e-business strategy and effective execution. Read on and learn what others are doing about the challenge, and most important, what your company can do!

To Patch or Not to Patch?

Application infrastructure is so fundamental to all businesses and business processes that its role and importance are too often ignored. For established companies, there are no short cuts on the journey toward creating seamless integration. The difficulty in creating integrated applications is the reason why many Internet startups are often able to overthrow seemingly impregnable leaders.

Consider the case of Citibank, a pioneer of online banking. Citibank decided to abandon many of the expensive, proprietary computer systems it had built in the last decade and create a new Internet banking and investment service. Citibank aims to replace the core back-office computer systems on which it keeps customer accounts—systems that it had built and maintained at a cost of hundreds of millions of dollars. The bank is taking such a radical action to catch up with a new generation of competitors such as E*TRADE and more nimble, established companies such as Charles Schwab that have seized the initiative on Internet financial services.[1]

Citibank had to address the question of *whether to create a fresh new Infrastructure* or *patch the existing infrastructure.* Many companies will be required to face the same question in the coming decade. Instead of patching existing systems and incrementally enhancing them, Citibank's plan to discard its legacy systems might be the best way for large companies to catch up with new companies. Much attention in the initial phases of e-business is spent on patching existing systems and wrestling with them to meet the needs of new business models.

However, for large, established companies, patching existing infrastructure is often the only choice. Here the number one challenge is integration. According to Delta Airlines' CIO, "A Web site is like an iceberg. What you see looks small and simple, but below it you have infrastructure integration issues with maybe 40 or 50 databases. So building a Web infrastructure can be a pretty serious risk for older companies."[2] What large companies are looking for is a blueprint that provides a logically consistent plan of activities and coordinated projects that guides the progression of an organization's application systems and infrastructure from its current state to a desired future state.

The number two challenge for large companies is building a seamless infrastructure on a fragmented application base. The seamless imperative is obvious, as customer retention and market-share growth have become critical in the face of boundless competition from incumbents and startups. Integrated service/ delivery platforms mark a fundamental change in the way a business runs. Such integration is not simply an IT issue, but a matter of creating the right structural foundation to facilitate e-business.

The number three challenge is knowing when to walk away and start over. How can senior management know when to start fresh and when to enhance existing infrastructure? When incremental change is insufficient, companies must be prepared to undertake fundamental change that could reshape the application foundation on which the company operates. Change on this scale is hard to plan and harder still to manage. All corporations resist change, and those with a long history often resist with tenacity. CEOs frequently complain that they seem to be pushing all the right buttons at the top, but nothing changes down below. Overcoming the inertia of a large organization calls for a new set of skills that we call e-business blueprint planning.

e-Business blueprint planning fills the gap between strategic planning and applications and provides a common language that executives from marketing, information technology, and manufacturing can all understand. The blueprint planning process joins the business model, applications, and performance objectives into a cohesive whole.

Competition in the digital age is based on how companies use an integrated infrastructure to serve the customer. Managers everywhere are realizing that the first step in creating new business designs is to create an effective foundation. The e-business blueprint provides both information and a decision context that enables management to arrive at a usable foundation. The blueprint creation process includes both infrastructure and application projects, as well as providing standards, guidelines, and other support for the set of activities that must be accomplished to reach the desired strategy goals.

Creating an enterprise blueprint for large companies can be tricky if they have acquired a lot of stand-alone applications over the years that refuse to talk to one another. It's important to arrange the different application categories in your company in a way that helps you understand where everything fits. There are four levels of application use in business:

- **Level 1: Isolated applications.** Each application is a collection of components and modules combined into one unit that performs a single function on a limited scale, for example, a simple order-taking application.

- **Level 2: Integrated applications.** A complex collection of many applications capable of performing an independent function on a large scale, for example, call-center applications.

- **Level 3: Application blueprint.** A large, widespread collection or family of applications functioning together to achieve a common purpose, for example, customer relationship management (CRM).

- **Level 4: Enterprise framework.** A collection of application blueprints—CRM, supply chain management (SCM), and so on—tightly integrated to support the business model.

Most companies are at level 2. Level 3 is a fairly new layer that has mushroomed with the advent of integrated packages such as SAP. As a result, we have witnessed a steady migration from level 2 to level 3 because companies realize that new business models require new structural capabilities. Nevertheless, it's still a challenge to ensure that all the application blueprints work together to support the e-business design. *At which level is your company?*

As it turns out, level 4 is changing the way market leaders do business. Companies such as Dell, Cisco, and Amazon.com, among others, have raised the bar. Today, many companies are worried about what's happening to their markets as customers become increasingly restless and demand innovation. These companies realize that systematic blueprint planning that is aligned with business goals is a matter of life and death.

The deeper we move into "the value decade," the clearer it is that effective e-business blueprint design not only differentiates, but also offers value. More and more CEOs are discovering that good blueprint design is good business, a means for achieving their strategic goals. The strategic solution is that management must get better at conceiving, developing, and launching new integration efforts—not just extensions and incremental improvements, but new blueprints that provide a sustainable competitive advantage. This strategy translates into better management of the e-business innovation process.

Evaluate Your Own Company

The typical corporate infrastructure involves multiple application packages and multiple legacy systems. The problem is not so much the diversity but the fact that there is no cohesive management. Take a hard look at your company and the way its e-business blueprint is being managed. Do you see the following disturbing things?

- Platform projects are taking too long. When managers are asked why, the standard answer is that everyone is working as hard as possible, but people are stretched across too many projects. The result is project gridlock: too many "strategic" projects in the pipeline.

- Many substandard projects that were once good ideas have been in the pipeline for years and have lost their value. They are siphoning off resources from worthy projects.

- Almost all the projects are long-term, multimillion-dollar, big-bang efforts. Many of the projects are high reward, but at the same time high risk. High risk implies that there's a high probability of technical or commercial failure. There are few quick hits to balance the risk.

- Almost all projects appear to be reinventing the wheel, resulting in wasted effort. There's overlap, and no one is taking advantage of established key elements.

- It's hard to make decisions. Today's technology is very complex, as simple integrated applications give way to proliferating layers of servers, operating systems, application languages, network protocols and routers, databases, hardware, and software. Not surprisingly, it's getting harder and harder to ascertain the long-term impact of any technology choice.

- Project interdependence is hard to manage. The integration between business units and between functions means that a change in one system often affects dozens of others, some in other organizations. And the accelerating pace of technological change combined with product life cycles that are now only a few months long is a further barrier to good IT decision making.

- Lack of communication and business-side buy-in. Often technology is deployed in a vacuum and users resist it. The IT side does not have the buy-in from the managers in charge of the business processes. This delays implementation and results in slower return on investment.

Overall, while some individual projects are very well executed, few employees get the big picture. Often strategy is unfocused or embraces too many projects, which spreads resources too thin over too many marginal-value projects. The result is a poorly balanced application strategy that doesn't support corporate strategy.

If you have these problems, you need a blueprint strategy that can create value through integration. For those who resist blueprint planning, ponder for a moment the costs of poor integration. Think about how much money an organization would save if everything were done correctly right from the start. We estimate that most companies throw away about 25 percent of their sales revenue on order rework, incorrect orders, and errors due a lack of integration. *How much money could integration save your company?*

e-Business Blueprint Creation Is Serious Business

Top management should play a strong role in the blueprint planning process for three reasons:

1. Blueprint decisions are among the most important a company makes.

2. Blueprint decisions may cut across several product lines or divisional boundaries.

3. Blueprint decisions frequently require the resolution of cross-functional conflict.

Top management's participation is also needed because making good blueprint decisions requires making complex trade-offs in various areas. e-Business blueprint planning influences the products/services that a company introduces into the market in a five- to ten-year period, the types and levels of capital investment to be made, and the integration agendas for suppliers. Creating a blueprint is a pervasive, all-encompassing topic. It's more than selecting projects that will meet strategic needs, although that's part of it. It's much more than resource allocation, although that's part of it, too. And it goes beyond simply developing a list of priority projects.

One problem with blueprint creation is that everyone sees it differently, depending on where he or she sits:

- The chief strategist sees it as developing an "ideal portfolio" to support the business vision.

- The CFO looks at the e-business blueprint as a way to optimally allocate financial resources.

- The CIO sees it as vehicle to foster the right infrastructure to support business.

- The chief marketing officer hopes it will yield better customer retention and more sales.

- The CEO prays that it will keep competitors at bay and deliver positive financial results quickly.

Blueprint creation can do all these things and more *if* top management is committed to it. *How committed is your management?*

The Problem Is Not Technology: The Problem Is Leadership

For large, established companies, the single biggest impediment to e-business blueprint planning is lack of consistent attention from top management. Without deep investments of time and energy from CEOs, and senior executives, companies simply cannot achieve the cultural, strategic, and technical changes required to navigate their ships in e-business waters. The seeds for failure for most e-business projects are usually sown at a project's beginning. There's not enough communication with users and not enough buy-in from the right management levels. The top three reasons for project failure most often cited are poor planning or poor project management, change in business goals during the project, and lack of business-management support.[3]

The root cause of bad planning is delegation. We know you're busy and that good managers delegate. But in the case of e-business, managers don't know what cannot be delegated. For example, one nondelegable role is sitting on the blueprint committee (when companies go into an e-business initiative, they often create a committee to guide and coordinate various projects). Of course, approval of the vision and direction is inherently nondelegable. Senior executives must set the goals, and there's no escaping the need for senior executives to participate in the deployment process (to identify what needs to be done to reach goals, provide the resources, and assign responsibility).

Executives must personally review performance against strategic goals, just as they've always compared performance with sales and profit goals. And upper managers should always be there to hand out rewards personally at recognition events. (Of course, top managers must also revise the reward system to include infrastructure initiatives.) The fact is, if senior executives don't participate, it sends a negative message about the importance given to e-business.

Ask yourself the following questions about your company's executive commitment:

- *Is your company doing e-business piecemeal or is it focused on it as a comprehensive vehicle for business transformation?*

- *Is there senior-level management involvement in e-business decision making? Is the CEO promoting the CIO to the role of a key advisor?*

- *Is top management attempting to sell the value of integration to decision makers?*

- *Has your company recognized that improving e-business investment management is a long-term process and should be planned accordingly?*

- *Has your company ensured that e-business investment decisions are strongly linked to strategic business objectives?*

- *Has your company built a shared e-business vision through different management levels? Has the e-business vision been presented in terms relevant to line-of-business managers?*

Media hype and stellar initial public offerings have made the road to e-business look smooth, inviting, and easy to navigate. There are plenty of consultants ready to take companies to the Promised Land with the "one-minute guide to e-business glory." Don't believe it for a moment. Around the first curve, conditions start to change, the road gets bumpier, and after a while you begin to see that the road you're on won't take you where you want to go because various earthquakes (customer priorities) have changed the terrain. So, you plan alternative routes. To quote Robert Frost, "Two roads diverged in a wood, and I— / I took the one less traveled by, / And that has made all the difference" ("The Road Not Taken"). Similarly, executives face many forks in the road. *Does your management team have the vision to take the right roads on your e-business journey?*

All roads ultimately lead to Rome, which in this case is a **real-time integrated** enterprise that can support customer needs better than the competition can. That brings us to the critical question that forms the backdrop of this chapter: *How should senior management create an integrated vision?*

Basic Steps of e-Business Blueprint Planning

Before charging into what techniques work best, let's reflect on what blueprint creation is. *Blueprint creation is a dynamic process whereby a business's list of active projects is constantly updated and revised.* In this process, new projects are evaluated, selected, and prioritized; existing projects may be accelerated, devalued, or killed; and resources are allocated and reallocated to the active projects. Uncertain and changing information, multiple goals, strategic considerations, interdependence among projects, and many decision makers shape the decision process. Finally, it's about balance, about the optimal investment mix of risk and return, cost reduction versus growth, and short-term versus long-term goals.

The key to good blueprint strategy is to plan carefully, considering every possible option and then identifying the likely projects from start to finish. So much effort is obviously time-consuming, but for many e-business strategic decisions, the sums at stake are large enough to justify the effort. The three basic steps of e-business blueprint planning are as follows.

1. **Prioritization blueprint.** Define the blueprint strategy, model, and initiatives. Select goal-focused rather than means-focused projects.

2. **Business case for action.** Which are the projects worth pursuing and how can we justify them to management?

3. **Application implementation.** How do we execute the projects that have been approved?

Figure 12.2 depicts the interdependencies between the three phases, and Table 12.1 lists the questions that arise in each phase.

The prioritization blueprint helps plan for long-term success. This planning involves proactively managing streams of innovation rather than reacting to a single innovation. Managing innovation streams is like juggling a set of balls. There has to be a shift away from an internal focus on automating functional silos to one on how to manage technology and innovation so they yield sustainable growth.

Once projects have been screened, it's critical to detail the findings of the

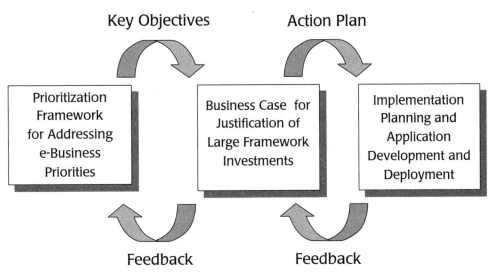

Figure 12.2: e-Business Blueprint Planning

blueprint plan in an e-business case for senior management's approval. This is the final stage prior to implementation, so it's important that the blueprint be attractive and clearly defined.

Then comes the messy part: execution. The battle is won not in the boardroom but in the trenches—in programming shops, on factory floors, and at service counters. Application execution is the platform for successful strategic attacks and defenses. Companies that fail to fully exploit the strategic power of applications will be both limited in their attacks and vulnerable to attack.

Table 12.1: Blueprint Planning Questions

Prioritization blueprint	*What aggregate set of enterprise framework projects do we need to initiate to improve our position and open up new business opportunities?*
Make the business case for action	*How can application framework decisions be strategically aligned to achieve business goals?*
	Can we make a compelling case to the key decision makers about the need for change?
Application implementation	*How do we take our journey along the chosen path?*
	Are we following our plan? How do we keep the plan relevant?

Doing the Right Projects: A Prioritization Blueprint

Organizations with complex portfolios of information systems must take a structured and disciplined approach to enterprise framework planning and investment in order to manage risk. Managers can learn from builders. As any builder will tell you, designing a house from the ground up can be a breeze compared with adding on to an existing structure. When starting from scratch, you can pick and choose the features you want. But adding on can be a headache because you have to seamlessly mesh new and old structural elements, and often the old structure dictates the materials, design, and extent of the addition.

The same problems exist in application infrastructure. As companies race toward e-business, the old infrastructure is creaking and groaning under the strain. Fixing the problems requires careful and deliberate investment in integration. **How should companies most effectively prioritize investment in their structural foundation to build an integrated application infrastructure?**

How Should You Invest in Integration?

To successfully build an integration blueprint, every company needs prioritization processes for capital budgeting, investing in new technologies, and allocating scarce resources among competing business groups. In almost all companies, managing enterprise framework creation focuses primarily on individual projects. Yet in reality, most established companies juggle multiple, concurrent projects.

Thus, senior managers often have to decide how to allocate resources among various enterprise framework application portfolios to achieve strategic objectives. Like money managers, they need to build a blueprint that optimizes their application investments. Management of resource allocation constitutes a critical part of e-business blueprint planning. It must help define the new integrated strategies, select winning application projects, and achieve the ideal balance of projects.

All firms have a set of application projects that are on an active list, that is, projects that have been started but not yet completed. Relatively few firms arrive at such a list through a systematic process of review and decision making about what the e-business application portfolio ought to be. As a result, many companies struggle from the strain of embracing e-business and end up choosing a quick-fix solution. One easy solution is to hire top-dollar consultants to help define an e-business strategy, implement e-business systems, and continually enhance and extend these solutions. However, good managers realize that creating a strategic plan that is the basis for business transformation requires a much more disciplined approach.

What is the right approach? Companies need to use a blueprint planning approach to specify the type and mix of projects that a company plans to undertake to achieve strategic objectives. Laying out the blueprint explicitly makes it possible to balance the demands of application projects for resources. The investment choices made today determine what the business product offerings and market position will be in the future.

The importance of application decisions that constitute the structural foundation cannot be overstated. The wager executives must place on their firms' ability to compete through technology is increasing. The cutting edge of technology management, however, goes beyond systems implementation; the rules of the game have shifted for the second time in less than a decade. Let's look at the issues managers currently confront in developing a prioritization plan.

Current Way of Prioritizing Projects

Although e-business blueprint planning looks systematic, it's really not. Whereas corporate planners look ahead several years, project prioritization still tends to be an annual ritual. Once a year, corporate headquarters asks its various operating units to submit application spending wish lists. Line-of-business managers, in turn, pose three questions to their subordinates:

- *Where do we need to spend money on application enhancements?*

- *How much will each of these enhancements cost us?*

- *What will we get for the money we spend?*

The result of this process is a separate wish list for all the various divisions—far too many for review. Each division checks for inconsistencies and redundancies among the wish lists prepared by its own site and functions. Once problems are resolved, each division forwards its wish list to corporate headquarters, where a quick summation typically reveals that full funding of all of the requests simply is not in the cards.

What target should we set for next year's capital spending? Answering this question often involves hours of discussion and negotiation among a company's highest levels of management and finance. Once the capital-spending target is set, a portion of it is allocated to each operating division in the form of a capital budget.

The managers tend to make a game of the system. They know that rarely will every project on the wish list get funding. Instead, each sees the other lines of business as competitors for a limited pool of dollars. Experienced managers tend to be even more sophisticated players of the capital-spending game. How they are measured, rewarded, and penalized largely determines how they spend capital. For example, leaving capital on the table at the end of the budget cycle is considered to be bad management in most companies, despite advances in performance measurement techniques during the last decade.

Therein lies the paradox: Integration is mandated from the top but it gets lost in the jungle of capital budgeting. How do you fix the current way of allocating resources? The first step in developing a resource allocation plan is to define clearly the types of projects a company needs.

Types of e-Business Projects

There are essentially three types of projects in e-business: incremental, breakthrough and platform.[4] Incremental, or improvement, projects are those that are derivatives, add-ons, and enhancements of existing projects. These projects include incremental feature changes with little or no major structural changes. These projects often require fewer resources and less risk because they leverage existing artifacts and enhance their functionality. If you look around your company you can find a lot of these projects.

Breakthrough and radical projects are those that involve substantial changes in the foundation of the firm. The breakthrough projects often spearhead the entry of the firm into a new area of business. These projects are often risky and have a high probability of failure. These are the kind that startups usually undertake because these projects are more amenable to a clean-slate approach.

Platform, or next-generation, projects are in between incremental and breakthrough projects. These projects, such as e-commerce, supply chain management (SCM) and others, result in the creation of a new structural foundation that can be leveraged across multiple areas of business. When carefully planned and executed, enterprise framework projects create an infrastructure on which various strategic initiatives can be undertaken. The move toward enterprise framework projects is driven by business—companies see the need for being able to move quickly through adaptive architecture.

Investment planning for framework projects is challenging for three reasons. First, companies have to balance strategic choices with practical realities. A market orientation is often a missing ingredient in framework planning. Second, cross-functional problem solving and integration is critical for success. The new framework planning process is multifunctional and requires active participation of the core groups from different areas. And third, getting agreement on final specifications is very difficult, albeit important. Don't attempt to design all functionality in the world into one framework. Such things don't exist. Be realistic and shoot for what functionality you need to serve customer priorities.

Figure 12.3 depicts an e-business funnel and shows how the e-business blueprint evolves from a high-level design into execution through a series of review and decision points called screening criteria. An example of a screening question is, *To what degree does the project align with strategy?*

Roadmap to an Enterprise Framework Prioritization Plan

e-Business success or failure is largely decided in the first few plays of the game, in the steps that precede actual execution. We have identified six steps for creating an enterprise framework prioritization plan.

1. Do solid, up-front homework on current infrastructure and customer priorities to support sharp blueprint definition.

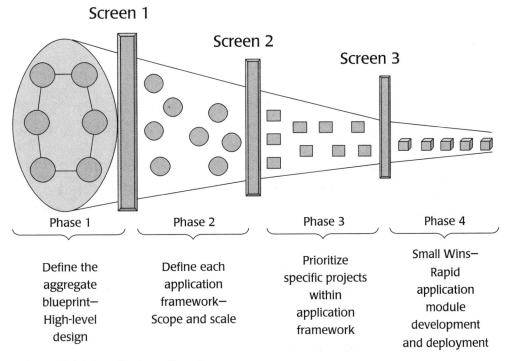

Figure 12.3: The e-Business Funnel

2. Review your own portfolio of active projects across the firm. Avoid reinventing the wheel.

3. Determine what needs fixing. Define the types and classes of enterprise framework projects that are to be covered by the aggregate blueprint.

4. Don't forget to build in differentiation at every opportunity.

5. Establish the desired future mix of enterprise framework functionality by type: e-commerce, SCM, or CRM.

6. Decide which enterprise framework projects to undertake.

The steps outlined here are not easy, nor can they be done overnight. However, they provide an excellent foundation for creating an aggregate blueprint plan. Once the enterprise framework mix is decided, it's time to move to the next step, creating a detailed evergreen business case (see Figure 12.4).

Putting It All Together: The e-Business Blueprint Case

Every execution phase should begin with creating a business case. Why? When a new technology emerges, invariably people ask, "Why develop a business case?

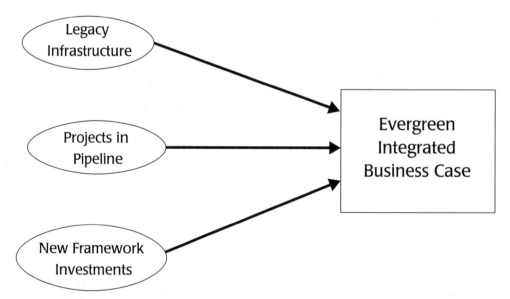

Figure 12.4: Need for a Business Case

Aren't the benefits obvious? Shouldn't we automatically stay up-to-date with technology?" Even when the benefits of new technology are significant and visible, a business case is a powerful tool for establishing project direction. Management will not commit any money unless they're absolutely convinced it's the way to go.

A good business case eliminates two problems immediately: the tendency to do nothing ("let's wait and see") and the tendency to treat e-business as just another run-of-the-mill project. Most managers will not move until an opportunity is crystal clear. By then it's often too late, because the competition didn't hesitate and is either enjoying the lion's share of the market or has so much momentum that it's extremely difficult to derail them. e-Business is as much about creating and shaping customer needs as it is about serving well-identified customer requirements. Good managers understand that customer needs and requirements are not static. They learn about and shape customer needs even as they implement applications.

e-Business applications should not be treated as business as usual. Because managers already handle a number of other projects, all with a particular planning sequence, it makes sense to adopt the same procedure for new projects. However, the planning sequence for existing projects is based on well-understood execution and deployment capabilities—factors that don't necessarily apply to new Internet applications.

Constructing a business case for a new e-business blueprint is a difficult thing to do, but formulating a clear business case helps formulate clarity of purpose. The goal of the e-business case is to develop clarity of purpose that allows scarce resources—human, capital, and technological—to be targeted for maximum results. A properly developed e-business case ensures that the work will be done right the first time. It also makes it possible to orchestrate simultaneous progress by diverse team members across all key functions in the enterprise.

A strong business case channels forces and accelerates project approval and implementation by coordinating work across functional silos, creating buy-in by most users, yielding consensus and clarity of objectives, earning active top management sponsorship, and communicating critical information among diverse participants.

Who Develops the e-Business Case?

Developing a business case is usually a cross-functional process requiring broad participation and a variety of skills. Fortunately, most of these skills exist in most organizations. Various executives and their respective organizations may play critical roles in developing the business case. Since e-business will affect every-thing in your company, make sure key executives are involved in creating the strategy. Consider the following key roles.

Chief Information Officer and the Information Technology Organization. Ini-tially, the IT group leads the effort in researching the project, thus playing a crit-ical role in developing the business case. The IT organization provides the guidance needed to understand e-business application features, the enterprise's IT architecture, the technology infrastructure, and the resources required to im-plement large-scale packaged software.

Chief Financial Officer and the Finance Organization. The CFO, and the finance organization, is usually involved in the decision to undertake a reengineering and/or enterprise application effort. The finance organization provides the ana-lytical skills necessary for estimating costs and benefits. Often, the CFO and CIO together provide the overall leadership for developing the business case.

Operating Vice Presidents and Their Respective Organizations. The involve-ment of senior-level management is critical in developing a credible business case. Each representative must be highly familiar with his or her organization's business processes and the potential for enhancing those processes.

Chief Executive Officer, President, Chief Operating Officer, or General Manager. The senior executive of the organization also plays a key role, because an imple-mentation of this type often has an impact on most of the organization. The se-nior executive sets the overall tone for the organization and is critical to the decision-making process.

The Role of Senior Management. Achieving a return on investment (ROI) from an e-business application implementation requires high-level managers to effec-tively guide and support the project. Significant change cannot occur or be sus-tained without the visible, active support and involvement of senior management.

Some level of specialized outside expertise may also be required for develop-ing the e-business case. Some of the areas in which external support may add sig-nificant value are listed in Table 12.2.

Key Elements of a Business Case

The content of a business case includes justification for the project, assessment of the preliminary scope of the project, and assessment of feasibility.

Table 12.2: External Support

Functional specialists	If the team members and their respective organizations are not familiar enough with the functionality to determine its benefits, then outside expertise may be required.
Project planning	External support from specialists experienced in implementation may be needed to develop the high-level project plan upon which the e-business case is built.
Process improvement benchmarks	Estimating and quantifying the process improvement opportunities may be difficult. Outside experts who have access to process improvement benchmarks from previous implementation experience may enhance the analysis.
Facilitator	Outside facilitation support can greatly assist with e-business case execution by allowing the internal team members to concentrate on the analysis while the facilitator leads the overall process and acts as a sounding board for the team.

Justification for the Project

An e-business case is crucial to obtaining top-management support. The scope and complexity of reengineering business processes and implementing new technology often require a solid business justification before senior management will commit the time, resources, and funding for the initiative.

Assuring management that their investment in enterprise applications will create value is of key importance. To achieve this, it must be made evident that the investment will be coherent with the overall strategy of the firm and that it will be efficiently managed. The e-business case provides justification for the project along strategic, operational, technical, and financial dimensions.

- **Strategic justification** means identifying the significant new capabilities that enterprise apps will provide for achieving its business objectives. The company's competitive landscape is surveyed and the company's current standing in the market is assessed. Based on this information, it's estimated where the company will stand in the future.

- **Operational justification** requires identifying and quantifying the specific process improvements that result from reengineering processes and integrating enterprise apps with those processes.

- **Technical justification** involves identifying how enterprise apps support the overall technology strategy of the company. It shows how the technology will enable improvements in the cost and capability of the IT infrastructure.

- **Financial justification** determines the costs and benefits of the proposed project and quantifies those values into performance measures meaningful to the organization, such as net present value, internal rate of return, or return on investment.

A detailed, technical appraisal in the e-business case must focus on the plausibility of a project. That is, customer needs and wish lists must be translated into technically and economically feasible solutions. This step might involve some preliminary design work, but it should not be construed as a full-fledged execution project.

An operations appraisal also must be done, investigating issues of integration, including cost, and the amount of investment required. A strong technical appraisal will also diminish forces that slow implementation and lead to analysis paralysis, by avoiding conflicting agendas, reducing unwillingness by participants to share information, and dissolving mistrust of technology. Finally, a detailed financial analysis is conducted to guide senior management.

Assessing Preliminary Scope

Perhaps the most fundamental issue associated with affecting a firm's business strategy is committing money and human resources in the face of business risks and uncertainties. The preliminary scope analysis can help.

By deciding on an initial set of project boundaries in the business case, you define the project's preliminary scope. Key elements to consider are as follows.

- **Organizational.** Which business units, locations, organizations, and processes will be included?

- **Functional.** Which business functions, activities, and modules will be used?

- **High-level application architecture.** A firm should develop a high-level application architecture that supports the business case. This enables your company to assess an e-business application's degree of potential fit with the desired business process capabilities of the organization.

- **High-level project plan.** The plan should include estimates of the implementation process, timetable, key milestones, and benefits. Each of these components is essential for supporting the discussion and decision-making process.

- **Resource requirements.** The business case is a powerful tool for identifying the internal skills and resources needed for action. In addition, a business case can be used to determine if outside resources are required for specialized tasks or to overcome limitations in internal skills.

Assessing Feasibility

After the preliminary scope of the project is set, you must then do the project feasibility analysis along the following three dimensions.

- **Financial.** Assess the feasibility of the project's cost and define the total cost of ownership; assess whether the project's benefits will outweigh the cost of the implementation.

- **Organizational and Cultural.** Assess the ability of the organization and the culture to accommodate a highly integrated enterprise system.

- **Technical.** Assess whether the information infrastructure can support new apps or be upgraded.

Once feasibility is established, the arduous process of aligning support for the project begins. A sound business case is invaluable for communicating, educating, and garnering widespread acceptance of a project.

Communicate, Communicate, Communicate

Once senior management is convinced, the next step is to build consensus—the buy-in needed to move a company toward an e-business architecture. Again, common values are very important. Getting companies organized along processes is an unbelievably difficult task. It is not necessarily a good idea to just generate new ideas at the top and push them down.

Getting stakeholder buy-in is critical. Before moving into the implementation phase, you need to work out the details of the blueprint and develop a list of projects. Each of these projects might have to be sold to the affected stakeholders. This is the final hurdle prior to the implementation stage, the last point at which the project can be killed before financial commitments are made. To sell your e-business case, follow these rules:

- **Be nontechnical.** Most managers understand that the primary way to inform decision makers is to present the functional or business case to management. This is the human side of IT, and it should be as nontechnical as possible.

- **Address cost, risk, and benefits.** Cost, risk, and benefit should be included in the analysis of alternative investments. Where possible, the analysis should be stated in fiscal terms, although other considerations, such as mission criticality, should be weighed in final decisions.

- **Be brief.** We recommend that when presenting the business case to review boards, managers should be succinct. Experience shows that summaries of around ten pages (supported by as much additional detail and analysis as warranted) make up a workable package for senior managers.

Stakeholders are often concerned about the definition of the project. They often subject the business case to a lot of "must meet" and "should meet" criteria. Here agreement must be reached on a number of key items before the project proceeds into the implementation stage. These items include definition of scope, specification of an integration strategy, delineation of product benefits to be delivered, and agreement on essential and desired features, attributes, and specifications.

Communication Best Practices

Keep these best practices in mind when trying to create shared values.

Create a cross-functional architecture team. By allowing members of the business units to participate in discussions about the architecture and its effects on the company, you're more likely to get buy-in. Think of the team members as your ambassadors. They can help sell the benefits and foster support at the grass-roots level.

Take baby steps. One way to sabotage the effort is to start talking about major changes. You have to ease into this type of change or you'll face resistance. Start small by demonstrating the positive effects of the new architecture. Get buy-in by selling the benefits of streamlining inefficient systems or improving turnaround on time-consuming tasks. Baby steps help win converts.

Clearly communicate plans and the benefits of the new architecture. Regularly publish an architectural strategy statement. This document will allow business units to have a handy reference of exactly what technologies your organization is pursuing. Many companies update these statements on a quarterly or as-needed basis to keep up with changing demands and trends.

Document success and publish the results. Company intranets and newsletters are good forums for some positive PR. Highlight tangible results, such as increased access to legacy information, faster turnaround time to data queries, or improved customer satisfaction scores. This publicity is also an opportunity for managers to show how technology is benefiting their units as well as the company.

Anticipate resistance. When it comes to creating an e-business architecture, the resistance to the process often comes from the IT units rather than the business groups. Loss of control, the perception of decreased importance, and the elimination of technologies or applications that the IT staff views as its domain are the primary reasons. Be sensitive to these conflicts and sell the project as strongly to the IT group as to the business units.

e-Business Project Planning Checklist

Setting the business direction shouldn't be an academic exercise. It should be preceded by a hard look at the realities of the marketplace and at the company's circumstances. Once that's accomplished, managers must document the strategic plan. Use these guidelines to clarify your planning work.

- **Develop a goal statement.** A goal statement is fewer than 20 words and provides a succinct statement of what the project is all about. It describes who will benefit from the project and how it fits in the overall scheme of things.

- **Set measurable goals.** Goals, which flow from the goal statement, define what the project will accomplish. Try to limit goals to no more than five. By using a consensus process, prioritize each goal according to its importance to the business.

- **Set objectives.** An objective is an action statement of what is to be completed under each goal during the specified time frame. Use a consensus process to prioritize objectives.

- **Identify strategies and tactics.** Strategies and tactics describe how to achieve the objectives set forth under the goals. Such statements isolate action items that the firm intends to implement during a specified time.

- **Develop short- and long-term action plans.** Action plans consist of time lines, process changes, technology planning, people responsibility assignments, and budget allocations. It's desirable and possible to achieve both short- and long-term results. When properly balanced, the two complement each other. Long-term benefits are really a series of incremental short-term improvements that support the higher-level organizational requirements.

- **Gain approval.** Review action plans with management. Get buy-in from key players. Make necessary revisions or adjustments. This step requires communication and more communication.

Some managers think that building an e-business case is simply an exercise in getting funding, and it is. But as you've gleaned from this chapter, it should yield considerably more important results. Building an e-business case speeds implementation, reduces risk, and helps maximize (or optimize) the benefits to be gained today and tomorrow. Unfortunately, few firms provide managers with effective guidelines for preparing an e-business case. Keep this chapter as a resource in mapping future cases.

Doing the Projects Right: An Execution Blueprint

New applications come to life by transforming ideas into working prototypes with detailed design and engineering that are tested and refined in preparation for enterprisewide deployment. The e-business execution funnel defines the way in which an organization proposes and prioritizes needs and how these needs converge to define and design specific applications. At the other end of the spectrum, day-to-day problem solving at the working level drives choices about the details of the design.

Somewhere between the broad architecture of the funnel and the details of the specific tasks, however, lies a whole set of choices the firm must make about the overall execution process. These choices include how projects should be sequenced, how work should be organized, how efforts should be led and managed, what milestones should be established, how senior management will interact with the project, and the way problems should be framed and solved.

In short, the detailed blueprint must lay out a pattern for execution. This may require companies to overhaul project management. For instance, in an SAP R/3 financial application project, McKesson chopped an unwieldy 40-member business steering committee down to four executives: CIO, CFO, the controller, and the vice president of shared financial services. At the same time, McKesson transferred the week-to-week project management from a single business executive to a four-person "project office" that had business knowledge, SAP knowledge, and a deep understanding of the complex legacy systems. No one person had all this knowledge. There wasn't even a person who knew even two aspects.[5]

A detailed execution blueprint can have a powerful impact on execution, and the devil's in the details. Creating it requires senior management's focused effort and attention because the execution process is a complex set of activities that extends over a considerable time period. In trying to understand the nature and role of the execution process, let's walk though an example of customer relationship management (CRM).

Developing a CRM Execution Blueprint

The CRM business perspective describes how the business works. It includes:

- The goals and objectives with respect to customer acquisition, service, and retention

- Basic flows of customer information in each of the products and services

- The functions and cross-functional activities performed in CRM business processes

- Major organizational elements and the interaction of all these elements

The CRM perspective includes broad business strategies and plans for moving the organization from its current state to its future state. The CRM blueprint looks at the overall structure and defines where and under what conditions different customer interactions are triggered, what value needs to be provided to the customer, what information will be collected centrally and locally, and where and how other applications will be involved.

The CRM blueprint defines the architecture, but the execution process is more detailed and specific. It describes how the various applications will be integrated to provide customer value, how the operational processes work, and how problems are solved and customers are serviced. To produce an outstanding CRM application, an outstanding execution process is required. This calls for careful planning of applications, information flows, and technology.

Rapid Execution Is the Norm

In the past, application frameworks were implemented slowly. However, in today's competitive world you don't have that luxury. For instance, CRM implementation can either accelerate or impede an organization's ability to adapt to changing business conditions.

Table 12.3 illustrates four implementation imperatives: speed, efficiency, flexibility, and quality. To succeed, implementations must be responsive to changing customer demands and competitor moves. This means that they must have short time-to-market cycles. The ability to identify opportunities, organize execution, and bring to market new capabilities quickly is critical to effective competition. At the same time firms must bring new capabilities to market efficiently. Resource allocation among competing projects is critical.

Table 12.3: Execution Imperatives

Required Capabilities	Driving Forces	Implications
Fast and responsive	Changing customer expectations; accelerating value migration	Shorter time-to-market cycles
High execution productivity	Scarce resources; wrong moves can destroy company	Make better management decisions about resource allocation and project selection
Flexible configurations	Continuous innovation; changing customer needs	Make architectural decisions that allow flexibility
Distinctive applications	Demanding customers; intense competition	Creativity combined with integrated solutions

However, being fast and efficient is not enough. Today's CRM implementations must be flexible. They must fully meet business requirements and be flexible enough to integrate new and emerging technologies without compromising daily operations. The new e-commerce solutions must also meet the demands in the market for value, reliability, and distinctive performance. Demanding customers and capable competitors drives up the ante. Requirements of performance, reliability, ease of use, and total value increase every year. More and more this means developing applications that not only satisfy but also surprise and delight customers.

Transition Management

A critical part of execution is the transition from old applications to new applications. Transition issues can derail a company. Samsonite, the world's leading luggage maker, is a good example. Samsonite product shipments in the United States nearly ground to a halt in the first 20 days of July 1998 because of problems in converting to new financial, manufacturing, and distribution applications. The system problems even disrupted Samsonite's invoicing and its electronic data interchange communications with its retail stores, resulting in inventory stockouts and lost sales at the retail level. The IT troubles contributed to a shocking $29.9 million loss, a subsequent drop in stock price, and numerous shareholder lawsuits against the company.

Large CRM projects create transition change in three stages. The first stage entails redefining jobs, establishing new procedures, fine-tuning applications, and learning to take advantage of the new streams of information created by the platform. The second stage involves skill execution, structural changes, process integration, and add-on technologies that expand the application functionality. The third stage is one of transformation, where the synergies of people, processes, and technology reach a peak.[6]

A transition to e-business needs a tightly coordinated approach. Coordination flies in the face of traditional application execution, which is usually characterized by a number of independent groups working on various aspects of an issue. This latter approach is like building an airplane by having one group go off on its own to design the wings, another to build the landing gear, and still another to develop the fuselage, with no group ever communicating with the others. *Would you fly in a plane built in such an ad hoc way?*

Why e-Business Initiatives Fail

Companies without effective blueprint management face several challenges. Indeed, many problems that beset application execution initiatives can be directly traced to a lack of effective blueprint management, resulting in an aging infrastructure plagued with problems from decades of deferred maintenance. Here are some agonies that firms endure when they don't have proper blueprint management in place.

First, weak blueprint management can set the company adrift in a sea of too many projects. There is no consistent mechanism for evaluating and, if necessary, killing weak projects. Instead, projects seem to take on lives of their own, like runaway trains that don't stop at review points. Further, new projects get added without considering whether there are resources available or how they will affect other projects already in the works. The result is a total lack of focus and a strain on available resources.

The problems don't stop there. A lack of focus and too many active projects mean that resources and people are spread too thin. As a result, projects are starved for resources and end up in a queue—a serious bottleneck in the process—and the cycle time increases. Suddenly, there are complaints about projects being behind schedule and taking too long. Then everyone starts to scramble, with predictable results: Quality of execution starts to suffer. So, not only are the projects late but their success rates drop.

Lacking effective blueprint management also means there are no rigorous and tough decision points, which in turn leads to poor project selection decisions. Excessive reliance on ROI to rank projects pushes cost-saving and incremental-improvement projects to the top of the list, while breakthrough projects languish. That emphasis often results in too many mediocre projects in the pipeline that yield only marginal value to the company. Consequently, many of the applications yield disappointing results. Even more insidious is that the really good projects are starved for resources, so they are either behind schedule or never achieve their full potential. And that costs the company huge opportunities.

Without a rigorous blueprint, the wrong projects often get selected for the wrong reasons. Some companies' investment decisions have more to do with high-clout sponsorship than good business. Instead of decisions being made on fact, some decisions are based on politics, internal disputes over territory, and emotion. This environment stifles innovation at the execution level, forcing lower-level executives to work outside normal channels. In the end, too many of these ill-selected projects fail anyway.

If your business faces any of these problems—long cycle times, a high failure rate, lack of strategic alignment—perhaps the root causes can be traced back to ineffective blueprint management. Table 12.4 illustrates some classic reasons why e-business projects fail. Ask yourself if your organization has any of these symptoms.

Memo to the CEO

Let's take a deep breath and examine our current predicament. Managers everywhere have been given identical marching orders from top management: Create a blueprint for the integrated enterprise and, in the process, develop supporting information and application architectures. This blueprint must exploit new technologies, such as the Internet, and new application frameworks, such as supply chain management, in hopes of garnering a competitive edge.

The goal of an integrated enterprise is to reduce information float, that is, the time between when data is captured in one place in the system and when it becomes available and usable ("actionable") in another place. Integration is a business transformation initiative. More than just a way of saving time in a business process, integrated strategies determine ways to link processes in different departments, locations, even different enterprises in faster, more closely knit ways.

Why should you care? New application infrastructure represents the modern pillars of the e-corporation. Top management at many companies now recognizes that application integration is critical to carrying out business strategies across a dispersed organization. Many profound changes are forcing organizations to rethink and broaden their views on integration,[7] including:

Table 12.4: Ten Ways to Fail at Turning Strategy into Action

1. Design the application blueprint on your own, in your own department—in a vacuum. After all, you know best, and cross-functional teams are a waste of time!

2. Don't do any homework or auditing. You already know what the problems are in the company, so jump immediately to a solution.

3. Don't bother looking at other companies' methods, such as their best practices, business models, execution snafus, and so on. You have nothing to learn from them.

4. If you do assemble a task force, meet several times in private. Then present your grand e-business design and expect other managers to applaud, even though they haven't been involved.

5. Don't seek outside help. Just read trade magazines and design your blueprint based on a generic model. If you do seek help, hire a brand-name guru who knows nothing about technology or blueprint management.

6. When other managers have questions, become defensive and rail at these "cynics" and "negative thinkers" who simply don't get it! Refuse to deal with objections—even valid ones—and never modify initial designs because they belong to you.

7. Don't worry about communicating. Most of this e-business strategy stuff is obvious anyway. Anyone can get it if they think hard enough.

8. Speaking of communication, make sure that the blueprint document is three binders thick, full of checklists and spreadsheets. If in doubt, overwhelm the reader with volume.

9. Don't bother with the process or project management because the e-business design is so good it will be automatically implemented.

10. Don't waste time taking baby steps to execute. You want the big bang effect. Turn off the old set of applications and completely switch the organization over to the new way of doing things.

- Heightened competition and increasingly sophisticated customers are forcing companies to present a single, near-real-time view of their customers and their relationship to the company, even though information about them is spread across multiple stovepipe applications.

- The current integration approaches are no longer timely enough for many applications. This is particularly apparent in supply chain management, where competitive advantages are increasingly coming from near-real-time data collection and propagation.

- A new style of event-based application is emerging. Activities in one area, such as a debit to inventory, must cause a number of other applications in other areas—from replenishment applications to modeling spreadsheets—to perform a related action.

- Mobile and wireless computing is quickly becoming a way of life. Unfortunately, such technology is fundamentally incompatible with legacy application architectures.

Clearly, integrated applications are the next step in the evolution of online systems. In fact, the ability to deliver integrated applications is a significant competitive differentiator in many industries and an operating requirement in others. Even just to maintain parity in their industries, businesses need to move beyond their current family of applications.

The road to blueprint planning is often bumpy and not clear. Every execution planning effort must include the following to minimize risk:

- An application framework prioritization process that helps focus the spotlight on important infrastructure projects. Unfortunately, e-business blueprint planning is often given scant attention by senior management. Our recommendation to companies is to establish a special task force to do the planning on a companywide basis.

- A systematic way to put together business cases for each infrastructure project. This includes a detailed plan with schedules, milestones, roles, and responsibilities. It also includes communication forums to explain strategies, implementation and success requirements, and the roles and responsibilities of organization members.

- A development strategy that implements great ideas. We need to be able to learn from each implementation in order to improve the overall planning process. Hence, particular attention must be paid to performance measurement and tracking metrics.

Are companies going to build from scratch to achieve integration? Not necessarily. Most organizations are finding more value in purchasing packaged applications and modifying them to suit their needs. As a result, the structural foundations of many companies are made from blueprints such as SAP, Baan, and PeopleSoft. They're connected together over the Internet in new, more sophisticated ways that enable them to exchange information more quickly than ever before. This connectivity accelerates business processes in which multiple departments or multiple companies work together. However, it accentuates the need for careful integration planning between these disparate application frameworks.

As the digital age progresses, companies must react more quickly to customer needs, bring products to market with greater speed, and respond more completely to changing business conditions. The ability to manage information is a prerequisite for success. To manage information transparently, organizations need an e-business blueprint—an approach that allows them to build on existing technology to create efficient, integrated applications that collect, manage, organize, and disseminate information throughout an enterprise. Ultimately, the effectiveness of an e-business blueprint depends on how managers use it and how well it fits into the day-to-day processes and culture of a company.

Endnotes

Chapter 1

1. Information asymmetry is a core concept in economics. Basically, it means that buyers have less information than sellers. The business of intermediation stems from this concept, as intermediaries attempt to reduce the gap.

2. John Seely Brown, ed., *Seeing Differently: Insights on Innovation* (Boston: Harvard Business Review Book Series, 1997).

3. "The Internet Retailing Report," Morgan Stanley, U.S. Investment Research, 28 May 1997; from http://www.ms.com/

4. "Microsoft Moves to Rule On-Line Sales," *The Wall Street Journal*, 5 June 1997, sec. B, p. 1.

5. Online travel agents charge $10 commissions, whereas traditional agents demand $50.

6. The term "e-business community" (EBC) was first introduced by the Alliance for Converging Technologies in their multiclient study "Winning in the Digital Economy."

7. The largest purchase item is a home. According to the National Automobile Dealers Association (NADA), the industry's largest dealer organization, $293 billion was spent by consumers in the United States in 1995 on new vehicles, representing 14.8 million new units.

8. Clinton Wilder, Online Auto Sales Pickup, *Information Week,* 9 February 1998.

9. For more examples of market leaders that responded and those that did not, see Gary Hamel and C.K. Prahalad's *Competing for the Future* (Boston: Harvard Business School Press, 1997).

10. e-Business architecture design and implementation is bound to emerge as one of the fastest-growing consulting businesses of the decade, because it will enable firms to do electronic commerce.

11. Ravi Kalakota, "Investing in Electronic Commerce—Lessons from the Field," working paper, E-Business Strategies Inc., Atlanta, Georgia, 1999.

12. Credible social and business prophets, notably Peter Drucker (*Managing in Turbulent Times*, 1980) and Alvin Toffler (*Future Shock*, 1970), among others, have been anticipating this business environment of ever-increasing rate of change for decades. Therefore, no organization, no manager, no person should be caught off guard.

Chapter 2

1. Address to the shareholders by Michael Eisner, Chairman and Chief Executive Officer, The Walt Disney Co., annual stockholders meeting, Kansas City, Missouri, 24 February 1998.
2. A 1997 report by the U.S. Department of Commerce estimates that overall data traffic on the Internet is doubling every 100 days.
3. "Trend-Spotting: Anyone Can Play," *Business Week,* 2 March 1998, p. 12.
4. Evan I. Schwartz, "How Middlemen Can Come Out on Top," *Business Week,* 9 February 1998, p. 4.
5. Annalee Saxenian, "The Origins and Dynamics of Production Networks in Silicon Valley," working paper, Institute of Urban and Regional Development, University of California, Berkeley, April 1990.
6. "Sara Lee's Plan to Contract Out Work Underscores Trend among U.S. Firms," *Wall Street Journal,* 17 September 1997, sec. A, p. 3, and "Sara Lee to Retreat from Manufacturing," *Wall Street Journal,* 16 September 1997, sec. A, p. 3.
7. Bob Violino, "Technology Spending—The Billion Dollar Club," *InformationWeek,* 25 November, 1996, p. 27.

Chapter 3

1. "Point and Click for Prozac," *Business Week,* 19 October 1998, p. 156.
2. Richard Lueckie, *Scuttle Your Ships Before Advancing* (New York: Oxford University Press, 1994) pp. 165–166.
3. This strategy was quite common in the 1960s and 1980s. Between 1959 and 1979, American Express acquired a staggering 350 companies, including Avis, Continental Baking (Wonder Bread, Twinkies), Sheraton, and Hartford Insurance.
4. Anthony Bianco, "The Rise of a Star," *Business Week,* 21 December 1998, p. 60.
5. "The Power of Virtual Integration: An Interview with Dell Computer's Michael Dell," *Harvard Business Review,* March/April 1998, p. 72.
6. Suzie Amer, Alessandra Bianchi, Sean Donahue, Steven Ginsberg, Michelle Jeffers, Lee Patterson, and Carol Pickering, "America's Best Technology Users," *Forbes,* 24 August 1998, p. 63.
7. Source: A speech by Jan Baan, founder and CEO of Baan Corporation.

Chapter 4

1. Bill Gates, "The Digital Nervous System" [online]. http://www.microsoft.com/dns/overviews/DNSoverviews.htm.
2. Clinton Wilder, "Booksellers' Battles Head for the Web," *InformationWeek,* 3 March 1997, pp. 62–63.
3. "America's Best Technology Users," *Forbes,* 24 August 1998, p. 63.
4. "Appliance Firm Gives Pricing System a Whirl," *Computerworld,* 23 March 1998, p. 1.
5. "Wal-Mart's IT Secret: Extreme Integration," *Datamation,* November 1996.
6. Stage 5 is predicated on the assumption that business models have a powerful predisposition to mutate and evolve. This idea is similar to so-called business ecosystems, made popular by James Moore in his book *The Death of Competition* (New York: HarperBusiness, 1996).

Chapter 5

1. Source: Sybase Customer Asset Management Solutions, http://www.sybase.com/.
2. "Biggest Sales Mistake: Asking Your Customers," *American Salesman,* November 1996, p. 22.
3. "Live to Ride," *Financial World,* 26 September 1995, p. 6.

Chapter 6

1. "We Sure as Hell Confused Ourselves, but What about the Customers?" *Marketing Intelligence & Planning,* April 1995, p. 5.
2. "Producing Unique Goods—and Headaches," *Inc.,* May 1998, p. 24.
3. "Smart Managing/Best Practices," *Fortune,* 10 November 1997, p. 283.

Chapter 7

1. Tim Minahan, "Enterprise Resource Planning," *Purchasing,* 16 July 1998, p. 112.
2. "3Com Corporation: Success Story" [online]. Available at http://www.sap.com/success/index.htm. File: 50020231.pdf. After its merger with U.S. Robotics in 1998, 3Com, headquartered in Santa Clara, California, now employs 13,000 people across 160 R&D, manufacturing, sales, and service sites worldwide.
3. "GM Picks SAP to Improve Information Technology," *Wall Street Journal,* 13 November 1997, p. 2.
4. Source: Glovia International, http://www.glovia.com/about/direction.html.
5. Bob Francis, "The New ERP Math," *PC Week Online,* 26 October 1998.
6. Legend has it that IBM turned down a contract to customize the production planning software of ICI's German subsidiary. The five programmers took the contract on themselves, founding SAP as a result.
7. Business process reengineering was believed to cure everything from corporate bloat to quality woes. It caused much woe to the tens of thousands of workers and executives who were "downsized" as a result.
8. Joseph B. White, Don Clark, and Silvia Ascarelli, "Program of Pain," *Wall Street Journal,* 14 March 1997, p. 6.
9. "The Software That Drives Microsoft," SAP case study.
10. Thomas H. Davenport, "Putting the Enterprise into the Enterprise System," *Harvard Business Review,* July/August 1998.
11. Source: Analyst Reports, Investext CD-ROM Database.
12. "Managing the ERP Equation," *PC Week Online,* 26 October 1998.

Chapter 8

1. Carol Hildebrand, "Beware of the Weak Links," *Enterprise CIO,* 15 August 1998, p. 20.
2. Andrew E. Serwer, "Michael Dell Turns the PC World Inside Out," *Fortune,* 8 September 1997, p. 76.
3. *Journal of Business Strategy,* November/December 1997, 25.
4. Andy Reinhardt and Seanna Browder, "Fly, Damn It, Fly," *Business Week,* 9 November 1998, p. 150.

5. "America's Best Technology Users," *Forbes*, 24 August 1998, p. 63.

6. Jennifer Bresnahan, "The Incredible Journey," *CIO Magazine*, 15 August 1998, p. 56.

7. Firms providing early versions of advanced planning capability include SAP, I2 Technologies, Manugistics, and Logility. More sophisticated systems that integrate production planning and transportation planning are under development.

8. Damark International, 10 K Filing with the Securities and Exchange Commission, http://sec.edgar.gov/.

9. It's estimated that American companies spend about $500 billion owning, holding, and moving inventory, including wrapping, bundling, loading, unloading, sorting, reloading, and then transporting goods.

10. "Gaining A Competitive Edge," speech by M. Anthony Burns, Ryder Systems, at the Economic Club of Detroit, Michigan, 21 April 1997.

11. Marshall Fisher, "What is the Right Supply-chain for your Product," *Harvard Business Review*, March 1997, p. 105.

12. T. R. "Ted" Garcia, Starbucks Senior Vice President, Supply Chain Operations, interviewed in *APICS—The Performance Advantage*, August 1997, p. 45.

Chapter 9

1. Roy Anderson, "Implementation of Web-Based Requisitioning," speech delivered at the E-Commerce Conference, 10 November 1998. Retrieved from http://www.napm.org/Education/NovDailymondaymorningec1.cfm.

2. "Holding the Line on SG&A," *CFO Magazine*, December 1996.

3. Fara Warner, "Ford Motor Uses the Internet to Slash Billions of Dollars from Ordinary Tasks," *Wall Street Journal*, 14 October 1998, p. 4.

4. Source: Industrial Distributors Group and S-1, filed 22 May 1998 retrieved from http://sec.edgar.gov/

5. AMEX Consulting Services, T&E Management Process Study, 1997 retrieved from www.extensity.com

6. "Reaping 'Net Savings—Microsoft's Online Buying App Slashes Costs," *Internet Week*, 4 August 1997.

7. Source: Microsoft Web Site, www.microsoft.com.

8. Source: Ariba Technologies Web site, www.ariba.com.

9. Erick Schonfeld, "The Exchange Economy," *Fortune*, 15 February 1999, p. 67.

Chapter 10

1. Exchange Applications, S 1/A prospectus filed with the Securities and Exchange Commission.

2. Knowledge tone is related to the notion of MicroStrategy's QueryTone. For more on QueryTone, see www.strategy.com.

3. Norbert Turek, "Decision into Action—Closed-Loop Systems Are Making Retailers More Responsive to Inventory Adjustments," *InformationWeek*, 26 October 1998.

4. Janet Novack, "Database Evangelist," *Forbes*, 7 September 1998, p. 66.

5. Steve Alexander, "Printer Manufacturer Tracks Your Inventory," *Computerworld*, 16 November 1998, p. 67.

6. Sun Microsystems, "British Telecom" [online]. Retrieved from: http://www.sun.com/products-n-solutions/telco/success.stry/ss10.britele.html.

7. Marina Bidoli, "Managing a Giant," *Financial Mail*, 16 October 1998, p. 80.

8. Source: Forrester Research Reports.

9. Michael French, "Mining for Dollars," *America's Network*, 15 April 1998, p. 24.

10. Janice Maloney, "Healtheon: Internet-Based Health Care Information and Services," *Fortune*, 8 July 1996, p. 88.

11. Source: Forrester Research, 1997.

12. Lawrence S. Gould, "What You Need to Know about Data Warehousing," *Automotive Manufacturing & Production*, June 1998, p. 64.

13. *DBMS*, August 1998, 36.

Chapter 11

1. Securities and Exchange Commission Form 10-K405 for OfficeMax, filed on 21 April 1998.

2. Stephen J. Wall and Shannon Rye Wall, "The Evolution Not the Death of Strategy" *Organizational Dynamics*, 22 September 1995, 6.

3. David Diamond, "Hold on Tight: Trends in Electronics Industry in 1998," *Electronic Business*, December 1998, p. 70.

4. Peter Drucker calls this set of interrelated assumptions the "theory of the business." Gary Hamel and C.K. Prahalad, in *Competing for the Future* (Boston: Harvard Business School Press, 1994) expand this concept, maintaining that "every manager carries around in his or her head a set of biases, assumptions, and presuppositions about the structure of the relevant 'industry,' about how one makes money in the industry, about who the competition is and isn't, about who the customers are and aren't, about which technologies are viable and which aren't, and so on" (p. 35).

5. Evan I. Schwartz, "OK, Retailers, Why Do Your Own Marketing When You Can Make 100,000 Other Web Sites Do It for You?" *New York Times*, 10 August 1998, sec. D, p. 3, col. 1.

6. Robert Hiebeler, Thomas Kelly, and Charles Ketteman, *Best Practices: Building Your Business with Customer-Focused Solutions* (New York: Simon & Schuster, 1998).

7. Ruth Owades, interview by John Metaxas, *In the Game*, Cable News Network, Transcript 97060318FN-l02, 3 June 1997.

8. Scott Kurnit's talk at Esther Dyson Adventure Conference 1997.

9. For more on supply chain design, see I2 Technologies' Web site at http://www.i2.com.

10. Gary Hamel and Jeff Sampler, "The E-Corporation," *Fortune*, 7 December 1998, p. 80.

11. Joseph C. Picken and Gregory G. Dess, "Right Strategy—Wrong Problem," *Organizational Dynamics*, 22 June 1998, p. 35.

12. Source: The Juran Institute.

13. Stephen Harper, "Leading Organizational Change in the 21st Century," *Industrial Management*, 15 May 1998, p. 25.

Chapter 12

1. Saul Habsell, "Citibank Sets New On-Line Bank System," *New York Times*, 5 October 1998, sec. C, p. 1, col. 5.

2. Clinton Wilder, "E-Commerce—Myths & Realities," *InformationWeek*, 7 December 1998.

3. Clinton Wilder and Beth Davis, "False Starts, Strong Finishes," *InformationWeek*, 30 November 1998.

4. For more details concerning these types of projects, see *Managing New Product and Process Development,* by Kim Clark and Steven Wheelwright (New York: Free Press, 1993).

5. Clinton Wilder and Beth Davis, "False Starts, Strong Finishes," *InformationWeek,* 30 November 1998.

6. Bruce Caldwell and Tom Stein, "Cultural, Organizational Shifts Move Beyond Software," *Computer Reseller News,* 7 December 1998.

7. Peter Houston, "Integrating Applications with Message Queuing Middleware," white paper, Microsoft Corporation, Redmond, Washington, 1998.

Index

Addison-Wesley Computer and Engineering Publishing Group

How to Interact with Us

1. Visit our Web site

http://www.awl.com/cseng

When you think you've read enough, there's always more content for you at Addison-Wesley's web site. Our web site contains a directory of complete product information including:

- Chapters
- Exclusive author interviews
- Links to authors' pages
- Tables of contents
- Source code

You can also discover what tradeshows and conferences Addison-Wesley will be attending, read what others are saying about our titles, and find out where and when you can meet our authors and have them sign your book.

2. Subscribe to Our Email Mailing Lists

Subscribe to our electronic mailing lists and be the first to know when new books are publishing. Here's how it works: Sign up for our electronic mailing at **http://www.awl.com/cseng/mailinglists.html**. Just select the subject areas that interest you and you will receive notification via email when we publish a book in that area.

3. Contact Us via Email

cepubprof@awl.com

Ask general questions about our books.
Sign up for our electronic mailing lists.
Submit corrections for our web site.

bexpress@awl.com

Request an Addison-Wesley catalog.
Get answers to questions regarding your order or our products.

innovations@awl.com

Request a current Innovations Newsletter.

webmaster@awl.com

Send comments about our web site.

mary.obrien@awl.com

Submit a book proposal.
Send errata for an Addison-Wesley book.

cepubpublicity@awl.com

Request a review copy for a member of the media interested in reviewing new Addison-Wesley titles.

We encourage you to patronize the many fine retailers who stock Addison-Wesley titles. Visit our online directory to find stores near you or visit our online store: **http://store.awl.com/** or call **800-824-7799**.

Addison Wesley Longman
Computer and Engineering Publishing Group
One Jacob Way, Reading, Massachusetts 01867 USA
TEL 781-944-3700 • FAX 781-942-3076